THEOLOGY AFTER READING

THEOLOGY AFTER READING

Christian Imagination and the Power of Fiction

DARREN J. N. MIDDLETON

BAYLOR UNIVERSITY PRESS

Cover Design by Matthew Greenblatt, Centerpointe Design

Library of Congress Cataloging-in-Publication Data

Middleton, Darren J. N., 1966-
  Theology after reading : Christian imagination and the power of fiction / by Darren J.N. Middleton.
        p. cm.
  Includes bibliographical references and index.
  ISBN 978-1-60258-158-6 (cloth : alk. paper)
  1. Fiction--Religious aspects. 2. Fiction--Religious aspects--Christianity. 3. Fiction--20th century--History and criticism. I. Title.

  PN3351.M53 2007
  809.3'93823--dc22

                          2008008640

Printed in the United States of America on acid-free paper with a minimum of 30% pcw recycled content.

To Jonathan,
who polishes my soul.

There's nothing written into the universe.
Nothing that says
one day,
perhaps soon,
You'll rise with the sun and find
Your soul
polished, Petoskey stone smooth.
But when You do
Tarry not to wonder
how
In this, Your little boy,
A new day has come. Think
But only of grace,
God's gesture. Your sign
That no life is so marked by rough edges
As to remain coarse forever.

—Darren J. N. Middleton, "Compline"

This is the lesson for today—
narrative, narrative, narrative . . .

—Charles Wright, *The Appalachian Book of the Dead IV*

CONTENTS

ACKNOWLEDGMENTS

I delight in expressing thanks to those who made this book possible.

Betsy Flowers, as always, for her kindheartedness. And our son, Jonathan Middleton, for allowing Daddy some time at the office. From now on, I promise to help you "bend it like Beckham."

Carey C. Newman, my instructive and exceedingly patient editor at Baylor University Press. And to J. David Holcomb, who favored the book with his enthusiasm at its outset.

Texas Christian University and R. Nowell Donovan, its Provost and Vice Chancellor for Academic Affairs, who acknowledged my need for a research leave, spring 2007. I also appreciate C. David Grant, TCU's Religion Department Chair, for kind and generous support along the way.

The late Daryl D. Schmidt, for his friendship and commitment to religious literacy.

The late Kenneth T. Lawrence, for his prudent counsel and sheer verve.

S. Brent Rodriguez Plate, for thought-provoking insights into what happens at the beguiling interface of religion and the arts.

Mallory K. Bolduc, Megan A. Johnson, Austin S. Lingerfelt, Ellen Schwaller, student assistants who read and responded to the manuscript at various stages.

Students in my "Christianity and Literature" class, 1998–2006, who were among the first to hear and then challenge my understanding of the personalities and themes featured in this book.

Prompt and courteous assistance at Texas Christian University from interlibrary loan.

My friends at the Bay View Association of the United Methodist Association, Bayview, Michigan, especially Rev. Robert R. Kimes, Director of Religious Activities, for the opportunity to present a substantial part of this book as The Nellie Gordon Blasius Lectures, June 2005.

The Anselm Class at the First Baptist Church of Memphis, Tennessee, the Inquirers' Class at South Hills Christian Church, Fort Worth, Texas, and the Family Covenant Class at University Christian Church, Fort Worth, Texas, for initial encouragement and sustained curiosity.

Patroclos Stavrou, an extraordinarily kind and accommodating man, for permission to quote from all texts authored by Nikos Kazantzakis and/or his wife, Eleni Kazantzaki (Helen Kazantzakis).

Paul Thigpen, for granting an interview during his busy schedule and for general support as well as keen interest.

Friends who read and commented on selected chapters of the book in manuscript form: Stella Mae Barber, Peter Bien, Amy Bressler, Jennifer Coggins, Daniel A. Dombrowski, Iva Lou Flowers, Ray D. Hatton, Lewis Owens, Ashley Pillow, and Jeff Pool.

Courteous and efficient publishing representatives: Elizabeth Cardone (Strang), Bette Graber (Random House), Elley Mytton (Andre Deutsch), as well as Christianne Squires (Strang).

And last but by no means least, I gratefully acknowledge use of the following:

From *The End of the Affair* by Graham Greene, copyright 1951, renewed copyright 1979 by Graham Greene. Used by permission of Viking Penguin, a division of Penguin Group (USA), Inc.

From *Sula* by Toni Morrison, copyright 1973 by Toni Morrison. Used by permission of Alfred A. Knopf, a division of Random House, Inc.

From *The Wine of Astonishment* by Earl Lovelace, copyright 1982 by Earl Lovelace. Used by permission of Andre Deutsch.

"Map of Hell" image taken from Paul Thigpen, *My Visit to Hell* (Lake Mary, Fla.: Realms, 2007), xiii. Used by permission.

Darren J. N. Middleton
October 29, 2007

INTRODUCTION

It's Fiction: What's Theology Got to Do with It?

A good deal! This is the short answer to my book's leading question. But even though I spend the next five chapters describing and illustrating what happens at fiction and theology's interface, I have decided from the outset to avoid what someone in my position—a theology professor as well as an ordained minister—might otherwise feel tempted to do: I will not discuss Dan Brown. Since many scholars have traveled down this road, it seems only appropriate to take another one. But it will not be the pathway known as Tim LaHaye and Jerry Jenkins; I intend to leave those two behind. Please do not misconstrue me: I do not dismiss such authors maliciously. In point of fact, I suspect the church and the academy has many things to thank them for, not the least of which is the way they incite us to treat literature as a resource for thinking theologically.[1] Love it or loathe it, *The Da Vinci Code* has made us think about Jesus of Nazareth, both before and after the early church's credal pronouncements about him. This is no small matter. But biblical historians such as Darrell L. Bock and Bart D. Ehrman have addressed the merits and demerits of Dan Brown's story already.[2] It is time to explore other theologically infused novels, such as Graham Greene's *The End of the Affair*, Toni Morrison's *Sula*, Nikos Kazantzakis' *The Last Temptation of Christ*, Earl Lovelace's *The Wine of Astonishment*, and Paul Thigpen's *My Visit to Hell*.

Some secular fiction has made it to church book clubs and undergraduate seminars. Even so, I have discovered that Christian readers tend to dismiss secular fiction as theologically scandalous, because it promotes ideas that violate the so-called permissible bounds of traditional Christian speculation.[3] It seems only fair to concede that some of the aforementioned novels *are* unorthodox. But this is partly because their writers are famous for having once lived on the borderlands between belief and unbelief. Greene and Kazantzakis are two very good examples.[4] Some Christians find this spiritual liminality troubling, and perhaps on one level it is, but it need not be viewed as entirely problematic. After all, even some of the most established theologians found themselves occupying similar territory at one time or another. Read Augustine's *Confessions.* Here the father of Western theology emerges from his own pages as an experienced, ardent man who wrestled persistently with his own weaknesses and feelings. He was often caught betwixt and between, someone whose relentless search for truth drove him to adopt a variety of intellectual positions at different times. And like Augustine, our novelists once struggled or continue to struggle with theological issues, not to mention themselves. Yet I think their example, like Augustine's, helps those of us who seek to work out our faith in fear and trembling.

A BIBLICAL FAITH STILL IN THE MAKING

I find our novelists most helpful when I learn to think of them, and certainly their stories, as contributing to a biblical faith still in the making. The Bible is the holy book of Christians. Its canon was closed in the fourth century, after much debate about what New Testament writings were acceptable to the early Christian communities. Talk of "a biblical faith still in the making" does not mean that the Bible's contents are endlessly revisable but that the inspiration energizing the biblical writers has continued across the centuries.

Traditionally, the word "inspiration" has been understood to mean that God supplies every word of the Bible, rendering the text inerrant. But I am not using this definition here. For me, inspiration denotes each biblical writer's *graced* desire and attempt to comprehend the world in light of God's revelation. God lies at the center of this interpretive process, otherwise it would be inappropriate to speak of *grace*, but I do not think the resulting overlays—the four gospels and the Epistles, say—somehow lose their human, fallible flavor during their composition. Theologically speaking, God need not bypass our historicity and contextuality—our createdness, if you will—in the process of gifting us with divine grace.

Our createdness is crucial. But this does not mean that inspiration is self-generated; it is God's gift to us. And looking back on Christian history, I sense this gift of inspiration everywhere, incarnate as the search for significance, both throughout and within almost numberless men and women, some famous and some far less so. I detect it in Anselm's attempt to balance faith and reason, in Hildegard of Bingen's sense that God sustains life's interconnectedness, and in Dietrich Bonhoeffer's so-called secular Christianity. But inspiration is not restricted to those who add building blocks to the grand cathedrals of the Christian mind; inspiration may be found in ordinary women and men, those "who lived faithfully a hidden life, and rest in unvisited tombs," to steal George Eliot's last line in *Middlemarch*.[5]

Inspiration may also appear in the work of those novelists, whether inside or outside the traditional circle of Christian faith, who have used and continue to use their creative imagination to gesture toward Mystery. When I speak of our featured novelists as contributing to a biblical faith still in the making, I am saying that I view them the way I view all peoples, Christian or not, as men and women who sometimes find themselves engaged in a graced search for theological meaning.[6] We will not always agree with the meaning such novelists, or anyone for that matter, derive from serious reflection on God, life, and reality. However, we can admire the struggle along the way.

Whenever women and men, past or present, gesture toward Mystery, and risk, like Jacob, becoming disabled in the struggle, there we can find a biblical faith still in the making.[7] The novelists I take up in this book are part of this graced tradition. They are part, that is, of an entire history of theological reflection, one that is still being articulated every time Christians think about the world and God's purposes. And even though the novelists and the stories I have selected are edgy and unconventional, in ways that trouble some Christians, I still think they promise to enrich our faith. Much depends on having the eyes to see and the ears to hear, and so, to prepare the way for the theology-based literary criticism that I pursue throughout the following five chapters, I want to pause for a moment and reflect on stories—why we read as well as interpret them and, ultimately, how they can make a difference.

"I Love to Tell the Story"

I adopt a reading strategy that examines stories and provides interpretation from a decidedly Christian perspective.[8] To this end, I make a series of general claims about the nature of stories and about reading, drawing on several sources to develop a way of treating novels—our focused genre—as other worlds that we, as readers, are invited to visit, and challenged to view charitably. Various connections to Christianity will surface at appropriate points, thereby making it possible for readers to sense that what follows is as much about theology as it is about fiction. The following six points explain my understanding of narrative. And they indicate how reflecting on stories might guide us in the direction of theological humility as well as toward leading more hospitable lives.

1: *Stories occupy the very center of our experience as human beings.* This is because they capture, delineate, and evoke our basic as well as common feelings of longing and loss. We live by the stories we craft and tell—stories characterized by joy and sorrow as well as by accomplishment and disappointment.[9] "Narration is as much part of human nature as breath and the circulation of the blood," A. S. Byatt asserts.[10] Reynolds Price agrees. "The need to tell and hear stories is," he says, "the second most important need after food."[11] And since Christianity's origins lie in the so-called greatest story ever told, I suspect most Christians would acknowledge Byatt's and Price's point. Jesus was by no means the first Jewish religious teacher to teach in parables, but he certainly used this method of vivid and memorable storytelling effectively. His initial followers remembered as well as recorded his parables and, down the ages, Christians have found ways to live out their truths, and thus continue Christ's work on earth. Today, popular hymns such as "I Love to Tell the Story" and "Tell Me the Story of Jesus" espouse the narrative quality of Christian existence.

2: *Stories cultivate and promote the quest for wisdom.* "Reader and writer," Eudora Welty declares, "we wish each other well. Don't we want and don't we understand the same thing? A story of beauty and passion, some fresh approximation of human truth?"[12] When we listen to stories, in other words, we commit ourselves to an important task—the search for significance. And this search is an extraordinarily complex process. Stories most certainly involve reader and writer, as Welty implies, yet literary critics like Roberto Callaso think they involve God as well. "Literature is never the product of a single subject," he announces. "There are always at least three actors: the hand that writes, the voice that speaks, the god who watches over and compels."[13] Yet how does God watch over and compel us? It is hard to say. Perhaps God inspires us to craft prose that gestures toward Mystery, theologian Paul S. Fiddes wonders; if so, then Calasso's remark represents another way of describing fiction and the fiction writer as part of a graced search for meaning.[14] I suspect most Christians would welcome such observations, because they uphold the alliance between, not to mention the preoccupation with, both truth and God—twin themes in any believer's self-understanding.

3: *Stories honor life's labyrinthine qualities, the way events and people twist and turn, sometimes unexpectedly so.* Unlike the systematic theologies that today's Christians find so appealing, stories are seldom neat and orderly. Instead, they often appear as chaotic as the lives they chart and the world they mimic. Consider Charles Dickens. He populates his carefully wrought worlds with characters whose lives so oscillate between emotional extremes—Skimpole in *Bleak House* and Pecksniff in *Our Mutual Friend*—as to defy tidy categorization. And then there are some novelists, like Martin Amis, who intentionally invert their narratives to create stories—*Time's Arrow*—that unravel like a film playing in reverse. This strategy enables such writers to show us the tricks time often plays on our consciousness. Stories also resist clear answers as well as provide few final endings. And whereas theologies committed to propositions and formulas often seek to close things down, to draw boundaries around what can and cannot be said about life and God, stories open out, often fitfully, and sometimes stimulate several interpretations or overlays. Stories operate in this way because language functions likewise. Calasso writes:

> Words are scattered archipelagos, drifting, sporadic. The mind is the sea. To recognize this sea in the mind seems to have become something forbidden, something that the presiding orthodoxies, in their various manifestations, whether scientistic or merely commonsensical, instinctively avoid.[15]

This observation entails that there is everything in language and story but closure. This notion troubles some theologians, of course, for they are used to securing Final Meaning through the practice of conceptual rigor and logical exactitude. For Calasso, however, literature—as a form of story—"grows like the grass between the heavy gray paving stones of thought."[16] Literature thus resists conceptualization; and it frequently presents itself to us "in all its recklessness: irresponsible, metamorphic, carrying no identity card that a desk sergeant might examine, deceptive in its tone . . . and, finally, subject to no authority."[17]

Language and story offer theology a return to humility, where theological humility means avoiding God-talk that speaks as though it takes God's point of view. Rowan Williams makes this point in his book, *On Christian Theology*. And it is no small matter that in addition to being a theologian and Archbishop of Canterbury, Williams writes and publishes poetry. Sensitive to words, especially to their unruly drift of meanings, he knows that serious reflection on language and story relativizes our ambitious theological pronouncements—it shows, in other words, that any attempt at a Final Say or a Total Perspective is impossible.[18] Yet Williams is far from one-sided at this point. He knows, as perhaps every good theologian ought to know, that when Christians use language, engage stories, and consult literature, they need, certainly at some point in their quest for understanding, to stop, pause, and ask what difference, if any, Christian theology makes to their efforts. For Williams, the theologian makes his or her difference by insisting on doctrine's ability to help us find some way through life's labyrinth:

> Theology of this sort nags away at the logic of our generative religious stories and rituals, trying to set out both in its speech *and* in its procedures what the logic entails. It will understand doctrinal definition as the attempt to make sure that we are still speaking of *God* in our narratives, not about the transactions of mythological subjects or about the administration of religious power.[19]

On this model, theology may best be seen as coming after the story, there to insure that the so-called God-overlay prevails. I promote *theology after reading* throughout my book. This approach requires first, reading a novel on its own terms and, then, working with its many features—plot, imagery, characterization, and symbol—to see how they come together and stimulate, perhaps even provoke, theological reflection.[20]

4: Stories invite us to take time out of our busy, perhaps even comfortable, routines to visit other worlds. We often leave town when we are on vacation. And sometimes being on holiday inspires us to journey overseas and transcend our cultural boundaries. I liken the act of reading fiction to the task of exploring another country. In each case, questions need to be asked, plans drawn up, and decisions made. When traveling abroad, for example, we often need a passport, perhaps a guide to the host culture's customs and language, not to mention its sights and sounds. We frequently need access to different currency, and, perhaps most importantly, we need to cultivate a curious attitude, one that does not automatically assign cultural inferiority to the place where we plan to spend some time. It is much the same with reading novels.

Novels are like other countries. And to adventure in the foreign land represented by the novel is to enter like a good tourist and roam around the fictional terrain that each writer creates, taking note of its many sights and sounds, the small but not insignificant details that constitute the novel's otherness. We visit novels in this way by surrendering our everyday self to the imaginative possibilities suggested by the narrative's province, then by encountering and opening ourselves up to other, fictional selves along the way, and, finally, by finishing the story, exiting its world, and returning to our everyday world, sometimes even transformed.[21]

The words I use are not without meaning for the Christian reader. This is because words such as "surrender" and "transformation" display religious resonance, an echo perhaps of the Christian language of conversion. Like God, novels require an outpouring of self coupled with an openness to change. C. S. Lewis puts it succinctly: "The first demand any work of art makes upon us is surrender. Look. Listen. Receive. Get yourself out the way."[22] If we surrender to the novel, then we stand poised and ready to be transformed, even by those views we dissent from or abominate, he declares.[23] To run with this metaphor is to suppose that God, as the author of our lives, sometimes requires us to abandon self, to "let go and let God," as my evangelical friends phrase it, and to make ourselves vulnerable to the transforming power of the divine, even when to do so feels like the hardest thing in the world.[24]

5: Stories dare us to assess them. "The test of a book lies in its power to map or transform a life," according to literary critic Mark Edmundson, and this pragmatic approach entails that "the question we would ultimately ask of any work of art is this: Can you live it?"[25] Of course, any answer to this question—either yes or no—launches us into the debate surrounding the so-called ethics of reading, or, the how and why of interpretation. For his part, Edmundson follows Matthew Arnold in believing that great stories can now take the place of religion; Edmundson's ethics of reading are shaped, therefore, by humanism. However, because "I Love to Tell the Story," my ethics of reading reflect my Christian commitment.[26]

When Christians sing this familiar hymn, as I often do, they mean the story of how and why a tender, merciful God visits and redeems us through Jesus of Nazareth, the Christ. But Christians must not simply *tell* this story. The New Testament demands that they *live* it, and they must live it in ways that show the story makes a difference. What this means is that our own tenderness toward others is the final yardstick of our own commitment to the Christian story of the God of tender mercies. If we extend charity and hospitality to others, and perhaps especially to those we might be tempted to think of as somehow beyond charity's and hospitality's official range, then we show ourselves to be Christians who not only tell the story but, in truth, embody it. There are stories, just as there are people, that we, as Christians, will find both difficult and troubling, maybe so troubling that we find ourselves tempted to dismiss them. What I am suggesting here, though, is that we suspend judgment in such situations, forgive any possible offense, and work to view either the story or the person charitably. Augustine coined a phrase for this Christian model of interpretation. He called it "the hermeneutics of love."[27] And these days numerous thinkers uphold the usefulness of this approach both textually and existentially. Alan Jacobs speaks of reading with *caritas*, Valentine Cunningham talks of reading with tact, and Nancy M. Malone addresses how reading enlarges our sympathies.[28] "In fiction," Malone says, "I come to know and understand people I may not have met otherwise. And thus I am persuaded to a more compassionate, generous, and loving response in my life beyond books."[29] Stories not only take us outside ourselves, into other lives, they also challenge us to read or interpret such lives graciously.

6: *Stories impact communities of readers as well as individuals—maybe, certain texts can only be understood rightly as communal texts.* In one sense, my theory of reading reflects a broadly humanistic endeavor; it says that reading changes lives.[30] Our society concurs by sending out the signal that reading stimulates delight and fosters civility. Part of me responds to this signal enthusiastically, at least as much can be inferred from the fact that I am spending this summer reading aloud to Jonathan, my toddler, as part of the Fort Worth Mayor's 2007 Reading Challenge.

Reading brings pleasure. It also brings peril, though, and this is because reading is powerful. It is powerful when an Israeli boy confronts anti-Semitism in Christopher Marlowe's *The Jew of Malta*. Reading is powerful when teenage girls consult romance fiction obsessively. And reading most certainly proved powerful for John David Chapman. His favorite novel growing up was J. D. Salinger's *The Catcher in the Rye*, an account of a neurotic adolescent who rebels against what he considers the phoniness of modern society. In 1980, shortly after firing several shots into John Lennon, Chapman dropped his gun and calmly took out his copy of Salinger's novel, sat down on the curb, and read until the police arrived.[31] Reading is powerful. It is powerful when a young couple commit suicide after reading William Shakespeare's *Romeo and Juliet*, and, more abstractly but no less powerfully, when teenage boys read James Joyce's *Portrait of an Artist* and suppose that forsaking community and forging out as an individual, unaccountable to no one and no thing, is the hallmark of hip, the very meaning of cool.

This last example is especially interesting to me as a Christian reader. I say this because reading, especially reading in Western literature, is powerful precisely because it often celebrates rather than challenges the reader. It frequently honors, sometimes to the point of glamorizing, the seemingly irrefutable subjectivity of the romantic hero, the lone searcher, the rugged individualist, and the withdrawn quietist. But this trend only unhinges me. I thus side with literary critic Wayne C. Booth.[32] He says that reading should never be something for the individual alone. What matters, he says, is the company we keep. And this means that some of our best reading will very likely need to take place in community, because communities hold our views in check, scrutinize our interpretations, and challenge our opinions. If and when they function this way, communities make it harder for us—at least in principle— to become carried away with ourselves.[33]

Christian reading should stress congregational accountability. Believers read best in an *ekklesia*, in the faith assembly, where there is godly wisdom within our group discussions. I am not saying that Christians should simply run out and join one of the many book clubs that we see scattered around our churches today. Doing so would be a start, to be sure, but it is not everything. Rather, I am saying that Christians read best when they gather together and view stories from the foot of the cross, so to speak, and in full view of its shadow. Golgotha represents part of the story that Christians love to tell. And the knowledge of Christ's self-sacrifice on Calvary corrects any theory of reading that glamorizes self. Of course, there is no guarantee that what I say here or elsewhere will foster theological humility and inspire more hospitable lives. I can only hope that it might, though, and we would do well to recall that some Christians, like the Apostle Paul, feel that hope saves us. Malone writes:

> We hope for all kinds of things from a book—pleasure, knowledge, insight, intimacy, greater understanding of others and ourselves,

beauty. But reading can also, in a deeper and more inchoate fashion, *give* us hope. Hope that there is a God whose extravagant fecundity is the source of the mysterious creative impulse of the artists among us. That the care and attention writers lavish on their characters are bestowed on us by our Creator. And that there is in life the kind of wholeness achieved in a great work of literature—a master narrative in which, though we cannot always see how, your story and mine have their part.[34]

THE BOOK'S OUTLINE

Fascinating things happen when theology and fiction come together. And in the next five chapters I outline as well as explore what such things are. In doing so, of course, I leave behind some of the theoretical notions covered in this introduction and, where appropriate, apply some of them more specifically. Overall, in what follows we see how traditional Christian theologians have attempted to formulate both the questions and answers of religious faith into systematic doctrine and, in turn, we explore how recent novelists, alongside certain post-WWII Christian theologians, appear to challenge, invert, reinterpret, and sometimes even affirm, the basic questions and answers of these more traditional theologians. In examining what happens when we think theologically after reading fiction, we acquaint ourselves with some of the basic ideas in Christian doctrine as well as recognize their expression as themes in selected works of literature.

Even though its chapters adopt and proceed out from a certain structure, *Theology after Reading* does not template Christian doctrinal categories onto literary texts; I do not shoehorn fiction into theology. Such a strategy—theology *before* reading—would be artificial at best and misleading at worst. My book's structure thus serves heuristic purposes only; in other words, working through various doctrines via various authors has a mapping function to it. Following critic Richard Lansdown, I find it difficult to argue against literature's autonomy, so the novel always comes first in my mind, yet I arrange things the way I do because this is how fiction stimulates or provokes me.[35] Theology *after* reading.

The book's first chapter addresses how Greene's *The End of the Affair* portrays Maurice Bendrix's struggle to accept faith in God, as he moves away from unsettled atheism into unsettled belief. This novel helps us think about divine existence and agency, especially in the form of miracle(s), providence, and grace.

Next, I examine how Morrison's *Sula* describes the friendship between Sula and Nel as they move from girlhood to womanhood, and how the author uses such characters to explore good and evil's uneasy affiliation. This novel helps us think about human nature, particularly our createdness, sin, fallenness, and our need for redemption.

The third chapter investigates how Kazantzakis' *The Last Temptation of Christ* imaginatively recreates a controversial life and death of Jesus. This novel helps us think about Christ's person and work, above all his humanity and the notion of salvation as deification (*theosis*).

After Kazantzakis, I delineate how Lovelace's *The Wine of Astonishment* registers the effect of the *Shouters Prohibition Ordinance*, which Trinidad and Tobago's colonial government passed in 1917, against a small community of Spiritual Baptists ("the Shouters"). Charting the church's survival between 1917 and 1951, the year the government lifted its ban, Lovelace links ecclesial witness to anticolonial resistance and, in so doing, offers an arresting portrait of non-Western Christianity. This novel helps us think about the church's nature and mission, especially in our increasingly global world.

The last chapter tackles how Paul Thigpen's *My Visit to Hell* graphically, and sometimes animatedly, retells Dante Alighieri's *Inferno* for our postmodern age. This novel helps us think about eschatology, the so-called last things, and especially death as well as judgment. An appendix features an interview with Thigpen, enabling us to grasp how and why he wrote his end times fiction.

For Further Reading

W. Dale Brown interviews a dozen contemporary writers on their faith and art in *Of Fiction and Faith: Twelve American Writers Talk about Their Vision and Work* (Grand Rapids, Mich.: W. B. Eerdmans, 1997). David S. Cunningham examines how key phrases in the Apostles' Creed emerge as cultural themes in *Reading Is Believing: The Christian Faith through Literature and Film* (Grand Rapids, Mich.: Brazos Press, 2002). In *Why Read?* (New York: Bloomsbury, 2004), Mark Edmundson discusses the difference books make in our lives. Paul S. Fiddes explores the relationship between human imagination and divine revelation in *Freedom and Limit: A Dialogue between Literature and Christian Doctrine* (Macon, Ga.: Mercer University Press, 1999). Justo L. González outlines the contours of Christian theology in *A Concise History of Christian Doctrine* (Nashville, Tenn.: Abingdon Press, 2007). D. Bruce Lockerbie offers an account of the antitranscendental trend in literature from Matthew Arnold to the present day in *Dismissing God: Modern Writers' Struggle Against Religion* (Grand Rapids, Mich.: Baker, 1998). Nancy M. Malone's *Walking a Literary Labyrinth: A Spirituality of Reading* (New York: Riverhead Books, 2003) investigates how fiction changes us religiously. Ian S. Markham's *Understanding Christian Doctrine* (Malden, Mass.: Blackwell, 2007) is an energetic introduction to key Christian beliefs, with special focus on areas of contemporary concern. Alister E. McGrath has authored as well as edited numerous texts that appeal to Christians. His edited volume of primary sources, *The Christian Theology Reader*, third edition (Malden, Mass.: Blackwell, 2007; 2001, 1996), offers brief excerpts from many theologians across the centuries. He both groups his selections thematically and provides short introductions for each anthologized entry. His own text, *Christian Theology: An Introduction*, fourth edition (Malden, Mass.: Blackwell, 2007; 2001, 1996, 1993) accompanies the *Reader*. Another edited volume, *Christian Literature: An Anthology* (Malden, Mass.: Blackwell, 2001) collects writings on prayers, sermons, and poems, covering all major periods in the English language. Gaye Williams Ortiz's and Clara B. Joseph's edited volume, *Theology and Literature: Rethinking Reader Responsibility* (New York: Palgrave, 2006) reiterates the reader's importance in the act of interpreting texts. Finally, Michael Ryan's *Literary Theory: A Practical Introduction*, second edition (Malden, Mass.: Blackwell, 2007; 1999) outlines currents in contemporary literary theory with special reference to recent fiction and film.

Selected Web Sites

1. http://www.pepperdine.edu/sponsored/ccl/
   The official site of the Conference on Christianity and Literature, an academic society that explores the relationships between the two subjects.

2. http://www.iclnet.org
   An impressive gateway to sites concerned with creeds, confessions of faith, denominational histories, theological themes, and Christian personalities.

3. http://www.ccel.org
   Calvin College's comprehensive site for online versions of primary sources in Christian theology.

4. http://www.kristisiegel.com/theory.htm
   Constructed and maintained by the Director of the English Graduate Program at Mount Mary College, Milwaukee, Wisconsin, this site offers an excellent introduction to the notoriously complex field of modern literary theory.

1

GOD

Graham Greene's *The End of the Affair*

Driving his readers to identify with characters beyond the customary limits of pity, the English Roman Catholic author Graham Greene has created some of modern fiction's most paradoxical figures. One such figure is God, particularly the God featured in *The End of the Affair*, Greene's 1951 novel about ill-fated love in the ruins of World War II London.[1] Written during the middle period of Greene's career, *The End of the Affair* is his most impressive—and perhaps most disturbing—theological novel. For in it, Greene suggests that God is reckless and severe: an invidious Lover whose strategies of seduction are as appalling as they are strange. If and when seen through traditional Christian spectacles, this figuration of God strains theological credibility. Greene's deity, it might be said, is much too sinister and unpredictable to warrant our worship. His God is not traditional Christian doctrine's enduringly good Lord. And yet, before we make any expeditious judgments, let us regard Greene's vocational self-understanding. "A writer's job," he told critic Philip Toynbee in 1957, is "to try to engage people's sympathy for characters outside the official range of sympathy."[2] As we will see, Greene problematizes the limits of permissible Christian theological speculation, chiefly through his use of dramatic suggestiveness, in order to secure our warmth for God. If God is torn, Greene claims, between tenderness and barbarism, between love and hate, as we often are, then God suffers internal division and strife, as we often do. Greene, then, perceives his God as a more real, and thus sympathetic character.[3]

With this first chapter I begin my examination of the relationship between Christian doctrine and modern fiction through an analysis of

Greene's controversial but potentially sympathetic characterization of the divine. This characterization, as we will see, has links to several literary and theological figures and themes that Greene energetically defends or disputes. In the tradition of Thomas Hardy, for instance, he develops the thought that an ironic God resides at the heart of life, hovering over us, its earthly quarry, while seemingly indifferent to our concerns. By drawing upon Robert Browning's poetry, particularly "Bishop Blougram's Apology," Greene also suggests that all Christians frequently find themselves embracing both faith and doubt, if honest, blending both qualities within their conflicted souls.[4] Read theologically, *The End of the Affair* addresses various arguments for God's existence as Greene grapples with topics discussed by theologians as diverse as Anselm of Canterbury, Thomas Aquinas, William Paley, John Henry Newman, and Baron Friedrich von Hügel—topics concerning how the world's intricate design proves that God exists, how Christian doctrine develops across time, and how the genuine religious impulse lies much deeper than the intellect. The twofold purpose of my first chapter, then, is first to show how these literary and theological thinkers and concepts come together around one problem in Greene's writing, the notoriously intractable question of the existence, nature, and activity of God, and, second, to assess whether or not Greene's answer, his imaginatively ironic portrait of the divine, should enlist our sympathy.

This chapter has four major sections. First, I sketch Greene's life and literary art, paying particular attention to his so-called Catholic agnosticism, which helps to create the distinction he often draws between faith and belief. Second, I examine the views of certain makers and remakers of the Christian doctrine of God, concentrating on those whose works directly impinge on Greene's novel. For example, since Richard Smythe, the earnest rationalist in *The End of the Affair*, refutes the traditional arguments for the existence of God, I focus on the theological concepts and considerations associated with Anselm, Aquinas, and Paley. Furthermore, I delineate and comment on Newman and von Hügel's particular Catholic theology, as Greene admired the personal, not strictly logical, approach to God and faith favored by both thinkers. In the third and major section, I offer a Christian theological reading of *The End of the Affair*, focusing on how the Christian doctrine of God surfaces as a cardinal theme at decisive points in Greene's narrative. And in the final section, I try to evoke sympathy for Greene's ideas by accenting the biblical basis to his portrait of an ironic God.

GRAHAM GREENE: LIFE AND LITERARY ART

Greene was born the fourth of six children in 1904 in the Hertfordshire region of England. Shortly after his father was appointed headmaster at Berkhamsted School in 1911, Greene grew exceedingly ill and acutely depressed. At only seven, he entered an intense period of psychoanalysis and underwent a six-month convalescence in London. In 1922, he went up to Oxford, where he spent three years reading history. There he edited the *Oxford Outlook*, flirted with membership in the Communist Party, published some experimental verse, formed important friendships, and met Vivien Dayrell-Browning, his future wife. After graduation, Greene worked as a journalist in Nottingham. Upon taking catechism classes from Father Trollope, he converted to Catholicism in 1926 and a year later married Dayrell-Browning—two of the most momentous occasions of his life. At this point, he accepted a job working with the staff of the London *Times*. His first novel, *The Man Within*, was published in 1929, prompting him to leave journalism to concentrate on travel and writing. Always somewhat restive, Greene satiated his wanderlust, not to mention his desire for copy, by traveling to places such as Burgundy, Cologne, Sweden, and West Africa. While he produced several critically acclaimed novels, travelogues, movie scripts, and somewhat controversial film reviews between 1931 and 1937, the 1938 publication of *Brighton Rock* garnered the attention of numerous Christian readers, clergy and laity alike.

The first of four so-called Catholic novels, *Brighton Rock* chronicles the fallout from gangland warfare in an English coastal town at Whitsuntide, and it plays with the provocative idea that God's limitless mercy reaches down and saves those whom we are tempted to believe irredeemable, beyond salvation, or outside the official range of divine sympathy. Greene's travels through Mexico, which he undertook in 1937–1938, inspired his portrayal of an irreverent priest hunted down by God and the state in *The Power and the Glory* (1940). And his 1942–1943 tour of duty in Sierra Leone for MI6, the British Secret Intelligence Service, shaped *The Heart of the Matter* (1948), which addresses the thorny issue of suicide as a mortal sin. As I explain in the next section, Greene outlined *The End of the Affair* (1951), the last installment in this Catholic tetralogy, on Capri in 1948.

Later travels in Indochina, Kenya, Vietnam, Cuba, Haiti, the United States, and Argentina yielded experiences that Greene wove into the fabric of his more political novels, such as *The Quiet American* (1955), *Our Man in Havana* (1958), *The Comedians* (1966), and *The Honorary Consul* (1973). Throughout the 1970s and into the early 1980s Greene authored several plays, a number of novels, and two autobiographies, but ill health in the late 1980s forced him to ration his literary output. Greene died in 1991 in Vevey, Switzerland.

While Greene often informed his friends and contemporaries that "a ruling passion gives to a shelf of novels the unity of a system," critics of his literary art have found it extraordinarily difficult to define and discuss the content of this "ruling passion."[5] Perhaps this is because Greene's own character seems so paradoxical, even ironic. In many of his recorded interviews, for example, Greene comes across as a taciturn man both haunted and fortified by an inner core of faith and doubt, of self-interest and self-effacement, and of loyalty and disloyalty. He looks for evidence of humanity in what most of us would think of as inhuman characters. Moreover, he seems to believe that evil contains within itself the seeds of good and that authentic faith pulsates at the heart of the unconventionally pious. Ostensibly able to coagulate numerous contradictions within his own embattled soul, Greene divides his allegiances without any anxiety—except, of course, in his fiction—and he consistently loiters on what Browning calls "the dangerous edge of things."[6] Browning's influence is worth noting at this juncture because he helps us understand Greene's primary theological conviction, his commitment to a life marked by ambiguity and irony.

Born in London in 1812, Browning was educated at home by his extremely well-read father. An independent spirit, he left the University of London after only a year, choosing to follow his own, self-directed reading plan. He married Elizabeth Barrett in 1846, and they settled in Florence until her death in 1861. Browning's *Collected Poems*, published in 1862, established him as one of the most heralded poets of the Victorian period (1832–1901). After his death in 1889, he was buried in Westminster Abbey's Poet's Corner.

"If I were to choose an epigraph for all the novels I have written," Greene reveals in *A Sort of Life*, "it would be from *Bishop Blougram's Apology*," one of the poems featured in Browning's *Men and Women*, first published in 1855:

> Our interest's on the dangerous edge of things.
> The honest thief, the tender murderer,

The superstitious atheist, demirep
That loves and saves her soul in new French
    books—
We watch while these in equilibrium keep
The giddy line midway.[7]

"With Robert Browning," Greene divulges, "I lived in a region of adulteries, of assignations at dark street corners, of lascivious priests and hasty dagger thrusts, and of sexual passion far more heady than romantic love."[8] Under Browning's influence, he cultivated a spirit of contradiction—an intoxicating zeal to practice divided loyalties, to entertain competing ideologies, and to honor the conflicting emotions and impulses that swirl and rage within us, struggling for our unbroken attention. This spirit of contradiction explains Greene's well-known narrative sleight-of-hand, as well as his fondness for creating characters marked by manifold incongruities: the unorthodox clergyman who experiences the gratuity of the divine Self-gift and the secret agent who embodies sincerity in the midst of his duplicity. As one of Greene's critics, Penelope Gilliatt, writes: "He is moved most by characters who have to be strong because they are weak, who have to be good because they think themselves sinners."[9]

Greene's interest in the mystery of sin and the desire for salvation forms a secondary theological commitment that stems from his awareness of life's ambiguities and paradoxes. Not black and white, Greene insists, human nature is black and gray, which entails that both good and evil can always find a place in our lives. We are marked by an intricate duality that stains and pains us and from which we desperately seek some way of escape. Our souls frequently resemble war zones with emotional and spiritual shrapnel exploding everywhere; at such times we crave only peace, whether temporary or ultimate.[10] Greene's literary art is replete with examples of this struggle. Consider Major Scobie, Greene's symbol of fragmented consciousness in *The Heart of the Matter*, who feels torn between the competing values of pity and pride, or else Alden Pyle, Greene's symbol of innocence and experience in *The Quiet American*, who feels caught on the borderland between naïve intrusiveness and informed engagement, never sure exactly which way to turn. Pyle and Scobie eventually escape their predicament. But we, as readers, come to their stories' end to find that Greene has challenged us to ponder the ambiguous nature of their salvation or escape.

For Greene, anxiety—the precondition of sin—occurs when we realize the almost numberless moral and spiritual dilemmas in any day's course. Such dilemmas appear to exist outside of us, exerting some hold on the way we live; they seem to chase us down, to nip at our heels. Many of us feel pursued, Greene avers, by conscience, by others, and especially by God. We possess an awareness that something or someone hunts us, like a bloodhound chasing after prized quarry. This awareness forms another of Greene's theological convictions.[11] One thinks here of Francis Andrews, the smuggler in Greene's first novel, *The Man Within*, who spends most of his beleaguered life running from fellow smugglers as well as from himself, particularly his past. And then Pinkie, the embodiment of wanton malevolence in *Brighton Rock*, who feels himself cornered both by Ida Arnold, his avenging angel, and God, whose strange and appalling mercy refuses to let him go.

Greene holds that God pursues us with an offer of salvation, an invitation to escape anxiety and sin, but he also believes that God's offer presents itself to us as a peculiar providence. In other words, Greene's God comes across as furtive, severe, even dastardly, someone who shocks us into submission through violent grace. In *The End of the Affair*, the self-absorbed, hate-filled, God-scorning Maurice Bendrix does not deserve God's good favor, yet he suffers the sneaky tactics of the divine who forces him to move from his own apprehensive atheism to the brink of belief. As the critic William Cash states, "The strange mercy of God was an obsession with Greene; the more unlikely the recipient the better."[12]

Greene's understanding of faith as troubled commitment derives from his own theological convictions—the paradoxical character of our world, the mystery of sin and salvation, and the anxiety of being hunted by a God whose mercy seems caught in a bizarre concoction with cruelty. Greene's construal of faith has a personal history, one that begins with his conversion in 1926, when he took the spiritual name of the doubting disciple Thomas. Greene the Doubter went on to model a faith marked by skepticism and distrust. He cared very little for the so-called proofs of God's existence, a trait shared by many of his characters, especially the protagonist in his short story "A Visit to Morin." Moreover, he found the doctrine of the Trinity highly unpersuasive, dismissing it as the end-product of bad mathematical reasoning. And while he was intrigued by the scholarly quest for the historical Jesus, he abhorred academic attempts to demythologize Scripture, particularly the Johannine account of Jesus' physical resurrection. In short, Greene approached things of the spirit by blending faith and doubt into his own careworn soul. In the following conversation between Greene and his confessor, Father Leopoldo Duran, one catches a glimpse of Greene's religious outlook:

> "Each day I have less and less faith," said Graham.
> And I replied: "Yes, but you have often told me that with every passing day you find you have less 'belief,' but more 'faith.'"
> Graham was silent. He suddenly came out with the most perfect remark on the subject. "The trouble is I don't believe my unbelief." No more precise sentence could have been uttered to define the faith of this man, to describe his spiritual life . . . I can testify that Graham Greene's faith was in a state of constant inner struggle with itself and that it obsessed him.[13]

Browning's influence appears to hover behind Greene's irresolute spirituality. Recall Greene's fondness for "Bishop Blougram's Apology" and now consider the following stanza, which articulates Browning's borderland religion:

> All we have gained then by our unbelief
> Is a life of doubt diversified by faith,
> For one of faith diversified by doubt:
> We call the chess-board white,—we call it
>   black.[14]

Greene's own borderland religion is best known by another term, "Catholic agnosticism," which he uses in numerous interviews. This term denotes a way of experiencing life that is both loyal and disloyal to the official teachings of the church—an unsettled, quizzical approach to any and all authorized patterns of Christian faith and practice. For example, Greene was particularly impatient with theologians such as Anselm and Aquinas who spent their time intellectualizing not only God's existence but also God's nature and activity. According to Greene, any attempt to conceptualize the divine, especially divine providence, yields little or no positive result, because life is replete with those inexplicable moments that reason appears powerless to explain. He believes that God's nature and activity are deeply inscrutable. And this sense of theological mystery inspires the strategic distinction Greene makes between the rational and irrational aspects of Christianity:

There's a difference between belief and faith. If I don't believe in X or Y, faith intervenes, telling me I am wrong not to believe. Faith is above belief. One can say that it's a gift of God, while belief is not. Belief is founded on reason. On the whole I keep my faith while enduring long periods of disbelief.[15]

As we will see, Greene's distinction between faith and belief surfaces in the latter part of *The End of the Affair,* when Bendrix appears forced by a succession of unfathomable events to consider the possibility that God is at work in his life, seeking sheer trust from his—Bendrix's— tormented, indecisive soul. Thus, having struggled with Greene's chief theological convictions, but before I offer a Christian theological reading of his novel, I turn to sketch the Christian doctrine of God.

THE DOCTRINE OF GOD: A SELECTIVE SKETCH

Centuries of serious and detailed readings of the Christian Bible (the Hebrew Bible and the New Testament) has led to what scholars now recognize as the traditional doctrine of God. Working from Scripture, Christians of the Patristic period (100–451) came to believe that certain traits properly belong to God alone.[16] For them, God is one, not many; God stands as the supreme being at the heart of the cosmos, and God exists as an eternal spirit, which entails that there never has been a past nor will there be a future void of God's presence. God is holy and personal, which means that God possesses mind, will, and feelings, attributes made positively manifest through equitable, tender, and beneficent means; God fully immerses Godself in creation, active as its originator and sustainer, though not to be conflated with this natural realm; God is omnipresent, omniscient, and omnipotent. God cannot change, and God is genuinely consistent in all that God does; finally, God seeks to reveal Godself to God's people. Countless theologians across the centuries have shaped, evaluated, rejected, reshaped, and demonstrated this description of God.[17]

Elaborate discussions about God's existence and activity became enormously popular in the years during and after the rise of the monasteries and the universities in medieval Europe (1050–1300).[18] Anselm and Aquinas were two of the most influential Christian scholars of this time, and their theological convictions constitute Christianity's intellectual scaffolding. Since Greene writes *The End of the Affair,* at least in part, to dismantle such scaffolding, I focus on both medieval thinkers, noting the development of their ideas as well as their importance for contemporary Christian theology. I introduce Paley after discussing Aquinas, since Paley's suggestion that a watch proves a watchmaker, and our universe proves God, builds on Aquinas' idea that behind the universe's design, however simple or complex, lies the Designer, God.

Anselm, Aquinas, and Paley

Born in 1033 in Aosta, Piedmont, now modern day Italy, Anselm traveled at age twenty-six to Normandy, France and settled at the Benedictine monastery of Bec. At this time, Bec's prior, the successful scholar and lawyer Lanfranc, launched him on his course of religious and intellectual development. He encouraged Anselm to read Aristotle and Augustine, for example, and Anselm completed this task with considerable enthusiasm, eventually acquiring an appreciation for their use of dialectic as a tool in philosophical and theological argumentation. In the late 1070s, though, Anselm became increasingly aware that his mentor's administrative and practical interests contrasted with his own more academic and theoretical passions, so he disengaged himself from Lanfranc's mentorship. Anselm next produced several books, which rightfully earned him a reputation as the fountainhead of Scholasticism (1200–1500). Later he became the prior and then abbot of Bec. Anselm lived his last sixteen years as the Archbishop of Canterbury, obliged to leave France for England after numerous public disagreements with various kings concerning church-state relations.

In his *Prayers and Meditations*, composed sometime between 1070 and 1075, Anselm claims that the life of the intellect and the life of prayer are not in opposition, as many Christians of his day believed, but rather that they serve as vital and necessary concomitants. While Anselm refutes that unaided knowledge of God is possible, holding that the content of the Christian faith is revealed, he nonetheless teaches that our intellect is a gift from God, that "a true and effective mind" is, at least partially, a step toward genuine Christian devotion, and that faith is illuminated by reason.[19] In his view, sound Christian theology rests on a "faith that seeks understanding"—*fides quaerens intellectum*.

Anselm's *Monologion*, written in 1075–1076, contains his first attempt to blend reason and faith in an argument designed to establish God's existence. Drawing upon Plato's notion of the Form of the Good, as well as neo-Platonist ideas, Anselm connects the varied good things of our observable world to "that which is good through itself."[20] This supremely good being is that reality through which anything good is good; it rules and regulates all things and is best understood as the God of Christianity. Anselm further develops this argument in *Proslogion* (1077–1078). Here he asserts that God is best defined as "that-than-which-a-greater-cannot-be-thought." Building on this terminological premise, Anselm insists that if God is defined as the greatest conceivable being, and if it is generally agreed that to exist in reality is greater than to exist in thought alone, then we can only think of God as existing in reality as well as in the mind. This enables Anselm to proclaim that God exists. In his own words:

> You exist so truly, Lord my God, that You cannot even be thought not to exist. And this is as it should be, for if some intelligence could think of something better than You, the creature would be above its Creator and would judge its Creator—and that is completely absurd. In fact, everything else there is, except You alone, can be thought of as not existing. You, alone, then, of all things most truly exist and therefore of all things possess existence to the highest degree; for anything else does not exist as truly, and so possesses existence to a lesser degree.[21]

Existence, Anselm concludes, is God's very essence—a predicate, a defining characteristic, without which God would not be God.[22]

Later philosophers, most notably the seventeenth-century thinkers René Descartes and Benedict Spinoza, would augment and refine some of Anselm's basic points. Others, however, such as the eighteenth-century philosophers David Hume and Immanuel Kant as well as the twentieth century's Bertrand Russell, would dispute Anselm's general assumption that existence defines anything, especially God. All things considered, Anselm's basic approach to God, couched as it is in the form of prayerful reflection, has challenged countless women and men across the centuries.[23] But the medieval scholar Aquinas ranks as one of the thinkers most moved by Anselm's work.

Born in 1225 near Naples, Italy, Aquinas was educated under the Benedictines and joined one of the first Christian monasteries, Monte Cassino in Italy, eventually moving to Paris in 1244 as part of his controversial decision to join the newly formed Dominican order. He lived at the Dominican house of studies in Cologne from 1248 to 1252, working with Albert the Great. Aquinas became full professor at the University of Paris in 1256, producing a steady stream of brief commentaries and short treatises until 1259, when he decided to return to Italy to take his teaching and writing in a different direction. Aquinas' Italian sojourn lasted six years, during which time he completed the *Summa contra Gentiles*—a theological manual designed to inform Christians how to convert unbelievers. A short stay in Rome around 1265 inspired Aquinas to begin his *Summa Theologiae*, an architectonic account of Christian theological method and truth designed to assist the spiritual and intellectual formation of priest-scholars. Aquinas resumed his teaching duties at the University of Paris in 1268, lecturing and writing on his own brand of Christian Aristotelianism. However, a terrifyingly sublime experience during Mass on 6 December 1273 left Aquinas with grave doubts about the overall spiritual usefulness of his work. He died in 1274, shortly after uttering one of the most famous phrases in Christian theological history, "All I have written now seems like straw." As a result, he left the *Summa Theologiae* unfinished.[24]

Although Aquinas ultimately finds God in Godself unfathomable, he maintains in his *Summa contra Gentiles* that it is still possible to arrive at some understanding of the divine through two basic methods. One method uses analogical language when speaking of God. According to Aquinas, God possesses the best human characteristics, such as knowledge and goodness, but in an incomprehensibly better form; put differently, what is good in this world is, by analogy, better and truer of God. Countless theologians since Aquinas have found this analogical method both persuasive and serviceable.[25] A second method involves reflecting on natural features of our world, thereby interpreting life's beauty and complexity as evidence of God's benevolent handiwork, a procedure whose roots lie in Aristotle's metaphysical works.[26] Unlike Anselm, Aquinas heeds Aristotle's counsel to begin with the world (*a posteriori*), not the mind (*a priori*), and thus he demonstrates divine existence by appealing to God's effects in nature.[27]

Drawing upon this second method, Aquinas offers five ways to prove God's existence.[28] As part of the first way, he invokes Aristotle's axiom that "nothing can come from nothing." On this view, cosmic change does not explain itself; rather, something or someone must initiate it, for without an initiator, there can be no reason for change. Nothing can come from nothing. Life's own initiator is unchanged, though, for something that both moves and is moved by others does not explain cosmic change comprehensively. Aristotle calls this unique, initiating power the "Unmoved Mover," but it is enough for Aquinas to call it "God."

Aquinas' second way describes life as a series of causes and effects. And in any given event, he says, one cannot have a last cause, or even an intermediate cause, unless one posits a first cause also. But why invoke a *cosmic* First Cause? Surely its alternative, the idea of an endless causal chain, explains life sufficiently? Aquinas disagrees. In his view, one fails to fully explain life by taking its numerous causes and effects and extending them back into eternity; life requires an ultimate explanation. And so Aquinas posits a First Cause—namely, God.

The third way concentrates on notions of contingency and non-contingency. Our world, Aquinas asserts, is contingent, which means there was a time when it was not and there will be a time when it does not exist. Yet following Aristotle, Aquinas once again maintains that "nothing can come from nothing"; events must have an origin. And this origin must be a reality marked by non-contingency (eternal, self-existent, or necessary being). This non-contingent reality is God. If God did not exist necessarily then nothing could exist, for our world depends upon God's non-contingency to exist at all.

In the fourth way, Aquinas draws attention to degrees of perfection in the world, such as goodness and truth, structuring his argument around the analogy of heat made famous by Aristotle:

> One finds among things that there are some more and some less good, true, noble, and so forth. But 'more' and 'less' are said of different things insofar as they approach, in their different ways, something that is the maximum, as in the case of a thing being said to be hotter insofar as it most nearly resembles that which is hottest. There is, therefore, something that is truest, something best, something noblest, and, consequently, something that is most fully in being, for those things that are truest are most fully in being, as it is written in *Metaphysics*. It is said in the same book that the maximum in any genus is the cause of everything in that genus, as, for example, fire, which is the maximum heat, is the cause of all hot things. Therefore there must also be something that is to all beings the cause of their existence, goodness, and every other perfection; and this we call God.[29]

Expressed differently, God represents, defines, and inspires the perfection to which we all strive.

The fifth and final way appeals to the overall presence of teleology, or purposeful aim, in the world. Nothing happens by accident, Aquinas holds, for there seems to be an underlying purpose in every action or behavior. This intelligence, which grounds and guides the world, we call God.

Aquinas' fifth way eventually leads to Paley's argument from design, first presented at the beginning of the nineteenth century. Born in Peterborough, East Anglia, England in 1743, Paley prepared for Anglican holy orders by attending Christ College at the University of Cambridge. Three years after his 1743 graduation, he joined his *alma mater's* faculty, spending the rest of his life writing and lecturing on the reasonableness of Christian doctrine. By the time of his death in 1805, he was a celebrated Anglican divine, an established church theologian with a popular reputation earned from such books as *A View of the Evidence of Christianity* (1794) and *Natural Theology, or, Evidences of the Existence and Attributes of the Deity, Collected from the Appearances of Nature* (1802).[30]

In *Natural Theology*, Paley draws the now famous analogy comparing the world to a watch and God to a watchmaker:

> In crossing a heath, suppose I pitched my foot against a *stone*, and were asked how the stone came to be there; I might possibly answer, that, for anything I knew to the contrary, it had lain there forever: nor would it perhaps be very easy to show the absurdity of this answer. But suppose I had found a *watch* upon the ground, and it should be inquired how the watch happened to be in that place; I should hardly think of the answer which I had before given, that, for anything I knew, the watch might have always been there. Yet why should not this answer serve for the watch as well as for the stone?[31]

Paley answers his own question by claiming that the watch displays ample evidence of craftsmanship; its presence on the heath leads him to posit a watchmaker's existence. Paley then claims that the world displays ample evidence of purpose and design: the five senses, the parts and functions of animals and vegetables, and the circadian rhythms of life. Such evidence, he says, requires an explanation, just like the watch on the heath. Thus, Paley posits a celestial watchmaker who crafts the world into being and becoming.[32]

Newman and von Hügel

Over the years, numerous thinkers have scrutinized and qualified the arguments for God's existence associated with Anselm, Aquinas, and Paley. And two such thinkers—Newman and von Hügel—have made it a point to insist that there is an existential fissure between rational proof and sheer trust. Both Newman and von Hügel's arguments greatly influenced Greene's theological views.[33]

Newman was born in London in 1801 and, as a young man, took "great delight in reading the Bible." He formed his earliest religious opinions—broadly Calvinist and evangelical—soon after converting to Christianity at 15, an experience he records in his *Apologia Pro Vita Sua*, published in seven parts between spring and summer 1864. After graduating from Trinity College, Oxford in 1821, he remained in the city to serve as a curate. In 1828, he was appointed the vicar of St. Mary's in Oxford. From this church's distinguished pulpit he preached many influential sermons, several of which decisively shaped early nineteenth-century Anglican theology and polity. By his own admission, his status in the Church of England rose to its height in spring 1839, but by the end of 1841 he lay, as he stated, "on my death-bed, as regards my membership with the Anglican Church." Realizing his own "Catholic sense" of the Thirty-Nine Articles and sensing that he could not "defend our [Anglican] separation from Rome and her faith without using arguments prejudicial to those great doctrines concerning our Lord, which are the very foundation of the Christian religion," Newman deconverted. The Roman Catholic church received him in 1845, and he used his considerable administrative and teaching skills to found oratories in Birmingham and London. Pope Leo XIII appointed him Cardinal in 1879, eleven years before Newman died of pneumonia in 1890.[34]

Newman's voluminous writings attest to his personal struggle with religious doubt and his energetic quest for religious certainty. This struggle and quest are best understood, critics say, when viewed as Newman's own response to the Victorian crisis of faith, a crisis traceable to the Enlightenment (1648–1800) belief that human reason alone determines and judges all our commitments.[35] By the middle of the nineteenth century, many ordained and lay Christians were wondering about the relationship between the intellect and faith, especially in light of Hume and Kant's devastating critiques of the various arguments for God's existence. In his 1870 *A Grammar of Assent*, Newman analyzes the grounds for religious belief. In this text, he confirms the so-called canon of reason by showing that the act of assent—to a belief, say, in the one God—is a rationally proper and justifiable act or state. Assent is a willful act, of which apprehension is a condition and reason (informal as well as formal) and conscience are antecedents. The "illative sense"—Newman's term for informal reasoning—is central to the act of assent because illation enables us to advance through probabilities to certitude.[36] In arguing that the roots of religious belief lie at a much deeper level than those of strict logic, Newman recognizes, first, the personal character of assent and, second, the ambiguous apprehension of religious faith. In *The End of the Affair*, these two themes form a vital part of Sarah Miles' characterization. By a process of internal assent, she moves uneasily from a state of anxious atheism to a state of troubled theism, both in response to an ironic God who seems to stalk her every move and in opposition to the evidence of sight and reason.[37]

Newman's sense of the personal conditions of religious belief in God harmonizes with theological themes taught by von Hügel, whom Greene also read and admired. Born the son of an Austrian nobleman in 1852, von Hügel lived in Tuscany and Brussels before moving to England in 1857. Although he was plagued by ill health and hampered by the absence of formal schooling, he eventually became a noted author and orator, as well as the catalyst behind the so-called modernist or revisionary strain within late nineteenth- and early twentieth-century Catholicism. His most celebrated book, *The Mystical Element of Religion as Studied in Saint Catherine of Genoa and Her Friends*, written between 1898 and 1908—at the height of the crisis caused by modernism—discusses three main elements of religion. While von Hügel concedes that the "historical and institutional" and the "analytic and speculative" elements of religion have their place, he emphasizes the element that involves personal intuition, emotion, and feeling.[38] Only mysticism penetrates the heart of Reality, he avers.[39] And thus von Hügel dedicated himself to the church's spiritual direction throughout his life and work, collaborating with numerous writers, including Evelyn Underhill, the noted Anglican author, on the challenge of cultivating an everyday mysticism. Although he was awarded the prestigious Gifford Lectureship for 1924–1926, ill health forced him to resign the lectureship. Von Hügel died in London in 1925.

The personal dimension in religion is paramount, von Hügel believes, because our experience of God is immediate and direct. As our "truest dignity and deepest disquiet," God reveals Godself within, before, and ahead of us, fructifying every aspect of life and beckoning it toward its richest realization. All genuine religious belief originates from an abundant Existence separate from our own. And this Existence requires our unwavering worship. Central to von Hügel's theology and spirituality is his belief in God as the "Infinite Spiritual Interiority," the religious life's ground and grammar, who grants us "indefinite opportunities for actualizing our own degree and kind of spiritual possibility and ideal." Persistent devotion to God, not philosophical reasoning, thus signifies our "deepest requirement and characteristic."[40]

In his introduction to the 1974 collected edition of *The End of the Affair*, Greene describes von Hügel's influence on his 1951 novel, which he wrote during his December 1948 visit to Capri:

> I have always imagined it [*The End of the Affair*] was influenced by the book I was reading at the time, a selection from Baron von Hügel, in particular passages from his study of St Catherine of Genoa [*The Mystical Element of Religion*]. I have a habit of marking the books I read, and yet I can find no passage marked on St. Catherine which has any relevance. But in another essay of Hügel's I come on this underlined: "the purification and slow constitution of the Individual into a Person, by means of the Thing-element [divine action], the apparently blind Determinism of Natural Law and Natural Happenings . . . Nothing can be more certain than that we must admit and place this undeniable, increasingly obtrusive, element and power *somewhere* in our lives: if we will not own it as a means, it will grip us as our end."[41]

Set within its wider context, this quoted passage reflects von Hügel's belief in a personal God who presses in upon us as the source of our spiritual growth ("purification"). In other words, we may personally experience God as the momentum for individual transformation, the one who energizes us to leave behind our small-minded egoism and develop an expansive, tender, other-focused personality. God offers us this transformation or development as a gift. And we accept (or not) this gift as an assignment—that is, the daily and costly surrender of self to the over-flowing, all-encompassing reality of God as Other. As Greene's jealous and jaded narrator in *The End of the Affair*, Bendrix illustrates von Hügel's theory of the production of personality. Though repulsed by Sarah's dramatic switch from atheism to theism, he is slowly "purified"— not without his feeling much annoyance and antipathy—by an ironic God, who uses underhanded methods and sinister tactics in order to "grip" Bendrix as his end (of the affair).[42]

In summary, this section's theologians generally believe God is ontologically and valuatively perfect; is holy, personal, and tender toward the world, and is worthy of our devotion. They use the process of rational reflection to come to the conclusion that we may demonstrate God's existence and activity. Yet some warn against the dangers of intellectualizing God, of abstracting the divine, or of turning God into the neat and tidy conclusion to a cleverly crafted syllogism. Such theologians, as we have seen, emphasize that God is personally experienced, which entails that God transcends logic, that the origin of the genuine religious impulse lies much deeper than the intellect, and that faith is a form of internal assent. Not surprisingly, the aforementioned personalities, themes, and ideas both appear and reverberate throughout my theological reading of *The End of the Affair*, to which I now turn.

Under the Green(e) Eyes of Heaven
A Christian Theological Reading of *The End of the Affair*

The End of the Affair is narrated through the perspective of Maurice Bendrix, an English novelist struggling with the conclusion of his torrid romance with Sarah Miles, the neglected wife of an unadventurous civil servant, Henry Miles. Although the novel opens in 1946, almost two years after the end of the affair, Bendrix quickly looks back to his first encounter with Henry in 1939. The two men come together when Henry allows Bendrix to investigate his daily duties and home habits in preparation for a book he plans to write. In the course of his research, though, Bendrix meets and falls in love with Sarah. Their adulterous alliance ends abruptly after an afternoon making love to the sound of V1s exploding on London's Clapham Common (June 1944). One such bomb comes too close to Bendrix's apartment, ripping into its windows and walls, causing him to stumble and fall down several flights of stairs. Seeing her lover spread-eagled on the parlor floor, seemingly dead, Sarah prays to God to save his life. In her appeal to the Almighty, she strikes a bargain, vowing to end her affair on the condition that God allows Bendrix to survive. Bendrix then manages to regain consciousness. He picks himself up, and returns to the bedroom, where he finds Sarah alone, calling out to God. Sarah brings their relationship to a close, leaving him to experience alone the resulting fallout: the wounding shrapnel of bitter rejection that quickly lodges itself inside his besieged soul.

Eighteen months later Bendrix finds himself on the Common, conversing with an apparently listless Henry, who now seems quite worried about how much time his wife spends away from home. Fearful that she has taken a lover, Henry tells Bendrix he is considering engaging the services of a private investigator, Mr. Savage, but then he quickly decides against it. During this conversation, which opens the book, Bendrix shows himself to be an unreliable narrator. He speaks of arbitrarily choosing his story's beginning, which is this first meeting with Henry after an extended absence, yet we suspect that he exercises an almost god-like prerogative at the novel's outset, seeking to control our view of the other characters in his story. Bendrix would have us believe, for example, that the story he tells is not his at all but rather one that belongs to others, namely, to ". . . Sarah, Henry, and of course, that third, whom I hated without yet knowing him, or even believing in him."[43] We have our doubts, however, because Bendrix seems much too intrusive, even overbearing, forcing himself into their story at decisive moments. Moreover, he pesters us into excusing his scandalous behavior by claiming that some devil sits on his shoulder and lures him into mischief. Overall, Bendrix's manipulative presence is glaringly obvious, and his thoughts are passionately laid bare. Almost two years have passed, yet he confesses he still hates both Sarah and whatever it was that invaded and pried open the tiny space between them—"that other, in whom in those days [1939–1944] we were lucky enough not to believe."[44] One wonders, though, if deceit lurks beneath Bendrix's candor. As his narration unfolds, that is, we cannot help but wonder whether it is love, not hate, and faith, not doubt, that pulsate at the heart of his story.

The oblique references to "that other" and "that third" stand out as two of the novel's earliest references to God. Before long, however, other references appear, demanding the reader's serious attention, like the air raid sirens announcing an oncoming German attack. Against Henry's wishes, for example, Bendrix employs the private investigator that Henry had considered engaging, and Mr. Parkis, an associate of Mr. Savage, along with Lance, his boy, begins to monitor Sarah's every movement. They trail her to a Roman Catholic church where the sight of Sarah sitting in the pew causes Parkis to question her faith. Bendrix demurs, because the Sarah he recalls "believed in God as little as I did. Or so I thought then and wonder now."[45] During their affair, Bendrix and Sarah had agreed to "eliminate God" from their lives, like Pierre Simon de Laplace, the French natural scientist, professing no need to think or speak of God as an explanation for what happens in their world ("*Je n'ai pas besoin de cet hypothèse*").[46]

Yet God refuses to eliminate Bendrix and Sarah from God's world. Like the protagonist in Francis Thompson's "The Hound of Heaven" poem, the God at work in *The End of the Affair* is on the prowl, dogging Sarah's and Bendrix's every footstep. When, two years after the end of the affair, Lance breaks into the Miles' house and retrieves something that resembles a love letter, Bendrix suspects that he has a new rival. But little does he realize that his contender is none other than God, arguably the supreme example of the jealous lover. Sarah's florid prose hints at an intimacy that both repels and compels Bendrix. He wastes no time in asking Parkis and his boy to track down his new adversary, root him out, and bring him to Henry's attention. A lover's extreme jealousy motivates Bendrix, and his self-protectiveness appears nakedly disagreeable. However, perhaps God's jealousy is the cause for concern at this point. After all, it appears that God adores Sarah enough to chase after her and intervene in her world, saving Bendrix to win her devotion. And yet, if this is how God acts, it prompts us to question the *character* of divine providence: is God's desire for Sarah so strong, so obsessive even, that the best way to view the miracle of Bendrix's survival is to treat it as the dastardly tactic of a green(e)-eyed rival-in-love?[47]

God's miracle ("a stranger's influence") in the midst of the V1 blast serves as the pivotal moment in Greene's novel, for it is upon this tense and ambiguous episode that all other episodes turn.[48] From Bendrix's side of the story, he survives the explosion (". . . I woke after five seconds or five minutes in a changed world") and finds his way back to the bedroom in time to discover Sarah crouched on the floor, deep in prayer "to anything that might exist."[49] At this point, Sarah comes across as a "superstitious atheist" (Browning), because she calls on the very God she previously agreed to eliminate from her world. In this respect, she typifies the Greenean protagonist, capable of coagulating numerous contradictions within her tortured soul, and it is through her that Greene masterfully calibrates the issue of doubt and faith. Dismissing her prayer as impractical, Bendrix seems utterly surprised by Sarah's superstitious atheism; he is entirely shocked to discover that Sarah petitions God after she finds him motionless and concludes she has lost him:

> "I don't understand. I knew for certain you were dead."
> "There wasn't much to pray for then, was there?" I teased her.
> "Except a miracle."
> "When you are hopeless enough," she said, "you can pray for miracles. They happen, don't they, to the poor, and I was poor."[50]

Sarah's remark about her poverty is best understood as a figure of speech for her troubled commitment to God, which has only just begun to express itself at this juncture in Greene's narrative. In the middle of this war-torn, dread-filled moment, Sarah discovers she is spiritually bankrupt, dolefully bereft of the religious resources—sheer trust in God, for example—that another kind of person might cash in at such a critical time. She claims not to understand what, if anything, God has done to save Bendrix, and I suspect that her word choice is one part of Greene's multifaceted theological strategy in *The End of the Affair*. If we recall Newman's and von Hügel's jointly-held belief that the origin of the genuine religious impulse lies much deeper than either logic or intellectual understanding, then Sarah's declaration that she does not comprehend God's nature and activity is highly instructive. Perhaps Greene uses Sarah's confusion not simply to signify her transition away from anxious atheism and toward troubled theism but also to promote the von Hügelian belief that a religion of the head and not of the heart creates the conditions under which one quickly becomes spiritually insolvent.

Sarah's parting words to Bendrix support these reflections, for they indicate a shifting in her soul: "Love doesn't end. Just because we don't see each other . . . My dear, my dear. People go on loving God, don't they, all their lives without seeing Him?"[51] Sarah begins to view God as her "truest dignity and deepest disquiet" (von Hügel), an abundant Existence pressing in upon her as well as the strange source of her spiritual purification. It appears that the God who rescues Bendrix and who now expects Sarah to keep her bargain is deeply enigmatic, like the *noir* atmosphere that pervades Greene's tale. In face of an experiential God as opposed to a rational deity, it seems that Sarah's decision to take leave of Bendrix is her "internal assent" (Newman) to an Elusive, Ironic Presence that subsequently stalks her every step.[52]

If Sarah is like a superstitious atheist when she's on her knees bargaining for Bendrix's life, then she is even more so when she decides to visit Richard Smythe, Greene's principal symbol for fervent rationalism. Smythe, who stands out as much for his birth-marked face as for his debating skills, spends his time on the Common preaching that God is nothing more than a psychological projection, the discreditable effect of our having spent too much time drunk in the taverns of hope and the cellars of fear. In Sarah's diary, which Bendrix acquires by stealth, we discover that she consults Smythe because she wants him to convince her that all talk of miracles is groundless, full of sound and fury. As she writes, "If he can persuade me that nothing happened, that my promise doesn't count, I'll write to Maurice and ask him if he wants to go on again."[53] Sarah wants to discredit her experience because it is the only thing holding her to her promise.

During one of her visits, Smythe dismisses his theological "enemies" and asserts that their "case" is "specious" because it is utterly reliant upon an inexcusable wish to avert cosmic loneliness by creating, telling, and handing down fanciful etiologies.[54] God, he protests, is a chimera, held fast in an appropriation process of the most passionate but largely uninformed inwardness. Ironically, Sarah finds faith because of Smythe's "fanaticism," although such faith does not deter Smythe, atheism's archabbot.[55] When Bendrix visits him, for instance, Smythe notices a faint glimmer of faith in Bendrix, some quality of the soul that hints at Bendrix's own form of superstitious atheism. Smythe moves fast to extinguish this flame, lest it become a giant conflagration:

> "I don't need to be converted, Mr. Smythe. I believe in nothing as it is. Except now and then."
> "It's the now and thens we have to deal with."
> "Pride can masquerade as hope. Or selfishness."
> "The odd thing is that those are the moments of hope."
> "I don't think that has anything to do with it at all. It happens suddenly, for no reason, a scent . . ."
> "Ah," Smythe said, "the construction of a flower, the argument from design, all that business about a watch requiring a watchmaker. It's old-fashioned. Schwenigen answered all that twenty-five years ago. Let me show you . . ."[56]

Smythe derides the traditional arguments for God's existence, especially the arguments associated with Aquinas and Paley, yet Smythe's refutations move neither Bendrix nor Sarah.[57] In fact, Sarah suspects Smythe is banging a drum that has long since failed to emit any sound. She pities him, particularly for the way his spent energy seems inversely proportional to the number of people interested in his message.

We might explain Smythe's furious energy by noting that he feels decidedly insecure about the strawberry mark on his face. Faith in God is easy when one is beautiful, Smythe tells Sarah, "but why should I love a God who gave a child this [his facial malady]?"[58] Yet dressed as it is in the garb of intense philosophical reductionism, Smythe's protest theodicy indicates he is more than an incredibly insecure young man.

In fact, it appears Smythe lives a life of doubt diversified by moments of faith (Browning). Sarah herself even wonders if Smythe's reasoning belies an inverted belief; for anyone to "be so serious, so argumentative about a legend," she conjectures, something other than plain and simple insecurity must be at stake.[59] Furthermore, after Smythe's initial skepticism, he appears to make room for the possibility of a God. Following Sarah's untimely death, he prays to her, as if to a saint, and discovers that his face clears up. Perhaps Smythe prays to Sarah rather than God because he feels that women and men are far more accessible; once Smythe believes in Sarah, so to speak, the leap to God becomes more manageable. In any event, he starts to use the word "miracle" as a way to name his experience. Even though Bendrix tries to dissuade him from using this "foolish newspaper word," Smythe eventually accepts and owns his newfound vocabulary of faith, which is based upon an apparently amazing grace.[60] As a result, his trust in God begins when and where his thinking leaves off. At the same point in time, a deceased Sarah visits Parkis' boy, Lance, and heals him of a raging fever. And if we add Lance's healing to Smythe's "miracle," we are on our way toward grasping the central drama of Greene's tale.[61]

This drama pits coincidence, the impersonal mechanism that drives life, issuing in one strange and random event after another, against providence.[62] To explore the limits of this drama, let us return to the scene of the V1 blast, this time viewing it through Sarah's eyes, a luxury that Greene affords us as he temporarily switches point-of-view, from Bendrix to Sarah, via her stolen diary. Here Sarah's voice becomes theologically instructive, because it reinforces the fact that we are in the fictional world Greene creates, "in the territory of uncertain meanings," a territory marked by plurality and ambiguity, where thinking and writing come together as "a gesture toward mystery."[63]

In her June 17, 1944 entry, Sarah reveals that during the first few moments following the V1 blast, she experienced sheer terror, the sort of nervous tension that inclines even the most skeptical soul to close his or her eyes and pray to God. Sarah records the contents of her prayer:

> I knelt and put my head on the bed and wished I could believe. Dear God, I said—why dear, why dear?—make me believe. I can't believe. Make me. I said, I'm a bitch and a fake and I hate myself. I can't do anything of myself. *Make* me believe. I shut my eyes tight, and I pressed my nails into the palms of my hands until I could feel noth-

ing but the pain, and I said, I will believe. Let him be alive, and I *will* believe. Give him a chance. Let him have his happiness. Do this and I'll believe. But that wasn't enough. It doesn't hurt to believe. So I said, I love him and I'll do anything if you'll make him alive. I said very slowly, I'll give him up for ever, only let him be alive with a chance, and I pressed and pressed and I could feel the skin break . . .[64]

This diary entry offers us a window onto Sarah's grief-stricken soul. With her love in ruins, quite literally, she lays some kind of Pascalian Wager, gambling her happiness against Bendrix's survival, her actual doubt against her potential faith. In time her bet with God appears to pay off. Not only does Bendrix live, but Sarah experiences moments of temporary relief and the stirrings of faith.[65]

Sarah models a faith that seeks understanding. Her diary entries are addressed to a God whom she struggles to trust. Such entries connect her to Anselm, whose own theological work appears in the form of a prayer. Moreover, Sarah's words suggest that she is aware of—even torn by—the existential fissure between that which her mind can verify and the sheer trust that God now demands.[66] Here we find Newman's influence on Greene apparent as Newman holds that the personal character of religious assent is intense, perhaps painful, since the objects of such faith—God and divine providence—can never be apprehended unambiguously. Although Sarah initially feels that her prayer has been answered, she is unsure whether it is providence or coincidence that has saved her lover. Additionally, in von Hügelian terms, Sarah's diary reveals how far and to what extent God seems to be pressing in upon her. While she repeatedly likens her life without Bendrix to a life lived in a desert, she nonetheless resists God, the abundant Existence who strives to moisten her emotional, psychological, and spiritual aridity.[67] "I want ordinary corrupt human love," Sarah pointedly protests, not God's love, which rains on the just and on the unjust.[68] Thus, in the midst of her despair, she looks to Smythe, hoping that he might convince her of her vow's silliness. But soon after she encounters him, Sarah finds herself praying, "Let me be of use to him."[69] This "use" becomes obvious when she miraculously heals Smythe's face, ridding it of the grotesque birthmark.[70]

Critic William Cash has recently argued that the life and writings of St. Thérèse of Lisieux, doctor of the Roman Catholic church, count as an important, if admittedly imprecise, influence behind Greene's depiction of Sarah's signs and wonders. In her short life, St. Thérèse was famous for both her simple existence and her phenomenal curative powers. Lady Catherine Walston, Greene's mistress in the late 1940s, was drawn to St. Thérèse's uncomplicated yet effective spirituality. And she was "obsessively reading" St. Thérèse's autobiography, *The Story of a Soul*, precisely when Greene was writing *The End of the Affair*. Moreover, Cash reports that Greene wrote to Lady Walston in 1950 "after a 'bad' day's work on *The End of the Affair*," describing how he had been praying "at the feet of St. Thérèse," enlisting her help in his attempt to love Lady Walston "through all this life." In early March the same year, Greene and Lady Walston visited St. Thérèse's basilica and shrine in Lisieux, France. Cash admits it "odd" that Greene never cites St. Thérèse. "Perhaps," he conjectures, "it was just too personal; or possibly he didn't want people to know just how important an influence St Thérèse had been during the final months of writing the novel, when Sarah herself is turned into a miracle-curing saint."[71]

In addition to helping Smythe, Sarah wants to help Bendrix—to take her former lover's pain away, to redeem him, after a fashion. Bendrix, however, is much too self-absorbed to accept her (and God's) help. This said, God transmutes Sarah's pain and disbelief, as evinced by Sarah's diary entry for February 10, 1946, mostly through Bendrix's envy:

> He [Bendrix] was on Your side all the time without knowing it. You willed our separation, but he willed it too. He worked for it with his anger and his jealousy, and he worked for it with his love. For he gave me so much love, and I gave him so much love that soon there wasn't anything left, when we'd finished, but You . . . But even the first time, in the hotel near Paddington, we spent all we had. You were there, teaching us to squander, like you taught the rich man, so that one day we might have nothing left except this love of You. But You are too good to me. When I ask You for pain, You give me peace. Give it him too. Give him my peace—he needs it more.[72]

Sarah reserves a place for Bendrix's covetousness within her own view of God's purpose for her life. Sin breeds sanctity, or as critic Kenneth Tynan puts it, "dunghills sprout daisies."[73] In any event, this Sarah is a far cry from the Sarah of a few months earlier, when she agreed to eliminate God from her life. Bendrix, on the other hand, remains steadfast, refusing to see life theistically. We sense as much when he closes Sarah's diary—"I couldn't read any more," he divulges, "over and over again . . . a passage hurt me too much . . ."—and secretly follows her to the Catholic church.[74] While sitting in the pew, he ascertains that Sarah's

new lover, God, requires unwavering devotion over philosophical reasoning. But Bendrix refuses to concede defeat:

> She loves us both, I thought, but if there is to be a conflict between an
> image and a man, I know who will win. I could put my hand on her
> thigh or my mouth on her breast: he [Jesus, the crucified God] was
> imprisoned behind the altar and couldn't move to plead *his* cause.[75]

Ironically, an immutable God uses this tense moment, bathed as it is in
a vespertinal glow, to plead God's cause: Jesus, as the crucified God,
bears the ultimate pain and loss of rejection, not Bendrix, meaning that
such pain and rejection make possible God's reconciliation of all sinners—Bendrix as well as Sarah—back to Godself.

To avoid further subterfuge, Bendrix reveals himself to Sarah and
admits to stealing her diary. In the process of his confession, their conversation hints at an explicit contrast between mutually exclusive ways
of "seeing-as"—namely, coincidence versus providence. The accompanying image of Sarah "huddled there [in the church] at the edge of candle-
light," seems to signify a woman in conflict with God, yet she is also
inexorably drawn toward the divine, like a moth bewitched by a flame.[76]
Everything is in God's capable hands, she claims, and this perspective
marks her out as a theist, albeit a troubled one. For his part, Bendrix
seems wounded by Sarah's fresh fondness for "that third" in whom he
does not believe. According to Bendrix, life is the result of an almost
endless interplay between chance and order. There is no God, he defi-
antly proclaims, only an impersonal mechanism randomly activating an
evolutionary advance.[77] This difference between Sarah and Bendrix is
a difference in "seeing-as," or what the contemporary American novelist
Doris Betts terms "overlay":

> Once you have listened to what he [Greene] says, even the thrillers
> have those little moments when something ticks into place. Some guy
> stands in front of a shop window and there's a cross in it, and that's
> all he says. He just moves on. What I see in that is exactly what I
> think the book of Job says—that there really is no way to prove the
> existence of a Divine Creator who oversees the world. If you see it,
> you will see it. If you don't see it, no one can persuade you. It is not an
> argument in nature or events. It is an overlay that you place on things
> or don't. Once you place it, you are in an impossible situation for per-
> suading modern people.[78]

Sarah sees Bendrix's survival as a sign and wonder, as God's specific action in her particular world. This way of perceiving is the interpretive "overlay" that she places on a strange set of circumstances, the overlay that puts her in an "impossible situation for persuading" her relentlessly skeptical, dialectical ex-lover.

Sarah's untimely death increases Bendrix's pain because it opens up a new wound—namely, the sharp sense that God "had certainly won in the end," had intruded into their lives "like a strange relation returned from the Antipodes" and spirited Sarah away.[79] But this wound and its ensuing pain also indicates a transformation within Bendrix—a new, though troubling, overlay that senses God's all-consuming control. Not surprisingly, Bendrix's rage appears as a last-ditch attempt to defy God. And he demands cremation of Sarah's body:

> I wanted her burnt up, I wanted to be able to say, Resurrect that body if you can. My jealousy had not finished, like Henry's, with her death. It was as if she were alive still, in the company of a lover she had preferred to me. How I wished I could send Parkis after her to interrupt their eternity.[80]

We eventually discover that Sarah converted to Catholicism prior to her death, as her final letter to Bendrix attests and Father Crompton, her confessor, confirms. This revelation illustrates a notorious feature of Greene's theological thinking: corruption breeds grace.[81] Throughout Greene's fiction, some moment of human misery serves as the basis for an outpouring of divine grace, especially where it is least expected or deserved. Through Sarah's letter we sense how her own torment gives rise to God's mercy, a severe mercy, as well as to her own form of fideism, and we learn that love, really, constitutes the best epistemology:

> But what's the good, Maurice? I believe there's a God—I believe the whole bag of tricks, there's nothing I don't believe, they could subdivide the Trinity into a dozen parts and I'd believe. They could dig up records that proved Christ had been invented by Pilate to get himself promoted and I'd believe just the same. I've caught belief like a disease. I've fallen into belief like I fell in love.[82]

Sarah illustrates von Hügel's theory of the production of personality, since it is God who presses in upon her, prizes her away from Bendrix, secures her soulful devotion, and, in the end, inspires in her the trust that becomes her deepest requirement and characteristic. In contrast, Bendrix hates God, especially the seemingly sneaky manner in which God inclines Sarah to proceed out from adultery and toward a kind of sainthood. Not surprisingly, the hues of Bendrix's bitterness fleck the novel's final pages. Standing before Henry, Smythe, Parkis, Father Crompton, and Mrs. Bertram, Sarah's mother, he decries God's peculiar providence. Nonetheless, Bendrix arrives at his tale's end only to find himself at the brink of faith, delivered there by a series of extraordinary events, against which his ironic detachment seems utterly powerless.[83]

Greene's interest in "the dangerous edge of things," to cite Browning one last time, has pushed Bendrix to a precarious position. He teeters on the edge of an emotional abyss, struggling to keep "the giddy line midway" between love and hate, faith and doubt, truth and duplicity. At the Golders Green crematorium, he implores Sarah—addressing her as if in prayer—to save him from dinner and a one-night stand with Sylvia, assistant to the literary critic Mr. Waterbury. Amazingly, Mrs. Bertram appears from nowhere and asks Bendrix to take *her* out to dinner. This meal becomes an uncomfortable alternative, however, because Mrs. Bertram uses it as an occasion to reminisce. She remembers how she took Sarah on holiday to Normandy when Sarah was only two, and how, against her husband's wishes, she had a local Catholic priest baptize Sarah. "I always had a wish that it [the sacrament of baptism] would 'take,'" she reveals, "like a vaccination."[84] Bendrix next finds himself painfully aware that some kind of divine mercy has perhaps followed Sarah all her days.

Placing Mrs. Bertram's strange disclosure alongside the "miracles" of Smythe and Lance Parkis, Bendrix grudgingly concedes that God must be at work in his life, pushing him toward theism, albeit an unsettled theism. But in looking back over his affair with Sarah, he rails against God's action: "He was as underhand as a lover, taking advantage of a passing mood, like a hero seducing us with his improbabilities and his legends."[85] Come what may, then, God grips his man at the end, just as von Hügel claims in the second volume of *The Mystical Element of Religion*, which Greene was reading during his writing of *The End of the Affair*. The final pages of the novel hint at Greene's theology of an irresistible God.

This said, Bendrix's parting words—"I found the one prayer that seemed to serve the winter mood: O God, You've done enough, You've robbed me of enough, I'm too tired and old to learn to love, leave me alone for ever"—suggest that the love wars are far from over or, to use von Hügel's terminology, that "the purification and slow constitution of the Individual [Bendrix] into a Person, by means of the Thing-element [divine action]," is incomplete.[86] While Bendrix moves toward the brink of faith, he lacks a sense of trust in God, and thus appears to be a typical Greenean character: "riven by doubts, perpetually uncommitted."[87] In his troubled theism, Bendrix remains a broken supplicant. But his broken supplication also indicates that however unsympathetic he might appear to us at first, it is *possible* at the end of his story—the story of his vulnerable gesture toward unfathomable Mystery—to feel sympathy for him, especially for the way he handles his nascent faith.[88] Thus, Bendrix's anxious commitment at the novel's finish signifies an admirable trace of humanity in the midst of apparent inhumanity.

Is Greene's God beyond Sympathy's Official Range?

Greene's controversial figuration certainly adds an element of inscrutability to Bendrix's story. Just when God's ways seem clear and comprehensible, Greene offers a twist in the tale that simultaneously stuns and stimulates us into upholding the mystifying nature of divine providence. Perhaps the nameless Catholic priest in Greene's *Brighton Rock* says it best when he warns Rose, Pinkie's girlfriend, "You can't conceive, my child, nor can I or anyone the . . . appalling . . . strangeness of the mercy of God."[89] Such "appalling strangeness" is what I attempt to convey in describing Greene's God. His deity moves in ways that sometimes seem severe, implying that God appears shadowy, even knavish, and certainly incongruous—in a word, ironic. The basic purpose of irony, moreover, is to animate creative writing with life's ambiguity. And in *The End of the Affair*, Greene fosters theological ambiguity through a complex process of defamiliarization, scrambling our conventional understanding of deity by inverting our traditional sense of God's basically tender character. Such an inversion might have a religious function, oddly enough, because the adventure of faith partly involves trusting that which frequently appears untrustworthy. Our sympathy for Sarah as well as Bendrix stems from a recognition of life's paradoxical nature and the difficulty of faith in the midst of such paradox. Bendrix's struggle is, in many ways, Greene's struggle. To feel sympathy for Bendrix's plight is to acknowledge Greene's. But do we and can we accept Greene's God?

One answer to this question involves highlighting the biblical background to Greene's way of picturing the divine. In his Pulitzer prize-winning *God: A Biography*, historian Jack Miles describes how different books in the *Tanakh* (a designation for the Old Testament or Hebrew Bible) reflect various views of God. Sometimes God surfaces in a story and seems recognizably and reassuringly kindhearted—appearing as Friend of the Family (Gen 25:12-50:18); Father (1 Sam); Wife (Hag, Zech, Mal), and Counselor (Ps). At other times, God appears exasperatingly ambiguous—emerging as Fiend (Job); Recluse (Lam); Puzzle (Eccl), and Absence (Esth). When we consider this information carefully, we recognize that the God who evolves through the course of the *Tanakh*'s multifaceted narrative is experienced differently, interpreted through varied overlays, and internally divided. Miles writes:

> The Lord God's character is contradictory [read: incongruous, ironic], and he is trapped within its contradictions.
>
> If he were, for example, either the omnipotent Lord of Heaven or the solicitous Friend of the Poor but not both, he could escape the trap. But he is indeed both, and he cannot escape. What is a problem of theodicy for the poor man whose suffering is not alleviated ('How can a good God . . . ?') is a conflict of identity for the God who does not alleviate it. Again, if he were only the tender, solicitous husband of Second Isaiah and not also the sword-in-hand butcher of Joshua, he could escape. But he is both, and he cannot escape. He is trapped as Hamlet is trapped—in himself.[90]

David Penchansky also points to an ironic God in the biblical tradition. In *What Rough Beast?: Images of God in the Hebrew Bible*, he observes the presence of an insecure God in Genesis 3; an irrational God in 2 Samuel 6; a vindictive God in 2 Samuel 24; a dangerous God in Leviticus 10; a malevolent God in Exodus 4:24-26, and, finally, an abusive God in 2 Kings 2:23-25. He exclaims, "God in these passages is rough, violent, unpredictable, liable to break out against even his most faithful followers without warning."[91] In light of *this* God, then, it is hardly surprising that some Christians think these stories are scandalous. Even if they are, though, they command our attention because they provoke us to think through our faith. Unsurprisingly, not every Christian agrees with such inquiry. Some even assume that questions and doubts about God exhibit arrogance, even unbelief; but, according to Penchansky, skepticism beats inside all faithful Christian hearts. And skeptical Christians know that at the center of these six troubled and troubling narratives lies an invitation to serious and multilayered theological investigation:

> Certainly these stories suggest a kind of Promethean agnosticism. The following quotes might elucidate a bit of what I mean: 'If this is what YHWH is like, I want nothing to do with him!' Or, 'Because I can't imagine a god being like this, I can't imagine God at all.' And gradually, 'God can't possibly be like this: What other ways might God be?' And so, finally, ultimately, such stories become tremendously hopeful. What begins as Promethean rebellion might be transformed into a bold creative activity, akin to worship, but a kind of worship that embraces human dignity, encourages questions, and accepts the ambiguity that seems to permeate human experience.[92]

Like the writers of the aforementioned six biblical passages, Greene challenges us to make sense of life within a religious framework. He uses the many characters in The End of the Affair to show us that there is something constructive in scrutinizing God and our existence.

If it is correct to say (a) that there is continuity between the God of the New Testament and the God of the Tanakh/Hebrew Bible, (b) that God evolves within the pages of both texts and the religious imagination of the many writers responsible for them, as well as (c) that there is an interpretive play of reader-believers across the centuries, then Greene's theo-poetical reflections do not appear to be scandalous after all. Rather, they seem to be part of a legitimate, if admittedly unsettling, biblical faith still in the making.

For Greene, faith in God's existence is not difficult. Rather it is God's seemingly ironic nature and activity that poses problems. Perhaps we struggle to feel sympathy for Greene's God because Greene himself struggled to feel any such sympathy. But this struggle to feel sympathy for—or what could be reconstrued as faith in—God is part of a long tradition, one beginning with the biblical authors, who seldom shy away from thinking of God as terror. For too long theologians have, somewhat ironically, turned a blind eye to this important tradition. But the fact that many of us leave The End of the Affair somewhat unsettled and disturbed indicates that Greene has uncovered a truth we ignore at our peril—that the troubled theism lurking within our own souls finds an echo in life's ambiguity.

CONCLUSION

Greene converted to Christianity in 1926 and, until his death in 1991, waged one constant war with God. *The End of the Affair*, first conceived in the late 1940s and published in 1951, is a conspicuous salvo. This novel's theological tenability, at least in terms of the Christian tradition, is uncertain, as the God who stirs within its pages is a strangely elusive and markedly ironic character. To my mind, this characterization of God reminds those of us who live in the light and power of the Christian story that we have little option, especially in the face of our ambiguous world, but to uphold theological mystery. *Fides supponit rationem et transcendit eam*: faith supposes reason and yet goes beyond it.

FOR FURTHER READING

Karen Armstrong's *The History of God: The 4,000-Year Quest of Judaism, Christianity and Islam* (New York: Alfred A. Knopf, 1994) is an architectonic account of the idea and experience of God at the heart of the three Abrahamic faiths. John Bowker's *God: A Brief History* (London: DK Publishing, 2002) is a lavishly illustrated survey of different conceptions of God from around the world. It concludes by suggesting that worship is our primary experience of God. Although Paul E. Capetz's *God: A Brief History* (Minneapolis, Minn.: Fortress, 2003) carries the same title as Bowker's book, it is quite different. Capetz traces the encounter between the Hebrew Bible's active, personal God and Greek metaphysics, and he shows how this encounter inspired divine trinitarianism. B. Jill Carroll's *The Savage Side: Reclaiming Violent Models of God* (Lanham, Md.: Roman and Littlefield, 2002) is a lively and energetic argument against contemporary Christianity's apparent domestication of God. William Cash's *The Third Woman: The Secret Passion that Inspired Graham Greene's* The End of the Affair (New York: Carroll & Graf, 2000) is a fascinating account of the love affair between Greene and Lady Catherine Walston. A. F. Cassis' *Graham Greene: Man of Paradox*, with a foreword by Peter Wolfe (Chicago: Loyola University Press, 1994) collects various interviews and impressions by numerous friends and acquaintances. Diana Culbertson's edited volume, *Invisible Light: Poems about God* (New York: Columbia University Press, 2000) features classic and modern writers—John Donne, William Blake, Denise Levertov, and Anne Sexton, et al.—reflecting on God in the first, second, or third person. C. Michael Curtis' anthology, *God: Stories* (Boston: Houghton Mifflin, 1998), promotes mostly North American short fiction on the concept and activity of God, featuring writers such as James Baldwin, Louise Erdrich, Bobbie Ann Mason, Cynthia Ozick, John Updike, Eudora Welty, et al. Quentin Falk's *Travels in Greeneland: The Complete Guide to the Cinema of Graham Greene*, revised and updated third edition, with a foreword by Neil Jordan (London: Reynolds and Hearn, 2000) offers an illustrated survey of the very many cinematic adaptations of Greene's films, including the two movie versions of *The End of the Affair* (1955, 1999). Patrick Henry's *The Ironic Christian's Companion: Finding the Marks of God's Grace in the World* (New York: Riverhead Books, 1999) imaginatively explores the relationship between God, ambiguity, mystery, and irony, emerging with a fresh grasp of what it means to be a Christian in today's fragmented and dissolute world. Wm. Thomas Hill, editor, *Perceptions of Religious Faith in the Work of Graham Greene* (New York: Peter Lang, 2001) is an edited anthology of specially commissioned interpretive essays on Greene's religiosity. Anton Houtepen's *God: An Open Question*, translated by John Bowden (London: Continuum, 2002), wrestles with the philosophical ambiguity and confessional plurality of our postmodern world to arrive at a fresh way of thinking about God. Alister E. McGrath makes an impassioned plea for doubt's importance in Christian discipleship in *Doubting: Growing Through the Uncertainties of Faith* (Downers Grove, Ill.: InterVarsity Press, 2007). William J. O'Malley's *God: The Oldest Question* (Chicago: Loyola University Press, 2000) engages atheism, science, and the challenge of religious diversity, and argues for God's contemporary relevance. Jack Miles' *God: A Biography* (New York: Alfred A. Knopf, 1995) is an award-winning literary study of the character of God in the Hebrew Bible. David Penchansky's *What Rough Beast?: Images of God in the Hebrew Bible* (Louisville, Ky.: Westminster John Knox, 1999) situates ironic portraits of God at the center of Israelite theology, not at the margins, as some might say. Finally, A. N. Wilson's *God's Funeral* (New York: W. W. Norton, 1999) examines Christianity's decline in Western Europe, especially England, focusing on the Victorian crisis of faith and doubt, which serves as the mood and background to Greene's work.

SELECTED WEB SITES

1. http://www.carm.org/dictionary.htm
   This is an online theological dictionary, which provides useful standard and instructive definitions of words used throughout this book.

2. http://www.religion-online.org
   A cyber-depot of texts and articles related to Christianity.

3. http://www.crosssearch.com/
   An impressive search engine for Christian Web sites.

4. http://www.grahamgreenebt.org/index.php
   This is the Internet location of the Graham Greene Birthplace Trust.

2

HUMANITY

Toni Morrison's *Sula*

When we talk about God, we inevitably reveal something of ourselves. In other words, our interpretation of the divine is, in part, an extension of our own background, experiences, and context. We only make sense of God from our particular human location. This process means that theology, at least in one sense, presupposes (or *is*) anthropology.[1] Most theologies then see the doctrine of God as unfolding into the doctrine of human nature. As the Creator points us to the created, the created points us back to the Creator. We have a responsibility, then, to examine our humanity if we are to talk about God.[2]

Theologians interested in the doctrine of humanity ponder our nature and destiny. Most begin with the idea of human createdness. Here they ask questions such as: what does it mean to think of ourselves as created in God's image? Do we have special duties or responsibilities toward the rest of creation? And what, if anything, does our being created male and female teach us about ourselves? Christian theologians also consider the twin notions of sin and salvation as essential to the human experience. They ask: how are we "good" and "evil"? What does it mean to say we are "free" or "predestined"? How do we "fall" from God's grace? And what is "original sin"?

Because it emphasizes that God created us in God's image, the Christian tradition explores how we are different from other living organisms. Human nature and human ethics are inextricably linked. We are able to think about our environment and universe in a way that other animals do not. We also have a sense of right and wrong, which entails that we have moral choices and that we are responsible for their consequences. Understanding the difference between vice and virtue is, according to many theologians, humanity's distinctive quality. Whatever else we are, we are moral creatures.

Theologians are certainly not alone in their concern with our human nature and thus our ethical duties. Numerous novels and poems explore the relationship between good and evil and subsequently challenge our sense of human morality. With this second chapter I continue my examination of the relationship between Christian doctrine and modern fiction through an analysis of the African American writer Toni Morrison and her second novel, *Sula*, published in 1973. In *Sula*, Morrison presents an outlook on good and evil that scrambles conventional Christian beliefs. For example, Augustine claims that all have sinned "in Adam," and as a result we are born sinful and in need of divine forgiveness and grace. This is the doctrine of "original sin," and many Christian thinkers across the centuries owe a great debt to Augustine for developing it.[3] According to Morrison, however, people are neither wholly good nor wholly evil; instead, they blend both impulses within their own souls, and sometimes what people intend for the good appears evil, and vice versa. Moreover, she challenges what traditional Christianity conceives of as good and evil, often confusing its ethical base. Traditional Christianity, for example, has tended to promote discussion of good and evil in individual terms only. Yet Morrison calls her readers to consider not only the way in which communities instantiate these values but also the way in which some communities clash with others—white with black and black with white for example—creating power imbalances, oppression, and sometimes rupture within these communities. Good and evil, therefore, display a social as well as an individual face.

This chapter has four major sections. First, I sketch Morrison's life and literary art, noting how and why she sees herself as a writer who proceeds out from, and gives voice to, African Americans' frequently intense and often sorrowful experiences. Second, I engage certain makers and remakers of the Christian doctrine of humanity, beginning with the architects of the traditional theory of human nature: two classical theologians who uphold the notion of an individual, autonomous self. Several contemporary theologians now question this notion, and in the greater part of this second section I showcase particular feminists and womanists, who reimagine human nature in ways that eschew individualism, accentuate sin as ruptured relationality, and celebrate grace as the God-given desire for wholeness. In the third and major section I offer a Christian theological reading of *Sula*, concentrating on how good and evil, construed individually and socially, serve as the fulcrum around which everything in Morrison's novel turns. A final section commends *Sula*'s intense existential vision to Christians and also urges learning from the womanist-inspired tendency to consult novels for theological insight.

TONI MORRISON: LIFE AND LITERARY ART

Born Chloe Anthony Wofford in Lorain, Ohio, in 1931, Morrison is the second of four children in a family raised on an aesthetic diet of oral folklore and music (gospel, blues, opera, and jazz), twin impulses that inform her experimental narrative strategies and overall fictional style.[4] Even though her hometown was less segregated than most Northern cities, its racial tension ran high, especially during the Great Depression, when her community and its white—mostly Greek and Italian—neighbors competed for scarce jobs and lived off meager wages.

By all accounts Morrison loved literature during high school and so, after graduating in 1949, she left Lorain and attended Howard University in Washington, D.C. This experience proved bittersweet. Although Morrison was the first woman in her family to attend college, she found her professors unwilling to venture outside the standard American literary canon. She read some black writers, men like Richard Wright and James Baldwin, but it was not until many years after Howard that she first read and enjoyed Zora Neale Hurston, the famed folklorist and novelist.

A spell in the Howard University Players, the school's drama club, took Morrison to the American South during her summer vacations, where she witnessed the black plight under Jim Crow. And it was at this time that she also began calling herself "Toni," an abbreviated version of her middle name. After obtaining degrees from Howard in 1953 and then Cornell University in 1955, Morrison returned to Howard to teach in 1957. The following year she married the Jamaican architect Harold Morrison, with whom she had two sons; they divorced in 1964.

She moved to New York City in 1968. Here she worked as senior editor for Random House. In 1970 she published her first novel, *The Bluest Eye*. Written in the tragic mode, this haunting tale chronicles the unhappy childhood of Pecola Breedlove, who craves acceptance from her family and friends. When she finds herself reviled and ridiculed,

however, she thinks that people simply dislike her skin color; blackness, she concludes, equals ugliness. Pecola soon dreams of having
blond hair and blue eyes, like Shirley Temple, but this dream quickly
develops into the nightmare of her unquiet mind, an insanity caused by
confused identity.

Morrison's second novel, *Sula* (1973), focuses on an eccentric character, Sula Peace, whose community, the Bottom, finds her experimental lifestyle peculiar at first and then positively wicked. As much as
Sula repels the Bottom townspeople, however, she also compels them to
become more cohesive; that is to say, she defines evil for them and, ironically, her vice galvinizes their virtue.

At the center of the highly mythopoetic *Song of Solomon* (1977) lies
Macon Dead III (Milkman), a Ulysses character whose odyssey to
retrieve his family's buried treasure leads him to something far more
lucrative than material riches—namely, a rewarding sense of his own
history and heritage.

Tar Baby (1981) explores the affair between Jadine Childs, an international male model, and a young drifter, Son Green, who meet, fall
in love, become alienated, and eventually reconcile, but only after they
jointly comprehend the agonizing truth that racial injustice holds all
black women and men in thrall.

Grounded in research that Morrison undertook for *The Black Book*
(1974), her edited, documented history of African American culture,
Beloved (1987), reimagines the story of ex-slave Margaret Garner, who
ran away from her Kentucky plantation in 1856. When her white owner
eventually cornered her in Cincinnati, Garner picked up a knife and
killed her own baby daughter. In Sethe, Morrison's Garner, we see what
happens within slavery's brutal field of force from one of its victim's
viewpoints.

Jazz (1992), set in 1920s Harlem, uses the characters of Violet, Felice,
and Joe, among others, to illustrate the power of community and ancestry to unite black women and men seeking to negotiate life and love in
an urban environment.

Drawing on themes central to Christian theology, such as redemp-
tion and resurrection, *Paradise* (1998) describes Ruby, Oklahoma, an
Eden-like small town first settled by nine black families after the Civil
War. Over the years Ruby's residents see themselves as living in utopia,
in paradise even, and so come to fear the Outside. In 1974, though, the
Outside, represented by the Convent, threatens Ruby's cohesiveness,

and an orgy of violence ensues. When the women of the Convent eventually absolve Ruby's menfolk, especially Deacon Morgan, for the part they play in the mayhem, grace and generosity prevail.

Most recently, in *Love* (2003), Morrison pulls us into the tale of William Cosey, whose reputed wealth attracts the attention of the many women in his life shortly after his death. Some of these women, like Heed and Christine, war with one another as they lay claim to understanding Cosey best of all. In their struggle, as with the struggles of others like May and Vida, we steal several looks into Cosey's life and, finally, into love itself, which ties this story's women together.[5]

The recipient of numerous awards, including a 1998 Pulitzer Prize for *Beloved* and the Nobel Prize for Literature (1993), Morrison has also written musicals (*New Orleans* [1983]), plays (*Dreaming Emmett* [1986]), literary essays (*Playing in the Dark: Whiteness and the Literary Imagination* [1992]), song cycles (*Honey and Rue* [1993]), and even books for children (*Remember: The Journey to School Integration* [2004]). These days, she teaches creative writing at Princeton University.

Morrison's boundless talent has never been self-serving. Instead, she testifies to what she calls "the elaborately socialized world of black people."[6] Scattered throughout her work, for example, are many references to events and figures in African American history. She often delineates this history within the context of tight-knit neighborhoods. And in her hands, such places sometimes give strong sustenance to people struggling to be free and sometimes, rather tragically, they go to wrack and ruin, losing all community cohesion in the process.[7]

Relationality and rupture mark the "whole world of Black people in this country," Morrison claims, and her novels explore how and why this is so.[8] Characters like Jadine and Pecola frequently find themselves challenged to confront society's many dualisms—beauty and ugliness, love and hate, good and evil—by learning to live intensely and well.[9] But nobody ever survives by self-regard in Morrison's fictive universe; her characters simply cannot exist outside of community, critics observe.[10] As a result, words such as "church," "ancestor," and "chorus" anchor Morrison's writings. But such words are not words only. They are fundamental features of the "black cosmology" that Morrison chronicles for us, her readers, and we gain much by examining their function in her books, she advises.[11]

Any talk of "church" and "cosmology" naturally inclines us to question Christianity's place in Morrison's life and literary art. It is hard, however, to answer this question.[12] While she certainly recognizes Christianity's power in the African American community, she reveals very little about her own faith and devotion. Morrison famously safeguards her personal life. If she ties herself to a particular religious tradition, then I am unaware of it, even if her work—both fiction and nonfiction—makes many Christian theological allusions.[13] It is certainly possible to examine *Sula* through Christian theological spectacles. Morrison even encourages it. In some of her interviews, for example, she alludes to the Garden of Eden, the divine Trinity, and life before the Fall to describe why good and evil's uneasy alliance focalizes *Sula*.[14] But before I offer a Christian theological reading of her novel, I need to address the Christian doctrine of humanity.[15]

THE DOCTRINE OF HUMANITY: A SELECTIVE SKETCH

The Christian doctrine of humanity's origins lies with Genesis, the first book of the Hebrew Bible, and its two creation stories. In the first story, which probably dates from about 500 B.C.E., the writer sets everything out in seven precise and tidy sections, matching our seven week days, opening with light's appearance on the first day and closing with humanity's arrival on the sixth.[16] God rests on the seventh day, which explains the origins of our own holy day of rest, the Sabbath or Lord's Day. In the second story, which hails from about 850 B.C.E., the writer begins his story differently, not with the waters of the first story but with earth as a wasteland. He also omits the time it took to create things, structures the order of creation differently, and he provides names—Adam and Eve—for the first humans.[17] Adam and Eve eventually succumb to temptation and are exiled from the Garden of Eden as punishment for their sin. Overall, this second creation story explains how and why the world God intended for good has fallen into disarray. Some of the early makers of the Christian doctrine of humanity, like Irenaeus and Augustine, take their cues from its suggestion that we can blame the world's evil and suffering on Adam and Eve.

Irenaeus and Augustine

Irenaeus of Lyons was born and raised in Smyrna, present-day Turkey. After spending some time in Rome, he moved to southern France and became Bishop of Lyons in 178. From this position he engaged some of the most serious heretical threats to late second-century Christianity.[18]

Writing in his most famous work, *Adversus Haereses* (*Against Heresies*), Irenaeus rejects the idea that we were created perfect in the beginning. In humanity's formative years, he says, we were incapable of receiving the perfection God intended for us. Spiritually, we were young and not fully formed. Yet this infancy did not last. Eventually we realized our freedom and the possibility of error. And through self-schooling and progress in the knowledge of good and evil, we grew and matured, became capable of receiving the knowledge of God in Christ, and we entered spiritual adulthood. On this view, then, our world is neither wholly good nor wholly evil; rather, it is shot through with examples of each. Here we control the scales of vice and virtue, chiefly through the choices we make, and this power to choose makes freedom integral to our personal growth.[19]

Belief in God's sovereignty over God's creation, and particularly God's prevenience in the salvation process, inclined Augustine to disagree with Irenaeus and, ultimately, to minimize—some might even say deny—our freedom, once Adam fell from grace.[20]

Born in North Africa to a Christian mother and a pagan father, Augustine was raised in a comfortable and cultured environment. He studied law and philosophy. He converted to Manichaeism in the fourth century's final few decades. This ancient Persian religion divides the universe into two general principles, Light and Darkness. It teaches that since our souls originate from the Light, and that all things temporal come from Darkness, we are not responsible for evil. Augustine was initially drawn to this theory of evil's origins, partly because he was so fascinated with explaining what went wrong with our world. However, his unremitting desire for truth eventually led him to entertain various intellectual positions at different times in his life. After teaching rhetoric in Rome in 383, he moved to Milan. Here he encountered the Christian bishop Ambrose, who baptized Augustine in 387. Under duress, Augustine was ordained Bishop of Hippo (now Annaba in modern-day Algeria) in 391. That same year he began drafting his most famous book, *Confessions*. He spent over thirty years working as a bishop, writing, and creating Christian community.[21]

Augustine believes that a supremely benevolent and tender God created an essentially good world—not one that is generally bad, as the Manichaeans held. We have ruined it, he says, by using our freedom incorrectly; evil is the product of liberty's misuse. All have sinned "in Adam," the original human being, and as a consequence, all have fallen short of God's purpose for creation. We are born sinful, then, and even though we have some small amount of freedom in our post-Eden state, we are essentially powerless to help ourselves. Given this scenario, we all stand in desperate, as well as urgent, need of God's grace, particularly if we hope for forgiveness and redemption. Very generally, this understanding represents the Augustinian doctrine of original sin. God's prevenient grace—not personal training and growth in the knowledge of good and evil—enables us to reach the point where we are capable of receiving the perfection that God intends for us.[22]

Morrison neither mentions Augustine nor Irenaeus in her writings. She does speak of a "Western" approach to evil, though, albeit critically, and Augustine may profitably be seen as one of the influences behind it. In addition, Morrison frequently asserts that we make something of ourselves as human beings by experience and correction, not by running from what we dislike or find difficult but by wrestling with it—an idea that I find decidedly Irenaean. Her distinctive and provocative contribution to this debate, though, is to suggest that black people, perhaps because of their difficult history, have proved themselves far more adept than others at understanding freedom's problems and possibilities:

> When I was writing about good and evil, I really wasn't writing about them in Western terms. It was interesting to me that black people at one time seemed not to respond to evil in the ways other people did, but that they thought evil had a natural place in the universe; they did not wish to eradicate it. They just wished to protect themselves from it, maybe even to manipulate it, but they never wanted to kill it. They thought evil was just another aspect of life. The ways black people dealt with evil accounted in my mind for how they responded to a lot of other things. It's like a double-edged sword. It accounts for one of the reasons it's difficult for them to organize long-term political wars against another people. It accounts for their generosity and acceptance of all sorts of things. It's because they're not terrified by evil, by difference. Evil is not an alien force; it's just a different force. That's the evil I was describing in *Sula*.[23]

Born of the freedom that seems so necessary to the creation of persons, good and evil signify natural and vital concomitants in *Sula*'s fictive community—as they do in life, according to Morrison and Irenaeus.

Reinhold Niebuhr and Feminist Theology

The seventeenth- and eighteenth-century Enlightenment thinkers dismissed the traditional understanding of the Christian doctrine of humanity, especially in its Augustinian form, as both empirically unverifiable (there is no evidence for an original Fall) and ethically repugnant (there is little or no sense in holding people culpable for an innate blemish). Today, many Christians accept their criticisms. However, this acceptance does not mean that there is little or no interest in reenvisioning the traditional model. On the contrary, several theologians now hold that "the meaning of the doctrine is true—there is a root sin that alienates humankind from God, generating personal and social evil—but that the insight into what this means and how to express it adequately to modern believers requires more than repetition of its classical formulation."[24]

The attempt to modernize the traditional understanding of the Christian doctrine of humanity is nowhere more clearly seen than in the work of Reinhold Niebuhr. Born in Wright City, Missouri, in 1892, Niebuhr studied theology at Eden Theological Seminary and Yale University before becoming a Detroit-based pastor in 1915. This first church appointment changed him dramatically. Shocked by the Ford Motor Company's reckless disregard for its workforce, Niebuhr both stood up and spoke out. He railed against industrial capitalism. He supported the labor movement. And he embraced Christian socialism. Later books, like *Moral Man and Immoral Society* (1932) and *The Nature and Destiny of Man* (1941–1943), emerged from his Detroit experience. Both texts draw attention to sin's social as well as individual face, twin themes that he returned to repeatedly during his thirty-two year teaching career at New York City's Union Theological Seminary. Niebuhr died on May 31, 1971.[25]

Niebuhr holds that God's image is not something we own or control, like reason or our rational faculty, but is, instead, an alliance with God that we may or may not appreciate.[26] When we fail to appreciate our alliance with God, it is only because we deny our "creatureliness" and, in short, pretend to be more than we are.[27] According to Niebuhr, we are creatures marked by freedom and finiteness; that is to say, we are "both free and bound, both limited and limitless."[28] Yet this existentially tensive truth often causes us to become anxious. We worry ourselves with impossibly high standards of perfection, he says, or else we fret for our insecurities. Such disquiet inclines us to hide our limits. We veil our limited knowledge. And then temptation strikes—the temptation to either "deny the contingent character" of our lives through pride and self-love or else to flee from our freedom through sensuality.[29] Sin is inevitable, therefore, even if we are responsible for its particular manifestation.[30]

In explaining how and why sin manifests itself, Niebuhr deepens and disciplines the traditional theological analysis of humanity, which privileges our epistemic and ethical autonomy, by focusing on our sociality, the way we relate to others. For example, sin as pride appears not just personally but organizationally. All groups are comprised of individuals. But Niebuhr thinks empirical observation shows us that "the pretensions and claims of a collective or social self exceed those of the individual ego."[31] No group has ever existed without making "unconditional claims" for its "conditioned values."[32] We might call this situation "institutional idolatry" or "structural sin." And its ability both to transcend and constrain the behavior of the individuals who participate in it troubles Niebuhr.

Several contemporary non-theological models of humanity also speak of our tendency toward behavior that distorts our communication with others. Morrison falls into this category. In the following interview, for example, she outlines why Sula seems evil. Notice how her commentary eschews the individualism that we might associate with the traditional Christian doctrine of humanity, especially in its Augustinian form, and how she, like Niebuhr before her, equates vice with whatever ruptures relationality:

> Sula's behavior looks inhuman, because she has cut herself off from responsibility to anyone other than herself, she is afraid of that area of commitment. She hasn't the tenacity and that sort of salt of the earth quality that Nel has. Even when Nel was in despair she takes good care of the children . . . Now, mind you, Sula was living in a period during which human beings had to take care of each other and she's living in a town in which it's absolutely necessary. That's why the townspeople don't understand her. You see, there were no agencies then. Neighbors, individuals, plain human beings used to do that— take care of the helpless or needy. She, Sula, put her grandmother away. That is considered awful because among Black people that never happened. You must take care of each other. That's more unforgiveable than anything else she does, because it suggests a lack of her sense of community. Critics devoted to the Western heroic tradition— the individual alone and triumphant—see Sula as a survivor. In the Black community she is lost.[33]

Even if it is tempting to think that Morrison's own words rule in certain opinions and rule out others, I think we would do well to resist judging Sula summarily. Sula is an extraordinarily complex character. And it is possible to view her in numerous ways. Some, like Niebuhr, might view her experimental lifestyle as destructively selfish. Yet others, like recent feminist-influenced theologians, might disagree.

Convinced that throughout history women have been reduced to silence and submission, feminist theologians like Daphne Hampson question Niebuhr's link between power and sin.[34] Male structures and male expectations have always joined forces to contain women in society, they claim. And this is what "patriarchy" means. It means women frequently find themselves relegated to a so-called lesser or trivial sphere. And here their creaturehood before God is denied.[35] Moreover, patriarchy gives all the power to men. As a result, feminist theologians do not find it in the least bit surprising that Niebuhr treats power as one of the two great temptations. It is—but for men only.[36] Women find it far more tempting *not* to exercise power:

> For the temptations of woman *as woman* are not the same as the temp-
> tations of man *as man*, and the specifically feminine forms of sin—
> 'feminine' not because they are confined to women or because women
> are incapable of sinning in other ways but because they are outgrowths
> of the basic feminine character structure—have a quality which can
> never be encompassed by such terms as "pride" and "will to power."
> They are better suggested by such items as triviality, distractibility,
> and diffuseness; lack of an organizing center or focus; dependence on
> others for one's own self-definition; tolerance at the expense of stan-
> dards of excellence; inability to respect the boundaries of privacy;
> sentimentality; gossipy sociability, and mistrust of reason—in short,
> underdevelopment or negation of the self.[37]

Sula never succumbs to triviality's allure, as we will see, and she refuses to rely on others for her own identity. Her organizing center or focus is all her own. But does she sin? Given much recent feminist theology, it is hard to say. One thing we can say, though, is that Morrison's novel is not a straightforward parable about good and evil; indeed, it is full of twists and turns. And viewing *Sula* through the lens of womanist as well as feminist theology illumines several intricacies.

Womanism and Womanist Theologies

Womanism resembles feminism in many ways, certainly in the way it takes delight in women's experience, but it differs from feminism in that it upholds the need for *black women* to make sense of *their* experience. By and large, black women have not always felt included by feminists and their intellectual projects.[38] The 1970s feminist movement promoted the Equal Rights Amendment (ERA), for example, and many white women took up better jobs and careers as a result. But black women witnessed little, if any, progress in their lives. And some even sensed racism's presence and persistence among ERA-liberated white feminists. More than anyone else, the African American writer Alice Walker helped black women respond to this specific crisis by crafting womanism's general principles, which first appeared in 1983.

A womanist is "a black feminist or feminist of color," Walker declares, and she frequently acts in ways that appear "outrageous, audacious, [or] courageous." Womanists often want "to know more and in greater depth than is considered 'good'" by others; they desire to act or be "in charge" and "serious" about life. They also love other women—their culture; "emotional flexibility," by which Walker means their tears and laughter, and their determined strength. Womanists are not separatists. Even though they may avoid men from time to time, often for "health" reasons, they are "committed to the survival and wholeness of entire people, male and female." Womanists love the earth and its many riches, like music and food, and they see meaning in life's struggles and joy in loving oneself.[39]

Most womanist theologians find Walker's work instructive. And some view it as axiomatic, certainly in its emphasis on black women's experience.[40] Experience teaches us that black women have shouldered the burden of at least three evils or structural sins across the years—racism, sexism, and classism. Despite this struggle, though, society underappreciates black women, and it often treats them indifferently. Seeking to correct this oversight, womanist theologians encourage black women to honor their life situations by sounding their voices unashamedly.[41]

When black women speak, they frequently address their need to work with others to guarantee survival. Racism, sexism, and classism are society's principal as well as powerful forces. In the face of such evils black women teach themselves how to hang on and to adapt, even to flourish, by cooperating with others. They forge alliances as well as establish networks. Slowly but surely, relationality represents every black woman's story and song.[42] Yet womanist theologians know that black women often find it difficult to tell relationality's story and sing its song. This is because the boundaries in which black women are often compelled to act or refrain from acting are less than ideal. Choices are limited. Womanist theologian Katie G. Cannon puts it this way:

> The real-lived texture of black life requires moral agency that may run contrary to the ethical boundaries of mainline Protestantism. Blacks may use action guides that have never been considered within the scope of traditional codes of faithful living. Racism, gender discrimination, and economic exploitation, as inherited, age-long complexes, require the black community to create and cultivate values and virtues in their own terms so that they prevail against the odds with moral integrity.[43]

On this view, then, "the quality of moral good is that which allows black people to maintain a feistiness about life that nobody can wipe out, no matter how hard they try."[44] Sula is nothing if not feisty, as we will see.

Cannon holds that virtuous living is whatever enables black people to "strain against the external limits" in their lives.[45] Sometimes such virtue shows up as the desire to promote black solidarity, especially in the face of suffering, and sometimes it shows up as expressive individualism, often in the form of personal protest or outright rejection of life's external limits. At other times, though, virtue shows up as "unctuousness," "invisible dignity," or "unshouted courage."[46] These last three terms are not synonyms for timid obsequiousness, however. Unctuousness is "the quality of steadfastness, akin to fortitude, in the face of formidable oppression," Cannon says.[47] And "unshouted courage" is "the often unacknowledged inner conviction that keeps one's appetite whet for freedom."[48] Frequently expressed in communities as well as individuals, the virtue of "unshouted courage" appears, moreover, in black people's "incentive to facilitate change, to chip away the oppressive structures, bit by bit, to celebrate and name their experience in new ways."[49]

Seen through Cannon's womanist lens, Morrison's multidimensional novel protests and scrambles our traditional understanding of right and wrong. Sula certainly strains against the limits imposed on her life. She is full of verve and spontaneity. And these creative, but sometimes dangerous, impulses incline her to strike out against boredom and convention. Sula lives freely and experimentally. And thus, from a certain perspective, she lives virtuously. In another sense, though, she lives viciously. Sula's expressive individualism frequently runs the risk of falling into distorted or ruptured relationality, because it often places her somehow outside or above communal accountability. Such ethical self-transcendence indicates that Sula is lost, Morrison avers.

Then there is Nel. She often plays within the rules and by the book. Consequently, she seldom strains against society's limits. Her reliability means she helps to anchor her world, the community of Bottom, but it also means she rarely stands out or up for anything provocative. Perhaps in one sense, then, she lives life viciously, since she appears to confront suffering and injustice with an air of resignation rather than defiance. Yet, to be fair, perhaps Nel lives virtuously. After all, her unshouted courage shows up as the buried, but sometimes effervescent desire to be other than she is, to live differently, and to recast her own experience in cathartic ways.

Besides Sula and Nel, we must not overlook the Bottom townspeople. They seek wholeness through neighborliness. And relationality, or at least the desire for it, reflects their story and song. In this respect, the Bottom community lives virtuously. But it also lives viciously. Sula's presence highlights difficulties for them, as we will see, and in time they come to abhor her feistiness, even as they benefit from it, slowly and quietly, in the form of reinforced solidarity.

Ruptured Relationality
A Christian Theological Reading of *Sula*

Tricked by his slaveowner, who had convinced him that land up in the Ohio hills was "the bottom of heaven—best land there is," a black man one day accepted this land as payment for performing some hard tasks.[50] He called it "the Bottom." Shortly after settling way up there he discovered that his white master had duped him. The so-called bottom at the top was little more than a place "where planting was backbreaking, where the soil slid down and washed away the seeds, and where the wind lingered all through winter."[51] In time, though, the Bottom's townspeople learned to cope with their misfortune by laughing about it. Humor has helped them, in other words, to create community and, imaginatively, to strain against the structural sin—racism—that both figuratively hovers over them and literally exists below them, among the white inhabitants of the valley town of Medallion City. From the outset, then, *Sula's* fictional world is topsy-turvy; the bottom is at the top and the top is at the bottom. This inversion is the first of many in Morrison's novel. It illustrates the "interplay of paradoxes" that womanist theologians like Cannon see not only in black women's fiction but also in the "real-lived texture of Black life."[52]

Sula showcases the complex, dynamic, and sometimes paradoxical friendship between Nel Wright and Sula Peace, outlining the nature and course of their moral maturation, which spans the years 1922–1965. They first forge their friendship in 1922, shortly after turning twelve, but to understand who they are and how they move from girlhood to womanhood, we must go back before this time and examine their early family life. "A woman who won all social battles with presence and a conviction of the legitimacy of her authority," Helene Wright gave birth to Nel in 1910, nine years after her marriage to her grandmother's nephew, Wiley Wright.[53] Because of Wiley's long absences as a ship's cook, Helene raised her child alone. According to Morrison's narrator, she "rose grandly to the occasion of motherhood," insuring that Nel learned how to behave politely and obediently, especially in church.[54] Most days Helene's "dark eyes arched in a perpetual query about other people's manners,"[55] and in her self-appointed role as the Bottom's moral guardian she would often dismiss "slackness," her word for anyone she judged to be living permissively. On such grounds she disapproved of Hannah Peace, Sula's "sooty" mother.[56]

The first of three children born to Eva Peace and a man named BoyBoy, Hannah grew up in a strange and stressful environment. Her father left the family cabin after five trying years of marriage to Eva. Shortly thereafter Eva abandoned Hannah, Pearl, and Plum to a neighbor, Mrs. Suggs, for eighteen months. When a rich but one-legged Eva eventually returned, Hannah watched while Eva became the "creator and sovereign" of one of Medallion's largest homes, leasing rooms to numberless cousins and nameless strays.[57] Unsurprisingly, Eva was a woman around whom much speculation swirled, with rumors flying like an uncontrollable squall. Her role in Plum's death and the origins of her disability became the two most talked-about topics in the neighborhood.[58]

While some folk said that Eva lost one of her legs after she purposefully placed it under a train in order to secure a pay off, others insinuated that she sold it to a local hospital for $10,000. Disabled but playfully prosperous, and so not without her fair share of gentlemen callers after

BoyBoy's disappearance, Eva's legacy to her daughters was "manlove," an erotic energy for maleness, and "Hannah simply refused to live without the attentions of a man."[59] Growing up austerely, Hannah eventually married Rekus, "a laughing man," who died three years after his wife gave birth to Sula, their only child.[60]

Eva and Hannah's lively womanism contrasts with the Bottom's apparent lack of movement and development. There is an ordering mechanism within the town, for example, and this conservative impulse shows up in numerous ways, some of them quite bizarre. Every January, for example, the crazy WW1 veteran Shadrack leads the townspeople in honoring National Suicide Day—a walking ritual that helps folk confront life's dangerous unpredictability. Shadrack scares others at first. In time, though, people become comfortable with him and his peculiar behavior. No weddings ever take place on National Suicide Day, twists of fate are credited to it, and even the local church organizes some of its teachings around what Shadrack says and does.[61] Herein lies the Bottom's story and song of black relationality; a simple-but-strange ritual binds people together and enables them to negotiate the topsy-turvy world they live in, and pass through. For their part, though, Eva and Hannah cultivate and maintain a feistiness about life that nobody in the Bottom, or even down below the Bottom, can wipe out, to paraphrase Cannon. Here the point is not so much that Eva and Hannah avoid Shadrack or disparage his ritual. Rather, the point is that they live self-sustaining lives, emotionally unaffected by community custom or habit.[62] Defined as the attempt to live outside or beyond communal accountability, autonomy signifies an aspect of Eva's and Hannah's womanism that Sula inherits and makes her own.[63]

Readers who work their way to the end of Morrison's novel ask one basic question: why would Nel and Sula become friends in the first place? After all, Sula comes across as reckless and unruly, perhaps even repulsive, especially when she appears to watch with interest when her mother, Hannah, burns to death. By contrast, Nel seems conventional and dependable, one of those individuals who embody the minor as well as major virtues—someone who accomplishes her work with impressive efficiency yet without great fanfare. Nel and Sula are quite different individuals. Still, they come together because there seems to be an element of both in each of them. Nel and Sula are mutually creative selves-in-relation, as various commentators point out.[64]

Injured by Helene's repeated attempts to drain every last ounce of originality and creativity out of her existence, Nel craves Sula's independence and verve. And in time, despite her mother's prissy protestations, Nel gravitates toward Sula and finds relief in her intractable personality.[65] By the same token, Nel's devotion and consistency help Sula recover from the wound she incurs when she learns that her mother dislikes her.[66] In the words of Morrison's narrator, Nel and Sula met in 1922 and "found in each other's eyes the intimacy they were looking for."[67]

Various episodes in Nel and Sula's friendship reinforce their harmony and understanding. When a gang of lascivious young boys corner them, for example, Sula decides to save her and Nel's modesty by slashing off the tip of her finger. Like Orestes before the Furies, Sula accepts the small loss to redeem her and Nel's whole lives. Indeed, Sula's self-inflicted sacrifice, a "scrap of flesh, like a button mushroom, curling in the cherry blood that ran into the corners of the slate," frightens the fearless young boys. Moreover, they stare in disbelief as she inquires, "If I can do that to myself, what you suppose I'll do to you?"[68]

While other incidents test Nel's and Sula's camaraderie, especially their questionable role in Chicken Little's drowning, these two young women continue to drift along, as if caught up in a dream, until 1927, the year Nel courts and subsequently marries Jude Greene, a waiter at the Hotel Medallion.[69] Described by Morrison's narrator as "a handsome, well-liked man—the tenor of Mount Zion's Men's Quartet, who had an enviable reputation among the girls and a comfortable one among men," Jude adds a fresh dimension to Nel's and Sula's intense companionship.[70] Viewing Nel as "someone sweet, industrious and loyal to shore him up," Jude marries Nel but, on their wedding day, Sula disrupts the celebrations by leaving the Bottom hastily.[71] She avoids friends and family for ten years.[72]

When Sula eventually returns, the townspeople launch a series of blistering attacks on her decade of experimental living. Eva accuses Sula of being narcissistic for not finding a husband, for not settling down, and for not making babies. In her reply, which she punctuates with expletives, Sula declares forcefully: "I don't want to make somebody else. I want to make myself."[73] The ensuing row, which seems so crucial to the novel's subsequent directionality, takes us to the center of Sula's evil. And it highlights one of the differences between Sula and Nel—namely, Nel's lack of belligerence:

". . . It ain't right for you to want to stay off by yourself. You need . . . I'm a tell you what you need."

Sula sat up. "I need you to shut your mouth."

"Don't nobody talk to me like that. Don't nobody . . ."

"This body does. Just 'cause you was bad enough to cut off your own leg you think you got a right to kick everybody with the stump."

. . . "Pus mouth! God's going to strike you!"

"Which God? The one watched you burn Plum?"

"Don't talk to me about no burning. You watched your own mamma. You crazy roach! You the one should have been burnt!"

"But I ain't. Got that? I ain't. Any more fires in this house, I'm lighting them!"

"Hellfire don't need lighting and it's already burning in you . . . "

"Whatever's burning in me is mine!"

"Amen!"

"And I'll split this town in two and everything in it before I'll let you put it out!"

"Pride goeth before a fall."

"What the hell do I care about falling?"

"Amazing Grace."[74]

Like John Milton's Satan, Sula displays an impertinence that is as wicked as it is unpleasant.[75] And, according to the Bottom's ethical conventions, her sassy and successful attempt to place Eva in a nursing home comes across as sinful—where sin signifies anything that ruptures relationality. Here theologian Kevin Vanhoozer notes the role that language ("pus mouth") plays in such sinfulness:

> . . . there are patterns of distortion in our communication with God and others, and with ourselves. Non-theological thinkers recognize distortions in patterns of communication [and Morrison certainly thinks Sula's lack of relationality leaves her "lost"], but only theology names these communicative distortions *sin*. Indeed, the most dangerous member of the body may be the tongue (James 3:5-10). Distorted patterns of communication eventually lead to a deformed or misshapen self. Hell is not others, as Jean-Paul Sartre wrongly maintained, but rather the inability to relate to others.[76]

Unafraid of falling from grace, though, Sula does not care what others think of her actions.

Sula strikes out on her own, sleeping first with Jude, Nel's husband, and then with the husbands of other women from the Bottom. And in her attempt to justify her licentiousness, Sula castigates her opponents for what she sees as their own sins of triviality, distractibility, and diffuseness.[77] From Sula's perspective, the Bottom's women lack an organizing focus; they rely on others, especially their menfolk, for their own self-definition, and they underdevelop or even negate their personalities. Given what feminism and womanism say about such sentiments, Sula seems strangely justified in turning the tables on her detractors, seeing sin in their passivity:

> She [Sula] saw how the years had dusted their bronze with ash, the eyes that had once opened wide to the moon bent into grimly sickles of concern. The narrower their lives, the wider their hips. Those with husbands had folded themselves into starched coffins, their sides bursting with other people's skinned dreams and bony regrets. Those without men were like sour-tipped needles featuring one constant empty eye. Those with men had had the sweetness sucked from their breath by ovens and steam kettles.[78]

On the surface, Sula signifies a classic type of evil impulse. And yet womanist theology inclines us to quarry much deeper in our analysis of her (and Nel's) character. "Black female protagonists are women with hard-boiled honesty and down-to-earth thinking," Cannon claims, "the ones who are forced to see through the shallowness, hypocrisy, and phoniness in their continual struggle for survival."[79] Equipped with a feistiness about life that nobody can tamp down, not even her family and friends, Sula sees through the life-destroying powers of white and black patriarchalism, and she survives, creating and cultivating values and virtues on her own terms.[80] If, as Cannon says, virtuous living involves "creatively straining against the external restraints in one's life," then Sula lives virtuously.[81] But we need to acknowledge that Sula also lives viciously. So much of what she says and does ruptures relationality: Sula betrays Nel, harbors ill-feelings toward her neighbors, abuses her extended family, and treats the Bottom's menfolk like sexual toys. Sula is an interplay of good and evil.

Nel's life is of a mingled yarn as well. There is little of Sula's liveliness in her, as I have noted, and if Nel sees through the phoniness and shallowness of some of the Bottom's women, then she keeps her judgments and complaints to herself. Is Nel's approach to life an example of living viciously? Perhaps. There is an element of meekness and acquiescence to her existence, and such traits do not seem to harmonize with

Cannon's womanist hymn to hard-boiled honesty and down to earth thinking. Nel accepts and accomplishes her small tasks unreservedly, lives within the law, seldom seeks out life's unconventional or experimental moments, and lacks any sense of drama and fanfare. In this respect, of course, she resembles the Bottom's women more than Sula.[82] And we know what Sula thinks of such women—that their own timidity indicates lack, lapse, and failure. But there is another way to examine and assess someone like Nel, and this approach also involves using Cannon's womanism. There are times, for example, when Nel responds to the less than gracious boundaries in which she lives by creating and cultivating "unctuousness," "invisible dignity," and "unshouted courage"—three virtues that we might connect to Nel's characterization, even if Cannon first ties them to Hurston's fictional heroines.[83] Such qualities describe Nel accurately, and we can appreciate how her virtue balances her vice; like Sula, Nel is an interplay of good and evil.

What attracts Nel to Sula and Sula to Nel is, as this section indicates, the question that trumps all other questions in our examination of Morrison's novel. Morrison's 1976 interview with Robert Stepto offers us one way of answering it:

> . . . I wanted to say, as much as I could say it without being overbearing, that there was a little bit of both in each of those two women, and that if they had been one person, I suppose they would have been a rather marvelous person. But each one lacked something the other had.[84]

Morrison also notes that while she wrote *Sula* by thinking of Sula as an evil force and Nel as good force, "sometimes good looks like evil and sometimes evil looks like good—you never know what it is. It depends on what uses you put it."[85] Sula, for example, comes across as vicious, especially for the way she ruptures the Bottom's relationality. But Morrison's characterization of Sula seems subtle. Sula not only ruptures relationality, for example, she also creates and cultivates it, by inspiring goodness in others. To paraphrase feminist theologian Denise Carmody, Sula displays "arrogant grace," since she is self-absorbed yet generous.[86]

Upon Sula's return to the Bottom after a decade of experimental living, others treat her as the town pariah, viewing her as evil's essence. However, Sula's malevolence soon rejuvenates her adversaries. "Other people seemed to turn their volume on and up when Sula was in the room," according to Morrison's narrator.[87] Over time, the Bottom's townspeople watch Sula "more closely than they watched any other roach or bitch in the town, and their alertness was gratified."[88] First, Teapot's Mamma, a normally indifferent woman, misreads Sula's desire to help young Teapot when he falls and fractures his leg, and, as a result, Teapot's Mamma sobers up, becomes clean and industrious, and abandons her reprehensible policy of sending her son to Dick's for a calcium-free breakfast of Mr. Goodbars and soda pop.[89] Second, the Bottom's women, insulted by Sula's promiscuity, resolve to take better care of their menfolk.[90] Here Morrison's narrator indicates that Sula's sin holds within itself the seeds of salvation for the people of Bottom:

> Their conviction of Sula's evil changed them in accountable yet mysterious ways. Once the source of their personal misfortune was identified, they had leave to protect and love another. They began to cherish their husbands and wives, protect their children, repair their homes and in general band together against the devil in their midst. In their world, aberrations were as much a part of nature as grace.[91]

In sharp contrast to the permissively free Sula, Nel seems "more terrified of the free fall."[92] While Nel "was the one person who had wanted nothing from her [Sula]," she nonetheless practices the moral prudery associated with the people of Bottom, and "virtue, bleak and drawn, was her only mooring."[93]

Described by Morrison's narrator as "the color of wet sandpaper," Nel seems serene, occasionally languid, and often terrified by life's messy verities. Yet she is also measured, disciplined, and reliable.[94] By contrast, Sula's coloring—Morrison's narrator describes her as "heavy brown with large quiet eyes"—hints at the possibility of difference and otherness.[95] Marked by an intensity that would make most blush, Sula lives without a thought for the approval of others, her passions exploding and erupting at a moment's notice, sometimes in vicious ways. Individually, Nel and Sula are very different characters; when they come together, though, the reader detects unanimity:

> Morrison's exploration of the female voice struggling toward maturity and authenticity climaxes in Sula and Nel's discussion at Sula's death-bed. There they confont the limitations of their respective moral visions. Frightened by Sula's detachment, even in the face of death, Nel is unable to hear Sula's truth; irritated by Nel's self-sacrifice in

the name of conventional goodness, Sula fails to appreciate Nel's pain. In the final actions, Sula and Nel openly and reciprocally care for the other in a recognition of interdependence.[96]

When Nel declares that she and Sula "was girls together," an insight that appears toward the novel's end as she leaves the cemetery where Sula lies buried, Morrison's narrator finally reveals what we have suspected all along. Nel and Sula are one girl, one woman, one person—able to coagulate contradictions, blend paradoxes, and fuse seemingly incompatible subidentities together.[97] Their personalities, could they have been merged, would have amounted to one whole person: an embodiment of *both* "unshouted courage" (Nel) *and* "hard-boiled honesty" (Sula) in one satisfyingly real soul.

Such "evil twin" or "doppelgänger" characterization echoes famous storylines within the Hebrew Bible. As we saw with Graham Greene in the last chapter, Morrison challenges Christian readers to reread the Scriptures, especially its more troubling texts. As a result, we discover sympathy for characters we initially locate outside sympathy's official range.

First, Nel and Sula illustrate the ancient concept of evil twins, as found in the biblical story of Cain and Abel as well as Jacob and Esau. Here one character represents the green-eyed foil of the other; the good and evil twin share in the societal value system and yet, as one of them inverts the system's ethics, so the evil twin embodies the dual opposite to his good counterpart. We initially refuse sympathy for the evil twin. After all, Cain rationalizes murdering Abel, and Jacob supplants Esau remorselessly. But, upon close reading and further reflection, we eventually appreciate that God protects the evil twin and makes it clear that he belongs to the Creator unreservedly. Reading about Cain and Jacob introduces us to scriptural antagonists whose jealousy and duplicity mark them out as ethically suspect. They are not so questionable that God abandons them altogether, however. On the contrary, and not without some irony, God transforms their evil into good. If God works through someone like Jacob, an insincere man who comes to faith after finally seeing God's face in Esau's compassion, then God, as Christians put it, works through all things, including the worst of sinners, and even us. We possess as well as display our own evil twin, the dark and knavish impulses within our souls. Reclaiming Cain and Jacob involves learning to countenance the evil as well as the good that competes for our attention. Scripture often functions like a mirror that we hold up to our face. Its stories become our stories. And through its many and varied tales we find an accurate reflection of who and what we are as human beings. Something similar occurs when we read *Sula*.[98]

Second, if we push the notion of doppelgänger even further, Morrison has us question the conventional construal of good and evil. Sula's dark skin marks her for life. The Bottom's townspeople treat the childhood Sula disdainfully, using darkness as an excuse to question her ethics. Sula fights her community's animosity, creating a conflict that perpetuates hostility and ill will. While we might initially wonder about such lifestyle choices, we can appreciate her struggle to survive. Like Jacob, who must overcome his father's favoritism toward the dull-witted Esau, Sula must manipulate and negotiate life at the bottom of the Bottom. Sula's impudent attempts to survive against all odds is the womanist embodiment of Jacob's all-night struggle with God. To be sure, womanism forces us to rethink traditional ethics and celebrate the sass, verve, and wit that resurrects and redeems Sula.

Through her narrator's frequent hint that Nel and Sula are one person split into two, Morrison suggests that a double lurks in every person. This insight can be expressed in theological terms used by Irenaeus: good and evil exist within us all as vital and necessary concomitants. Far from paradisal life is, instead, a hostile but basically benevolent environment wherein we struggle to become authentically human by learning how to tolerate and negotiate our impulses toward vice and virtue. For womanist theologians, as we have seen, the point of this struggle is to master our impulses, channeling them in the service of self-other relationships that advance mutuality and reciprocity, qualities that womanists trace to our being made in God's image and, ultimately, to the divine life itself.

THE NOVEL'S PALPABLE HUMANITY

Christians in my class often ask about my use of *Sula*. Some questions come from students who sincerely do not see how I could use this novel, especially its ethically suspect set of characters, to remark upon Christian doctrine. Many young women and men find Sula's actions disgusting, for example, and several wonder if she has any redeeming qualities whatsoever. I appreciate their objections. Without a doubt: *Sula* is a challenging read. But Morrison's novel repays our close attention. And I think we can learn something when we come to view it not only through the prism of the Christian doctrine of humanity, as I note, but also through what Christians say about Jesus of Nazareth.

Certain beliefs about Jesus reside at Christianity's doctrinal center. One such belief claims that Jesus was God "incarnate." This means God became a human being and so Jesus, as the next chapter will explore, is both human and divine. If Christians take this belief in incarnation seriously, then the most instructive way to study and resolve thorny theological topics such as sin and grace is to observe and ponder them in palpable, flesh-and-blood depictions. As I say to my students: a Christian theology of reading recognizes, even celebrates, how novels like *Sula* afford us beguiling insights into what serious theological concerns look and feel like in realistic or true to life—incarnate—situations.

Personal and Social Sin

Sula's insights are two-fold. First, I think Morrison's novel concerns itself with two theological questions: how does right spoil, and how can wrong be redeemed? *Sula* answers these questions by showing Christian readers that good and evil reside in all of us, that it seldom takes much to tip the ethical scales one way or the other, and that what happens at the novel's end—the realization of partnership, the apparent union of opposites, at-one-ment as atonement—suggests grace's indomitable power to reconcile and make whole. Morrison's story has deep insight into human nature, since her description of Sula's and Nel's possibilities and perils rings true for us. We resemble both characters because, like them, we battle constantly with our strengths and weaknesses. When we are placed under pressure, as Morrison's characters so often are, good and evil are right there with us, though we do not sin to grow. Wrestling with vice and virtue helps us to develop and mature. There is no shadow without light, and this notion, common to *Sula* as well as Scripture, means we have to learn to live with our shadow side in order to live healthy lives.

Second, *Sula* tells us as much about our relationship with others as it does about ourselves. Traditional Christian doctrine discusses sin and evil in individual terms only, as we have seen, but Morrison and more recent theologians do not permit us this luxury. Indeed, they understand good and evil as structural as well as personal realities. Social sin often takes the form of racism, as it does in *Sula*, where it is embodied by Medallion City's white inhabitants. This group represents the greater evil in this novel: they are the top people who first manipulated the folks at the bottom but now, ironically, desire the bottom for land development. And even though white people are unspoken characters who lurk at *Sula*'s edge, they nonetheless control the black community's sense of vice and virtue; white people are both principal and powerful.[99]

Besides racism, social sin also takes the form of ruptured relationality, the examples for which are legion in Morrison's novel. Perhaps the most profound sense of brokenness occurs when Sula decides to upend her values by leading an experimental lifestyle; the Bottom's townspeople cast her out, so to speak, and Sula disappears for a decade. Everything and everyone subsequently goes to wrack and ruin. The community disintegrates, and evil occurs. Conversely, grace appears in the spirituality of persistence personified not only by individual characters in *Sula* but also by the Bottom's townspeople; here, grace is the God-given desire for order and wholeness in a topsy-turvy, fragmented world.[100] When Sula returns to the Bottom after ten years away, her evil facilitates her community's good.

This lesson, that we always need the other to flourish, appears in the resolution at the novel's end: "We was girls together." It remains the chief reason why I think Christians should read *Sula*. Such an integration upholds two profoundly theological notions, which call us to come face to face with the fact and meaning of our existence today: whatever ruptures our relationality represents the most insidious evil in our midst, the novel declares, and whatever helps us become increasingly attentive of our need for each other, even for God, heralds grace.

Literature and Womanist Theology

By now it should be clear that womanist theologians develop their understanding of what it means to be human not only by reflecting on "the real-lived texture of black life" but also by examining the black woman's literary tradition.[101] This observation is important to make, given my book's overall interest in what happens at theology's and literature's intersection. With Greene in the last chapter and Nikos Kazantzakis in the next, we observe theology informing literature. In the present chapter, however, the tables turn. Here we witness literature informing theology. Besides using Walker's work, for instance, Cannon traces the talk of "unctuousness" and "unshouted courage" to Hurston. Other womanist theologians use poets and writers such as Nikki Giovanni, Gwendolyn Brooks, Paule Marshall, and Phillis Wheatley.[102] But why? Why are womanist theologians ready and willing to use literature as a resource for thinking theologically? It is because they situate black literature, especially black women's literature, at "the nexus between the real-lived texture of black life and the oral-aural cultural values implicitly passed on and received from one generation to the next."[103] Novelists like Morrison are, therefore, like "conduit[s] for the tribe."[104] As a faithful recorder of African American existential struggles, Morrison, like so many of her fellow black women writers, "can be trusted as seriously mirroring black reality."[105]

Literature's medium allows *all* authors not only to provide compelling explorations of their characters' personal journeys; it also stimulates us to address important theological questions: why is there anything at all, and not just nothing? What is it in me that causes me to be alive, even to become what I am not yet? The answers to such questions are legion, as numberless as the narratives that women and men have produced across the centuries, not simply for entertainment but so that we might orient ourselves in this vast universe and live more purposeful lives. We are storytelling bipeds, as some commentators aver, and literature's most serious challenge to Christians is to "take up and read" spiritually (*lectio divina*).[106] In the words of Eugene H. Peterson, theologian and biblical translator:

> Reading today is largely a consumer activity—people devour books, magazines, pamphlets, and newspapers for information that will fuel their ambition or careers or competence. The faster the better, the more the better. It is either analytical, figuring things out; or it is frivolous, killing time. Spiritual reading is mostly a lover's activity—a dalliance with words, reading as much between the lines as in the lines themselves. It is leisurely, as ready to reread an old book as to open a new one. It is playful, always anticipating the pleasures of friendship. It is prayerful, convinced that all honest words can involve us is some way, if we read with our hearts as well as our heads, in an eternal conversation that got its start in the Word that "became flesh." Spiritual reading is at home with Homer as well as Hosea.[107]

CONCLUSION

Sula illustrates one black woman writer's contribution to an understanding of black life and, perhaps, to the Christian doctrine of humanity also. Here Morrison shows how "black people creatively strain against external limits in their lives, how they affirm their humanity by inverting assumptions and how they balance the continual struggle and interplay of paradoxes."[108] Good and evil are natural and vital concomitants in *Sula*, as they appear to be for several theologians mentioned in this chapter, particularly the womanists, and life's challenge involves learning how to comprehend as well as coagulate these impulses in search of a meaningful identity, both individually and collectively.

FOR FURTHER READING

Mark E. Biddle's *Missing the Mark: Sin and Its Consequences in Biblical Theology* (Nashville, Tenn.: Abingdon Press, 2005) proceeds out from Scripture and constructs an understanding of sin that holds considerable promise for those engaged in Christian ministry. Ron David's *Toni Morrison Explained: A Reader's Road Map to the Novels* (New York: Random House, 2000) is a quirky yet informed introduction to the novelist's quite complex work. Eleazar S. Fernandez's *Reimagining the Human: Theological Anthropology in Response to Systemic Evil* (St. Louis, Mo.: Chalice Press, 2004) takes racism, classism, sexism and "naturism," as the starting point for an entirely fresh understanding of what it means to be human. Stacey M. Floyd-Thomas' *Mining the Motherlode: Methods in Womanist Ethics* (Cleveland: Pilgrim Press, 2006) explains, among other things, how literature shapes womanist theology. Her edited volume, *Deeper Shades of Purple: Womanism in Religion and Society* (New York: New York University Press, 2006) assembles and showcases some of today's brightest and best womanist minds. C. David Grant's *A Theology of God's Grace* (St. Louis, Mo.: Chalice Press, 2004) outlines an approach to divine grace that takes our postmodern world seriously. David P. Gushee's *Only Human: Christian Reflections on the Journey Toward Wholeness* (San Francisco: Jossey-Bass, 2005) provides an excellent survey of ancient and contemporary discussions of our nature and destiny. Therese E. Higgins' *Religiosity, Cosmology, and Folklore: The African Influence in the Novels of Toni Morrison* (New York: Routledge, 2001) represents one of the most accessible and informative overviews of Morrison's work to date, emphasizing the traditional African qualities in her writing. Dwight M. Hopkins' *Heart and Head: Black Theology–Past, Present, and Future* (New York: Palgrave, 2003) introduces some of the movement's key personalities, themes, and developments. Hopkins has also published *Being Human: Race, Culture, and Religion* (Minneapolis, Minn.: Fortress, 2005), an attempt to comprehend what it means to be human in light of African American experience. Daryl Koehn's *The Nature of Evil* (New York: Palgrave, 2005) utilizes popular literature to address violence and beauty, twin impulses in human nature. John Portman's *A History of Sin: Its Evolution to Today and Beyond* (Lanham, Md.: Rowman & Littlefield, 2007) chronicles sin's intellectual history. And Gloria Grant Roberson's *The World of Toni Morrison: A Guide to Characters and Places in Her Novels* (Westport, Conn.: Greenwood Press, 2003) contains over eight-hundred brief encyclopedia entries on her work.

SELECTED WEB SITES

1. http://www.tonimorrisonsociety.org/
   This site belongs to the official Toni Morrison Society.

2. http://www.ku.edu/~phbw/
   A clearing house for archival, documentary, and scholarly research in African American literature.

3. http://www.library.ucsb.edu/subjects/blackfeminism/ah_womanisttheol.html
   An introduction to womanist thought.

3

JESUS

Nikos Kazantzakis' *The Last Temptation of Christ*

While some Christians believe that every New Testament story and traditional doctrinal claim about Jesus of Nazareth is worthy of assent, and
therefore beyond dispute, others hold them open to question. Varying
interpretations of Jesus' significance inspire hostile reactions among
Christians. Such is the case with the Cretan author Nikos Kazantzakis,
whose 1951 novelistic re-creation of Jesus' life, *The Last Temptation of
Christ*, ranks as one of the most contentious construals of Jesus in history.[1] Since other scholars have documented the furor surrounding
this text, I will not restate their observations. Instead, I continue my
examination of the relationship between Christian doctrine and modern
fiction by considering both the sources and intent behind Kazantzakis'
allegedly scandalous story.

There are three major sections in this chapter. In the first, I delineate Kazantzakis' energetic life and prolific career, focusing on his
imaginative use of Henri Bergson's evolutionary philosophy. In the second section, I sketch some of the traditional claims made by Christians
about Jesus and the christological formulas articulated by the church.
As I show, Christians have defined their faith by affirming both Jesus'
divinity and humanity. Yet this so-called christological complementarity has sometimes been achieved at the expense of emphasizing Jesus'
full humanity; I trace a line of thinkers who question this approach,
urging that a thoroughly divine Jesus is entirely irrelevant to our experience. Major examples here include two Christian writers Kazantzakis
both read and admired: Nicholas Cabasilas, the Byzantine mystic, and
Ernest Renan, the French Catholic historian.

The third section explores how Kazantzakis affirms Jesus' full humanity in the context of an evolutionary Christology. For Kazantzakis, the Messiah moves through four stages of vocational formation. Yet this Messiah never loses sight of his humanity en route to full union with God. I conclude, then, that Christians should neither repudiate nor ignore Kazantzakis, for his work displays deep spiritual longing as well as provides parallels with other writers inside the Christian tradition.[2]

NIKOS KAZANTZAKIS: LIFE AND LITERARY ART

Kazantzakis was born in Iráklion, Crete, in 1883.[3] After completing his secondary school education in 1902, he left the island for Athens, where he studied law. During his undergraduate years, Kazantzakis ventured into creative writing, and published a first novel, *Serpent and Lily* (1906). Enthused by critics' initial praise, Kazantzakis abruptly left for Paris, the writers' capital of the world, in 1907.

In Paris, Kazantzakis encountered numerous philosophers, poets, and artists, whose influence would prove enduring. Two of the more significant were Bergson, whose lectures on evolutionary philosophy he audited, and Friedrich Nietzsche, whose philosophical writings he devoured. Nietzsche actually inspired the dissertation Kazantzakis published in 1909, shortly after returning to Crete via Italy. Eager, upon his return, to introduce and promote progressive ideas, Kazantzakis lectured on Bergson's philosophy.[4]

In 1914, Kazantzakis made a pilgrimage to the Holy Mountain, Athos, the so-called axis of Eastern Orthodox monasticism.[5] Surrounded by Athos' sacred atmosphere and action, he spent forty days in various monasteries, reading Bergson's *Creative Evolution*, the Buddha's biography, Cabasilas' *The Life in Christ*, Dante Alighieri's *Divine Comedy*, and the canonical gospels. Sensing Christ's living, suffering presence during his time on the Holy Mountain, Kazantzakis embraced this religious sentiment and then folded it into *Christ*, one of three plays he wrote in 1915.

Kazantzakis spent the next fifteen years traveling Europe, which, in turn, further fed his literary imagination. While mining lignite in the Peloponnesus around 1917, for example, he encountered the Dionysian workmate George Zorbás, whom he later immortalized in *Zorba the Greek* (1946). In 1919, he agreed to help the Greek government repatriate several thousand Greeks trapped in the Caucasus, an experience that later served as copy for *The Greek Passion*, his fictional transfiguration of Christ's final hours (1954). Passing through Berlin and Vienna in

1922, where he encountered Freudian psychology and read the Buddhist scriptures, he began outlining *The Saviors of God: Spiritual Exercises*, later published in 1927. Kazantzakis made a pilgrimage to Assisi in 1924—a site he would visit again and again, eventually expressing his devotion to the Poor Man of God through *Saint Francis* (1956). Between 1924 and 1929 Kazantzakis also traveled across the Soviet Union, Palestine, Cyprus, Spain, Italy, Egypt, and Czechoslovakia. At various points along the way, he completed numerous drafts of the *Odyssey*, his modern sequel to Homer's epic, later published in 1938. Throughout his international travels, Kazantzakis never knowingly overlooked events in Greece, especially its civil war in 1949, which inspired his novel, *The Fratricides* (1963).

In 1941, during the autumn of his literary career, Kazantzakis explored his commitment to Bergsonian-Nietzschean philosophy through novels. As early as 1942 he planned a work about Jesus, but this initial effort—"Christ's Memoirs"—did not lead to anything concrete until *The Last Temptation of Christ*, which was published—finally, after much official religious consternation—in 1955.

Kazantzakis' religious fiction disturbed numerous Christians. In 1953, the Eastern Orthodox Church condemned portions of *Freedom or Death* and *The Last Temptation of Christ*, even though the latter was unavailable in Greek. In 1954, Pope Pius XII placed *The Last Temptation of Christ* on the Roman Catholic Index of Forbidden Texts, prompting Kazantzakis to cite Tertullian, the North African father of Latin theology, in his defense.[6]

In 1955, after a short illness, Kazantzakis sketched his spiritual autobiography, *Report to Greco* (1961), and visited the German Lutheran theologian and medical missionary Albert Schweitzer.[7] Like Kazantzakis, Schweitzer was an unorthodox yet deeply religious thinker; together, they admired the teachings of Jesus, even if they could not affirm Jesus' uniqueness. A trusted soulmate, Schweitzer nominated Kazantzakis for the Nobel Prize for Literature, which he lost by one vote in 1956. He was also present when Kazantzakis died at the hospital in Freiburg, Germany, in 1957.

Bergson and Kazantzakis: Process Philosophers

Kazantzakis' literature can be seen as a poeticization of Bergsonian philosophy. The recipient of the 1927 Nobel Prize for Literature, Bergson promotes a worldview—evolutionary vitalism—that stresses existence's flux and mutability. In life, he says, nothing remains fixed and settled, not even the self, because everything evolves:

> Like eddies of dust raised by the wind as it passes, the living turn upon themselves, borne up by the great blast of life. They are therefore relatively stable, and counterfeit immobility so well that we treat each of them as a *thing* rather than as a *progress*, forgetting that the very permanence of their form is only the outline of a movement.[8]

An endless battle between two opposing forces—spirit and matter— characterizes "reality," Bergson continues. While the *élan vital*, life's energizing spirit, surges upward and onward toward creativity and novelty, matter pushes downward toward stillness and equilibrium.[9] The universe advances, then, because a vital impulse or disembodied creativity launches itself into matter and immediately sets about unmaking itself (dematerialization).[10] This unstoppable struggle—mobility against immobility—breaks out in everything and everyone, he claims.

Following Bergson's lead, Kazantzakis maintains that the *élan vital* triggers evolutionary change. It does this by inviting everything, especially us, to transubstantiate all matter into spirit.[11] He moves beyond Bergson, though, because he equates "God" with this palpitating life force. More significant, however, is that with this equation Kazantzakis also moves beyond traditional Christianity, which developed alongside Greek philosophy, especially the Greek idea of the One and the Many, or permanence and change.[12] In accord with Greek permanence, traditional Christian doctrine portrays God as a transcendent, immutable deity who grounds a static, unchanging world. But Kazantzakis challenges this way of picturing God.[13]

"Saving" God

The Saviors of God, Kazantzakis' primary religious statement, represents his attempt to think theologically in light of evolutionary philosophy. It controversially rejects God as unchanging and understands God as an integral part of the world's formation and growth, evolving with us through time, even affected by us, sometimes to the point of needing our help to advance into the future. Kazantzakis' God is not, therefore, all powerful; indeed, his God seems doomed to remain forever incarcerated in matter unless we assist God's release—the spirit's dematerialization— through spiritual exercises. As a result, we have a duty to "save" God.

Kazantzakis develops this evolutionary theology by analyzing our human condition. He describes it as a process involving three duties and four conceptual steps. Our first duty involves using our *minds* to develop a rational, coherent understanding of our world or, more specifically, an intelligent vision of how the cosmos mediates God's struggling presence. Our second duty, to follow our *heart's* depth of feeling in search of life's essence, rests on an abiding faith in existential and ecological unity. Our third duty entails overcoming whatever vision and sentiment *intelligence* and *feeling* offer us. We must liberate ourselves both from "the simple complacency of the mind that thinks to put all things in order and hopes to subdue phenomena" and "from the terror of the heart that seeks and hopes to find the essence of things."[14] Overcoming *mind* and *heart* entails embracing nihilism, the view that nothing of any value exists:

> Our body is a ship that sails on deep blue waters. What is our goal? To be shipwrecked!
>
> Because the Atlantic is a cataract, the new Earth exists only in the heart of man, and suddenly, in a silent whirlpool, you will sink into the cataract of death, you and the whole world's galleon.
>
> Without hope, but with bravery, it is your duty to set your prow calmly toward the abyss. And to say: 'Nothing exists!'[15]

Our attempt to discharge these three duties compels us to undertake a personal quest involving four conceptual steps. In the first step, we encounter an evolving God upon whom we are called to save. Here God's convulsive Cry tears at our entrails, entreating us to save God by facilitating *élan vital's* dematerialization. "Cry" is the English rendering of *kravyí*, which Kazantzakis often uses to denote his evolving, struggling God, especially the way God maneuvers matter into the future.[16] Used in the New Testament, *kravyí* means "an articulate or inarticulate loud cry."[17] In a Greek dictionary, it can mean bawl, yelp (in notification, tumult, or grief), croak (as a raven), or scream, screech, i.e., to call aloud (to shriek, to exclaim, or to entreat). For Kazantzakis, *kravyí* is more than just a loud noise; it is a declaration. In *The Last Temptation of Christ*, God cries; in fact, God even croaks, like a raven, and declares that Jesus must do all he can to avoid the devil's snare, which is ordinariness and happiness.[18] Attending to God's *kravyí*, as Jesus does in *The Last Temptation of Christ*, requires enormous bravery, even self-sacrifice.

The second of the four conceptual steps requires additional courage. At this point Kazantzakis enjoins us to transcend ego to discover and then appreciate the intellectual, social, and historical traditions that shape us. Such discovery and appreciation is followed by the third step, in which we surmount all provincialism and nationalism to embrace ecumenical togetherness. For Kazantzakis, our spiritual development necessitates a greatly increased awareness of our connectedness to all things, especially humankind's wider spirit. Most importantly, he reiterates how God's Cry echoes from the depths of our unfolding soul, beckoning us to ascend, evolve, and transform:

> "Lord, who are you? You loom before me like a Centaur, his hands stretched toward the sky, his feet transfixed in mud."
> "I am He who eternally ascends."
> "Why do you ascend? You strain every muscle, you struggle and fight to emerge from the beast. From the beast, and from man. Do not leave me!"
> "I fight and ascend that I may not drown. I stretch out my hands, I clutch at every warm body, I raise my head above my brains that I may breathe. I drown everywhere and can nowhere be contained."
> "Lord, why do you tremble?"
> "I am afraid! This dark ascent has no ending. My head is a flame that tries eternally to detach itself, but the breath of night blows eternally to put me out. My struggle is endangered every moment. I walk and stumble in the flesh like a traveler overtaken by night, and I call out: 'Help me!'"[19]

In Kazantzakis' writings, "Lord" and "God" are strong metaphors for our emerging cosmos' groans and travails. In the fourth and last conceptual step, therefore, we identify with our universe's evolutionary advance. Here we find that life's vital impulse (the *élan vital*/Lord/God) agitates us, as it agitates Kazantzakis' Jesus, to actualize our potential for formation and growth. Our final and supreme duty, then, involves collaborating with God as all reality makes its painful, arduous, and tireless evolutionary ascent from matter to forms of life increasingly more intelligent, purposive, and spiritual.

This evolving, struggling God operates within all created life. God as all-encompassing spiritual presence assumes tangible form— becomes incarnate—by taking on flesh and subjecting Godself to possible corruption, so that we, God's physical counterparts, may be able to assume a spiritual form. Our world serves, therefore, as the exacting arena wherein we act to further life's development and so save God.

We are constantly in-the-making, thus we are able to contribute to the *élan vital*'s unmaking, facilitate dematerialization, and save God. If and when we do, the process begins anew, in others if not also in ourselves. Existence evolves endlessly.

Kazantzakis believes that "life is a crusade in the service of God."[20] Though life's specific campaigns both begin and end, the overall hostilities never cease. God therefore needs valiant warriors to wage God's war (against the devil). Since Kazantzakis maintains that Jesus models this type of heroism, he envisions Jesus blazing ahead of us, eager to enlist us in the same struggle—the struggle to heed and assist God's Cry for help.

Mentally worn to shreds, Kazantzakis' Jesus (in *The Last Temptation of Christ*) entertains frequent thought-provoking qualms about the task God has elected him to accomplish and the agony that must attend it. An insecure and hesitant man, he cannot say whether the gestures he receives come from God or the devil, and he appears bewildered by his standing among his disciples. He also feels enticed by an earthly existence replete with material assets and bodily affection. Predictably, this Jesus has stirred controversy. As we will see, though, Kazantzakis struggled with the christological controversies that have haunted Christians since the fourth century.[21] In doing so he emerged with an indisputably fresh and genuinely sympathetic, if admittedly contentious, account of Jesus the Christ.

The Doctrine of Jesus: A Selective Sketch

The fourth-century Nicene Creed describes Jesus as the preexistent Son of God, the Second Person of the Trinity, who came down from heaven and became incarnate to save people from their sins. Before this creed, which the majority of Christians view as traditional Christianity's benchmark, the question "Who is Jesus?" caused much spirited, even tense discussion.[22] An examination of the Gospels, for example, together with other ancient literature that mentions Jesus of Nazareth, indicates that Jesus' initial followers exalted him with such lofty titles as Messiah, Son of God, Lord, Savior, and Redeemer. Over time, though, some of these followers affirmed the same thing but argued about the meaning. They formed factions, such as the Docetists and the Ebionites, and they soon offered their distinctive christological views.

The Docetists, a word taken from the Greek verb meaning "to seem," claimed that Jesus only seemed human. When Jesus came down from heaven, they said, he disguised his divinity in human garb. In contrast to the Docetists, the Ebionites, a group of Jewish Christians, upheld Jesus' humanity and opposed his divinity. They viewed Jesus as a charismatic prophet, the human son of Mary and Joseph, but little else. With their contrasting profiles of Jesus, the Docetists and the Ebionites caused considerable controversy within the early church. However, some second century church fathers eventually argued against both factions by affirming Jesus' humanity and divinity.[23] We might call this patristic affirmation of Jesus' God-man status "christological complementarity."

Debates about Jesus' divinity did not cease simply because Ignatius of Antioch and Ireneaus of Lyons defeated the Docetists and the Ebionites in the second century. In fact, theologians posed questions about Jesus' God-likeness for years afterwards. Most of these men were associated with either one of the two major centers of patristic theological excellence: Alexandria, located in today's Egypt, and Antioch, in today's Turkey. Writers from the Alexandrian school, such as Athanasius and Apollinarius of Laodicea, claimed that the Second Person of the Trinity assumed human nature, and, by doing so, ensured that it, human nature, was able to share in God's life. In other words, the preexistent Son of God came down from heaven and became human in order that humanity might become divine; an affirmation of Jesus' full deity, therefore, leads to an understanding of redemption as deification (theosis, becoming God-like). According to this view, Jesus mysteriously reunifies and deifies all things in God.[24] In contrast to the Alexandrians, the writers associated with the Antiochene school, such as Arius and Nestorius, affirmed Jesus' full humanity. And they stressed the importance of his ethical teaching.

These two schools played an energetic game of christological ping-pong in the years preceding the conversion of the Emperor Constantine. After Constantine's Edict of Milan in 313, this game reached a new level of competition with the Arian controversy. Arius' emphasis on the creaturely status of Jesus was successfully attacked by writers associated with the Alexandrian school. Only God has the power to cancel sin, for all creatures are naturally flawed, and so only God can redeem fallen humanity, Athanasius declared. Jesus must be God incarnate, therefore, and not just a mere creature, for the New Testament and the Christian liturgical tradition are alike in their adamant declaration that Jesus Christ is humanity's Savior.[25] The delegates at the Council of Nicea in 325 decided to accept Athanasius' affirmation of Jesus' full divinity, as the Nicene Creed makes clear.[26]

A strong reaction against Arianism, the Nicene Creed underscores Jesus' divine-human complementarity. However, the creed's authors pay little attention to the actual details of Jesus' earthly existence; they mention neither his words nor his deeds. On the subject of his Galilean vision and mission, his historicity, the Nicene Creed remains largely silent. Another version of this christological silence regarding Jesus' humanity appeared in the Chalcedonian definition of the Christian faith, in 451.[27]

After Nicea, Athanasius continued to argue for Jesus' divinity. Arius had been banished on account of his christological views but Arianism, the approach to thinking about Jesus for which Arius is famous, continued to flourish and, as a result, it fell to Apollinarius of Laodicea to mount a frontal assault on Arianism's belief in Jesus' humanity:

> We confess that the Word has not descended upon a holy man, which was what happened in the case of the prophets. Rather, the Word himself has become flesh without having assumed a human mind—that is, a changeable mind, which is enslaved to filthy thoughts—but which exists as an immutable and heavenly divine mind.[28]

Apollinarius' Christology is an instructive example of what happens when Christian theologians assert Jesus' full divinity at all costs. Notice the basic thrust of Apollinarius' argument: the human mind is the source of wickedness and so Jesus, as the sinless Son of God, did not possess a mind like ours; on the contrary, his mind was directed by God's pure and spotless providence.

Against Apollinarius, the late fourth century Cappadocian father Gregory of Nazianzus argued that unless the Savior assumes human nature in its entirety, he cannot redeem us:

> If anyone has put their trust in him as a human being lacking a human mind, they are themselves mindless and not worthy of salvation. For what has not been assumed has not been healed; it is what is united to his divinity that is saved . . . . Let them not grudge us our total salvation, or endue the Saviour only with the bones and nerves and mere appearance of humanity.[29]

The delegates who attended the Council of Chalcedon tried to avoid Apollinarius' mistake and to follow Gregory's lead. They affirmed the idea that Jesus possessed "two natures in one person" but, as indicated, they accomplished this task of a unified christological scheme without acknowledging either the content of Jesus' own message or the value of Jesus' original Palestinian context. While their normative creed asserts Jesus' humanity, it includes few details of his life and work. This strategy has had a ripple effect, in that traditional Christianity has expanded across the centuries by upholding Nicea's and Chalcedon's insights.[30]

While most Christians view *The Last Temptation of Christ* as theologically unorthodox, I hold that Kazantzakis' model of God's incarnational presence in Jesus affirms christological complementarity and thus harmonizes with the ecumenical creeds' general theological trajectory:

> Great things happen when God mixes with man. Without man, God would have no mind on this Earth to reflect upon his creatures intelligibly and to examine, fearfully yet impudently, his wise omnipotence. He would have on this Earth no heart to pity the concerns of others and to struggle to beget virtues and cares which God either did not want, or forgot, or was afraid to fashion. He breathed upon man, however, giving him the power and audacity to continue creation.
>
> But man, without God, born as he is unarmed, would have been obliterated by hunger, fear and cold; and if he survived these, he would have crawled like a slug midway between the lions and lice; and if with incessant struggle he managed to stand on his hind legs, he would never have been able to escape the tight, warm, tender embrace of his mother the monkey . . . . Reflecting on this, Jesus felt more deeply than he had ever felt before, that God and man could become one.[31]

Traditional Christian doctrine affirms the organic unity of body and spirit in Jesus' person and work. In my view, there is nothing in the above quotation that indicates Kazantzakis' rejection of this approach to christological speculation.

Today it is possible to look back on the Christian past and identify writers inside this tradition who offer insights into Jesus' humanity that other thinkers, especially those responsible for Nicea and Chalcedon, often overlook. Like Kazantzakis after them, Cabasilas and Renan have not always met with church approval. Their christological starting point, Jesus the man, differs from the starting point associated with traditional Christology, but they have helped to make and remake Christian doctrine.[32] And they have shaped Kazantzakis' novel immensely.

Cabasilas

Born into one of Thessalonica's most aristocratic families in 1320, Cabasilas studied under his mother's uncle, who succeeded Gregory Palamas, Byzantium's most illustrious theologian, in the office of the Archbishop of Thessalonica. Cabasilas also studied in Constantinople, the Christian East's most sacred city until Muslims sacked it in 1453. There he excelled in law, rhetoric, astronomy, and theology. Although he was a candidate for the patriarchate of Constantinople in 1354, he was passed over, and he subsequently devoted his life to serving the church as a layman. He died in 1390.[33]

As a layman Cabasilas wrote theology, liturgy, sermons, civil and canon law, and even poems. He also favored hesychast mysticism, the Byzantine Christian practice of meditating by combining certain vocal and bodily exercises to promote spiritual formation. Despite his fondness for meditation, which his opponents viewed as abstruse, Cabasilas was not an elitist who endorsed religious beliefs and behaviors affecting a select few only. Rather, he emphasized how all Christians could follow Christ personally.

Cabasilas wrested spirituality from its cloistered confines and set about democratizing discipleship by upholding the sacramental life's existential importance. He articulates this democratization of discipleship though his devotional classic, *The Life in Christ*, which Kazantzakis took with him on his 1914 pilgrimage to Athos.[34] Here Cabasilas endorses Athanasius' oft-cited remark: "He [Jesus] was made man that we might be made God."[35] Cabasilas suggests that we begin the process of becoming God-like when we enter baptismal waters, receive chrismation (the Eastern Orthodox church equivalent to confirmation), and take the Eucharist. In these three sacraments, God's agency commingles with our own, thus affording us an opportunity to participate in Christ's life.

In *Journey to the Morea: Travels in Greece*, Kazantzakis describes Cabasilas as "an old and revered figure, a great, long-forgotten Byzantine mystic," whose "remarkable book," *The Life in Christ*, contains several "lofty precepts."[36] The following four Cabasilian-Kazantzakian precepts influence my theological reading of *The Last Temptation of Christ*.

First, Cabasilas and Kazantzakis view life as God's workshop. Here God labors with us, God's coworkers, to transubstantiate materiality into divinity.[37] God facilitates transubstantiation by descending to us—as Jesus—so that we might ascend to God.[38] Significantly, we can trace this ascent-descent language, itself so crucial to the deification doctrine, to Palamas, and even to the early medieval Byzantine hymnodist, Symeon the New Theologian, who holds that all believers in Jesus, and thus in God's descending power, will rise above their sinful natures and ascend to God.[39]

Second, Cabasilas and Kazantzakis affirm Jesus' humanity. Both dismiss the Apollinarian error that assumes God replaces Jesus' human mind with God's own mind. A divine mind immunizes Jesus from doubts and struggles, they say, and thus problematizes his saving relevance for us.[40] In short, Cabasilas and Kazantzakis uphold Jesus' historicity.[41] But they do not commend Jesus' humanity only. Against any form of Ebionitism, they advocate christological complementarity, for they believe Jesus exemplifies divinity *and* humanity. Kazantzakis' claim that "great things happen when God mixes with man" compares favorably with Cabasilas:

> It was necessary that the remedy for my weakness be God and become man, for were He God only He would not be united to us, for how could He become our feast? On the other hand, if Christ were no more than what we are, His feast would have been ineffectual. Now, however, since He is both at once, He is united to those who have the same nature as Himself and coalesces with us men. By His divinity He is able to exalt and transcend our human nature and to transform it into Himself.[42]

Third, Cabasilas and Kazantzakis uphold christological complementarity by linking our development—our evolution or salvation—to Jesus' passion. For them, Jesus' death and resurrection models what it means to surrender oneself to God. And both describe Jesus as our ally, co-struggler, or as the archetype for our progress. "He has opened heaven to all," Cabasilas writes, "and has shown us the way and supplied wings that we may fly thither. Not content with this, He Himself leads the way and sustains us and encourages us when we slacken." Kazantzakis agrees: "We have a model in front of us now," he states, "a model who blazes our trail and gives us strength."[43]

Fourth, this exemplarist Christology means that Jesus is not simply an important historical figure, the Man from Nazareth who wandered through Palestine, but is, in addition, fully contemporaneous. According to Cabasilas and Kazantzakis, the Jesus of history becomes the Christ of faith, because, mysteriously, he approaches us, confronts us, and makes claims on our lives. Sometimes our response costs us heavily, but no other route exists, none but the Christ-like struggle to love wastefully, toward full union with God.[44]

Renan

Renan was born in Tréguier, France, in 1823. By all accounts, he was a pious young man who revered nature's splendors. Educated for the Catholic priesthood, he did not take orders, electing instead to teach. He specialized in ancient languages and religious history and, after spending some time conducting research in Syria, he settled in Paris, becoming the Collège de France's professor of Hebrew. Over time, Renan's academic tenure at the Collège generated several controversies. His 1863 *Vie de Jésus* (*The Life of Jesus*) was perhaps his most scandalous book. Within five months of publication, it had sold sixty thousand copies and been translated into several European languages. But many readers viewed it as highly problematic, for it treats Jesus as a purely historical figure.[45] Undaunted by ecclesiastical disdain, Renan published prolifically and widely, and, until his death in 1892, he was a leading proponent of French critical philosophy.[46]

Kazantzakis read Renan in October 1950. According to Peter Bien, Kazantzakis' main translator and critic, Kazantzakis' unpublished holograph notebooks from this time indicate that Kazantzakis copied down long passages from *The Life of Jesus* and then decided, less than a month later, to retell Jesus' life, calling it *The Last Temptation.*[47] Generally speaking, Renan and Kazantzakis share eleven points of theological consanguinity. First, they view the canonical gospels, including Matthew's—which they prioritize—as legendary biographies, instructive in their own way, but ultimately incapable of capturing Jesus' spirit.[48] Second, they claim Jesus was born in Nazareth, not in Bethlehem, an insight shared by many recent scholars.[49] Third, they stress the canonical and extracanonical apocalyptic sources behind Jesus' message; more specifically, both link Jesus to Daniel's "Son of Man," the Bible's enigmatic symbol of God's holy elect.[50]

Fourth, they hold that during Jesus' three years of teaching, preaching, healing, and traveling in Palestine, his messianic self-understanding evolved. Over time Jesus moved from being a parochial carpenter's son toward symbolizing both Daniel's "Son of Man" and Isaiah's "Suffering Servant."[51] Fifth, they assess Jesus' followers unenthusiastically. Together they lament John the Baptist's regressive influence, the disciples' pushy personalities, and Judas' narrow-but-benign outlook on life. While they treat Mary Magdalene sympathetically, neither is keen on the Apostle Paul.[52] Sixth, they underscore Jesus' central message, the kingdom of heaven, even if they concede that he preaches God's rule enigmatically. For both writers, Jesus proclaims the kingdom as *both* present *and* future. That is to say, Jesus speaks of God's not-yet-but-imminent reign *and* of God's dominion already begun. In evaluating both forms of the kingdom, Renan and Kazantzakis favor God's at-hand sovereignty, which Renan calls Jesus' "religion of the heart."[53] In this religion, the kingdom's citizens are those who internalize God's rule and respond to Jesus personally.

Seventh, they interpret Jesus' signs and wonders psychosomatically. By isolating various kingdom works to their first-century mythic (read: prescientific) context, they treat Jesus' miracles rationally. According to Renan and Kazantzakis, Jesus does not need miracles; he is the miracle.[54] Eighth, they note that Jewish and Roman authorities found Jesus' preaching and healing controversial and that he was crucified for sedition. What is interesting here, though, is that both Renan and Kazantzakis claim Jesus experienced doubts during his time on the cross. Renan writes:

> For a moment, according to certain narratives, his heart failed him; a cloud hid from him the face of his Father; he endured an agony of despair a thousand times more acute than all his torture. He saw only the ingratitude of men; he perhaps repented suffering for a vile race, and exclaimed: 'My God, my God, why hast thou forsaken me?' But his divine instinct still prevailed. In the degree that the life of the body became extinguished, his soul became clear, and returned by degrees to its celestial origin. He regained the idea of his mission; he saw in his death the salvation of the world; he lost sight of the hideous spectacle spread at his feet, and, profoundly united to his Father, he began upon the gibbet the divine life which he was to live in the heart of humanity through infinite ages.[55]

In other words, Renan says that Jesus hesitated, questioned, wondered, and, as Kazantzakis speculates, he even pondered *what if*—what if he had settled for domestic life, become the best carpenter in Nazareth, an ordinary husband and father, and not the world's Messiah? As we will see, Jesus' short-term indecisiveness forms the fulcrum around which everything else turns in *The Last Temptation of Christ*.

Ninth, they consider Jesus an example of how God wants us to live. In following him, we embody the gospel story in our lives, continuing Jesus' work, and, when this happens, we uphold both his historicity and contemporaneity. Relatedly, Renan and Kazantzakis focus on Jesus' spiritual resurrection only, pointing to the way his Mystical Presence triggers a chain reaction of personal and social transformation. In other words, Jesus lives on in spirit, beckoning us forward, inspiring our thoughts, transforming our hearts, and he gives us his power to be his compassion and strength in our world.[56]

Tenth, they expand their belief in Jesus' spiritual resurrection to suggest that there is more to God's saving activity than Jesus of Nazareth. Renan announces, "No transitory appearance exhausts the Divinity; God was revealed before Jesus—God will reveal Himself after him."[57] Likewise, Kazantzakis ends *The Last Temptation of Christ* by suggesting that the dematerialization process begun and ended in Jesus begins anew in each and every Jesus follower. Using more traditional Christian theological language, we might say that Renan and Kazantzakis deem Jesus the first of God's several sons and daughters. And in thinking of all men and women as holy partners in a heavenly calling, Renan and Kazantzakis uphold *theosis*, the doctrine of our ascent to God, our participation in God's life, our deification.[58]

Finally, both mourn the way various Christian theologians across the centuries have encrusted Jesus' message in dogmatic pronouncement and confessional formulae. In short, they handle the Christian doctrinal tradition skeptically. What is interesting, therefore, is that both seem to distinguish the historical Jesus from the credal Christ. Renan claims:

> The rock of metaphysical subtleties against which Christianity broke from the third century, was in nowise created by the Founder. Jesus has neither dogma nor system, but a fixed personal resolution, which, exceeding in intensity every other created will, directs to this hour the destinies of humanity.[59]

And writing to his friend, Börje Knös, in 1951, Kazantzakis echoes Renan's sentiments:

> I wanted to renew and supplement the sacred Myth that underlies the great Christian civilization of the West. It [*The Last Temptation*

of Christ] isn't a simple 'Life of Christ.' It's a laborious, sacred, creative endeavor to reincarnate the essence of Christ, setting aside the dross—falsehoods and pettinesses which all the churches and all the cassocked representatives of Christianity have heaped upon His figure, thereby distorting it.

The pages of my manuscript were often smudged because I could not hold back my tears. Parables which Christ could not possibly have left as the Gospels relate them I have supplemented, and I have given them the noble and compassionate ending befitting Christ's heart. Words which we do not know that He said I have put into His mouth, because He would have said them if His Disciples had had His spiritual force and purity. And everywhere poetry, love of animals and plant life and men, confidence in the soul, certainty that light will prevail.[60]

Novelizing the Nazarene
A Christian Theological Reading of *The Last Temptation of Christ*

In his unpublished notes on *The Last Temptation of Christ*, Kazantzakis pictures Jesus passing through four vocational stages: Son of the Carpenter, Son of Man (meek), Son of David (fierce), and Son of God.[61] At the onset of stage one, which coincides with the novel's first dream sequence, Jesus finds himself pursued, figuratively speaking, by devils and dwarfs. Soon his soul resembles a coliseum in which two powerful armies—matter and spirit—do battle. Kazantzakis draws our attention to habit's inertia, an important feature of Jesus' humanity, which the *élan vital* (God) casts behind it as it advances. With each subsequent transition in Jesus' vocational understanding, he struggles with the devil's temptations to happiness, begins to see life as charged with God's presence and, at the novel's end, emerges from the last dream sequence to effect union with God by learning how to transubstantiate matter into spirit. Since Jesus' four stages constitute *The Last Temptation of Christ*'s governing structures, I employ them to explain how he scales life's metaphysical mountain, moving from its base camp (ordinariness, convention, happiness) to its summit (meaningfulness, union with God, *theosis*).

Jesus as Son of the Carpenter

When we first encounter Kazantzakis' Jesus, he is, ironically, making crosses for the Romans. But cross-making unhinges him; he suffers from headaches and nightmares. Inside him, the soldiers of discontent march from his heart to his head and declare war on his soul. He blames himself for Joseph's immobility, Mary Magdalene's waywardness, and even for Israel's collective sin. He rebukes God, for God wants to drive Jesus away from Galilee and out toward something unknown, even as Jesus prefers to remain Nazareth's best carpenter. Jesus' headaches and nightmares persist, though, and in time he feels torn between happiness and meaningfulness.

Kazantzakis uses the bird of prey image to render this struggle between God and Jesus. On numerous occasions, God croaks like a raven or cries like an eagle, and Jesus constantly feels this bird's agitating presence. In one scene, for example, God's Spirit swoops down and incites Jesus to forsake his carpentry for the desert.[62] As a figurative device for God's agency, the bird of prey stands in ironic opposition to traditional Christianity's peaceful dove. For this reason, if not for others, many Christians reprimand Kazantzakis. Yet consider Mark 1:10, which describes how Jesus of Nazareth "saw the heavens torn apart and the Spirit descending like a dove on him," and then note the violent wording.[63] One might also compare the scene where Jesus encounters God as a vulture with Mark 1:12. Here God's Spirit "drives" or "shoves" Jesus into the wilderness; intriguingly, the Koine verb means "to cast out" (like an exorcism) or "to eject" (by force).[64]

Throughout Kazantzakis' novel, vultures suggest God's energizing spirit as well as the *élan vital*'s animating thrust. Women, on the other hand, symbolize domestic happiness. Witness Jesus' mother. Acutely distressed by her son's apparent inability to find happiness, Mary dislikes the fact that Jesus collaborates with the Romans by making crosses for condemned Jewish nationalists. She therefore tries to dissuade him from taking the "evil road" away from the "ways of men."[65] When rabbi Simeon suggests that his nephew might be divinely favored, she defies God to leave her son alone, to let Jesus taste happiness. Through the rabbi's voice ("if God listened to mothers we would all rot away in a bog of security and easy living"), Kazantzakis suggests that the devil snares us with domestic happiness, the joys of so-called normal life.[66] To resist Satan and therefore to secure spiritual evolution, Kazantzakis' Jesus must listen to God's Cry. And to do this he must surmount obstacles that women, among others, place in his way.

Kazantzakis scholars Adèle Bloch and Richard Chilson address the nature and function of women in Kazantzakis' novel. According to Bloch, Kazantzakis' women "can grasp neither the Messiah's abstract idealism, nor his dedication to soul and God." They are unable, she says, "to recognize the divine spark in one closely related to them." It therefore follows that "the Kazantzakian Man," including Jesus, "must escape from the maternal grip if he is to forge ahead on the evolutionary path."[67] In Jesus' first stage, then, he spiritually disengages himself from all the women he encounters, especially his mother. Women tempt him with domestic tranquility's promise, but Kazantzakis' Jesus doggedly resists, for only in doing so will his messianic formation unfold and ripen. Chilson writes:

> They [women] are a real source of temptation, almost symbols of the great temptation, the symbol of bodily embrace and wifely compassionship in God's law, against the harsh way of God alone and the symbol of the Cross. The final temptation of Jesus is to forsake his life of struggle for the life of domesticity. This is the greatest and most enticing threat to the great Cry of the Invisible.[68]

Compelled into the desert by God's thorn-clawed Spirit, Jesus eventually leaves Mary and Nazareth; he evolves. To illustrate what effect such an evolution has on Jesus' life, I consider one episode that occurs as Jesus shifts from "Son of the Carpenter" to "Son of Man." Here Jesus halts his wilderness pilgrimage, notices a butterfly on a tree, readjusts the butterfly's position, and then refers to it as "my sister."[69] Significantly, Kazantzakis uses butterflies as metaphors for the flesh's transubstantiation into spirit.

Butterflies connote the *élan vital*'s frenetic agency, especially as it launches itself into matter, intermingles with corporeality, and then unmakes itself. As the following remark from *Report to Greco* makes clear, the caterpillar-butterfly's unfolding career illustrates life's divinely-mandated drive toward creative evolution:

> It is impossible to express the joy I experienced when I first saw a grub engraved on one tray of the delicate golden balances discovered in the tombs of Mycenae and a butterfly on the other—symbols doubtlessly taken from Crete. For me, the grub's yearning to become a butter-

fly always stood as its—and man's—most imperative and at the same time most legitimate duty. God makes us grubs, and we, by our own efforts, must become butterflies.[70]

Critic Tom Doulis extends this butterfly metaphor by describing Kazantzakis' Jesus as "God in the cocoon of man."[71] On this view, *The Last Temptation of Christ* depicts the time it takes Jesus to emerge from conventionality's chrysalis, flap his wings, and fly toward God. This maturation process takes time, because at least four stages are involved in Jesus' becoming Christ. Doulis concentrates on the first two only.

In focusing on Jesus' transition from "Son of the Carpenter" to "Son of Man," Doulis draws attention to two monarch butterflies who set down on Jesus' bloodsoaked bandanna—a recent spoil from the Romans for helping to crucify a Zealot—as he wanders through the desert. This is how Kazantzakis' narrator describes the incident:

> They [the monarch butterflies] danced gleefully, frolicking in the sun, and at the very last alighted on the man's bloodied kerchief with their proboscises over the red spots, as though they wished to suck up the blood. Feeling their caress on the top of his head, he recalled God's talons, and it seemed to him that these and the butterfly wings brought him the identical message. Ah, if only God could always descend to man not as a thunderbolt or a clawing vulture but as a butterfly.[72]

The "identical message" that butterflies and vultures—note how Kazantzakis combines his two major tropes for God's agency—bring to Jesus seems clear-cut: God wants Jesus to transubstantiate matter into spirit. What we have here, then, is the first soundings of an evolutionary Christology.[73]

Other critics also note that transubstantiation lies at the heart of Kazantzakis' butterfly and vulture imagery. Andreas Poulakidas states that Kazantzakis uses this term to signify how God envelopes our developing world, rousing us in our restlessness. Daniel Dombrowski concurs. In Kazantzakis' world, he says, characters frequently find themselves caught between routine and adventure, between everydayness and God's Cry, which beckons them forward and upward (Bergson's dematerialization). Transubstantiation serves as these characters' turning point, the existential pivot around which happiness and meaningfulness swirl. Not surprisingly, it is all such characters can do to live in light of transubstantiation's activity and challenge.[74] Transubstantiation's activity and challenge touch everyone and everything, Kazantzakis proclaims, and the entire world feels its vitality. Dombrowski here summarizes Kazantzakis' philosophical theology:

> Human transformation of mundane existence into a glorious reign, into God, follows from the caterpillar who becomes a butterfly, from the fish who leaps into the air, from the silkworm who turns dust into silk.[75]

"Within Christianity," Dombrowski continues, "this eternal process of transubstantiation is focused on Christ."[76] Kazantzakis agrees. Like Cabasilas and Renan before him, he believes Jesus of Nazareth blazes our trail, because he "continually transubstantiated flesh into spirit, and ascended [note the gesture toward *theosis*]" to God.[77] In *The Last Temptation of Christ*, Jesus cooperates with life's transubstantiating impulse by willing his own metamorphosis. He evolves through four vocational stages and frees or saves God by heeding and responding to God's Cry for immediate release from matter's confines. Since Jesus cooperates with God, he pushes on ahead of us. He becomes, that is, One whose example fosters our personal change as well as our world's development. Poulakidas glosses Kazantzakis fittingly: "By partaking in the process of *metousiosis* (creative evolution), one grows in the spirit of God."[78]

Jesus as Son of Man

Cracks in Jesus' chrysalis appear during his "Son of the Carpenter" stage. He leaves home for the desert, for example, and spurns his mother as well as Magdalene. But this initial change is not enough. Further evolution or transubstantiation appears necessary. God therefore cries out to Jesus, shrieking like a vulture. Jesus hesitates before finally ushering in his second stage of vocational formation, the "Son of Man" stage.

Following Renan, Kazantzakis uses Daniel 7:13-14, where the "Ancient in Years," God, protects those who suffer and remain loyal to God's covenant. In *The Last Temptation of Christ*, Kazantzakis has this vision read to Joachim, the ailing abbot of the desert monastery that Jesus visits. Joachim, it transpires, has grown tired of advancing Roman imperialism and delayed apocalyptic promises. And so he entreats God to establish history's new and last epoch by sending the "Son of

Man." Bien holds that this specific incident constitutes the "watershed" between Jesus' former, "Son of the Carpenter" stage, and his new actuality as the "Son of Man." I agree. Lured by butterflies and thorn-claws, Kazantzakis' Jesus enters the monastery, reflects on Daniel's vision, and through God's agency transitions into his newest vocational stage.[79]

Jesus' time in the desert monastery causes all clouds of vocational unknowing in his life to lift and dissipate. Now purified by God, he declares his readiness to preach his Renanian gospel of love. As noted, Renan characterizes Jesus as a gentle, Galilean prophet who wanders up and down Palestine's rolling hills, both awed by nature's serene beauty and keen to preach as well as enact unconditional charity; in the "Son of Man" stage, Kazantzakis' Jesus mirrors Renan's so-called aesthetic Jesus. That is to say, Kazantzakis' Jesus endorses boundless tenderness; he reveres life.[80]

Jesus' reverence for life frustrates Judas Iscariot who, depicting Jesus' darker, demonic side, would rather see Jesus march upon Jerusalem and oust the Romans. Jesus' mother also seems disheartened.[81] In Bergsonian terms, she defies Jesus to treat the *élan vital* with contempt, disregard the divine Cry, and settle down. Jesus withstands Mary's temptation to happiness, however, and thus passes his messiahship's first real test: he averts possible mob violence, saves Magdalene's life, and preaches universal sin as well as unrestricted love. Symbolizing robust tendencies working in the opposite direction to dematerialization, to use Bergson's phraseology once more, Jesus' mother implores the crowds to ignore him. And she lambastes his apparent religious fanaticism. For his part, though, Jesus appears indifferent. When Mary begs him to return home, for example, and resume his carpentry, he demurs.[82]

Kazantzakis asks us to question Mary, not Jesus, and to see her as someone who impedes his vocational formation. I say this because Kazantzakis treats "satisfaction" as "the greatest sin of all."[83] Since Jesus' mother wants to arrest matter's transubstantiation into spirit by using domestic manacles, Kazantzakis wants us to view her, not Jesus, as sinful, where "sinful" means working against God's will (dematerialization).[84] On one level, then, Jesus' revolt against his mother appears virtuous; it is generous evidence that he has set out spiritually to evolve.

Accompanying Jesus' evolution from "Son of the Carpenter" to "Son of Man" is a development in the way crowds view and construe the way he thinks and acts. Consider how Philip and "simple Nathanael" respond to one of Jesus' short homilies:

> "I like him," said the gangling cobbler [Nathanael]. "His words are as sweet as honey. Would you believe it: listening to him, I actually licked my chops!"
>
> The shepherd was of a different opinion. "I don't like him. He says one thing and does another; he shouts, 'Love! Love!' and builds crosses and crucifies!"
>
> "That's all over and done with, I tell you, Philip. *He had to pass that stage, the stage of crosses. Now he's passed it and taken God's road.*"[85]

In contrast to enthusiastic Nathanael, Judas remains perplexed, unsure how to either designate Jesus or interpret some of his statements about loving one's enemies:

> I don't know what to call you—son of Mary? son of the Carpenter? son of David? As you can see, I still don't know who you are—but neither do you. We both must discover the answer; we both must find relief! No, this uncertainty cannot last. Don't look at the others—they follow you like bleating sheep; don't look at the women, who do nothing but admire you and spill tears. After all, they're women: they have hearts and no minds, and we've no use for them. It's we two who must find out who you are and whether this flame that burns you is the God of Israel or the devil. We must! We must![86]

Judas' theological struggles are prompted not by any personal faithlessness but by the fact that Jesus changes his mind constantly. On some occasions, Judas thinks Jesus speaks well, while at other times he vehemently disagrees with him. One such confrontation occurs outside Nazareth and illustrates Kazantzakis' treatment of matter's uneasy alliance with spirit:

> The redbeard [Judas] gave a start. Grasping Jesus' shoulder, he shouted with fiery breath: "You want to free Israel from the Romans?"
>
> "To free the soul from sin."
>
> Judas snatched his hand away from Jesus' shoulder in a frenzy and banged his fist against the trunk of the olive tree. "This is where our ways part," he growled, facing Jesus and looking at him with hatred. "First the body must be freed from the Romans, and later the soul from sin. That is the road. Can you take it? A house isn't built

from the roof down; it's built from the foundation up."

"The foundation is the soul, Judas."

"The foundation is the body—that's where you've got to begin. Watch out, son of Mary."[87]

As we will see, Jesus quickly discovers that Judas tells the truth.

Jesus as Son of David

Jesus' encounter with John the Baptist changes Jesus' mind once again. This is because John's fervently held apocalyptic eschatology — the idea that the Messiah must facilitate Israel's Day of Reckoning by taking an axe to Jerusalem's rancid fruit—challenges Jesus' initial belief in ethical eschatology, the idea that love alone effects personal as well as social transformation. Stirred by John's message, Jesus travels out to the desert, isolates himself, fasts, addresses God, resists the devil, and emerges with inklings of his next divinely appointed vocational stage.[88]

In the desert, Jesus encounters taloned birds, his mother's image, and crunching footsteps on baked sand. These images all serving as tropes for the devil's temptations. In one scene, Jesus watches crows descend on the carcass of a sacrificial (scape)goat sent out in the wilderness by priests to atone for Israel's sins. Seeing the goat's fate as figurative of his own destiny, he calls the carcass "brother" and immediately covers the dead animal with sand, thereby preventing the crows from continuing their tasty feed.[89] The angry birds divert their attention away from the goat's carcass and toward Jesus. For the crows, then, Jesus becomes the surrogate goat, fresh meat to stalk and pester. Kazantzakis uses this episode to suggest, once again, God's brutish assault on Jesus' soul. Kazantzakis also uses it as a hinge upon which "the Son of Man" is brought to fresh cognizance of his budding messiahship.[90] Other tropes ebb and flow as the devil tempts Jesus three times. In each instance, the primary images—serpent, lion, and consuming fire—together with the secondary images—rabbit, partridge, and a goat's carcass—evoke the matter-spirit dialectic, the progressive tussle between body and *élan vital*, and the duty to transubstantiate private struggle into public ministry. In short, the desert temptations accentuate Kazantzakis' evolutionary Christology.

Enticed by God's incremental agency (the *élan vital*), Jesus rejects his former stage, "Son of Man," with its ideals of brotherly love and universal forgiveness, and, instead, cultivates revolutionary antagonism as the "Son of David":

> Now begins my own duty: to chop down the rotted tree. I believed I was a bridegroom and that I held a flowering almond branch in my hand, but all the while I was a wood-chopper.[91]

Faced with Jesus' indecisiveness, his disciples lose heart rapidly:

> The companions grew numb. The voice was severe. It no longer frolicked and laughed; it was calling them to arms. In order to enter the kingdom of heaven, then, would they have to go by way of death? Was there no other road?[92]

Nearly all Jesus' followers fail to comprehend his spiritual complexity, have little or no knowledge of his interior world, and seem powerless to intuit Jesus' psychological anguish. They bicker constantly. And they vie with each other for leadership positions in the new earthly kingdom, which they mistakenly believe Jesus will instantiate soon. Between Jesus and Judas, however, there is an exceedingly close alliance.

As Kazantzakis' narrator remarks, "a terrible secret joined the two of them [Jesus and Judas] and separated them from the rest."[93] On many occasions Jesus and Judas converse late into the night, seem to know what the other feels and thinks, and treat themselves as somehow tied to the other's destiny. One explanation for this intimacy uses the matter-spirit dialectic that I described earlier. Here Judas depicts the fleshly driven antithesis to Jesus' spirit-filled, *élan*-urged existence. "The savior-martyr never stands alone," Chilson says, "but always with a savior-hero."[94] Jesus needs Judas to remind him of, and agitate him continually with, thoughts of Rome's imperial aggression and the need for political resistance, materiality's captivating lure. By the same token, Judas requires Jesus to preach ceaselessly a spiritual will-to-power which, although worked out in our earthbound lives, is not confined to temporal existence.[95]

Notwithstanding Judas, most who hear Jesus' message of divine fire and war find it religiously unsatisfying. In Capernaum, for example, Zebedee (father to two of Jesus' disciples in Kazantzakis' novel, as in the New Testament) invites Jesus into his home but confesses that he does not know what to make of him:

> So speak, son of Mary. Bring God again into my house! Excuse me if I call you son of Mary, but I still don't know what to call you. Some call you the son of the Carpenter, others the Son of David, son of God, son of man. Everyone is confused. Obviously the world has not yet made up its mind.[96]

With great fervor, Jesus brings God to Zebedee by preaching that "love comes after the flames," which means that one cannot love injustice. He tells him that God's impending conflagration will purify humankind's base metal, creating something infinitely valuable.[97]

God's holocaust begins in Jerusalem, but it does not appear as Jesus expects it. He confesses this to Judas, who listens as Jesus articulates his latest messianic understanding. Kazantzakis has Jesus discern this new vocational direction during one of his many visits to Golgotha. Here the Hebrew prophet Isaiah presents Jesus with a goatskin—the very goat that Jesus had buried in the desert—upon whose hide is written Isaiah 53, the Song of the Suffering Servant. Following Renan, Kazantzakis uses Isaiah's words as the new hinge to bring Jesus to full awareness of his destiny. And with this awareness, God's butterfly shrugs off his chrysalis and becomes airborne:

> For the world to be saved, I, of my own will, must die. At first, I didn't understand it myself. God sent me signs in vain: sometimes visions in the air, sometimes dreams in my sleep; or the goat's carcass in the desert with all the sins of the people around its neck. And since the day I quit my mother's house, a shadow has followed behind me like a dog or at times has run in front to show me the road. What road? The Cross![98]

Before Jesus can fully embrace Isaiah's prophecy, and thus evolve into his vocational formation's final stage, Jesus must fail as the "Son of David." This happens when Jesus storms the Jerusalem temple only to delay militant resistance, anguishing over his function as a servant-martyr rather than as a social reformer. The flame of armed insurrection fades and Jesus, together with his humiliated disciples, retreats to nearby Bethany. Because of this failure in the temple, Bien describes Jesus' third stage as "strangely regressive, a retreat rather than an advance."[99] Until this moment, Jesus, the "Son of Man," preaches dis-interested spirituality. As the "Son of David," though, he replaces this virtue with political messianism grounded in patriotic ardor. Failure as the "Son of David" underscores two essential points—one political and one psychological—about evolution's complexity.

As the "Son of Man," Jesus rejects hatred and violence and preaches humility as well as universal love. But his sermons fall like seed on stony ground. Hardly anyone appropriates Jesus' message; rather, the crowds upbraid and reject him. Jesus fails. However, this specific failure averts another, more vital loss. If Jesus' message had taken root, that is, and selfless love had been shown to be all that the world needed to effect its transformation, Jesus may have become smugly convinced that his mission had been accomplished. Therein lies the real danger, for, in Kazantzakis' world, satisfaction constitutes the worst sin. The best way to succeed, therefore, is to fail. Hence, Kazantzakis has Jesus fail in his "Son of Man" stage, regroup himself, and finally endorse what previ-ously he could only resist—namely, political messianism.

Bien notes that Kazantzakis has Jesus fail for psychological reasons as well as political ones. Throughout *The Last Temptation of Christ*, for example, Jesus tries to integrate his own soul, to harmonize psychic contrasts, but this can only be reached as Jesus wrestles with Judas, his darker side, transubstantiating evil into service of the good. Convinced by the Davidic messianic vision, Judas begs Jesus to oust the Romans and cleanse the Jerusalem temple. For its part, though, God's Cry lures Jesus differently. Adventuring to reconcile such competing impulses, Jesus learns how to love Judas, and in doing so he learns how to abide the swirling mass of bitterness, pride, and violence within his own soul. As "Son of David," Jesus discovers and appropriates his dark side, albeit temporarily, before evolving into his vocational formation's fourth and final stage.[100]

Jesus as Son of God

At the turning point between talk and action, Kazantzakis' Jesus renounces his political messianism, escapes into hiding, reprioritizes his mission, and surrenders himself in an act of apocalyptic self-immolation designed to inaugurate God's kingdom. He evolves, in other words, but not without Judas, whom Kazantzakis portrays as helping Jesus fulfill Isaiah's proph-ecy that the Messiah must suffer and die to redeem humankind.

Unable to disavow the body by himself, Jesus needs Judas' treachery to help him forgo material happiness, to enable him to throw off physical stagnation's fetters, to be in phase with the divine current which leads the way, and to ascend to God. Following Cabasilas, Kazantzakis views life as God's workshop, and God's laborers, he implies, include unlikely personnel, like Judas. Expressed in Bergsonian terms, Jesus and Judas assist the *élan vital*'s dematerialization; unless they collude, the transubstantiation of Jesus' flesh into spirit, *The Last Temptation of Christ*'s main theme and the signal of God's redemption, will not occur.[101] Judas, therefore, betrays Jesus, and the Romans crucify him at Golgotha. What happens next links Kazantzakis and Renan very closely.

As he draws what seems like his last breath, Jesus faints and imagines a Negro lad taking him down from the cross. In a scene evoking Abraham's binding of Isaac, the youngster convinces Jesus that God no longer requires his death—that his crucifixion has been lived in a dream, in other words, and that Mary Magdalene, symbol of earthly pleasure, awaits him.[102] Although disguised as God's angel, the Negro lad nonetheless signifies Lucifer's last temptation, and Jesus rises to the bait: he marries Magdalene, fathers her child, and lives contentedly. Even after she dies he marries again, produces more offspring, and the devil's victory seems assured:

> Jesus' face shone. "I've finished wrestling with God," he said. "We have become friends. I won't build crosses any more. I'll build troughs, cradles, bedsteads. I'll send a message to have my tools brought from Nazareth; I'll have my embittered mother come too, so that she can bring up her grandchildren and feel some sweetness on her lips at last, poor thing."[103]

Jesus' domestic composure steadily deteriorates with three incidents in his imagined life as an old man.[104] Yet only Judas, appearing once more as Jesus' demonic side, seems able and willing to remind Jesus of his original mission as a savior-martyr. After revealing the Negro lad's satanic origin, Judas castigates Jesus for succumbing to Lucifer's last temptation to be happy:

> "Where is the cross which was supposed to be our springboard to heaven? As he faced the cross this fake Messiah went dizzy and fainted. Then the ladies got hold of him and installed him to manufacture children for them. He says he fought, fought courageously. Yes,

he swaggers about like the cock of the roost. But your post, deserter, was on the cross, and you know it."[105]

With such trenchant remarks, Judas insinuates that heroic life on earth involves transubstantiating fleshly concerns into spiritual discipline. However, he sees Jesus, now aged and infirm, as little more than a decorated foot soldier in the Great Army of the Mediocre.

Struggling to escape the last temptation's allure, with Judas' remarks ringing in his ears, Jesus wishes himself back onto the cross and the dream sequence ends. Its ending recalls Bergson's belief that the *élan vital* constantly launches itself into matter, energizes it, transforms flesh into spirit, and then begins the process anew once it has unmade itself. Here Kazantzakis' narrator highlights how Jesus' death exemplifies this cyclical process—how the end of the dematerialization that Jesus labors for represents the beginning of the *élan vital*'s reentry into matter on another level:

> No, no, he was not a coward, a deserter, a traitor. No, he was nailed to the cross. He had stood his ground honorably to the very end; he had kept his word. The moment he cried ELI ELI and fainted, Temptation had captured him for a split second and led him astray. The joys, marriages and children were lies; the decrepit degraded old men who shouted coward, deserter, traitor at him were lies. All—all were illusions sent by the Devil. His disciples were alive and thriving. They had gone over sea and land and were proclaiming the Good News. Everything had turned out as it should, glory be to God!
> He uttered a triumphant cry: "IT IS ACCOMPLISHED!"
> And it was as though he had said: Everything has begun.[106]

The novel's ending recalls its beginning, which emphasizes Jesus as the model in front of us, blazing our trail. It also returns us to Cabasilas and Renan, even to the Gospels, because it upholds the belief—emphasized in all three sources—that Jesus is not only an important human figure, he is a living, if mysterious, presence who shares in our lives, and invites us to share in God's life. Seen through Cabasilas' and Renan's eyes, for instance, the "everything" that has "begun" is the invitation to us, Christ's followers, daily to live in Christ and, therefore, to participate in God. Also, Kazantzakis' use of "it is accomplished" echoes John 19:30. In the Fourth Gospel, "it is accomplished" is not simply a cry of relief that all Jesus' trials and sufferings are over; it represents his shout of victory.

On one level, then, John's phrasing signifies that Jesus' death completes his saving work. On another level, though, "it is accomplished" suggests that the salvific process has only just begun. And this new beginning is the summons to follow Jesus, to take up our own cross, and unite with God through him.

What was it about Jesus of Nazareth that caused people across the centuries and even today to follow him, and, in their following, show that God's saving activity is processive and not one single act? Kazantzakis answers this question by novelizing the Nazarene in light of traditional christological complementarity as well as evolutionary thought. His Jesus becomes Christ through a co-constitution of divine providence and his own heroic struggle. God works with Jesus and Jesus works with God, and "great things happen" when they merge. On this view Jesus serves as the paradigm for not only God's relationship to us but also our relationship to God. This alliance proceeds toward spirit.

SHOULD CHRISTIANS READ KAZANTZAKIS?

In his religiously sincere search to appreciate Jesus as someone in whom human and divine qualities are mysteriously united, Kazantzakis writes his novelistic re-creation of Jesus' life with two fundamental points in mind. First, he emphasizes God's coming into Jesus' human flesh, or, to use doctrinal language, God incarnating Godself. As the immanent life-force, the *élan vital*, Kazantzakis' God creatively fructifies Jesus' life with God's evolving Spirit. Hence, *the divine becomes human*. Second, Kazantzakis shows how Jesus struggles with his humanity and becomes God by surrendering to the *élan vital*, which carries Jesus forward and breaks through the conservative structures (marriage, progeny, career) that threaten his progress. Hence, *the human becomes divine*.

This second point seems especially worthy of our close attention, for, as theologian John Bowden points out, "throughout the history of the early church and even today, in much of the Christian tradition, popular understanding as well as academic theology finds great difficulty in seeing Jesus as *truly* human."[107] Kazantzakis never experienced such difficulty, as we have seen, but he identified with those who do, and he wrote his novel to encourage and fortify those struggling with what it means to say Jesus assumed our nature in order to heal it. Against those who neglect Jesus' humanity, like some Alexandrians, Kazantzakis holds, following churchmen like Gregory of Nazianzus, that God knows what it is to be human, to be a creature, as only a creature can know it. In Jesus, Kazantzakis claims, divine grace knots itself in an extraordinary rapture with human vulnerability—an insight that complements the spirit of the Scriptures and the ecumenical creeds. Christians thus repudiate or ignore *The Last Temptation of Christ* at their peril. There is, I think, much to be gained, theologically as well as spiritually, from reading this novel. Ethicist David S. Cunningham agrees:

> This problem has haunted Christian theology from the beginning: how to hold together the full humanity and full divinity of Christ. The words of the [Apostles'] creed—'Jesus Christ, God's only Son, our Lord'—offers us a statement that emphasizes the importance of holding these two elements together. However, it does not explain to us how we are to accomplish this rather monumental task. So we will always be in need of works such as *The Last Temptation of Christ* to remind us of just how difficult this task is—and how important it is that we attend to it, again and again, in every age.[108]

For me, the quality of Jesus' humanity discloses God in Kazantzakis' novel. His Jesus lives through the unruliness of those emotions that can destroy us all. Yet more than that: he transubstantiates them into adoration as well as love, and thus helps us advance toward God.

Following several Christian theologians from across the centuries, Kazantzakis holds that God's emerging Spirit in Christ acts like a neutron in an intricate chain reaction of personal and social transformation. Recall the novel's ending: Kazantzakis here suggests that the cross unleashes a creative energy within the historical process; as a result, he implies that God's (or the immanent life-force's) Christic vitality continually seeks to apprehend us, to energize us, and to make of our lives a crusade in the service of an evolving God. The Servant Christ, in other words, models authentic life for all who would follow him; and the Incarnation is, therefore, a perpetual reality.

As we have seen, this emphasis on the cross' soteriological implications resembles the Orthodox stress, traceable to Athanasius and Cabasilas, on *theosis*. Here we are not absorbed into God's essence; rather, God's energies penetrate and propel us onward and upward. For Kazantzakis, as for Cabasilas and Renan, even for Schweitzer, the Christian is one in whom God—revealed to us as Jesus the Christ—is forming Godself again and again, transmuting consciousness from fear and despair to life-affirming love. On such grounds, then, I think we can say that Kazantzakis' novel engages and utilizes Christian theological ideas, personalities, debates, and developments, in ways that repay our close attention. Furthermore, his Christology expresses insights into Jesus' human nature and the universal effects of Jesus' work that traditional theologians also employ. I advise Christians to read *The Last Temptation of Christ* for, when they do, they will find there a poignant portrait of Jesus, God's humanness, before he became encrusted in sophisticated doctrines, long-winded dogmas, and elaborate rituals.

Conclusion

In his "On the Rule of the Heretics," written in Latin in the third century's early years, Tertullian contrasts Jerusalem with Athens, and he questions the validity of attempts to relate the Christian gospel to pagan or secular philosophy.[109] This dissimilarity between two different centers of spiritual inquiry, a foil that symbolizes the tensive alliance between divine revelation and human reason, has led to other perceived contrasts in the history of Christian doctrine. What is there in common between Scripture and tradition, between faith and history, and between Christology and soteriology? I want to extend Tertullian's initial question in order to ask: what is there in common between Kazantzakis' rich theological fiction and Christianity's unfolding doctrinal history? While answers to this last question often seem unsympathetic to Kazantzakis' religious project, and hostility toward a Christian reading of his work is sometimes vigorous, we have seen that Kazantzakis comes close to some of Christian doctrine's many makers and remakers.

For Further Reading

Robert Atwan, George Dardess, and Peggy Rosenthal's assembled and edited volume, *Divine Inspiration: The Life of Jesus in World Poetry* (Oxford: Oxford University Press, 1998) presents almost three hundred poems about Jesus from across the centuries and around the globe. Christopher M. Bellitto's *The General Councils: A History of the Twenty-One Church Councils from Nicaea to Vatican II* (Mahwah, N.J.: Paulist Press, 2001) provides an excellent introduction to the authoritative theological statements that have shaped Christianity's two-thousand-year course. Jon L. Berquist's *Incarnation* (St. Louis, Mo.: Chalice Press, 2000) surveys the New Testament's most fundamental theme. Jon Binns' *An Introduction to the Christian Orthodox Churches* (Cambridge: Cambridge University Press, 2002) describes the churches of the Orthodox East from 312 until 2000, focusing on liturgy, theology, monastic life, iconography, and the East-West schism of 1054. Markus Bockmuehl's edited text, *The Cambridge Companion to Jesus* (Cambridge: Cambridge University Press, 2001), incorporates ancient sources and more recent scholarship to explore Jesus' past and present. Michael J. Christensen and Jeffery A. Wittung's edited volume, *Partakers of the Divine Nature: The History and Development of Deification in the Christian Traditions* (Grand Rapids, Mich.: Baker Academic, 2008), traces the concept of *theosis* throughout Eastern and Western forms of Christian doctrine and uses its findings to establish grounds for an ecumenical theology for our time. Donald Fairbairn's *Eastern Orthodoxy through Western Eyes* (Louisville, Ky.: Westminster John Knox, 2002) offers one of the most accessible introductions to Eastern Christianity on the market. *Theosis: Deification in Christian Theology* (Eugene, Oreg.: Pickwick Publications, 2006), Stephen Finlan and Vladimir Kharlamov's edited volume, collects eleven fresh and enlightening essays on one of the most noteworthy themes in Christian doctrine. David F. Ford and Mike Higton's *Jesus* (Oxford: Oxford University Press, 2002) offers an extensive collection of ancient, modern, and postmodern documents, which reflect an array of responses to Jesus over the last two-thousand years. Veli-Matti Kärkkäinen's *Christology: A Global Introduction* (Grand Rapids, Mich.: Baker Academic, 2003) provides an ecumenical, international, and contextual introduction to Jesus' person in contemporary theology. In addition, Kärkkäinen's work on theosis, *One With God: Salvation as Deification and Justification* (Collegeville, Minn.: Liturgical Press, 2004), demonstrates that salvation as union with God has roots in the New Testament, in the Eastern Orthodox tradition, in Martin Luther's theology, and in later Protestant theologies. Darren J. N. Middleton's edited volume, *Scandalizing Jesus?: Kazantzakis' The Last Temptation of Christ Fifty Years On* (New York: Continuum, 2005), reexamines Kazantzakis' novel and Martin Scorsese's film, acknowledging strengths and weakness to both. Marvin Meyer's and Charles Hughes' anthology, *Jesus Then and Now: Images of Jesus in History and Christology* (Harrisburg, Pa.: Trinity Press International, 2001), brings conservative and liberal theologians together to converse about faith, history, literary texts, and theology's overall purpose. Christopher Seitz's edited collection, *Nicene Christianity: The Future for a New Ecumenism* (Grand Rapids, Mich.: Brazos Press, 2002), presents internationally recognized contemporary theologians' investigations and expositions of the Nicene Creed's enduring legacy. Graham Speake's *Mount Athos: Renewal in Paradise* (New Haven, Conn.: Yale University Press, 2003) is a lavishly illustrated guide to Greece's most famous monastic preserve.

SELECTED WEB SITES

1. http://www.newadvent.org/cathen/14597a.htm
   This site offers an encyclopedia article on the historical development of christological thought.

2. http://www.historical-museum.gr/kazantzakis/
   This is the Society for Cretan Historical Studies Web site, with links to the Kazantzakis museum on Crete.

3. http://www.goarch.org/access/orthodoxy/
   Hosted by the Greek Orthodox Archdiocese of America, this site offers a primer on all things connected to Eastern Christianity.

4

CHURCH

Earl Lovelace's *The Wine of Astonishment*

The church does not mean only, or even chiefly, the purpose-built and consecrated building at the street's end. It is the vast assembly of women, men, and children called out to be separate from a world deemed antagonistic to God. Such is the root meaning of the New Testament term *ekklesia*, the Greek word for "church."[1] *Ekklesia* suggests an idea that carries at least two emphases. First, the idea of being *called* out to be separate entails that the church is more than an assembled group that we simply agree to join. It suggests that God—rather than a priest, say—gathers, sustains, and emboldens the faith community. Second, the idea of being called *out to be separate* means that once we feel ourselves saved from transgression, we demonstrate our new alliance with God by abandoning the everyday world with its persistent, disquieting concerns of money, power, and sex. The Christian doctrine of the church recognizes both emphases. Yet it acknowledges that these different emphases stimulate different "ecclesiologies" or views on what it means to belong to the church.[2]

Those Christians who stress their separation from the world frequently come together to condemn ordinary life as sinful. And their leaders—some of whom scrutinize would-be members carefully, teach moral standards strictly, and police members' behavior rigorously—often declare that individuals avoid divine displeasure by being saved out of the world by conversion. Once saved, converts believe they must wait for God-in-Christ to break into the world, set aside the moral wheat from the immoral chaff, destroy the world, and then establish God's kingdom.[3] Such waiting may take the form of withdrawn quietism or isolated counter-culturalism. However they wait, though, Christian groups resembling the above description exist throughout our world, often in small or close-knit communities. At the same time, there are Christians who model a different ecclesiology. They believe God created the world, declared it good, and redeemed it through Jesus Christ.[4] Even though they know people are sinful, and that wrongdoing permeates almost every aspect of life, they follow God in choosing not to abandon the world. God participates within the world, they say, inspiring believers to work within its structures to transform existence. Characteristically, such Christians do not wait for the day of divine judgment; instead, they hold that God has called them to assume the task of redeeming public as well as private life. By working to improve the world, they believe they are helping God usher in God's kingdom. Rather than see themselves connected to close-knit or small communities only, Christians of this type see themselves as part of a worldwide movement, one that transcends particular denominational structures to constitute an ecclesiastical unity that stretches back to Jesus Christ, the church's one foundation.[5]

There is a third approach to ecclesiology, one that blends grass-roots leadership with political analysis, and these new faith communities represent fresh ways of doing theology. In the Caribbean and Latin America, for example, Christianity arrived with the slave traders as well as the conquerors. Over time, disenfranchised peoples came to view Christianity as colonialism's weapon—an imperial stick designed to keep people in their place, tamp down dissent, and preserve the status quo. In recent years, though, decolonial and liberation theology has emerged to pose not just religious questions about how souls are saved but political questions about how to convert economic and cultural structures that hold people—especially the indigent—in thrall. Living near or south of the equator, such Global South theologians are reading Scripture with fresh eyes. And they are emerging from the experience with the belief that Jesus Christ advocates for those individuals pushed out to society's edges. The contemporary church's task involves working for freedom from all forms of oppression, many claim.[6] As we will see, this new way of "being a church" will have an impact on how ecclesiology is understood in the future.

To make the doctrine of the church straightforward to grasp, I have simplified matters from this chapter's onset. Of course the empirical reality looks far more complex. Among Christians there are many understandings of the word "church," for example, and these are located at various points in between the approaches to ecclesiology outlined above. Notice the common denominator in such approaches, however, for they all proclaim Jesus Christ's centrality. Today, most theologians see the doctrine of Jesus Christ's person and work, which I discussed in the last chapter, as unfolding into the doctrine of the church. Ecclesiology proceeds out from Christology and soteriology, they say. Through the life, death, and resurrection of Jesus Christ, God's Son and our Savior, we have all found our way back to God. This redemption leads to a new relationship between God and God's people, made concrete in the church, which continues Jesus Christ's work in the present.

Like the biblical writers and Christian theologians before them, many novelists and poets have used imaginative models to explore the relationship between God and the church.[7] With this fourth chapter I continue my examination of the relationship between Christian doctrine and modern fiction through an analysis of the Caribbean writer Earl Lovelace and his fourth novel, *The Wine of Astonishment*, published in 1982.[8] Focusing on a rural, so-called Shouters or Spiritual Baptist community, this novel explores the impact of British and American colonialism on Trinidad, especially its legacy of soul-destruction, and the attempts made by various members of the fictional Bonasse church to regain their sense of confidence as well as possibility. As we will see, the ecclesiology that emerges from *The Wine of Astonishment* reflects ideas traceable to various makers and remakers of Christian doctrine. First, Protestant theology finds an expression in Lovelace's protagonists, Leader Bee and Mother Eva, when they declare that fidelity to the Bible, the priesthood of all believers, personal holiness, and being set apart from the world constitute hallmarks of the true church. Second, the Bonasse congregation's anticolonial resistance, symbolized by its dignified protest of unjust laws as well as its struggle to keep its African heritage alive, is in line with several attempts in the last fifty years or so—chiefly by liberation or Caribbean decolonial theology—to treat engagement with the world as the most important task for the church today.

This chapter has four major sections. First, I outline Lovelace's life and literary art, focusing on how Trinidad and Tobago's landscape and history of slavery, as well as imperialism, informs his fiction. I also pay close attention to his theory of reparation—the idea of repairing selves crushed under colonialism's heavy weight. Second, I engage certain makers and remakers of the Christian doctrine of the church, beginning with selected biblical personalities and then moving to highlight those theologians who can illumine our reading of Lovelace's novel. In the third and major section I offer a Christian theological reading of *The Wine of Astonishment*, concentrating on how Lovelace's Spiritual Baptists both engage and set themselves apart from the British and American colonials who both literally and figuratively surround (read: oppress) them. A final section situates *The Wine of Astonishment*'s ecclesiology within the context of recent theological calls to heed those voices from the Global South. And it appreciates how such non-Western churches are shaping Christianity's present and future.[9]

EARL LOVELACE: LIFE AND LITERARY ART

Autobiographical references in Lovelace's *A Brief Conversion and Other Stories* (1988) indicate that he was born in Toco, Trinidad, on July 13, 1935.[10] Soon afterward he lived with his Tobago-based maternal grandparents before moving back to Trinidad in his teenage years, completing his high school education in Port of Spain. Work with Trinidad's Department of Foresty and, later, with the Department of Agriculture inspired him to undertake study at the Eastern Caribbean Institute of Agriculture and Foresty in the early 1960s. This work-study cultivated his deep admiration for Trinidad's landscape and peoples, especially in rural areas. His tenderness toward ordinary people and their struggle to work with their environment permeates his literary art. We observe such tenderness—perhaps at its best—in Lovelace's second novel, *The Schoolmaster* (1968), which he published shortly after spending some time in residence at Howard University. Here Lovelace contrasts the city's trials and tribulations with the village's unspoiled and tranquil atmosphere. Railing against the plantation owner, Paulaine Dandrade, especially her plans to educate the Kumaca villagers on her own terms, Constantine Patron and Father Vincent, the local Catholic priest, urge an insider's rather than an outsider's involvement in conscientizing the villagers. Tensions ensue. And in the greater part of the novel, Lovelace's symbols of city and rural life struggle to understand one another. The nameless schoolmaster in this tale only exacerbates matters, especially when what he teaches and how he acts eventually conflicts with the village's traditional family values.

Lovelace's first novel, the award-winning *While Gods Are Falling* (1965), introduces the themes—besides tenderness for rural life and peoples—that today serve as his hallmarks: his unconditional regard for black people's dignity and worth, his sense that anticolonial resistance facilitates such positive self-regard, and his belief that communities, including the church, must help repair the souls of those damaged by years of mental slavery. Here, the people of Trinidad's capital city gesture toward something outside themselves, something outside their individual and collective self, to overcome Port of Spain's hopeless poverty, senseless murders, and rampant chaos. Life seems much too arduous, however, and people soon find they can no longer rely on religious authorities, community leaders, the police and the law courts, parents, educators, and conventional values. Such "gods" have fallen. Plunged into poverty on account of his father's misfortune, Walter Castle, Lovelace's protagonist in *While Gods Are Falling*, spends the novel feeling trapped inside his unpromising socioeconomic conditions and his deteriorating sense of self. He fortifies himself, as his surname implies, by placing a symbolic moat around his vulnerable identity. And his tragedy is that this arrangement causes him to live isolated from the one thing that promises to save or repair him—his community.

A third novel, *The Dragon Can't Dance* (1979), appeared after Lovelace spent much of the 1970s working at various universities. He taught literature and creative writing at the Federal City College (now the University of the District of Columbia) between 1971 and 1973, and at Johns Hopkins University, from 1973 to 1974. Lovelace earned a Master of Arts degree in English from Johns Hopkins. He also lectured at the University of the West Indies, St. Augustine, Trinidad, between 1977 and 1987 and, briefly, at the University of Iowa, in 1980, shortly after receiving a Guggenheim Fellowship. An attempt to capture the many survival and resistance strategies adopted by poor, Trinidadian black men, *The Dragon Can't Dance* introduces such colorful characters as the Dragon, the Badjohn, and the Calypsonian, who subvert—sometimes through violence and sometimes by dancing—the political establishment's attempt to undercut their personhood and potential. Such protagonists are Bacchanalian, to use critic Funso Aiyejina's phrasing, using calypso and comedy to protest a society that privileges whiteness and marginalizes blackness.[11] The reader soon discovers, though, that in a world marked by neocolonialism, the dragon struggles to dance. For the disenfranchised Trinidadian black woman or man, life sways to a different rhythm. The carnival gives way to an altogether different dance, the dance of life, which is the struggle to find food, water, and shelter, not to mention a voice that might be heard.

Completed prior to *The Dragon Can't Dance* but published a little later, *The Wine of Astonishment* reintroduces Lovelace's readers to life in rural Bonasse, Trinidad. The novel is narrated by the mother of the Bonasse church, Eva, whose husband, Bee, pastors a people trying to practice their faith in light of the colonial government's 1917 decision to prohibit Spiritual Baptists, or Shouters, from worshiping openly and freely.[12] Known for their neo-African beliefs and liturgies, the Shouters were deemed heretical and banned on November 28, 1917. This ban was eventually lifted by R. A. Joseph, Trinidad's Minister of Education and Social Services, on March 30, 1951. Trinidad and Tobago now celebrates Spiritual Baptist (Shouter) Liberation Day on March 30 annually. Although marked by moments of fortune and misfortune, as we will see, the Bonasse church slowly emerges from colonial and neocolonial oppression, poised and ready to welcome the Spirit's movement into the future. Here, in this concise and compelling novel, Lovelace fuses African and Trinidadian religious elements together and creates an ecclesiology that teaches the Western church more than one lesson.

The winner of the 1997 Commonwealth Writer's Prize, *Salt* (1996) brings together two characters, Bango, a community activist with a dream to organize a racially inclusive holiday parade, and Alford George, a Trinidadian steeped in European values, who does not look at life the way Bango does. Bango tries to bring his community together, to repair the hurt that has come to mark various African, Chinese, Indian, and European immigrants to Trinidad. Over time, Bango's actions inspire Alford, creating space for the latter's transition from failed teacher to dignified human being.

The need for dignity concerns Lovelace greatly. We will not be able to welcome each other as human beings, he says, unless we help each other overcome any and all sense of inferiority. "We in the Caribbean have become satisfied with a degree of liveable freedom," Lovelace declares in a recent lecture, and this is "dangerous because our satisfaction with it could see us institutionalizing the permanent acceptance of ourselves as second-class citizens."[13] Overcoming such "second-classness" stands out as "one of the motive forces at the root" of *Salt*.[14]

Although well-known for his novels, Lovelace has written other material. He has penned several plays, for example, as well as two musicals and some short stories. Numerous contributions to periodicals illustrate that he has not forgotten his journalistic origins.[15] When he is not teaching at Wellesley College in Massachusetts, he is at work on a sixth novel, currently untitled, a book of essays on Caribbean life and culture, and a children's story.

Reparation Theory

Armed with its tremendous wealth and power, Europe began to colonize the world for economic and political profit from the fifteenth until the late nineteenth century. Flanking this imperial expansionism were the Christian missionaries who held that it was their Christ-mandated duty to convert the "pagans" who lived in the "uncivilized" world, such as Africa's "dark continent," and plant churches in places where none existed before. Although many missionaries failed to return from foreign lands because diseases such as malaria and typhoid cut short their lives, they saw themselves as enacting the Great Commission, turning unbelievers into church members.[16] In addition to bringing their religion to places such as Benin and Ghana, these missionaries also imported European ethics, often associating such values with holiness. Over time, though, indigenous Africans came to identify Christian missionaries with white colonization and the abuse that this involved. Seldom did Christian missionaries make any real or concerted effort to consider, much less appreciate, the centuries-old traditional African religions that surrounded them. Such indifference frequently led to the Africans being mistreated, and helped to create such evils as the transatlantic slave trade, which resulted in millions of Africans being captured, sold, and shipped to the Caribbean, South America, and the United States.[17]

The Caribbean was rife with sugar colonies by the middle of the seventeenth century. And most of the slaves who made it to this part of the New World from West Africa were forced to work on the new, bustling plantations. By most estimates, the various European powers that operated this region between 1651 and 1830 introduced almost five million Africans to the Caribbean. Despite this ample African presence, both colonial administrators and Christian missionaries dismissed the religions that Africans brought with them through the Middle Passage. In time, though, these religions developed a "syncretic" or "creolized" character—that is, Africans adjusted their religiosity so that it displayed recognizably Christian traits and retained identifiably African aspects. Although many such religions were initially outlawed, they clearly adapted to their new environment, and now we recognize them as Obeah (Jamaica), Santería (Cuba), Shango (Trinidad), and Vodou (Haiti). Today, it is hard to represent Caribbean Christianity without taking syncretism seriously. Many expressions of the church in the region, like the Trinidadian Spiritual Baptists, both preserve and promote their African heritage.[18]

In the middle of the last century, more colonized countries gained political independence. Caribbean peoples proclaimed liberation, and fresh leadership, often involving black governance, emerged. A new day dawned. But for many cultural commentators, Lovelace included, independence has inclined otherwise good people to labor under a false sense of freedom. The roots of this problem, certainly for Trinidad, which achieved independence in 1962, run deep. The country is roughly divided into 41 percent African and 41 percent Indian peoples, with the rest being made up of various Amerindians, Chinese, Europeans, and Lebanese. Ethnic and cultural fractiousness runs rampant. Lovelace traces such disunity to adjustments made by colonial administrators shortly after the 1834 Emancipation. In the years following Emancipation, for example, colonials welcomed Indian immigrants to Trinidad, because they represented a cheaper workforce than the newly freed slaves:

> This situation, of course, set up tensions from the very beginning between Africans, who by their struggles against enslavement bore the brunt of colonial opprobrium, and the Indians, who were seen by them as reaping the benefits they had worked for. Beneath the surface, then, of this and other relationships, there is resentment, competition, victimhood, shame, and guilt. Despite our great possibilities and the contributions made by each group within the spheres of its ingenuity, tensions consume our energies, and place each group on the defensive, and limit the quality of the creative address we might make to our future.[19]

Given this historical and cultural background, Lovelace wants to help Trinidadians "find a way to welcome each other into a New World of new, liberating and creative relationships."[20] Europeans lack the moral authority to help in this endeavor, he says, and the Indians are unable to make the welcome either. As recent arrivals, Indians have yet to plant their roots in the landscape. Africans are the best equipped, Lovelace claims, for "they, more than any other group, have made liberation the central theme of their existence, and have laid the foundation for a new society."[21] Yet, there is a long way to go. Emancipation, self-government, and independence are "important landmarks in our struggle for person-hood," Lovelace holds, but people still lack confidence and self-worth.[22]

The act of welcoming others involves pursuing "the full restoration of personhood for both the brutalised and the brutaliser, those who have been injured and those who in injuring others have injured themselves."[23] Lovelace calls this act "reparation (not reparations)" and, in his view, it represents our best ideal for life in the twenty-first century:

> As in any relationship where there has been a breach of trust, you have to repair the breach in order to start again, until the next time, when positions might well be changed, since human stupidity will not and cannot end . . . In relationships we can expect endless wrongs to be done to us, and we can expect that we will also do wrong countless times; this is what it means to be human. Being human also means saying you are sorry, and doing whatever it takes to restore the rela-tionship you violated.[24]

Genuine relationality, or what Lovelace calls "the act of welcoming others," requires, therefore, that we walk humbly, forgive one another repeatedly, and seek reciprocal flourishing.

Notice the way that Lovelace alludes to the Hebrew Bible in his understanding of reparation. He speaks, for example, of our need to "repair the breach" in the relationships that mark and divide our lives.[25] Interestingly, the New Testament writers prefer "reconcile" to "repair," though it clearly reflects the same sentiment. In the Apostle Paul's let-ters, for example, the "reconciliation" theme finds its most impres-sive exposition. Here, Paul states that since God has worked through Jesus Christ's life, death, and resurrection to reconcile all people back to Godself, the church's task now flows from its nature as a body of reconciled individuals. This "ministry of reconciliation" involves help-ing others overcome mutual enmity through mutual mercy.[26] Lovelace's Spiritual Baptists know their Bible only too well, as we will see, for they affirm people's humanity by welcoming them unconditionally and thus, in the end, may best be seen to promote an ecclesiology based around gestures of belonging.

Because "the process of being human is ongoing," reparation or rec-onciliation is never complete.[27] And this belief in our open-endedness is one reason why Lovelace thinks Trinidadians (and others) have labored under a false sense of freedom for such a long time. "There is the sense that once free from colonialism, I now become a finished project," he says. "None of us is a finished project. We are all unfinished projects."[28] But now is not the time for solo endeavors. "We need to envisage a communal project," he declares, and one that takes seriously what it means to be authentically human. "We were always involved in that but colonialism got in the way."[29] Together with educators and artists, today's church must be placed in service of this communal project of reparation or reconciliation. It must call us to account as humans, for example, and resolutely enjoin us to embody our highest ideal of what it means to be human.[30] The church accomplishes this task, at least in part, by working to cultivate those images that help people, especially Africans, rediscover their dignity after years of having their true personality denied. By welcoming and affirming people where they are, the church fulfills its New Testament mission to help us repair the faith we break with others and with God.[31]

THE DOCTRINE OF THE CHURCH: A SELECTIVE SKETCH

Christians met in one another's homes during their formative years. They did so because few formal places of worship existed. Many believers, like those featured in the New Testament's earliest surviving letter, viewed purpose-built structures as futile because, as they put it, Jesus was coming back soon to end the world.[32] Poverty and persecution also made it impossible to build churches. As the years rolled by, however, the church grew and developed. Small worship houses were constructed, and leaders of the church, called bishops, were chosen to watch over those districts where sizeable Christian groups congregated. Only with the Emperor Constantine's conversion to Christianity, which occurred early in the fourth century, did Christianity's status change. More churches were built, and this time some of them were quite majestic, like the Hagia Sophia in Constantinople, a city named after the Emperor himself.

As noted in the last chapter, one of Emperor Constantine's more significant tasks involved calling together the first ecumenical, or worldwide, council of the Christian church in Nicea, to discuss a variety of theological issues. The assembled theologians issued a statement, the Nicene Creed, which outlined how the early church understood its nature and function. Here, the church is described as "one, holy, catholic, and apostolic." In other words, God requires the church to (1) come together as a unified whole, (2) represent God's will on earth, modeling Jesus Christ's presence in the world, (3) understand itself as a *universal* congregation of believers, and (4) reflect Jesus' teachings as passed on through his apostles.[33]

Nicea's officially sanctioned ecclesiology held for several centuries, although there were always a few differences in what various Christians believed about the church. In 1054, for example, the two major centers of ecclesiastical excellence in the medieval world were separated in "the Great Schism," named after the Greek word ("schism") for "tear." From this moment, there were two major Christian churches in the world: the Catholic ("universal") church, led by the Rome-based Pope, and the Orthodox ("correct-thinking") church, run by the Constantinople-based Patriarch. The former church acquired considerable power during the Middle Ages. By the early sixteenth century, however, many Christians, some of them priests, became frustrated with the church's apparent abuse of such power.[34]

In 1517, the German priest Martin Luther nailed a provocative document on a door castigating many of the Catholic church's practices. This act of subversion was deeply transformative, setting in motion a chain reaction of ecclesiastical reform that quickly moved beyond Luther's Germany to affect other parts of the West as well. Many Christians believed, like Luther, that the Catholic church had lost its sense of vocation. It had become preoccupied with money, they said, even the world in general, and had turned a blind eye to the world's lost and hopeless, those whom Jesus had entrusted to the church's care.[35] Luther's protest changed the Western church's course forever, creating the space for Protestant churches to form and grow, chiefly by pulling away from Rome's influence.[36]

The Reformation was a complex moment in world history, much less Christian history, and the intellectual movements it inspired— Lutheranism and Calvinism, to name but two—are far too multifaceted and subtle to do them justice in this short summary. For our purposes, though, Protestantism's main beliefs and practices may be stated in the following way. God speaks through God's word, the Bible, and the Bible is the primary witness to Jesus of Nazareth, the Christ; Jesus mediates God's grace; Jesus alone is Savior; faith is God's free and unconditional gift to us; faith justifies sinners; the Holy Spirit sanctifies believers, helping us to love God because God first loved us; the church is a fellowship of justified and sanctified believers, and all believers are priests to each other.[37] Lovelace's Spiritual Baptists reflect most, if not all, of the aforementioned principles. As we will see, Mother Eva and Leader Bee reference the Bible closely and constantly. Leader Bee even functions as a Christ-like figure, mediating grace and helping people stand before God individually. Arriving as God's gift, faith holds the Bonasse congregation together as a fellowship of believers. To withstand the oppression that flanks them on all sides, the church draws its unifying strength from the Holy Spirit's sanctifying energy.[38]

The Baptists

Protestant churches began to pull away from Rome's power in the sixteenth century. The Reformation reached England, for example, when King Henry VIII was on the throne. Motivated by the desire to divorce and remarry, which angered Rome, he initiated several reforms and eventually declared himself head of the English church. Later monarchs, like Edward VI and Elizabeth I, continued Henry VIII's reforms and, indeed, went so far as to conjoin church and state, an action that appeared to guarantee uniformity throughout the land.[39]

More radical Christians opposed the established church. Such believers became known as Puritans, and they held that the church, not the government, should shape worship. The English Parliament disagreed, and many Puritans suffered persecution for their cause. Various "independent" or "free" churches nonetheless emerged in the seventeenth and eighteenth centuries, united by their unwillingness to conform to the state in matters of faith.[40] One of the best known of these nonconformist churches, the Baptists, now number 110 million adherents worldwide.[41] As we will see, the freedom to worship according to conscience links Lovelace's early twentieth century Spiritual Baptists with their Reformation forebears in faith.

Although here is not the place to elucidate what historian H. Leon McBeth calls "four centuries of Baptist witness," it is important to make clear that Baptists were influenced by the Protestant reformers.[42] They also found the English Bible inspiring. And from their earliest stirrings they saw themselves as a movement marked by an intense longing for spiritual reform. In the seventeenth century, two Baptist groups held sway. The General Baptists, as their name implies, cast their theological net widely. Following the Dutch reformer Jacob Arminius, they believed our volition factors into the salvation process; consequently, all who freely assent to Jesus Christ as God's Son and Savior will find their names in the Book of Life. In contrast, the Particular Baptists followed John Calvin, the reformer associated with the Swiss city of Geneva, by holding that God predestines and saves the elect only. McBeth notes that although they came into their own much later than General Baptists, the Particular Baptists eventually attracted more followers and their Calvinist theology, best symbolized by the 1644 First London Confession, subsequently shaped Baptist thought and practice immeasurably.[43]

Such beliefs and behavior were, at least by the 1700s, more or less in place and they may be summarized in the following manner:[44]

First, the early Baptists believed in one God who reveals Godself to the world as Father, Son, and Holy Spirit. The term "trinity" is now commonplace to describe the idea that there are three persons in one divine being.

Second, the early Baptists held that God guided the biblical writers to articulate God's will, word for word. The Bible is therefore infallible, without error, and supremely authoritative. This said, each believer has the right and the freedom to read and interpret the Bible in light of his understanding of the world.

Third, the early Baptists affirmed the efficacy of the atonement. But, as we have seen, General and Particular Baptists disagreed with one another concerning the *scope* of God's saving grace. A doctrinal fire stoked by tensions over allegiances to Arminianism and Calvinism respectively, this theological contrast influenced late seventeenth century views on such ecclesiastical activities as preaching and missions.[45]

Fourth, the early Baptists, both General and Particular, viewed the church as a gathered body of baptized believers, noted for its observance of the two primary gospel ordinances, believers' baptism and the Lord's Supper, and for its avowal of the priesthood of all believers. This latter notion captures the idea that all church members fully participate in every aspect of ecclesiastical life. Each church, moreover, has congregational autonomy. Since all believers are like priests to all other believers, each gathered community has the freedom to come together and make its own decisions, elect its own leaders, and administer whatever discipline it deems necessary to keep the church faithful to its calling as God's people.[46]

Fifth, the early Baptists followed two types of church leader, pastor and deacon, and although some were well-educated, many were not. Men and women served as deacons. Some women preached, especially among the General Baptists, but men often assumed such responsibilities. A third ecclesiastical office, the so-called messenger, became popular among General Baptists, but this position was phased out by the eighteenth century's close.

Sixth, the early Baptists subscribed to believers' baptism. Only people who are able and ready to comprehend as well as agree to the gospel, and who can articulate their personal decision to do so, are baptized by total immersion. "This practice conferred their name," McBeth explains, "and provided a vivid picture to distinguish them from others."[47]

Seventh, the early Baptists followed Ulrich Zwingli in treating the Lord's Supper as a memorial to Christ's death. However, Baptists differed on who could approach the table and share in the meal. While some Baptists favored "closed communion," the practice of allowing only baptized believers to participate in the Lord's Supper, others preferred "open communion," meaning that the meal was open to *all* who profess belief in Jesus Christ as God's Son and our Savior. In time, the latter approach won out.

Eighth, the early Baptists were divided on their relationship to national government. Unlike the General Baptists, who tended to eschew allegiance to authorities that persecuted them dreadfully, the Particular Baptists "followed their Calvinistic heritage in giving high value to political loyalty and patriotic participation in civil affairs."[48] Most General Baptists affirmed faithfulness to the monarchy. However, many also favored pacifism, which often led outsiders to suspect them of unfaithfulness or a lack of patriotism.

Ninth, the early Baptists declared the importance of religious liberty. Hostility and outright persecution, especially in the seventeenth century, inspired this belief and behavior. But Baptists did not claim such liberty for themselves alone. In fact, they made themselves thoroughly unpopular by insisting that the authorities allow non-Baptist groups, such as Catholics and Jews, to gather and worship freely.

Finally, the early Baptists placed their hope in Christ's eventual return. For the most part, they did not envisage this second coming in violent terms, but some did. And for a time, the members of the so-called Fifth Monarchy Movement, who take their name from an intriguing reading of Daniel 7, held sway. By the seventeenth century's close, however, most Baptists followed the general religious belief, observable in a variety of traditions, that Christ would return to earth imminently.[49]

Baptists and Trinidad

Enthused by the theologians linked to the nineteenth century's trans-atlantic religious awakenings, thirteen men associated with the Northamptonshire Association of Baptist churches gathered together on October 2, 1792 to think about preaching the gospel in foreign lands. Seated in "the back parlour of Mrs. Beeby Wallis's home in Kettering," they formed the Particular Baptist Society for the Propagation of the Gospel amongst the Heathen, the organization that we now recognize as the Baptist Missionary Society (BMS).[50] The response was overwhelmingly positive; a mission to India followed almost immediately.[51] By 1813, the BMS had made initial forays into the West Indies.[52]

Former slaves from the United States arrived in Trinidad in 1815. Drawn to the late eighteenth century religious revivals that were popular in states like Virginia, where many of the immigrants were from, these individuals had assisted the British during the War of 1812 and, for their efforts, had been promised safe passage out of the United States. By all accounts, the new settlers adapted to the island's cultural environment fairly easily. Historian Brian Stanley elaborates:

> The religion which Christian communities and preachers brought with them to the Caribbean was enthusiastic and experiential. It was a faith more of the Spirit than of the Word—a Christianity of the poor and non-literate. The uninhibited emotionalism of the "camp-meetings" of the American revivalist tradition held much the same attraction for the slave communities of both the southern States and the Caribbean. Revivalism enabled them to express the joy of new Christian experience in old cultural forms: slaves filled with the Holy Spirit worshipped in ways that their African forefathers possessed by the spirits of African traditional religion would have found not entirely unfamiliar.[53]

Black Baptists from the United States settled in Trinidad's southern region in areas that became known as "Company villages." Ethnomusicologist Lorna Michael claims that the Spiritual Baptists are their direct descendents.[54]

The BMS sent missionaries to plant a church, St. John's, in Port of Spain, somewhat removed from the south, and the initial success they met with buoyed their endeavors. However, the BMS president visited Trinidad in 1859 and, in his official report, expressed grave concerns about the "most unseemly" worship styles adopted by various Baptist congregations, especially those in the south. Such unseemly behavior included ecstatic dancing and vociferous praising. There was much work to do, according to the BMS officials. "In Trinidad," as Stanley remarks, "the problems of grafting the native Baptist plant into the British Baptist tree remained substantial."[55]

Although a fairly robust Baptist Union of Trinidad was established in 1860, St. John's Church found itself struggling to make ends meet by the nineteenth century's close. More official visits followed, and further complaints, directed toward the southern churches especially, were lodged. But, from the BMS' perspective, very little changed, and so the society withdrew from the West Indies mission field in December 1892.[56]

St. John's accepted an ecclesiastical grant from the British colonial government and, at the twentieth century's turn, they used this money to appoint a former missionary to the Sudan, J. J. Cooksey, as pastor of their own church and superintendent to the island's southern churches. He opposed the Spiritual Baptists or Shouters, the so-called native Baptist tradition, and was successful in banning them from meeting on BMS premises. This action eventually divided the Trinidadian Baptists, though, and it forced Cooksey's resignation. A young student from Bristol Baptist College, J. H. Poole, replaced him. In a ministry that lasted for the greater part of the twentieth century, Poole made many influential changes to Trinidadian Baptist life, not the least of which involved recognizing the value of the Spiritual Baptists and providing them with some measure of pastoral oversight. By 1945, though, Poole was so frustrated with the Shouters, especially their "old African superstitions," that he argued against native church autonomy, so to speak, and, instead, persuaded the BMS to resume their work in Trinidad. The first appointments, like Eva Waggot, arrived in early 1946.

Eight years after Trinidad and Tobago declared their independence from British rule in 1962, the BMS partnered with the island's Baptist Union to educate and establish homegrown pastors and church leaders. Outside influence did not disappear, however, for the Foreign Mission Board of the Southern Baptist Convention sent their own missionaries between 1970 and 1976. The Baptist Union of Trinidad and Tobago stopped accepting Europeans as pastors in 1980. From this time to the present day, Baptists in Trinidad and Tobago have been numerically weak, except among the Spiritual Baptists, yet they remain a vital presence on the island.[57]

While there are some scholars, like James T. Houk, who consider several theories concerning the origins of the Trinidadian Spiritual Baptists or Shouters, most trace the group to the previously mentioned black Baptists from the United States.[58] These women and men were part of the transatlantic slave trade, as I have noted, and this connection enables us to acknowledge and appreciate the foreign, especially African, roots to the Spiritual Baptist tradition. Recent academic work fortifies this link. For example, anthropologist Kenneth Anthony Lum associates the Spiritual Baptists with Trinidad's Orisha religion, which has its ancestry among the Yoruba, a region in West Africa and one of the foremost ethnic and religious groups in Benin and Nigeria.[59] As we will see, it is both the African and Baptist components of the Spiritual Baptists, as well as their Baptist-ness, that merit close attention.

The identifying features of the Spiritual Baptist tradition may be set out in the following way.[60] First, they worship in a variety of buildings, often called temples, and the architecture as well as furnishings now assume a fairly standard pattern. Most houses of worship revolve around an ornate pole that stands at the room's center. Believers often douse this pole with water at least three times, remove their shoes when approaching it, and regularly adorn the shrine with flowers, candles, bells, and copies of the Bible. Cruciform chalk markings are found at the pole's base. Benches encircle the pole. The church's leaders, often called "mother," "father," "leader," or "watchman," sit in special altar chairs. Additional flags and candles beautify this area. Since Spiritual Baptists also believe in Scripture as God's word, the pulpit's centrality on the temple's altar reflects preaching's importance.[61]

Second, the Spiritual Baptists are recognizably Baptist in many of their beliefs and rituals. Although contrasts with their forebears in faith certainly exist, their "essential rites are carried on," as the anthropologists Herskovits and Herskovits note, "beneath an overlay of conventionalized decorum."[62] This is to say, the Spiritual Baptists join other Baptists in believing in God's sovereignty, Jesus Christ as God's Son and our Savior, the Bible as God's word, and faith as the proper and primary response to the Holy Spirit's power. Each Spiritual Baptist church also views itself as a gathered, autonomous union. Even though there are certain specific leaders, and some reports mention as many as nineteen, every believer is like a priest to every other believer.[63]

Third, the Spiritual Baptists take their other name, the Shouters, from the experiential and emotional dimension of their faith. Many shake and shout during worship. Like the black Baptists from the United States, the Spiritual Baptists place enormous emphasis on Pentecost, when the first Christians experienced the Holy Spirit's spontaneous power.[64] And in their worship they try to recreate the kinds of experiences that changed the lives of the first followers of Jesus. The most abiding hallmark of the Spiritual Baptists, spirit possession, often manifests itself in ecstatic dances, exuberant prayers and praises, speaking in tongues, bell-ringing, often performed by the church's "mother," and trances as well as dream-visions.[65] Such manifestations reflect their African religious heritage.[66]

Fourth, the Spiritual Baptists say that believers join their temple by moving through a series of rites and rituals. Individuals who experience visions or dreams often approach a Spiritual Baptist leader. And this person invariably recommends baptism. Prebaptismal instruction, which often lasts weeks or months, establishes the believer's moral credentials. It also marks the moment when the leader presents the baptismal candidate with a Bible chapter or a hymn, which serves as a prompt during later worship services. A Spiritual Baptist frequently convulses or bellows when the congregation either cites his verse or sings her song. Baptism is by total immersion, often in a local river, and is commonly followed by additional visions or dreams. Such postbaptismal experiences normally inspire believers to practice "mournin' groun" rites.[67] This term describes a retreat, which affords the believer time to experience and receive the Holy Spirit's gifts, including healing and glossolalia.

Lastly, like their forebears in faith, the Spiritual Baptists have suffered as a consequence of their struggle for the freedom to worship according to conscience. *The Shouters' Prohibition Ordinance* of 1917, as I noted earlier, banned their activities and forced them underground. Trinidad's Attorney General, who sponsored this legislation, called the Spiritual Baptists "an unmitagated nuisance" because their rites were noisy and because other "practices which are indulged in are not such as should be tolerated in a well conducted community."[68] Ironically, the heavy fines imposed on those believers who violated the *Prohibition* adversely affected the colonial government. Persecution energized the Spiritual Baptists and drew sympathy for the group from other Trinidadians.[69] After the government lifted the ban in 1951, people began rethinking the role of the Spiritual Baptists on the island. And many came to value their honesty and decency—the sort of moral correctness that, in the words of Herskovits and Herskovits, may best be seen in the way the Spiritual Baptists "grant to each member a degree of actual and psychological participation that makes the individual worshipper feel that he or she is a useful, a necessary part of the world about him."[70] This observation recalls Lovelace's reparation theory, the ethic of welcoming each other:

> The creative spirit of God has been passed on to each and everyone of us, this idea has been emphasised and affirmed in the Spiritual Baptist religion and unless we see ourselves as second-class people we will understand that our task is to also create for our welfare and our delight . . . We need to learn to cherish each other.[71]

Caribbean Theology

Reflecting the trend toward engaging the world politically as well as religiously, first made popular in the late 1960s by various liberation theologians, the Caribbean Conference of Churches (CCC) was established in 1971 to promote interdenominational togetherness and teamwork in all dimensions of Caribbean life. By 1977, the theologians associated with the CCC were upholding the real and pressing need to "decolonize theology." This arresting phrase refers to the task of equipping congregations with tools to enable all Caribbean persons to develop an authentically postcolonial religious identity, an identity constructed around the twin notions of genuine black personhood and peoplehood before God.[72] Jamaican theologian Noel Leo Erskine writes:

> As the church in the Caribbean decolonizes theology, it must be willing to put aside a timeless, universal, metaphysical theology and become existential as it seeks to relate to the living history of blackness. This is consistent with biblical revelation, which took on historical particularity in the exodus and in the incarnation.[73]

Decolonizing theology remains the watchword of present-day Caribbean theologians. Here are the main ways of thinking and acting captured by this term.[74]

First, Caribbean theologians recognize the region's long and difficult history of colonialism and slavery. And they are committed to raising people's awareness of how and why such brutish realities continue to shape Caribbean identity. Many are convinced, as Lovelace seems to be, that Caribbean peoples live under a false sense of freedom after independence. Decolonizing theology involves conscientization, helping people appreciate the messy verities of their own history and heritage.[75]

Second, Caribbean theologians stress Christianity's paradoxical part in sanctioning as well as challenging colonialism and slavery. They critique the established churches, like the Anglicans, for imposing European and American models on Caribbean congregations. Yet Caribbean theologians also uphold the nonconformist or free churches, like the Spiritual Baptists, for the way they express their dissent by affirming indigenity, an incarnation of Christianity in neo-African form(s). Decolonizing theology involves locating and celebrating the native expression of Christ's Spirit in the Caribbean experience.[76]

Third, Caribbean theologians claim that oppression represents colonialism's and slavery's vestigial remains throughout the Caribbean. The church has addressed such oppression only infrequently, they say, and all too often, especially in recent years, it has been in the form of North American televangelists. Such imported, hit-and-run preachers deliver sermons that hurt rather than help the region. Their message of personal salvation and individual triumphalism masks the structural sins—persistent poverty, migration, cultural alienation, dependence, fragmentation, drug trafficking, and narcotic abuse—that exert principal and powerful influence over Caribbean peoples. Decolonizing theology involves naming and challenging such forces. It treats the postcolonial church in the Caribbean as the agent of emancipation for "the disvalued self," to cite the Antiguan theologian Kortright Davis:

> Is it not true that the most crucial human need in the Caribbean at this time is neither trade, nor aid, nor arms, nor even the liberation of the mind, but rather the *emancipation of the disvalued self*? Is it not true that this disvalued self is the product of our own misconception of truth, beauty, goodness, and human dignity, and that others have willingly joined us in our self-deprecating miscegenation of values? The culture of our mind has been assaulted by the culture of our environment, and our historical values have been radically disfigured by misguided modes of belief. We are trapped most of the time within the confines of our disvalued selves, and we seldom realize that we are.[77]

Davis' remarks remind us of Lovelace's ethic of welcoming and repairing each other. And they mirror *The Wine of Astonishment*'s main theme—the notion that the church's future lies in its faithfulness to Christ's emancipatory and reconciling Spirit. As we will see, Lovelace and various Caribbean theologians are united, for the most part, by the belief that the church is the bearer of a new identity before God.[78]

Finally, Caribbean theologians claim that the region's persistent poverty represents theology's methodological starting point. Decolonizing theology involves identifying with those caught in the web of socioeconomic suffering. It also invokes kenotic Christology—one interpretation of the Pauline vision of Jesus' powerful and yet humble servanthood in Philippians 2—as a way to "preserve the paradox of power and powerlessness of the gospel in an ethos of ecclesiastical and technological triumphalism," writes Caribbean theologian Romney M. Moseley.[79] Expressed in the form of a heightened "commitment to bear each other's suffering," the ecclesiology that flows from such kenotic Christology reflects "a covenantal ethic of responsibility."[80] Decolonizing theology involves striving for values that represent intrinsic goods: justice, emancipation, and what Lovelace calls "a sense of belonging, a psychic ease, the valuing of our contributions, a space in which to grow and the natural acknowledgment of our worth and dignity as human beings."[81]

"Africa in Us, Black in Us"
A Christian Theological Reading of *The Wine of Astonishment*

The height of the Second World War, when U.S. soldiers arrive in Trinidad and establish a base on the island, represents one part of this novel's setting. Another part reflects one congregation's response to the *Shouters Prohibition Ordinance*, which the British colonial government established on November 28, 1917. The "Shouters" was an unkind sobriquet for the Trinidadian Spiritual Baptists, and it derives from the tendency among devotees toward religiously ecstatic behavior. Before the ban on their activities was lifted in 1951, many outsiders viewed the group as overly emotional and dangerously unpredictable. Even so, Spiritual Baptists now enjoy legal, social, and political acceptance in Trinidad and Tobago, as Frances Henry's recent study shows.[82]

Lovelace's principal characters, Mother Eva and Leader Bee, do not live to experience such widespread recognition. Their fate involves helping a small, careworn group of Spiritual Baptists cope with the colonial oppression that literally and figuratively borders their congregational life. Fit tightly between the (military) Base and the (country) Estate, symbols of U.S. and U.K. imperialism respectively, the Bonasse believers battle against those who exalt Western virtues as well as weaken or run-down the value of their Africanized Christianity.[83] The novel's title, taken from the Authorized Version of Psalm 60:3, captures their struggle: "Thou hast shewed thy people hard things; thou has made us to drink the wine of astonishment."

Besides functioning as the community lifegiver, as her biblical name suggests, Mother Eva narrates Lovelace's novel.[84] She describes the "hard things," like the police raids on her church, which she and other Spiritual Baptists endure. The effects of the 1917 *Prohibition* echo throughout the island, especially in Bonasse, and Mother Eva, who has been married to Leader Bee for twenty-three years, encourages her husband to visit Ivan Morton, the local boy recently elected to political office. Morton has a new car, one that comes with his new status, and we soon learn that he is about to move into a new house, the Estate, which once served as home to wealthy English colonialists.[85] Leader Bee's audience with Morton goes badly. When he complains about the police raids, for example, Morton treats the Spiritual Baptists as an obstacle to Trinidad's civilization process. They stand for an unwarranted reversion to an ancestral, credulous religion, he says, and they symbolize an incarnation of Christianity that lags far behind other forms—Anglicanism and Roman Catholicism. In attacking the Spiritual Baptists in this way, of course, Morton echoes the approach taken—as previously noted—by the BMS missionaries as well as the Trinidadian government in the first half of the twentieth century.

Also known as Dorcas, an allusion to the kindhearted woman whom the Apostle Peter resurrects from the dead, Leader Bee finds Morton's views appalling:

> And Mr Civilize sit down there in the whiteman house on the whiteman chair with the whiteman tie and cuff-links and wristwatch on telling me: "We can't change our colour, Dorcas, but we can change our attitude. We can't be white, but we can act white." And all I want is to worship God in my way.[86]

While Leader Bee values the black creole church tradition, which celebrates the native expression of Christ's Spirit in the Caribbean experience, Morton sees it as an example of arrested development. At the novel's outset, then, we learn what is at stake for the Bonasse Spiritual Baptists: the freedom to engage in acts of prayer and devotion according to conscience. This stress on religious liberty, especially the high cost to be paid for securing it, links Lovelace's congregation to its seventeenth- and eighteenth-century forebears in faith.

In Leader Bee's absence, the Charlotte high school principal invites Mother Eva to send Reggie, her brightest son, to the school. When she hears about Morton's attitude, though, she expresses confusion. If schooling produces so-called civilized gentlemen, like Morton, who quickly and conveniently forget their roots, then why acquire an education? Faced with indifference from her own kind as well as the inability to worship freely, she sees her setbacks as part of discipleship's cost, her own cross to bear, and so she sings—albeit in the safety of her own home, away from the establishment's disapproving glare. She sings to God.[87]

Both Mother Eva and Leader Bee believe that the political and educational authorities have failed the Bonasse people. And this failure forms the wine of astonishment that the Spiritual Baptists are forced to drink, evinced by the way the church gathers one Sunday and, in Mother Eva's estimation, "when we open our mouths, it was to sing the hymn in the same lawful way, the same dead way, without bellringing or handclapping or shouting."[88] The *Prohibition* inhibits the group's emotionalism; here, in Mother Eva's cheerless words, we find an example of colonialism's soul destruction. Other characters feel similarly bereft. Besides Leader Bee and Mother Eva, no one more than Bolo, the community's prize-winning stickfighter, senses the imperial evil that surrounds and threatens to engulf the community. He attends church one Sunday, for example, and decries its timidly obsequious response to the Spirit's movement.

Described as a "special man," not just by women such as Sister Lucy and Miss Ellen, but by the entire community, Bolo laments the way the *Prohibition* has forced his church to become overly formal, even mannered. But ecclesiastical affectation is not his only concern. When the government bans the Carnival, the festival where he triumphs over other stickfighters, and the Americans establish their Base on the island, he feels deprived of effectiveness, spirit, or verve.[89] New money seeps into the community and

. . . fellars spring up from nowhere with clean fingernails and pointy tip shoes; lean fellars in zoot suits with long silver chains looping from the fob of their trousers to their side pocket, who, to see their eyes, you have to lift up their hat brims. What women see in them, I [Mother Eva] don't know; but these was the new heroes. And now, men who used to be dying for Bolo to take a drink with them was passing him in the street without a word of greeting. Bolo feel it. He feel it.[90]

For their part, the American soldiers recreate the carnivalesque environment in the Buntin shop; here, Bolo engages in mock stickfighting and Clem, the "chantwell," strums his guitar and sings his songs.[91] Yet this arrangement only alienates Bolo from the skill that once made him toast of the town. In mock stickfighting, it was "as if he was trying to dance back something that was going away," Mother Eva bemoans.[92]

Colonialism explains Bolo's "hyper-masculine behavior," according to literary critic Patrick Colm Hogan.[93] When the Spiritual Baptists respond to governmental repression meekly, for example, Bolo becomes angry, and he assaults those who serve as the novel's mimeticists, the black colonial immitators, who threaten his community's existence.[94] On this latter point, Bolo clashes with Mother Eva's cousin, Mitchell, who works his way into the American soldiers' affections and benefits from this alliance financially. Mitchell lambastes Bolo's conservatism, his apparent inability to move with the times, and Bolo strikes him down. After this manly and triumphant exchange, though, Bolo deteriorates. Walking through the Bonasse streets, "he didn't have that free easy stride, that smooth fluent joyful walk that we use to so admire. A stiffness come over him."[95]

In theological terms, Bolo counteracts his "disvalued self," to use Davis' term, by looking to Leader Bee's Spiritual Baptist church. Bolo wants the Shouters, whom he sees as the protector of traditional values, to mount some kind of resistance to the imperialism that emanates from the Estate and the Base. But as Mother Eva explains, Bolo's strategy fails. The government's "steady persecution," the direct result of the *Prohibition* itself, disables the congregation, and this state of affairs temporarily weakens the church's sense of confidence and possibility.[96] I say "temporarily" because, as we will see, the rest of Lovelace's story chronicles how the Bonasse Spiritual Baptists, with Bolo's improbable help, slowly but surely emerge from the tyranny that threatens them, ready to repair and affirm each other as well as welcome the Spirit's movement into an unknown future.

"We Church"

When Mother Eva first describes the Bonasse congregation, in the section of Lovelace's novel entitled "We Church," she helps us situate her local and gathered group of Spiritual Baptists within the broad historical and theological context outlined earlier in this chapter. First, we learn that blacks own and govern everything about their assembly. "We have this church," she announces. "The walls make out of mud, the roof covered with carrat leaves: a simple hut with no steeple or cross or acolytes or white priests or latin ceremonies. But is our own. Black people own it."[97] Caribbean theologians like Erskine emphasize the need to decolonize theology, and he thinks this task involves developing and instantiating a sense of black personhood and peoplehood before God. Self-governance is essential to this assignment, as we have seen, and from Erskine's perspective, we might say that the Bonasse Spiritual Baptists are on their way toward decolonizing theology. "Government ain't spent one cent helping us to build it or to put bench in it or anything; the bell that we ring when we call to the Spirit is our money that pay for it. So we have this church," Mother Eva declares.[98]

Second, we discover that the Bonasse believers affirm absolute and unqualified fidelity to the Bible. "We preach the Word and who have ears to hear, hear."[99] Many hear very well. Leader Bee's scripturally sound sermons work, Mother Eva notes, because they take the indigent and voiceless lives of those listening to them seriously. "We carry the Word to the downtrodden and the forgotten and the lame and the beaten, and we touch black people soul."[100] A theology of decolonization stresses solidarity with the poor, notes Caribbean theologian Moseley, and it does so by using the Bible's resources to emphasize God's own solidarity with human suffering through Jesus Christ's suffering.[101] Jesus Christ stands out as the primary mediator of God's grace in Lovelace's novel, and atonement's efficacy pulsates at the heart of the Shouters theological self-understanding.[102]

Third, Mother Eva reveals that her church upholds the doctrine of the priesthood of all believers:

> . . . after the service finish the brethren could discuss together how the corn growing, how the children doing, for what price cocoa selling, and the men could know which brother they should lend a hand to the coming week, and the sisters could find out who sick from the

congregation so we could go and sit with her a little and help out with
the cooking for her children or the washing or the ironing. And it was
nice at last to have a place to be together, where you could hear your
voice shouting hallelujah and feel the Spirit speading over the Church
as the brethren sing and dance and catch the power.[103]

The group's tendency to "catch the power" attracts followers. As Mother
Eva explains, however, no one is ever forced to join the Bonasse congregation. Rather, the initiation process is such that individuals first have
visions and dreams, which incline them to approach Leader Bee for
guidance. Genuine converts are baptized by total immersion in the local
river and then put out "on the Mournin' Ground to pray and fast and
wait for the Lord."[104] As the anthropologists Herskovits and Herskovits
informed us earlier, this ritual often creates the conditions for the new
member to feel called to serve in one of the nineteen positions of ecclesiastical headship within the Spiritual Baptist tradition.

Finally, we come to appreciate the relevance of an African heritage,
especially its cultural forms, in this congregation's ecclesial awareness
and formation. "We [the church] was going good—not the best but good
enough for a people who bring our bare hands with us from Africa and
go through trials and tribulations enough to make a weaker people surrender," Mother Eva proclaims.[105] And even after the government prohibits the Spiritual Baptists from worshiping freely:

> Enough of us remain to sing the hymns and clap hands and make a
> joyful noise unto the Lord who keep us and strengthen us to reach
> another day in this tribulation country far away from Africa, the home
> that we don't know.[106]

Here, Mother Eva ties the Bonasse church's African sensibility to the
transatlantic slave trade and British colonial history. She also connects
it to how her fellow believers worship "in ways that their African forefa-
thers possessed by the spirits of African traditional religion would have
found not entirely unfamiliar," to cite historian Stanley once again.[107]
Such improvised, bustling tumult, so seemingly typical of the Spiritual
Baptist tradition, throbs throughout *The Wine of Astonishment*, and in
Lovelace's hands, this lively experientialism becomes an opportunity
to espouse the Caribbean's cultural ties to Africa. When God's Spirit
possesses Sister Lucas, for example, she walks "in that sweet, graceful,
noble walk that black women alone have from generations of carrying
on their head buckets of water and baskets of cocoa."[108]

Leader Bee's followers, like all Spiritual Baptists, creolize their faith, blending disparate elements of traditional African religions with Western Protestant nonconformism. This native incarnation of Christ's Spirit helps them acquire, at least for a while, some sense of their full dignity as human beings before God. But then the authorities not only tamp down their fervor, they outlaw their activities altogether. "One day we was Baptist," Mother Eva announces, "the next day we was criminals."[109] Symbolized in the novel by Corporal Prince, the tall and intimidating black man who watches over the Bonasse church, the government runs a smear campaign against the Spiritual Baptists, one that equates their rites and rituals with Satanism. And their persecution works. The 1917 *Prohibition* marginalizes the Bonasse congregation; it literally and figuratively pushes them to the village's edge.

Working from this disenfranchised position, the church mimics their early Baptist forebears in faith by becoming countercultural, meeting in secret to discuss how to protest unjust laws and to worship according to conscience. God's Spirit moves among the believers, Mother Eva informs us, though it is with varying degrees of success. Women and men continue to dream and have visions, even organize hush-hush baptisms, but Prince creates problems for the believers, problems that become so huge that Bolo suggests killing him.[110] For his part, Leader Bee preaches the contrary; in fact, he takes the diplomatic route and approaches Morton.

Once revered by his community as a Moses figure, Morton now symbolizes what happens when someone acquires an education and cuts his community moorings. He sees the Spiritual Baptists as gullible, even uncouth, and, like his mother, he favors an established or socially acceptable form of Christian commitment, which explains why he leaves the Bonasse congregation to join the Roman Catholic church. Troubled by his departure, the villagers find Morton suspicious; Bolo dislikes him acutely. Morton competes with Bolo for the affections of Eulalie Clifford, the village darling, and wins. When Morton abandons Eulalie shortly after she gives birth to his child and then takes up with a light-skinned lady, Bolo's enmity for Morton only intensifies. Mother Eva concludes that the tension between them reflects a change in the village itself. Bolo plays the part of the warrior, at least in her mind, and Morton signifies the scholar. In traditional African cultures, the warrior often serves as the chief figure, the man others in the community consult and revere. But in Bonasse, the young man with academic credentials, the intellectual, represents the future. The village teeters, therefore, on the edge of an abyss. It stands poised to lose its cultural identity, mostly because Morton, the ardent mimic of the colonial bourgeoisie, now displays more influence than Bolo, whose stickfighting skills seem like a relic from the past.[111]

Reflecting the thoughts of an emotionally frayed pastor to a deeply divided people, Leader Bee's sermons show that, while he shares the community's frustration, especially with Morton's studied indifference, he disagrees with Bolo's urge to kill Prince. In light of the *Prohibition*, Leader Bee preaches emotional and liturgical restraint. His cautionary words work, at least initially, but then various congregants, particularly Bolo, begin to realize that concession leads ineluctably to inauthenticity. In Mother Eva's words,

> But the more we go on with this type of service, this soft praying and quiet singing, and not ringing the bell or catching the Spirit, the more we realize that we ain't solving the problem. All we was doing was taking away the ceremonies natural to our worship. All we was doing was watering down the beauty and appeal of our church.[112]

Aware that his church had become a place where believers "have to stifle hallelujah in our throat," and conscious of Bolo's presence in the pew, "like a hard question staring in everybody face," Leader Bee decides to change.[113] He reads the Bible, catches the Spirit, and then resolves to break the law.[114] At one Sunday meeting he mounts the pulpit and lets loose his stammering tongue. Since he reads and interprets the Scriptures from his social location, Leader Bee practices "calypso exegesis," to use Trinidadian theologian George M. Mulrain's term.[115] Here the interpreter's Caribbean culture shapes the Bible's contemporary application:

> The experience for Caribbean people has been one of slavery, oppression, colonialism, suffering, victimization, marginalization, anonymity. Hence, when Caribbean people read the Bible, the way they interpret the message will be affected by their knowledge of these situations. They read the Bible as the book which helps to reveal God. As far as they are concerned, the only God who makes sense to them, and whom they can communicate to their sisters and brothers in the faith, is a God who understands what they and their forebears have experienced and who sides with them in their sufferings.[116]

Like so many calypso interpreters, Leader Bee filters his own congregation's crisis through a contextual or vernacular reading of the Bible. He parallels his church's oppression with oppression in ancient Israel, for example, and the Bonasse believers soon see themselves mirrored in Scripture.

Their reflection also appears when Leader Bee links how God's Spirit possesses the first Christians at Pentecost, as recorded in Acts 2, with his own community's ecstatic experience of divine possession. Traditional African religions address religious possession, as I have noted, and yet, by connecting the Spiritual Baptists not only to Africa but to the first followers of Jesus, who also struggled with legal authorities (as Acts makes clear), Lovelace makes his main point exceedingly well: colonial oppression threatens Christian as well as African convictions.[117]

Not everyone favors this Spirit-filled, mother tongue theology of liberation and hope. Prince breaks up the meeting and arrests the entire congregation. The Shouters seem energized and defiant, though, for they sing hymns as they march to the local police station. When Morton endorses Prince's actions, Bolo reacts violently, but several officers beat Bolo remorselessly. The church itself takes a verbal thrashing when Leader Bee represents them before the Shouter-scorning magistrate. "You have the gall to stand and argue," the judge complains, "when all you doing is leading these poor people astray, making them jump and prance and shout to the devil as if you still in the wilds of Africa."[118]

Possessed by colonialism, to use a very deliberate trope, the church lapses once more. And then several events help the Spiritual Baptists regain their strength. The Second World War ends, for example, and the Americans leave the Base to return home. "By the time the war end," Mother Eva notes, "we in Bonasse was a different people."[119] Black nationalism intensifies, free elections occur, and the independence movement's first birth-pangs are felt throughout the island. As if seeing the writing on the wall, the British leave abruptly. Not unsurprisingly, the departure of the imperial forces leaves a leadership vacuum. In this new situation, education becomes all important. Morton has learning, for example, but Rufus George, his political opponent, does not. Since Bolo languishes in prison, the scholar displaces the warrior, so to speak, and the people elect Morton to lead the village. Life under Morton changes everything, and when the authorities eventually release Bolo, his reentry into Bonasse village life fails miserably. Although he tries to regain his status through stickfighting, for example, he attacks the people and their instruments during Carnival time. Stickfighting no longer pro-vides the cultural identity it once used to, and the "new Bolo" turns to alcohol and violence.[120]

"The Church Comes Back"

A onetime member of the Bonasse Shouters congregation but now an Anglican, Brother Primus approaches Leader Bee and Mother Eva for help in setting his daughters free from Bolo's clutches. When Leader Bee tries to reason with Bolo, however, Bolo takes him to task. It is strange, he protests, that the church seems passive to social injustice and yet livid over personal turpitude—as if individual failings take precedence over structural sin. Bolo thinks this situation is Bonasse's real tragedy, that the village's political timidity proves that the long-gone colonialists still continue to enslave the people.[121]

In the midst of this faceoff, Mother Eva dreams about Jesus. Her dream weaves Bolo into the action, giving us the impression that he, like Christ, will soon serve as the community's sacrifice. When the police confront and shoot Bolo, he falls to the ground, landing in a cruciform pose. The analogy seems complete. Only the mournful Muriel, Brother Primus' youngest daughter, cements the connection as she rushes to Bolo's body and assumes the position of a woman at the foot of the cross.[122]

"The church is the key to everything," Mother Eva states, shortly after Bolo's funeral, and she urges her community to realize that "the church is the root for us to grow out from, the church is Africa in us, black in us."[123] With such brief but stirring remarks, Mother Eva illus-trates the main point behind Josiah Ulysses Young III's Pan-African theology:

> The Spirit of recreation is moving across the waters of the Atlantic in a transcontextual consciousness of the peasantry and the underclass. Ancestral values of healing and wholeness are in the Spirit gaining ascendency over a privileged class who have turned their backs on the African heritage. New life is signified in the redemptive meaning of the humanity of God enshrined in the modalities of being of the black poor. In God the Creator-Liberator, the Incarnate Sufferer and the Revolutionary, the black poor receive in the heart a liberating gift of struggle that saves them from the absurdity of assuming the deformed image of their oppressors.[124]

Even if the Spiritual Baptists struggle to internalize Mother Eva's plea to retain the black, creole ecclesial tradition, the novel ends on a high note. The government repeals the *Prohibition* in 1951, and the congregation reassembles yet seems liturgically lifeless. Leader Bee and Mother Eva groan inwardly. Then, after church one Sunday morning, they stop and listen to a steel band playing nearby. The pulsating rhythms call to mind Trinidad and Africa, and they hear in the sounds that surround them an evocation of the same Spirit that once energized their people. This music makes everything seem generally good, "like resurrection morning," and the moment leaves them filled with the hope that the Bonasse believers will soon welcome and repair each other, recover their self-esteem, and welcome the Spirit's movement into an exciting future.[125]

Literary critic Norman Reed Cary claims that only an unwise reader thinks the novel's ending advocates religious faith. "This may seem the case at the beginning, when Eva accounts for persecution by trusting in God's providence. By the end, though, the answer that Eva proposes is less theocentric, for she has observed the particular suffering of two men [Bee and Bolo]."[126] I disagree. By the novel's end, one finds oneself invited to see God's Spirit poured out, especially in Bolo and Bee, the novel's Christ figures, yet also in a wider kenosis, in the music that marks Trinidad's soundscape.[127] Christianity is an incarnational religion; here, the holy is eternally renewed in the common. So I fail to see how Mother Eva's "less theocentric" self-understanding leads ineluctably to a purely "humanistic" reading of *The Wine of Astonishment*. Surely she knows, as most Christians ought to know, that the generous Spirit of God, breath of creation itself, blows and empowers where it will. I thus read the novel's end theologically: Leader Bee and Mother Eva seem open to the gracious gifting of God's Spirit, to the empowering presence of God's Spirit, and to the exploratory leading of God's Spirit.

Two final observations seem appropriate at this point. Both comments come together to illustrate how Spiritual Baptist theology expresses the Christian gospel against an African cultural background. First, I think Lovelace arrives at his story's conclusion and upholds the Spiritual Baptists for embodying an ecclesiology based around gestures of belonging. Individuals articulate their voice in this community, and women find opportunities to advance themselves. Through the relevance of their cultural forms, moreover, the Shouters eschew Western ecclesial mimicry, and they decolonize theology. In their struggle to cultivate and promote their full dignity as human beings before God, they also show themselves faithful to Christ's emancipatory and reconciling Spirit. Davis' words, albeit intended to summarize Caribbean ecclesiology in general, thus serve as an instructive gloss on the Bonasse congregation:

> We can do no better than to recognize that the Caribbean experience, with its shifting sands and changing circumstances, is always faced with tremendous paradoxes. There are crises of almost insurmountable proportions, and yet the people are thriving. There appears to be little to celebrate, and yet they sustain a Carnival spirit with which they infect all who deal with them. Crisis gives them a strong sense of resilience and survival, and Carnival gives them a strong sense of beauty and creativity. Religion serves as the integrative factor in all this, and the churches provide the avenues for ritual, ceremonies, hymnody, proclamation of the Word, communal discourse, a sense of belonging and spiritual expression, as well as a reason to hope for brighter days.[128]

Second, the allusion to Easter Sunday at the novel's end makes it quite clear that Christianity resides at the center of Leader Bee's and Mother Eva's self-understanding. But let us not forget that the Bonasse believers, like all Spiritual Baptists, Africanize their Christianity. If we look carefully, we will notice that *The Wine of Astonishment*'s final pages reference an artistic or material dimension of Africa's history and heritage—the drum—that comes back to life, so to speak, after repeated attempts to kill it. Banned in the late nineteenth century by the Trinidadian colonial government, African skin drums died their cultural death only to experience rebirth in the form of calypso steel drums. This death-rebirth motif testifies to the enduring legacy of traditional African religions within the African diaspora. Hogan writes,

> This common Caribbean view that African tradition is a spirit that persists and never dies is not mere metaphor or wishful thinking. It derives from a common sense of a history in which African traditions survived despite displacement and continued repression, a sense that, for centuries, there has been a recognizable continuity in Afro-Caribbean practices, leading all the way back to Africa.[129]

Knowing that Lovelace ends his novel with allusions to Africa *and* Christianity inspires me to reflect theologically and, ultimately, to ask a question that many Christians, especially the Finnish theologian Veli-Matti Kärkkäinen, are asking today: how will Christianity's rapid expansion near or south of the equator, in the so-called Global South—which includes Africa and Trinidad—shape our understanding of the church's future? It is to this question that I now turn.

THE CHURCH AND/IN THE GLOBAL SOUTH

Christianity's population and power pendulum has in more recent years swung away from the Western Hemisphere and toward the Southern Hemisphere. We have witnessed the remarkable accession to Christian faith in tropical Africa, for example, and the largest recession of faith in Europe.[130] The net result of this arresting development, which shows no sign of tapering off, is that Global South Christianity now represents normative Christianity. Such an occurrence requires us to rethink things theologically.[131] While a detailed description of this rethinking lies beyond the scope of my book, it is possible to run through some of the ways Global South Christians, like Trinidad's Spiritual Baptists, now shape the way we think about the church. Here are two issues to consider.

First, Global South Christians accentuate Christianity's incarnationality, and perhaps even bring it back into focus for Western Christians, by stressing the way God speaks in culture-specific terms. The word takes flesh in particular realities. And the gospel's success throughout history, if success is the right word, lies in its inherent vernacularizing tendencies—its basic ability, in other words, to tabernacle itself in and adapt itself to many languages and cultures. By professing Christianity in their mother tongue, then, either through Bible translations and/or indigenous cultural idioms as well as practices, Global South Christians witness to Christianity's origins as an embodied faith, missiologist Lamin Sanneh claims.[132] Trinidad's Spiritual Baptists utilize African and Caribbean cultural forms, as we have seen, and so testify to how God works within certain cultures to incarnate Godself both situationally and concretely. When Global South Christians accentuate and appreciate incarnationality, then, they challenge Western Christians to abandon any and all sense of their own intellectual or institutional privilege.

Second, Global South Christians decolonize the faith by empowering themselves theologically and ecclesiastically. Such self-determination shows up in attempts to cultivate, articulate, and celebrate local faith stories, and it appears in grassroots communities who uphold local church agency. Trinidad's Spiritual Baptists decolonize the faith, as we have seen, by valorizing the way God moves among them, by dignifying ancient or ancestral modalities, and by refusing to mimic European or North American church authorities. In other words, the Shouters proclaim the Spirit's energetic presence in their version of the gospel story—a story that provides, as we have seen, a sense of black personhood and peoplehood before God. The tale of the Spiritual Baptists is a local tale, tied as it is to Trinidad and Tobago's recent colonial and postcolonial history, but it is also part of the wider, unfolding narrative of the church. When Global South Christians read the Bible from their location and see things through their eyes, not the eyes of those far removed from their contexts, they challenge Western Christians to adjust their own vision, to focus less on the so-called Great Christian Thinkers—men such as Luther, Calvin, and Zwingli—and, instead, to examine those so-called fringe figures, people like Mother Eva and Leader Bee, women and men who take their stand in some remote or difficult place in God's world, and live the cost of discipleship in a quiet way. Historian Philip Jenkins writes,

> Particularly over the past quarter century, the history of Christianity has moved enthusiastically downward, to focus on the lived experience of ordinary believers, no less than the great deeds of celebrated leaders. In more senses than one, it has also moved outward, recognizing that the Christian experience cannot be contained within denominations but must be explored to the margins of orthodoxy and beyond. And perhaps most of all, it has expanded geographically, with a powerful emphasis on the global, non-Euro/American experience. Living in a world in which the most dramatic Christian growth occurs in Africa, Asia, and Latin America, how could historians do otherwise?[133]

With the advent of Global South Christianity, illustrated by Trinidad's Spiritual Baptists (but by no means confined to them), non-Western theological literacy may prove to be intellectually, spiritually, and pastorally necessary if we are to understand and appreciate the worldwide church's complexity.

CONCLUSION

Lovelace champions the Spiritual Baptists for the way they work to put reparation theory into practice, laboring to create for black people "a sense of belonging, a psychic ease, the valuing of our contributions, a space in which to grow and the natural acknowledgment of our worth and dignity as human beings."[134] In ecclesiological terms, we might say that the Shouters, committed as they are to a covenantal ethics of reconciliation and responsibility, come together and labor both to emanicipate the disvalued black self and to decolonize theology. Whether in fact or fiction, this growing congregation manifests the body of Christ in their local and lively experience; struggling but resourceful, they, like so many Global South Christians, stand ready to reshape the way all Christians think and act.

Since many Western Christians lack the time and the resources to travel to, and live among, Global South Christians, I like to view those novels that offer flesh and blood descriptions of indigenous responses to the gospel as exciting alternatives. Novels can never take the place of the real thing, to be sure, but if the reader delves into the story and then accepts the invitation to migrate mentally, the opportunity to see life differently heightens and the chance to witness God's generous Spirit intensifies.[135]

For Further Reading

Kortright Davis' *Emancipation Still Comin': Explorations in Caribbean Emancipatory Theology* (Maryknoll, N.Y.: Orbis Books, 1990) ranks as one of the classic examples of Caribbean theology in the late twentieth century. Noel Leo Erskine's *Decolonizing Theology: A Caribbean Perspective* (Maryknoll, N.Y.: Orbis Books, 1981) is another standard in the field. Susan VanZanten Gallagher's edited volume, *Postcolonial Literature and the Biblical Call for Justice* (Jackson: University Press of Mississippi, 1994) brings together twelve essays on a range of postcolonial writers and shows how their work resonates with Scripture's imperative to treat all peoples lovingly, hospitably, and fairly. While Lovelace is not featured in this volume, readers will discover writers like him, writers who pose provocative questions to the contemporary church. Frances Henry's *Reclaiming African Religions in Trinidad: The Socio-Political Legitimation of the Orisha and the Spiritual Baptist Faiths* (Kingston, Jamaica: University of West Indies Press, 2003) shows how the Shouters emerged from being the poor and the downtrodden within Trinidad, persecuted by colonial authorities, to enjoying legal as well as social acceptance. Philip Jenkins' *The Next Christendom: The Coming of Global Christianity* (Oxford: Oxford University Press, 2002) highlights the issues, personalities, and trends at the heart of the current debate concerning Christianity's explosive growth in the Global South. His more recent book, *The New Faces of Christianity: Believing the Bible in the Global South* (Oxford: Oxford University Press, 2006) explores the fresh and invigorating hermeneutical work emerging from Christians in the Southern Hemisphere. Veli-Matti Kärkkäinen's *An Introduction to Ecclesiology: Ecumenical, Historical and Global Perspectives* (Downers Grove, Ill.: InterVarsity Press, 2002) offers an introductory survey of ecclesiological themes in Christian history, with an emphasis on contemporary ecclesiologists. *A History of Christianity in Asia, Africa, and Latin America, 1450–1990*, edited by Klaus Koschorke, Frieder Ludwig, and Mariano Delgado (Grand Rapids, Mich.: W. B. Eerdmans, 2007) presents a comparative history of Christianity in three different parts of the world. To my knowledge, it is the first documentary source book of its kind. Earl Lovelace's *Growing in the Dark: Selected Essays*, edited by Funso Aiyejina (Trinidad and Tobago: Lexington Trinidad, 2003) provides us with a fascinating glimpse into the range of Lovelace's mind. Rebecca Moore's *Voices of Christianity: A Global Introduction* (Boston: McGraw-Hill, 2006) stands out as one of the best of the new readers in Christian history and doctrine, offering a forum for those international voices that Europeans and North Americans have often ignored. And finally, Lamin Sanneh's *Whose Religion Is Christianity?: The Gospel beyond the West* (Grand Rapids, Mich.: W. B. Eerdmans, 2003) uses a question and answer format to explain non-Western Christianity's impact on Western theology.

SELECTED WEB SITES

1. http://library2.nalis.gov.tt/Default.aspx?tabid=174

    This site provides an instructive overview of the history of the Spiritual Baptists or Shouters.

2. http://www.oikoumene.org/en/home.html

    Web site for the World Council of Churches, which formed in 1948.

3. http://www.bwanet.org

   Home of the Baptist World Alliance.

4. http://www.postcolonialweb.org

   A site devoted to postcolonial literature in English.

5. http://demo.lutherproductions.com/historytutor/basic/main_menu.htm

   Connected with Luther Seminary in St. Paul, Minnesota, this site features a "Christian History Tutor," focusing on major periods in the church's ongoing development.

6. http://www.div.ed.ac.uk/research_worldchris

   The University of Edinburgh, Scotland, has a site connected to its Centre for the Study of Christianity in the non-Western world.

5

ESCHATOLOGY

Paul Thigpen's *My Visit to Hell*

Pulitzer prize-winning author Ernest Becker holds that since we often refuse to think or talk about death, we frequently deny it.[1] We fear the unknown, he says, and sometimes fearing what we do not know is worse than fearing what we do. For those who do think and talk about it, death's unavoidability stimulates several questions whose answers do not come easily, if they come at all. Is there continued conscious existence after bodily death? What is the soul? Do we return to earth reincarnated? What is the resurrected body? Is there a heaven? Is there a hell? Such questions are religious. And today all the world religions believe in life after death, even if their eschatologies vary considerably.[2] With its root in the Greek word *eschaton*, which means final or last, Christian eschatology denotes the many and varied ideas that Christians entertain about time's or history's end.[3] Some envisage the end as otherworldly. Others view it as this-worldly. Either way, many associate the end with at least four things: death, judgment, heaven, and hell.

A robust belief in God's personal qualities, such as loving mercy and tender forgiveness, is one reason why Christians declare that God cares for us, people whom God created with the purpose of relating to God. Although we can relate to God on this side of the grave, Christians generally maintain that life after death promises this relationship's complete fulfillment. Jesus Christ's life, death, and resurrection grounds the hope of eternal life, they declare.[4] Judgment is an important issue also. For many centuries theologians have taught that heaven is God's reward for those who live life virtuously and hell is God's punishment for those who live life viciously.[5] Yet some Christians now question hell's reality. They believe that God will never abandon those whom God creates and loves, and so they prefer to think of heaven and hell as states of mind rather than places—a sense of closeness to God, that is, or else alienation from God. Others hold fast to belief in heaven and hell as literal places. As I write, it is Halloween; numerous churches across the United States are inviting non-Christians to so-called hell houses, which Christians present not simply as an alternative to haunted houses but as an intentionally graphic and gloomy pointer to what *really and truly* awaits the unsaved dead.[6]

Among the modern-day Christian literalists, it seems that many consult novels as well as the Bible when discussing the afterlife. Certainly, over the last fifteen or twenty years, book publishers have gone out of their way to promote "fictional eschatologies," and their frenetic work has paid dividends. Consider the astonishing success of the Tim LaHaye and Jerry Jenkins *Left Behind* series, Alice Sebold's *Lovely Bones*, and Mitch Albom's *The Five People You Meet in Heaven*. Such bestsellers are often discussed in Adult Christian Education settings. Many have been successfully adapted for the screen, and literary critics as well as religious historians and theologians have written about them at some length.[7] Yet there are other, less famous but no less imaginative examples in this broadly construed "end times fiction" genre. I plan to focus on one of them—Paul Thigpen's *My Visit to Hell* (aka: *Gehenna*), which retells Dante Alighieri's *Inferno* for our postmodern age.[8]

This chapter on eschatology, my last, appropriately enough, has four major sections. First, I sketch Thigpen's life and literary art. (An interview with him that offers detailed answers to pointed questions about his influences and intent appears in Appendix I, which follows this final chapter.[9]) Second, I engage certain makers and remakers of the Christian doctrine of eschatology, beginning with selected biblical texts and then moving to highlight those thinkers—Augustine, Thomas Aquinas, and Dante—who illumine our reading of Thigpen's novel. In the third and major section I offer a Christian theological reading of *My Visit to Hell*, concentrating on how Thigpen's protagonist, Thomas Travis, and his companion, Capopia (Miss C), help us grasp the author's Thomistic-Dantesque vision of the underworld. A final section situates *My Visit to Hell* within the context of recent theological calls to rehabilitate future eschatology.

PAUL THIGPEN: LIFE AND LITERARY ART

The current editor of *The Catholic Answer*, a national bimonthly magazine that fields inquiries about Roman Catholic faith and practice, Thigpen was born to Presbyterian parents in Savannah, Georgia, in 1954. He attended Yale University where, in 1977, he graduated *summa cum laude*, Phi Beta Kappa, with distinction in religious studies. Thigpen entered the Catholic church in 1993. He wrote about his experience in Patrick Madrid's *Surprised By Truth*, an anthology of Catholic conversion narratives.[10] He later specialized in historical theology and church history at Emory University, where he wrote his doctoral dissertation on Savannah's Catholic lay leadership. Thigpen earned his Ph.D. in 1995. Today, he works as the founder and executive director of The Stella Maris Center for Faith and Culture, a Savannah-based lay initiative of catechesis, evangelization, and cultural transformation for the Catholic church.

Most of Thigpen's adult life has been spent either assisting churches, teaching, or in writing. In the late 1980s, for example, he served as an ordained pastor on the staff of The Life Center, a nondenominational Protestant congregation in Dunwoody, Georgia. He also spent the mid to late 1990s as an assistant professor of religious studies at Southwest Missouri State University (now Missouri State University), as Fellow in Theology at The College of Saint Thomas More in Fort Worth, Texas, and adjunct professor at Savannah's Saint Leo University. A best-selling and award-winning writer, Thigpen has addressed many subjects in diverse genres—apologetics, Bible commentaries, children's books, devotionals, encyclopedia entries, fiction, poetry, and even radio scripts. To date, he has published over thirty books and more than five hundred articles. His work has been translated into several languages.

Besides *My Visit to Hell*, at least two other publications hold the key to Thigpen's eschatology. The first text, released in 2001 as *Blood of the Martyrs, Seed of the Church: Stories of Catholics Who Died for Their Faith*, is not as directly related to the doctrine of eschatology, but its emphasis on heroic suffering and death shows that it is certainly indirectly related. A second book, *Last Words: Final Thoughts of Catholic Saints and Sinners*, was published in 2006. It presents numerous death-bed anecdotes from various Catholics throughout history with Thigpen's own commentary on what we can learn from those who stand at the next world's threshold.

A trilogy evaluating "rapture fiction" also merits our close attention.[11] Here Thigpen indicates why North America has always been fertile soil for apocalyptic religion's seeds, and he convincingly demonstrates how and why the *Left Behind* novels promote anti-Catholicism.[12] One other text, currently in preparation, only promises to amplify Thigpen's eschatological voice.[13]

THE DOCTRINE OF ESCHATOLOGY: A SELECTIVE SKETCH

Christians have debated the doctrine of eschatology for centuries.[14] Many have proposed several different theories to explain the traditional belief in the return of Jesus Christ at the world's end to judge the living and the dead. Heaven and hell often serve important functions in such theories.[15] They signify the consequences of God's judgment, for example, and both the Bible and later literature (e.g. Dante) offer lively, often allegorical accounts of what to expect in either or both places. Consider hell. Frequently understood by Christians as an arena of never-ending anguish, especially for the depraved and dissolute, hell translates three emotionally intense words—the Hebrew *sheol*, the Aramaic *Gehenna*, and the Greek *Hades*—that recur throughout Scripture.[16]

Although there was little notion of personal survival after death among the ancient Israelities, most people prior to the third century B.C.E. seem to have believed in a deep pit—*sheol*—beneath the earth.[17] Belief in this bleak, inhospitable underworld prevailed until around 165 B.C.E., or shortly after the Maccabean Revolution, when many claimed that at the future Judgment Day God would reward those Jews who had died for their faith.[18] New Testament writers eventually developed this notion and, in various passages, we read that God rewards the righteous with paradise or heaven and punishes the unrighteous with hell or *Gehenna*.[19]

The Canaanites once offered children as burnt sacrifices to Molech at *Gehenna* and, when this practice ceased, Jerusalem's people used this valley outside the capital—the Valley of Hinnom—as an unremitting burning ground for the city's garbage. Such fires eventually became the image for hell, with its blistering brutality. Writing around 197, for example, Tertullian describes *Gehenna* as "a store of hidden underground fire for the purposes of punishment."[20]

The dead leave this world and enter the next through the gates of *Hades*. Here their postmortem existence is either boringly dull or unusually painful.[21] Scripture sometimes imagines *Hades* as a prison, a subterranean holding pen, or a resting place that Christ visits.[22] The church's official teaching only adds to such pictures. "He [Christ] descended into hell," the Apostles' Creed declares.[23] Between Good Friday and Easter Sunday, in other words, Christ's soul journeyed to earth's lower parts, into *Hades*, and set sinners free from original sin's penalty. This so-called harrowing of hell is an event that showcases the spiritual suffering that Christ underwent for us, many theologians and artists aver.[24] It also proclaims Christ's victory over the devil.

Talk of hell often leads Christians to speak of the devil—an English word for "slanderer," called *ha-satan* in Hebrew, and rendered *diabolos* in the Septuagint, the Greek translation of the Hebrew Bible. Long and complicated, the devil's, or Satan's, history may be summarized as follows.[25] His name signifies one of his early functions.[26] We meet him in the story of Job, for example, where we are told that in the Heavenly Court, the adversary or, to use modern jargon, "the prosecuting attorney," suggests that Job is only upright because God rewards him so generously.[27] Satan eventually tests Job by making him so ill that he begins to question God's goodness in his hour of need. Divinely appointed to patrol the earth and notify God of covenant violations, Satan is one of God's many sons. Only later does he evolve into an abhorrent character—an influential yet arrogant angel evicted from heaven; defiant toward God as well as envious of us; the underworld's pitiless ruler; cruel leader of a division of demons, who may enter our lives and exploit our inherited weaknesses, and the enemy of Jesus. Given Satan's principal and powerful force, it is little wonder that many Christians across the centuries have taken comfort from God's promise that Satan will sooner or later lose his power and perish in a fiery lake.[28]

At least one early church theologian had a hard time thinking about Satan and hell. In his *De Principiis* (*On First Principles*), for example, the Eastern theologian Origen emphasizes hell's curative pain only; its torment is real, he says, but it is provisional, designed simply to restore our sin-sick souls. Against the notion that recalcitrant evildoers face endless suffering, Origen favors *apocatastasis*, which is theological shorthand for the notion that God will save us all, including the devil and his angels, at time's end.[29] Such universalism contrasts with two other positions on hell—separationism (the belief that God will condemn and sever some sinners from God entirely) and annihilationism (the belief that God will wipe out the wicked completely). Recent theology entertains all three positions, and some thinkers are reviving Origen's ideas. We will notice, however, that Thigpen does not leave the debate over annihilationism so open in *My Visit to Hell*.[30]

Augustine

Augustine arrived in Milan, Italy, in 384 and immediately found himself drawn to the Milanese neo-Platonists, especially their conviction that we can grasp God (or the Good) through our own mind's resources.[31] By 396, however, Augustine had come to believe differently. Reading the Apostle Paul taught him that since we have inherited Adam's original sin, and thus fallen short of God's initial design for our lives, reason alone is insufficient for the task of grasping God's holy complexity. We need divine grace.[32]

Although we are created to serve God, we often settle for less, becoming citizens not of the City of God, to use Augustine's language, but of the earthly or secular city instead.[33] In this other city, we fail to adore God unreservedly. "Original sin," to cite Thomas Merton's gloss on Augustine's position, is "an act of spiritual apostasy from the contemplative vision and love of God," which breaks the link between ourselves and the divine.[34] Expressed differently, Augustine holds that we habitually try to deny our createdness by seeking to create ourselves. Yet when we rely on our own resources, not God's, we display our pride. The root of all evil, pride causes us to fall under the control of the devil who, in his envy for us, personifies pride's viciousness. If we are to be liberated from such captivity, then we must acknowledge our need for divine grace. Trusting in God's unmerited favor sets us free to embody the *caritas*, or love of God and neighbor, that Augustine sees as our divine purpose.

God's grace entered history in Jesus of Nazareth, the Christ, which means that Jesus is our reason to trust God. Through faith in Jesus, together with submission to the church that represents Christ's mystical body on earth, we become citizens of the City of God. Jesus is the only road to eternal life. All other roads lead to hell. Death is not the end, then, and Augustine's eschatological hope relies, not on neo-Platonic philosophy, but on faith in the risen Lord. Such faith makes sense, Augustine states, because we can show how and why Scripture grounds it, the church guarantees it, and reason justifies it. The saints, who trust and love God, will experience their bodily resurrection at history's end and enjoy eternal happiness in heaven, the City of God. The wicked, despite all objections, will face eternal punishment in hell, the devil's city.[35]

Augustine's eschatology, which he crafted by combining biblical images of God's ultimate justice with early Christian theories of the afterlife, appeared in the 400s. Death divides our mortal body from our immortal soul, he teaches, and follows from the spiritual apostasy that is original sin. When we die and cross the threshold, as it were, God judges our vice and virtue immediately. Augustine subscribes to a literal heaven, where the godly are rewarded for their faithfulness with the unspeakably glorious ability to see God face to face. He also believes in a literal hell, a pit where the ungodly are rightly as well as severely penalized, not annihilated, and where it is no longer possible for them to secure God's forgiveness for their sin.

The devil is the angel of the pit. God authored the created universe, Augustine maintains, but one of God's angels could not accept his createdness and, when his demands for equal powers were not met, the angel and his followers waged war in heaven. Not surprisingly, this compelling mental image eventually found its way into literature. "Better to reign in Hell," Milton's rebel angel Satan says in the epic poem *Paradise Lost*, "than serve in Heav'n."[36] Note that Augustine's view of the devil, which Milton and others accept, avoids imagining life dualistically. The dualist picture of the universe sees everything as an arena in which two opposing and equal impulses contest each other eternally. God's universe is fundamentally good, Augustine declares, which means that evil is a privation, or absence, of the good. In other words, God created the devil good and, like us, free to choose any course of action. But the devil freely elected to change or distort his nature by asserting his equality with God; he fell from his goodness, then, and became God's enemy. As the perfect man whom God admits as an acceptable substitute for our sinful ways, Jesus defeats the devil and so reconciles us to God. At the general resurrection that marks the world's end, Jesus will appear again to judge the living and the dead, Augustine upholds. Before such time, though, many will occupy purgatory, viewed as another stage, between earth and heaven, where souls may be purged, or purified through penance, and made ready for heaven.[37] Medieval theologians formalized the doctrine of purgatory in 1253.

Augustine's eschatology eventually became the theological default mode for the Roman Catholic church, and almost every other group in Christian history has had it in mind when thinking through their own teaching on the matter. Centuries after Augustine, Aquinas elaborated on the ideas of his forebear in faith, and some of these ideas now command our attention.

Aquinas

God creates and intends everything, but especially us, to unite to Godself, which means God is life's efficient and final cause, according to Aquinas.[38] Put differently: what is it in me that causes me to be alive? It is God. Created out of nothing, we are most authentically ourselves when we relate to the divine power on which we depend. And I am most alive, most truly myself, when I convert to the love of God and cultivate *caritas*, the charity of outpouring love, toward others. Sin's awful and abiding tragedy, at least from this perspective, is that we craft and sustain our identities apart from God.[39] Theologian Robert Barron drives the point home:

> And is it not the case that so much of the struggle of human life flows from this failure to see properly who we are? Why do we engage in violence? Why are we crippled by hatred and envy? Why do we fall so often into a life-denying self-absorption? Because, I would argue, we don't appreciate our creatureliness. When I realize that I am nothing but an outflow of the divine love, nothing but an ongoing gift, I realize there is no 'self' that requires defense. I am not one being among many fighting for primacy; on the contrary, I am a sheer dependency upon the divine grace. And thus my life need not be an awful struggle for dominance, a continual warfare against God, against nature, against my fellows, all those who threaten my "turf." The wonderful doctrine of creation, as articulated by Thomas Aquinas, enables me to let go, to relax, to find myself in losing myself.[40]

We cannot hope to attain our proper end, union with God, except by grace. To understand what this notion means, however, we must explore how Aquinas distinguishes between "nature" and "grace." Very generally, he uses the former term to signify creation's dependence upon God. Adam's sin corrupts nature, of course, but such corruption does not make it impossible for us to do things by ourselves. What happened in Eden does not obliterate our natural capacities, Aquinas claims. We can reproduce, for example, and build homes. To find our way back to God after the Fall, though, we need sanctifying grace, which directs and moves us to the work proper to us, "the full participation of the divinity," which Aquinas views as humanity's "true bliss."[41]

Grace does not compromise our ontological integrity. As ensouled bodies, we are always at liberty. Even as God sets about transforming us, we remain ourselves, free to make mistakes. If this were not so, grace would appear precipitous, too abrupt to prevent our self-identity's loss. In developing this part of his theology, Aquinas says that God in God's transcendence nonetheless acts immanently in what I freely elect to do, which means that God is the primary cause of an action, like my befriending someone lonely, and I am its secondary cause. Creation, therefore, possesses full integrity.[42]

Like Augustine, whom he often quotes favorably, Aquinas disdains dualism.[43] He thinks an omnibenevolent God created a world marked by marvelous complexity, variety, and integrity. God also created the devil who, for Aquinas, was good, but who has fallen into vice. On this view, evil is not metaphysically substantive, an entity; rather, Aquinas views it as an absence of the good. Evil does not compete with God in any way. It is not a force that is coequal with the divine; evil is lack, lapse, and failure—as such, it is something that God allows to exist, if "exist" is the right word, so that it might yield good.[44]

We live in this world of good and evil as wayfarers. Death separates our souls and bodies, and the soul's judgment follows immediately. If we choose the good and rely on divine grace, then God rewards us by assigning us to heaven. Aquinas also believes in a real and fiery hell, where sinners experience physical as well as mental and spiritual suffering. Purgatory represents an opportunity for us to be made ready for heaven. As Christians, then, we must live with hope, one of the most important theological virtues. Eschatological hope resides not simply in the soul's immortality, though, but in the body's resurrection, which Jesus Christ's second coming will one day facilitate; at this time God will perfect the bodies of the righteous departed. Such radically reconstituted, ensouled bodies will then experience what the Apostles' Creed calls "the life everlasting," the vision of God.[45] Finally, Aquinas upholds Augustine's belief in the so-called pleasures of the abominable fancy, the notion that heaven's blessed will one day celebrate the torture of hell's damned.[46]

Augustine and Aquinas shaped the strong view of hell that I outline above and many now link it with traditional Christianity. Whenever theology appears, though, literature is never far behind. Consider Jesus' parable of the rich man and Lazarus. This simple story paints a picture of the afterlife that made sense to the Jews and the early Christians.[47] Centuries later, Milton's *Paradise Lost* added more detailed thoughts on the same topic. By far the most famous piece of literary eschatology, though, belongs to Dante, the Tuscan theologian in verse.

Dante

Very little is known of Dante's life. Born into an Italian Florentine family in 1265, his father, Alighiero, seems to have acquired considerable wealth through usury and his mother, Bella, died when he was six. Dante was betrothed to Gemma Donati in 1277, shortly after turning 12, and their marriage, which occurred later, produced four children. However, Donati was not the only woman in his life. Literary scholar Peter S. Hawkins thinks Bice di Folco Portinari, an important Florentine who died in 1290, commanded Dante's real devotion, so much so that she represents his model for Beatrice, the poet's Christ-like guide through Paradise.[48] Educated at home, Dante studied the great Roman poets, including Virgil, known for his epic, the *Aeneid*, and by 1295 he had published poetry of his own, verse that effectively launched a new style. Numerous discussions with wandering Dominicans and Franciscans introduced him to the two giants of Christian theology, Augustine and Aquinas.[49] Dante entered local politics at the end of the century but, in early 1302, he became a casualty of civic unrest. He was eventually barred from Florence. Dante spent the next twenty years in exile, moving between various towns in north-central Italy as well as authoring provocative texts, until his death in 1321.

Dante began *The Divine Comedy* during his time in exile, probably around 1308, and then released its three *cantiche* over the next decade or so. *Inferno* was the first to appear, in 1314. Taken as a whole, *The Divine Comedy* describes Dante's pilgrimage through the three arenas of the afterlife, an event that occurs during the three days between Christ's passion and resurrection, the so-called Easter Triduum. Virgil guides Dante through hell and purgatory. But since Virgil lived life paganly, he is obliged to languish in limbo as Dante ascends out of these two arenas and progresses toward paradise. Beatrice picks up where Virgil leaves off, and Dante makes his heaven-bound journey with her assistance.

In the next section I view Thigpen's *My Visit to Hell* as a "postfigurative" novel, because its plot and action is "prefigured" in the mythic pattern associated with Dante's *Inferno*.[50] We must pass through the poem, then, before navigating the novel. [51]

Told by a voyager-narrator, *Inferno* begins on Good Friday, 1300. When we first encounter the poet he is thirty-five, adrift in "a shadowed forest," and surrounded by three ferocious animals, who represent tropes for various temptations. While the sunlit hill affords him a fleeting glimpse of salvation and the "path that does not stray," Dante continues to feel despondent; eventually, Virgil rescues and guides him down an alternative path, one that leads to two of the three eternal arenas that the poet must visit before he sees God face to face. Virgil warns Dante that in the first of these arenas, hell, he will "hear the howls of desperation and see the ancient spirits in their pain, as each of them laments his second death." [52]

Dante then passes through hell's gate, on which he finds the legendary inscription, "abandon every hope, who enter here," and finds himself in the ante-inferno. Populated by "the sorry souls of those who lived without disgrace and without praise," this pre-hell realm also includes "the coward angels" who tried to remain neutral in the heavenly rebellion led by Satan. Neither in nor out of hell, then, these "wretched ones" wander along "the melancholy shore of Acheron." The horseflies and wasps that sting them repeatedly reflect, perhaps, the sharp pang of their conscience. To enter hell completely, Virgil and Dante must use the ferry to cross the river Acheron. The aged "pilot of the livid marsh," Charon, at first refuses to transport Dante, on the grounds that he is a "living soul" rather than a dead one, but Virgil announces that God has "willed" the poet's pilgrimage, and so he and Dante eventually travel to the other side. [53]

Once across the river Acheron, Virgil steers Dante around, down, and through hell's nine concentric circles. And we discover that each new circle signifies more and more troubling layers of evil, ending with the most nefarious one of all, the home of those who betray their benefactors, where Satan resides. While sinners in each particular circle are made eternally miserable by the foremost sin they committed on earth, they justify and express no remorse for their past actions. Various beasts and spirits seek to block Dante's progress through hell; however, Virgil answers them by saying that the poet's journey to the deep has been willed on high.

The journey proper begins in the first circle, also known as limbo, where Dante encounters mostly noble pagans—virtuous souls who, despite their worthiness, either lived before Christ or went to their death unbaptized and outside the church.[54] The lustful reside in the second circle, where violent storms buffet their every move. Tormented by Cerberus, the beast with three throats, the gluttonous live in the third circle. The poet encounters the avaricious and the prodigal in the fourth circle; here, working in opposite directions to each other, they roll weights in semicircles. In the fifth circle, the slimy Styx sullies the wrathful and consumes the sullen. Crossing the Styx, Virgil and Dante then approach hell's lower part, the outset of which is the city of Dis. Entrance into Dis takes them into the sixth circle: "Here are the arch-heretics and those who followed them, from every sect; those tombs are much more crowded than you think."[55] Such false teachers burn in their sepulchres.

Guarded by the Minotaur, the seventh circle accomodates the violent, and is divided into three rings. The outer or first ring includes those who were violent against their neighbors; such sinners are immersed in a river of boiling blood. The centaur Nessus helps Dante and Virgil cross the river and enter the middle or second ring, home to those who were violent against themselves or against their possessions. Here vicious dogs chase as well as dismember the profligates, and the suicides appear as malformed, lifeless trees. The third or inner ring is composed of three zones for three sets of sinners—the violent against God, the blasphemers; the violent against nature, the sodomites; and the violent against art, the usurers. Fiery sands scorch each and every malefactor.

Dante and Virgil reach circle eight with the help of a winged monster, Geryon, and here they encounter the fradulent, who are located in a place called Malebolge. The poets find that Malebolge has ten pouches or ditches, each one corresponding to a certain type of fraud; seducers reside in the first pouch, for example, and falsifiers are punished in the tenth. Here, sinners are beset with strange diseases, covered in excrement, engrossed in boiling pitch, or else nailed to the floor. In the ninth circle, which the giant Antaeus helps Dante and Virgil enter, those who betray their friends and benefactors are frozen in an ice-cold lake, also known as Cocytus, and suffer in one of four concentric zones. The first zone, named for the biblical Cain, is for those who betray their family. Traitors to country or city, indeed any political organization, are housed in the second zone, named for Antenor, who betrayed his native Troy to the Greeks. Labeled to evoke the duplicitous captain of Jericho, Ptolemy, who invited people to a banquet and murdered them there, zone three contains those who betray their guests. The fourth and final zone, Judecca, includes those who betray their benefactors. Here Lucifer, or Dis, also resides, "the emperor of the despondent kingdom," his three mouths chewing on Brutus, Cassius, and Judas—a truly hellish, unholy trinity. Dante and Virgil eventually escape this painful universe by climbing Lucifer's fur, taking their leave through earth's center, emerging beneath a star-studded sky in the Southern Hemisphere, shortly before Easter Sunday's sunrise.[56]

"The Infernal Architecture"
A Christian Theological Reading of *My Visit to Hell*

Traditional pictures of heaven and hell may seem strange to contemporary Christians, perhaps even outdated, but Thigpen believes the warnings they give about turning our backs on God are as serious today as they ever were:

> I don't enjoy thinking or writing about sin and its tormenting consequences. But our culture's moral compass has become so skewed that the time seems right to do it. In fact, I'm not alone in this concern: just before the first edition of this book was published in 1992, several polls showed that a surprising number of Americans were thinking and talking about the possibility of final justice for the wicked in the afterlife. My guess is that such discussions have only multiplied and intensified.
>
> And no wonder—people don't have to look far to find candidates for hell. I could have clipped a hundred news items from the daily paper to paste in these pages, and you'd have hardly noticed the difference. Dante Alighieri, the Italian Christian poet who wrote a book called the *Inferno*, said nearly seven centuries ago: "I have found the original of my hell in the world in which we inhabit." I guess there's nothing new under the sun after all.[57]

This said, Thigpen does not intend for us to treat his novel as a Window giving directly on to Reality. Arriving at the story's end we will feel informed, because "the infernal 'architecture' described here simply reflects in its broad lines the moral theological tradition of the Western Church as laid out long ago by St. Thomas Aquinas," but we should resist viewing *My Visit to Hell* literally.[58] It represents "only the latest addition to a genre of such literature known as 'tours of hell,' and there are likely more to come," he declares.[59]

Real historical personalities appear throughout Thigpen's tale, just as they do in Dante's *Inferno*, and this fact highlights one of several textual parallels that incline me to treat *My Visit to Hell* as a postfigurative novel. Here again, though, Thigpen intends no literalism. His novel tackles specific sins, not particular transgressors, and "if you find yourself somewhere in its pages," he adds, then "keep in mind that I find myself there, too."[60] Following the Apostle Paul and Augustine, Thigpen holds that we have fallen short of God's intentions and need to be forgiven as well as restored. Having faith in Jesus Christ as God's Son and our Savior, and submitting to the church, is the only way to eternal life; whatever else it is, then, *My Visit to Hell* is a story that seems both personal and cosmic.

"The Great Crack"

Thomas Travis is roughly half of the biblically allotted age of 70, like Dante's voyager-narrator, and appears quite accomplished but lost as well as alone in the world.[61] He hints that childhood abuse at the hands of his father, Homer, explains such disorientation. Yet the novel opens *in media res*. We first encounter Thomas as an American, Southern academic who reflects his culture's worst stereotypes, racism and sexism.[62] His first name evokes doubting Thomas, the skeptical disciple, and his last sounds like "traverse," the verb to move through or cross over, which means it may even capture the Augustinian-Thomistic belief that we are wayfarers in the world.[63] Thomas is also a native of Waycross, a country town in Georgia that combines two words commonly associated with the early Christians. Waycross also hints at Thomas' identity struggle, an internal division perhaps, or else an actute feeling that he remains stuck at midlife's existential intersection.[64] As we will see, Thigpen incorporates Thomas' background and qualities into the novel's plot, especially in some of the more dramatic scenes that unfold in lower hell.

Initially set during a sweleringly hot June night in modern-day Atlanta, the novel opens with Thomas walking the city streets and reading *Paradise Lost*. Being lost in a book emphasizes Thomas' worldly detachment—an awkward remoteness or disconnectedness that suggests he cares more about the celestial war than he does about the race riots that have recently become part of his city's hustle and flow. When Thomas looks up from his book, however, he finds himself cornered by a "half-naked gang of three" black youths.[65] He tries to escape their

clutches by taking refuge in an abandoned building, though new pursu-
ants soon appear—rats and bats—and they, along with the rabble, force
him to take the termite-infested stairs, which eventually collapse under
his weight and plunge him into the building's deserted darkness. Only
his prayerful plea punctuates the moment's scary silence.[66]

In due course Thomas finds himself on solid ground, though when
he regains consciousness Thigpen draws our attention to "a single huge
crack, about a yard wide," stretching out to every horizon.[67] Read in
the context of later passages, this crack alludes to hell's harrowing. As
Capopia, the novel's other pilgrim-protagonist, explains: Satan was so
taken aback when Jesus descended into the abyss on Holy Saturday
and asked for hell's keys that the underworld's foundations shook and
an earthquake occurred, an eruption that allowed those whom Jesus
came to rescue to flee with Christ through the ensuing fissure.[68] At this
stage in the story, though, Thomas possesses no actual knowledge of this
event, and thus he proceeds out from ignorance as well as calamity.

When we discover that Thomas holds an earned doctorate in historical theology, his scriptural ignorance seems somewhat ironic, though
such irony probably illustrates how Thigpen, following Augustine,
upholds the mind's limits and grounds reason firmly in faith. Thomas
is a scholar. Yet the scholar's calm and abstract thought remains sub-
ordinate to faith, the novel infers.[69] This said, Thomas draws on his
book-learning after he tracks the crack's line to a manhole cover bear-
ing an inscription—"ABANDON ALL HOPE, YOU WHO ENTER
HERE"—that he recognizes as belonging to the gates of Dante's fictional hell.[70] Tracing the inscription's origins to Dante is one thing, however, but trusting its words to point the way to hell is another. Thomas
is a skeptic. Rather than read the inscription literally, then, he assumes
it represents some well-read government guy's amusing prank. Only
after Thigpen introduces Capopia, an escort who advises the professor
to advance cautiously, do we suspect that Thomas believes hell is for real
and that he must continue his journey with a chastened epistemology.[71]

Capopia, whose name translates into English as "I do not dispute
God," plays Virgil to Thomas' Dante. Yet her life counters the privileged
existence of the Latin poet whose function she assumes. An animist
enslaved and brought to America from southwest Africa in the middle
of the eighteenth century, Miss C was raped by a married, white clergyman, who then fed his infant son to hungry alligators to escape his wife's
ire. She also searches hell for her long-lost sister, Apangela, whose name

means, literally, "One who intends not to finish her journey," and Miss C appears destined, like the Virgil after whom she is modeled, to remain in limbo, home to the world's virtuous pagans.[72] Her story is excruciatingly sad. And Thigpen intertwines it with Thomas' own both masterfully and movingly.

Hell's Moral Topography

Thomas begins his tour at hell's vestibule,[73] where he encounters a group of so-called neutrals, "those who lived a lukewarm life that was neither hot nor cold, praiseworthy nor damnable."[74] Such women and men "made all of life a spectator sport, watching idly while others pushed the world toward good and evil."[75] If anyone or anything ever called them to a serious view of their responsibilities as human beings, then they simply shrugged their shoulders and allowed everyday life's illusions, like television, to provide them with an excuse for not listening. Here Miss C answers Thomas' protest of their treatment by using words that sound both Augustinian and Thomistic:

> "For *that* they deserve hell? Just for being ordinary human beings?"
>
> She shook her head sharply. "No—not ordinary human beings; in fact, hardly human beings at all. The human will was made to act, and when left unused it rusts like any tool until it corrodes into something less than human. This is the final end of such decay."[76]

When we are alive, in other words, we have to choose what we want to do and how we want to be, for we are free, though God has hardwired us to receive a call that we must not ignore—the call to examine our own existence. All neutrals once heard this call, she says, but they muffled or silenced it. Such sinners, like Thomas' cousin Virgil, do not so much get what they deserve as become what they are: motionless men and women marked by identities crafted apart from God.[77]

Hell's vestibule astonishes Thomas. One reason for such distress lies in his education. He is an academic heir of the philosophical Enlightenment, and this means he is unable to accept even the possibility that life continues beyond the grave and that evil could be personified. Thomas identifies himself as an atheist, situates his God-talk within the context of cultural Christianity only, and he dismisses the idea of a soul attached to a person's body and interacting with it. For her part, Miss C

MAP OF HELL

THE VESTIBULE The Neutrals

CIRCLE 1 (LIMBO) The Virtuous Pagans

CIRCLE 2 The Lascivious

CIRCLE 3 The Gluttons

CIRCLE 4 The Hoarders and Wasters

CIRCLE 5 The Wrathful and Sullen

CIRCLE 6 (SEMINARY OF DIS) The Heretics

CIRCLE 7 The Violent
- Ring 1 Violent Toward Others
- Ring 2 Violent Toward Self
- Ring 3 Violent Toward God

CIRCLE 8 (MALEBOGE) The Fraudulent
- Pit 1 Seducers and Panderers
- Pit 2 Flatterers
- Pit 3 Simonists
- Pit 4 False Prophets
- Pit 5 Grafters
- Pit 6 Hypocrites
- Pit 7 Thieves
- Pit 8 Evil Counselors
- Pit 9 Schismatics
- Pit 10 Falsifiers

CIRCLE 9 (LAKE COCYTUS) The Traitors
- Region 1 Traitors to Family
- Region 2 Traitors to Country
- Region 3 Traitors to Friends
- Region 4 Traitors to Benefactors

UPPER HELL
CIRCLES 2–5
Sins of Weakness

MIDDLE HELL
CIRCLE 6
Sins of Intellect

LOWER HELL
CIRCLES 7–9
Sins of Malice
(Injury and Fraud)

promotes the Augustinian-Thomistic notion that we are ensouled bodies. She rejects dualism, and she addresses how death momentarily separates our mortal body from our immortal soul, and upholds the belief
that God will unite and evaluate both—as one—on Judgment Day. As
his first name implies, however, Thomas doubts such convictions and
demands proof.[78]

Proof appears in the form of his former football coach. They
meet on Charon's boat, which, since Dante's time, has grown in size
to become an oil tanker, and their encounter changes everything.
Hell's "reality punched me in the gut with brass knuckles," Thomas
exclaims, "and thirty-three years of sin vomited up from my memory
into my mind."[79] Memory serves as an important theological resource
for Thomas, as it did for Augustine, whose own beliefs, according
to the *Confessions*, emerged from deep, personal distress. Before he
reaches the other side of the river Acheron, Thomas breaks down
and confesses as well as laments his many moral faults. He divulges
everything from stealing (not pears, following Augustine, but Zero
candy bars) to illicit sex, another of Augustine's weaknesses, and
intellectual pride, which shows up in Thomas' clever use of "the
faddish babble of the Deconstructionists . . . to impress the snobs I
called friends."[80] This epiphanic moment on Charon's boat will not
prevent Thomas from asking additional theological questions during
his journey, as we will see, yet, at this juncture, confession changes
him dramatically:

> A son of hell. *That's what I am*, I realized. And now I'm coming home.
> When this grimy tin tub docks, some politically correct committee of
> damned souls will probably be waiting there to deconstruct *me*.[81]

Thigpen is a confessing theologian. He reveals, for example, that
his religious life has changed over the years and that his theology
has matured alongside such developments. He entered the Catholic
church in the 1990s, as we have seen, and the reader who compares
My Visit to Hell with *Gehenna* will discern several changed story details
that reflect his spiritual journey and display fresh theological significance. The worship of the church on earth that shakes hell is now
referred to as the "Holy Sacrifice," for example, and Miss C now tells
Thomas that he has a "mother in heaven" interceding for him. The
silver cross is now explicitly a crucifix. Thigpen also adds "Feast of
All Souls" to the date after his name at the end of his new author's

note.[82] Whatever else it accomplishes, *My Visit to Hell* novelizes future eschatology from a Roman Catholic perspective.

Limbo, or, Circle One

Also known as limbo, hell's first circle introduces us to Miss C's friend, Lakshmi, whose Hindu name evokes Asia as Capopia evokes Africa. Both characters, like Dante's Virgil, represent noble or virtuous pagans; essentially decent, they nonetheless embraced something other than Christianity—Hinduism, Buddhism, animism—while they were alive, and limbo represents their punishment. Some virtuous pagans escaped from limbo during hell's initial harrowing, as noted earlier, but not all of them did. On the subject of another harrowing's possibility, furthermore, Thigpen has Miss C disagree with Lakshmi. Perhaps reflecting a belief in our fundamental goodness, Lakshmi hopes Christ will shake hell again, but Miss C, perhaps reflecting an Augustinian pessimism, remains unpersuaded.[83]

Prone to passionate exhortation, just like Augustine but unlike Aquinas, Thomas protests the virtuous pagan's predicament. These people are good, he says, and they do not deserve to languish in limbo. Thomas thus struggles to balance belief in a God of mercy or even justice with circle one's existence. And the anxiety as well as anger that this struggle stimulates becomes especially apparent when he sees the spiritually eclectic temple, an enormous mass of gray rock "sculpted into the stone equivalent of a freshman religion textbook—a random collage that slapped together every god and spirit the world had ever worshipped," etched against limbo's inauspicious horizon, both damaged and disused.[84] Thomas finally collects himself and, without denying his Augustinian intensity, serenely reveals that "my mind had stumbled over these ancient stones, and my heart had broken in the fall."[85] Limbo, or, circle one, like meeting Coach Schweiss on Charon's oil tanker, transforms everything, he admits:

> I could no longer say an easy "I don't know" about salvation, about the afterlife, about ultimate reality. Now I knew—not everything, but enough to push me farther down, all the way down to the bottom of things. I wanted to know what was at the bottom.[86]

Before Thomas journeys into hell proper, Miss C draws his attention to the Lake of the Innocents. This place is home to millions of unborn and newborn babies encased in little bubbles—blameless victims of various sins, like abortion, who—and note the Augustinian tenor of her remark— "died before the stain of Adam could be washed from their souls."[87] Each baby points a finger toward the Lake's bottom, an arresting detail that Thigpen eventually explains in the scene that appears just before his protagonists enter upper hell. Gathered to meet the Frankenstein-like judge whose job it is to consign people to various circles of punishment, some women and men find themselves identified as killers by the pointing fingers; "they [the unborn and newborn dead] are innocently reaching out one last time for the parents who rejected them before they are taken where they will forget—and their parents are taken where they will *never* forget."[88]

Upper Hell, or, Circles Two to Five: Sins of Weakness

Miss C's use of the "ancient words of waiver" guarantees safe passage into upper hell, where she points out that this region's architecture owes much to Dante and Aquinas.[89] "Sin is a single wretched rag that wraps the world," she says, "but some of it is dirty, and some of it moldy, and some of it bloody through and through."[90] All sins are not the same, therefore, even if they seem to originate from the same source, pride. In her words:

> The inhabitants of upper hell consistently chose something over God. Little by little they allowed some created good to matter more to them than God—food, lust, wine, money, whatever. They clung to their own little pleasures and possessions, feelings and moods, until they had to let go of what mattered most.[91]

Sin happens when, out of self-love, we deny our createdness and construct identities apart from our Creator. Hell's circles are thus concentric, each new level signifying greater and greater evil, and sinners are often punished in ways that reflect their earthly crimes. Lustful couples in circle two cling to one another for all eternity, for example, "screaming at each other as only infuriated lovers can," and circle four's hoarders and wasters play an endless TV game show to see who keeps or loses the most possessions.[92] These four circles thus punish sins of weakness or incontinence; in each instance, the guilty person failed to control a natural impulse and, instead, became controlled by it. We make our own hell. On this view, which echoes Augustine as well as Aquinas, evil is a privation of the good.

Thigpen is a novelist of divine mercy rather than of sin. And his grace-flecked eschatology appears in Miss C's understanding of God's tenderness toward our fallenness. On earth, weak-willed and sin-sick souls can confess their crimes, reach out, and "turn toward whatever means of grace may be nearby," she holds, and, "if they do, they will not end up here."[93] Called into relationship with God, we are dependent upon our Creator. Aquinas understands this as our "nature." We often make small, sinful choices that accumulate over time and create patterns of rebellion and wrongdoing. We wound God and ourselves. Yet grace still calls. Here God works through myriad forms of human life and culture to bring us back to Godself, the Thomistic notion that grace perfects or sanctifies nature. "If not for grace," Miss C asserts, "heaven would be empty of our race."[94] Hell is not empty, though, for many refuse to heed God's solicitous plea and, consequently, fail to repent; whatever their consigned circle, though, Miss C believes "they have gotten not simply what they deserve, but what they are."[95] And most sinners in hell, like Miss Hairdo in circle four and the sullen celebrity memorist in circle five, justify their behavior and appear unrepentant.[96]

Middle Hell, or, Circle Six: Sins of Intellect

Thomas and Miss C cross the River of Hate (Styx) and proceed toward the Seminary of Dis. The sins in this sixth circle concern the intellect's abuse. Some of the personalities we encounter here, like Augustine's nemesis Pelagius, are real historical figures, and some of the movements, like liberation theology, are actual cultural trends. But we would do well to remind ourselves that Thigpen asks us to pay attention to the sin rather than the sinner.

Built around four major halls, a combined library/cafeteria, a Tomb of the Ultimate Concern, and a cluster of small dorms, Dis' campus initially proves inaccessible, even though Miss C invokes the ancient words of waiver.[97] After Thomas solves a riddle about heretics, though, the demons let the travelers through. For her part, Miss C credits Thomas' accomplishment to God—the enigmatic agency of a grace that, while distinct from nature, still acts in a way that respects nature's integrity.[98] Yet God's grace also troubles Thomas. He finds the campus tour disturbing, for example, because he believes people with sincere, yet mistaken beliefs, do not deserve hell's punishment. Even toward the end of his time in circle six, after pestering Miss C with several questions, he begrudgingly advances to the next level, unsatisfied with her answers and craving further debate.

We can best understand Thomas' dissatisfaction by noting Thigpen's fondness for Flannery O'Connor. God's grace hunts people down in her stories, and occasionally it faces up to them violently. Consider how the symbolically named Mary Grace, armed with purple prose and a book on human development, confronts the self-righteous Mrs. Turpin and forces her to experience an epiphany that involves learning how Christ-like it is to withhold judgment on others. O'Connor wrote stories like "Revelation" because she found our modern, nihilistic culture worrying—and its loss of "mystery and manners" agitated her tremendously. In her view, we have willfully abandoned all feeling for the church's rituals and dogmas ("manners"), which mediate God's transcendence ("mystery"), and, in being so reckless, we now find ourselves unable to orient our created lives toward our Creator. We are alienated from God. But since God appears unable to use beauty to woo us back, God must stun us into faith and leave us uptight as well as afraid by what we experience, like the women in the Easter garden. Thigpen, following O'Connor, appears to agree with this shocking strategy, one we might associate with Aquinas: "Thomas, whatever the coolness or dryness of his tone, never forgets that grace is a word at which we are disturbed, a word that stirs us to reach out beyond the confines of our nature," writes theologian Frederick Christian Bauerschmidt.[99] In *My Visit to Hell*, Thomas finds himself unhinged by the Seminary of Dis, not simply because his own books and lectures might consign him there one day but because the grace that continues to call also continues to confound.

Several theological personalities live on Dis' campus. The Marcionites reside in Gnostic Hall, for example, and the Unitarians live in Arius-Socinus Hall. Thomas also encounters New Agers, Christian Scientists, and Mormons—even an Episcopal seminary professor of feminist spirituality who once urged women to be creative with the ancient symbols of goddesses from around the globe. Such people attend hell's seminary because they allowed intellectual conceit to define their earthly lives. Miss C acknowledges as much when she bemoans Pelagius' prideful peddling of unsound doctrine:

> She turned and pointed to one of the blazing dorms in the distance. "The arch-heretic Pelagius is there because he believed and taught

that we can find our way to heaven without grace—or without grace beyond what is already given to us in our nature. Yet the truth is that fallen human nature is grievously bent, and it cannot unbend itself unaided. Pelagius could not soar into the presence of God without grace any more than he could fly without wings. In both cases the futile attempt only leads downward to destruction."

"And you don't think he was fully sincere in that belief?"

"How could he have been? Even while he still lived on Earth, the evidence of his own daily failings would have been enough to prove that he was still in need of grace to reach moral perfection. But he proudly ignored the simple truth that would have shown his heresy for what it was."[100]

In the Seminary's Materialist Hall, furthermore, Thigpen positions Rudolf Bultmann, the German biblical critic, and Dr. Perdido, an invented symbol of liberation theology's nefarious tendency toward ideological smugness.

Bultmann taught at Germany's Marburg University from 1921 to 1951. He made headlines both there and elsewhere by promoting his so-called demythologization of the New Testament. This way of reading the Bible situates talk of the devil, spirits, and miracles within the context of the first-century's mythical worldview. Living lives on the basis of our modern, scientific worldview means we must reinterpret the New Testament world existentially; in short, hell-talk should be understood figuratively.[101] In circle six, though, the demons deride Bultmann pitilessly: "Go ahead! . . . Make my day! Demythologize *me*!"[102] Now, as I have said, Thigpen warns us about assuming authorial intention where he intends little or none, so we should not read too much into Bultmann's hellish predicament. The sin itself matters most. Being intellectually cavalier carries consequences, or so middle hell teaches, and this notion entails that during our lives we would do well to think—certainly about matters of the spirit—both guardedly and modestly.

With the liberation theologian Dr. Perdido, whose name means "damned" or "lost" in Spanish, we see another example of excessive pride, though in his case *hubris* hitches itself to naked ambition and unashamed two-facedness. We discover that while he was alive, for example, he stressed freedom from oppression, with the goal of transformation, but routinely quoted Scripture selectively, flunked those students who challenged his Marxism, and exploited grassroots congregations as the expedient way to securing top academic honors. In short, Dr. Perdido was aggressively duplicitous. Little wonder, then, that Dis' demons eventually ship him off to circle eight's sixth pit, home to hell's hypocrites, having concluded that his sins were more egregious than were at first suspected. Intriguingly, Thomas possesses enough integrity to implicate himself in his former professor's transgressions.[103]

Lower Hell, or, Circles Seven to Nine: Sins of Malice

"No longer were we sampling the spoiled fruit of human weakness or folly," Thomas says, upon entering lower hell, "here we could taste instead the poison of malice, dark, and bitter."[104] Circle seven accommodates the violent, and it is stratified into three concentric rings—the outer ring for those who were once violent toward others and their property, the middle ring for those violent toward themselves, and the inner ring for those violent toward God as well as nature. Cruel tyrants abound in the outer ring, as we might expect, and *My Visit to Hell* pictures Attila the Hun as well as Saddam Hussein marinating in a river of burning blood, the so-called Phlegethon, to a level corresponding to their crimes.

Accessing the middle ring costs both protagonists. Thomas gives his father's wedding band to an angry demon, for example, and Miss C offers her sister's silver crucifix.[105] This latter gesture provokes an intense theological discussion, one in which she explains how the crucifix not only reminds her of the lengths of suffering to which God in Christ has gone to redeem us but how it also serves as a sort of prayer to God for mercy. At history's end, though, Miss C thinks such mercy will overlook her for having been "born in the wrong time and place."[106] Moved to disagree with Miss C, Thomas notes his intention to escape hell, secure himself to heaven, and then petition God to rescue as well as redeem her.[107] Like Augustine, who thought Plato was useful and contained some truth, Thomas upholds the wideness of God's mercy.

The middle ring houses the suicides. Dante envisages these women and men as twisted thornbushes. When the poet breaks a twig off one of them, the sad, lonely soul trapped inside springs to life and narrates what led him to end his life prematurely. Something similar happens in Thigpen's novel. Here the suicides are isolated and confined to telephone utility poles. When Thomas pulls on a stray cable, it screams. God's grace once called to such persons—failed business men, women with eating disorders, and jilted lovers—but, in the end, they refused divine assistance and did not go gently into the good night.[108] This said, Miss

C hints that Christ's blood contains a plentiful redemption: "Perhaps all those of us who must face such a dreadful ordeal [an intolerably severe sickness for which euthanasia seems the only relief] are in the end judged more mercifully than we dare hope."[109]

The violent against God and nature occupy circle seven's inner ring. Here we discover that blasphemers as well as atheists wound God by invoking God's name improperly, either through profanity or mockery, and homosexuals as well as usurers injure the divine by behaving in ways that abuse God's created order, nature itself, which constitutes the Almighty's property. Thigpen captures this emphasis on violating nature quite adroitly. Consider the inner ring's geography. Instead of the flaming sand and fiery flakes in Dante's vision, Thigpen imagines an ungodly terrain, scorched as well as blackened by nuclear radiation—itself an atrocious outcome of an "unnatural" or "forced mutation of matter into energy."[110] Also note the presence of slave traders, those who take women and men made in God's image and sell them for something—cash—that is intrinsically inert; of course, their presence before Miss C only accentuates the novel's dramatic intensity.[111]

Sent to the outer ring for committing acts of sodomy, an attractive policeman eventually steers Thomas and Miss C away from the slavers who, despite the horrors of their sentence, continue to behave shamelessly. The policeman turns out to be an 80s movie star, Stone Jordan, whose screen-hunk, ladies'-man persona once masked his alternative lifestyle. He steals Thomas' trousers to avoid being caught by other demons and, with the help of Geryon the monster, they all travel to circle eight, where the fraudulent dwell.[112] The journey to hell's penultimate circle, also called Malebolge, an ancient word that means evil pockets or pits, blinds Stone. Insight soon follows because Stone, an Iowa homosexual with father-son issues, and Miss C, the former animist with an Augustinian angle on life, pause before entering the first of circle eight's ten pits and converse energetically. Thigpen uses what they say to calibrate issues of faith and doubt dexterously. In their exchange, we witness one cry for understanding, however unsteady, and one reiteration of Christian theology's traditional belief that all have sinned in Adam, the original man, and as a consequence we are all born sinful—"broken" is Miss C's word of choice—and in need of God's grace.[113]

When a pit one sinner brings news about Apangela, Miss C's sister, Thomas and his companion become sidetracked and lose one another temporarily, leaving Stone and Thomas to cross the bridges spanning the various pits. More theological reflections ensue. Stone wonders about an eventual amnesty for hell's inhabitants: "Don't you think these people [the seducers and the panderers] might finally cry 'uncle' and get a reprieve?" Thomas demurs. Sinners must repent, he says, sounding more and more like Miss C, and the time for saying sorry as well as reaching out for grace's life jacket exists in the upper world only.[114] In answering Stone in this way, Thomas upholds the Roman Catholic notion of freedom: that is, the power we have—while we are alive—to choose at any time between good and evil. Grace is not irresistible; we can shun the Spirit's lively scheming. "Maybe death commits us to all the choices we made before it," Thomas ponders.[115] All choices carry consequences, and hell represents "the place where all those consequences finally catch up with people."[116] On this view, hell's point boils down to one simple but horrifying truth: "You can't escape the torment, because you *are* the torment."[117]

Another query troubles Thomas, especially after he guides Stone through the first six pits, enduring the sight of everything from pit four astrologers with heads awry to pit five politicians stewing in vats of molten plastic, and we might express it this way: does divine grace ever expire? Judging by what happens in pit six, the answer to this question seems far from simple. A hypocrite exposes Stone's upper world duplicity—acting straight when really gay—and he, Stone, ultimately tumbles into a trench overflowing with other charlatans, where he soon finds himself condemned to spend eternity shuffling along wearing weighty clothes.[118] Thomas' interior monologue takes us to the heart of the matter: "But what about Stone? Had grace run out before it reached him? Had it reached him, only to be scorned?"[119] In theology, as in life itself, sometimes the quality of the questions we ask is more important than the answers we furnish.

Lakshmi reemerges in pit four, not long before Stone's ignominious end removes him from the novel's picture, and she informs Thomas to remain within Miss C's reach at all times, and to trust her alone. But the message arrives belatedly. He has *already* lost contact with Miss C, as noted earlier, and now he follows Stone's lead. Thomas eventually discovers the dead movie star's deceit, as we have seen, and he advances through two additional pits quickly. Grace then reaches down and teaches Thomas to pray—an entreaty that God appears to answer by reuniting Miss C and Thomas in pit nine, home to those men and women who spent their lives on earth sowing discord, the so-called schismatics.[120]

"Grace never runs out," Miss C teaches, "but in some cases it can wear thin, and if we tear in it a large enough hole, we can fall right through it."[121] Our ego-driven lovelessness for God and others often creates this hole; and such is the case with those in pit nine, like Homer, Thomas' father, whose bellicose racism tarnishes the tender, reconciling moment with his son. One glance at Miss C, for example, and Homer becomes truculent, discourteous, and determined to sunder charity's bonds. In hell, as we have discovered, we do not so much get what we deserve as become what we are. Schismatics tear people apart, and the punishment in this pit, as with the others, fits the crime. Here a chainsaw-wielding demon slashes at those who cut their ties to others cruelly.

We move toward God, Augustine teaches, not by walking but by loving. Yet Homer's hurtful strife shows that he lacks love for the Other. Without such love, he not only fails to see how the Other, made in God's image, reflects God, he offends the very Charity which gives, and is universal as well as unconditional. Little wonder, then, that Homer's hatred keeps him making the pit nine rounds, re-membering his wounded body until it becomes time for the butcher-demon to carve him up again.[122]

When Thomas protests his father's fate, and wonders if the damned might yet still apologize to God and be forgiven, Miss C reiterates her basically Augustinian view of hell:

> Have you yet seen anyone here repent? It is too late, Thomas, just as it was too late for Stone. Despite the good in his heart, the evil inside your father has conquered, and it will anchor him in hell forever. Even if he escaped that pit for a season, sooner or later he would return of his own will to be among those who share his hatred—or else he would end up farther down than before, as Stone did.[123]

The apparent austerity of this reply notwithstanding, the Virgil-like Miss C feels Thomas' pain. Her own father sold her into slavery, we discover, and her tour guide duties often force her to pass through the ice where he lies frozen, in region one of circle nine—the final resting place for those who betrayed their families. Each time she sees him, though, she informs us that she forgives him and accepts what she cannot change. Stunned by this revelation, and moved by her manner, Thomas enters hell's final circle chastened and renewed: "'Capopia,' I said softly. 'I'll call you Capopia from now on. Forgive me for failing to appreciate just how rightly you were named.'"[124]

Augustine believes in a penal hell, where sinners receive fitting justice, are not destroyed completely, and where saying sorry no longer matters. Over the years, though, Thigpen has modified his own views on such matters. In *Gehenna*, the first edition of the novel, he leaves the debate over annihilationism fairly open. When Thomas asks if God will one day destroy the wicked, for example, Capopia replies, "I fear there are no certain answers," but Thigpen omits this sentence from *My Visit to Hell*, the novel's second edition.[125] Again, in *Gehenna*, Capopia claims that "the tradition of the church leans strongly toward a conviction that eternal torment is the final reality," but "the tradition can be wrong," Thomas retorts. *My Visit to Hell* renders this exchange quite differently. Thigpen omits Thomas' line altogether, and Capopia now sounds categorical: "But the tradition of the church *insists that the correct interpretation* is this: eternal torment is the final reality."[126] Although Miss C ultimately refrains from providing an ample defense of annihilationism, she clearly favors it with her faith; in the last analysis, she believes that our imprecise understanding of eternity's relationship to time only adds to the mystery of what follows the Last Judgment.

Giants surround the frozen Lake Cocytus, otherwise known as circle nine, and here, in lower hell's final part, we learn of one region for each of the four different kinds of betrayal. Those who in the upper world practiced incest, adultery, and spousal abuse now personify the traitors to family of region one. Aborting parents may be found here also. All such sinners are frozen in ice, like Miss C's father, and even though they "never have the mercy of losing consciousness," the damned lack remorse for their crimes.[127] Traitors to country reside in region two and traitors to friends in region three; each is immersed to a depth corresponding to his or her crimes.

When Miss C informs Thomas that she once betrayed her stepmother, arguably her greatest benefactor, we realize why she feels unable to advance into circle nine's fourth and final region. Thomas thus faces the rest of his journey alone, an upset that becomes even more shocking when we discover that not only are he and Miss C related, which means that the Waycross racist has been wearing Africa's face all these years, but that Satan may imprison Thomas in region four also. It turns out that Thomas' father used his entire savings to convince Thomas' birth mother—Miss C's descendent—not to abort him. Homer thus sacrificed everything to adopt Thomas. Even though he knew nothing about this situation, Thomas acknowledges that his lifetime's willful resistance to his father typifies the worst kind of treachery.

Thigpen's theology of Satan avoids the ancient dualism that speaks of two separate and equal forces in the universe eternally in combat with each other. Rather, it reflects the traditional belief—associated with Augustine, Aquinas, Dante, and Milton—that honors God as creation's origin, sees goodness as the divine purpose for our world, and treats Satan as one of God's deceitful angels—the soul's enemy as well as the prince of darkness. Encased in ice on account of his treachery toward God, *My Visit to Hell*'s Satan displays an unholy trinity of differently colored faces that make him appear both sickeningly monstrous and stunningly attractive. Each face's mouth chews on history's most notorious traitors; for his part, Thomas concentrates on Judas:

> If you'd ask me to name the most despicable crime in history, I'd have told you it was Judas's treachery. Once again hell's architecture made sense: the ultimate human traitor of the ultimate Benefactor suffered the ultimate punishment in the ultimate dungeon.[128]

By crawling up Satan's furry back, sliding down his slick torso, and then aiming for the hole next to Satan's flabby belly, marking hell's exit, Thomas seeks to escape the devil's clutches. But his initial attempt fails. Dante's vision explains how the two poets escape through the hole, resurface on the other side of the world, and then continue their pilgrimage. In Thigpen's novel, however, Miss C reappears and sacrifices herself to insure Thomas' freedom; knowing that she betrayed her benefactor, she rushes into region four and diverts Satan's attention by promising him the "greater prize" of an escort to feast upon.[129] Heading for the hole, Thomas notices Apangela's crucifix, which Miss C returned to her sister when they reunited in circle eight. He picks it up, wields it like a weapon before the angel of the pit, and then dives into the hole. The long way down burns and browns his skin. When Thomas resurfaces he, like the *Inferno*'s travelers, finds himself in another hemisphere, in India, to be precise. Determined to keep the promise he made to Miss C before he saw her for the last time, he tells his story to the world: "'Jesus. Jesus. Oh, Jesus . . .' I kissed the feet of the Man on the cross in my hand, and I wept to know that grace at last had triumphed."[130] Such is the joyous, christocentric future eschatology that pulsates at the heart of *My Visit to Hell*.

HOPE FOR THE WORLD

While traditional Christians treat biblical eschatology as predicting our world's actual or chronological future, theologians like Bultmann dismiss such talk as outmoded as well as irrelevant. The world did not end when the biblical writers said it would, he protests, and thus their mistaken views need not be taken seriously today. We must reinterpret biblical eschatology existentially, Bultmann urges, so that it speaks to the here and now, and, in the process, we must reject future eschatology altogether. Such was the theological mood in the first half of the last century. By the mid 1960s, however, things began to change. And today, scholars credit the German Protestant Jürgen Moltmann, one of the later twentieth-century's most widely-read theologians, with breathing new life into the Christian doctrine of future eschatology.

Hope focalizes Moltmann's work. He grounds Christian hope in the dialectic of Good Friday and Easter Sunday. The crucified Christ's resurrection represents God's promise to us, he claims, and this promise not only problematizes our present reality. It also reveals our world's ability to open out to a future and a hope—the kingdom of God both around and within us. Christian hope is for our world's new creation, not for some other world to replace our world, and the church contributes to this new creation by loving wastefully, serving others, and promoting personal as well as structural change.[131] In Moltmann's words:

> If we simultaneously begin to think of God and future, faith and hope, we move in a new way close to the primitive Christian Easter message. We are able to understand it again eschatologically. We can recognize in the inexplicable *novum* of Christ the anticipation and the incarnation of the ultimately or universally new, which in the coming of the recreating God can be hoped for. God is the power of the future. God is the power of the new. Jesus himself has been translated into the future of the new. He represents this future and at the same time mediates it. . . . In him, who from the cross, God-forsakenness, and hell was raised, we become certain of a future which will conquer God-forsakenness and hell.[132]

It appears to me that Thigpen promotes his own, Catholic version of christocentric future eschatology. We see it, for example, in his passionate sense that hope shapes the structure of Christian existence:

Our anthropology is shaped by our eschatology—that is, our under-standing of what it means to be human is profoundly influenced by our understanding of the ultimate purpose of human beings. If we have truly been made by a good and loving God with the intended destiny of living in joyful communion with Him forever, then the knowledge of that truth has thoroughgoing implications for the way we live right now. In this sense, as the Scripture says, hope is the "anchor of the soul" (Hebrews 6:19), and everyone who has such a hope "purifies himself as He is pure" (1 John 3:3).[133]

There are at least three ways in which such eschatology also shows up in *My Visit to Hell*. First, Miss C believes Christ saves us from our self-imposed alienation from God. He alone reveals God's face and heart, full of grace as well as truth, and personifies the divine purpose for us all to journey toward God by loving. Believing in the crucified Christ, especially the Christ who descended into hell to snatch victory from the devil's jaws, and celebrating the risen Christ in church is the only way to shake hell and secure eternal life, she avers. Second, in Thomas' dialec-tic of destiny, he faces up to his weakness—his *hubris*, his malice, and his mortality—and in doing this he also meets head on, through grace, the justice and mercy of the supremely good and loving God. Third, hope permeates *My Visit to Hell*. Thomas experiences such hope dialectically—for the greater part of the novel, in other words, he hopes for heaven's righteousness in the midst of hell's moral poverty and for divine grace in the midst of the devil's torture. Hope also propels Thomas down through hell and back out into the upper world, whereupon he kisses Apangela's silver crucifix—the novel's powerful and poignant symbol of Christ's overcoming of hell—and declares himself ready and willing to help usher in the new creation by sharing his Augustinian story of sin, the fall into chaos, confession, forgiveness, and the conversion to the love of God: a story both personal and cosmic.

CONCLUSION

Some Christians detail hell's punishments, in order, it seems, to frighten people into confessing their sins, attending church, and leading ethical lives. Thigpen is not one of them. His novel displays astonishing imag-ery, and certain readers may find it moves them to reassess their lives, but it is not hellfire preaching in literary drag. On the contrary, *My Visit to Hell* represents an inventive attempt to help us orient our faith eschatologically—that is, to see our existence as tilted toward the life after this one. In such an outlook, hope, and not fear, motivates our discipleship. And hope inspires real, lasting joy. In Thigpen's words:

> Without God—without the hope of another world beyond this one, for which this one is longing—there could be no true merriment. There could be only the shallow giggle of flippancy or the hollow mockery of the cynic. To be truly merry is to live lightly in this world, to be unburdened with cares about things that are quickly passing away.[134]

And again:

> This eternal communion with God, face-to-face at last, is called the beatific vision—the vision of perfect blessedness. Human happiness knows no completion, no permanence, apart from it. Why not? Because the Creator has made men and women for Himself, and they will never be fully satisfied until they experience this final divine embrace.[135]

For Further Reading

James Alison uses *Raising Abel: The Recovery of the Eschatological Imagination* (New York: Crossroad Publishing, 1996) to issue a clarion call for contemporary Christians to resituate eschatology at the center of their theological thinking. Greg Carey's *Ultimate Things: An Introduction to Jewish and Christian Apocalyptic* (St. Louis, Mo.: Chalice Press, 2005) describes the main texts and themes associated with ancient apocalypticism. William Crockett's edited volume, *Four Views on Hell* (Grand Rapids, Mich.: Zondervan, 1997), explores literal and metaphorical understandings of the underworld. It also discusses conditional immortality, the idea that punishment after death is real but temporary, as well as the notion of purgatory. Paul Fiddes' *The Promised End: Eschatology in Theology and Literature* (Malden, Mass.: Blackwell, 2000) brings together critical theorists, novelists, and theologians to address the concept of "open" and "closed" endings in life as in literature. Written by Peter S. Hawkins, *Dante: A Brief History* (Malden, Mass.: Blackwell, 2006) outlines the Tuscan poet's life and theology, with special reference to the *Divine Comedy*. Various theories concerning continued conscious existence after bodily death are discussed in John Hick's *Death and Eternal Life* (Louisville, Ky.: Westminster John Knox, 1994). In addition to serving as an essential sourcebook for Thigpen's novel, Martha Himmelfarb's *Tours of Hell: An Apocalyptic Form in Jewish and Christian Literature* (Minneapolis, Minn.: Fortress, 1985) describes some of the ancient accounts of what follows Judgment Day. Henry Angsar Kelly's, *Satan: A Biography* (Cambridge: Cambridge University Press, 2006) contests that we have misunderstood Satan. A former Jesuit priest, Kelly uses the writings of the New Testament and the early church fathers to reconstruct Satan as a bureaucrat rather than a villain—someone appointed by God for a unique task. Alister E. McGrath explores hell's opposite in *A Brief History of Heaven* (Malden, Mass.: Blackwell, 2003). Most Americans believe in heaven, but their notion of paradise may be defective, writes Jeffrey Burton Russell, in *Paradise Mislaid: How We Lost Heaven and How We Can Regain It* (Oxford: Oxford University Press, 2006). Alan F. Segal's magisterial study, *Life after Death: A History of the Afterlife in Western Religion* (New York: Doubleday, 2004), offers the most comprehensive history of the subject to date. *The History of Hell* (New York: Harcourt Brace, 1993), written by Alice K. Turner, offers a richly-illustrated, multi-religious approach to the Great Below.

SELECTED WEB SITES

1. http://www.paulthigpen.com/index.html
   Paul Thigpen's personal Web site, featuring biographical essays, full list of publications, and several other resources.

2. http://www.newadvent.org/cathen/07207a.htm
   A link to an entry on "Hell" in a Catholic Encyclopedia.

3. http://dante.ilt.columbia.edu/new/
   Columbia University's Digital Dante site.

Appendix I

An Interview with Paul Thigpen

Paul Thigpen emerges from the following interview, which he gave just before *My Visit to Hell*'s May 2007 release, as an experienced, thoughtful, fervent man, single-minded in his search for the truth. In this sense, he resembles Augustine and Thomas Aquinas, his two main theological influences, because throughout their work reason also seeks to understand what faith believes. We observe, moreover, that Thigpen's well-stocked mind exhibits keen interest in what happens at the interface of theology and literature. This interview pays close attention to his beliefs concerning heaven, hell, and the devil, for example, and notes his response to recent end times fiction, the *Left Behind* novels particularly.

DM: For the benefit of readers who are encountering your name and work for the first time, please describe the major landmarks in your Christian formation, especially your transition from Evangelicalism to Roman Catholicism.

PT: I was reared in a Presbyterian home, a rather devout youngster who hoped to be a pastor when I grew up. But after reading some Voltaire at the age of twelve, I became an atheist materialist (in the philosophical sense). My reconversion to Christian faith came six years later at the end of my high school career, after reading C. S. Lewis, rereading the Gospels, and having certain personal transformative experiences that convinced me that certain fundamental claims of the Christian faith were true; including these:

- All things were created and are sustained by an infinite, almighty, transcendent, yet personal God, who made us in His image (with a rational intellect and free will) and who loves us beyond all telling.
- Through the abuse of that free will, our race has brought upon itself a profound brokenness that we are powerless on our own to heal completely; we are like people who have dug ourselves into a pit so deep that we cannot climb out of it without help.
- To heal us, God entered history nearly 2,000 years ago as a Man, Jesus Christ, who joined His divine nature to our human nature to remake it, offering to help us overcome our rebellion against Him and all its tragic consequences.
- The healing He offers is a free gift, but we are also free to reject it and to reject Him. (In this regard I parted ways with the Calvinist tradition of my youth, though I had never consciously encountered there the issue of free will and predestination.)
- Acceptance of this priceless gift and cooperation with it leads to eternal joy in perfect fellowship with the God who made us; rejection of this gift leads to eternal misery in alienation from Him.

The Christian circles in which I moved after my reconversion were largely Evangelical Protestant. But over the years, the more theology and Church history that I read, the more firmly I became convinced that the Protestant vision of the Christian faith—however nurturing and inspiring it had been for me—was nevertheless at its heart incomplete and even self-contradictory.

After long, careful years of demanding study (three degrees in religion) and agonizing prayer, even though I had been ordained as a Protestant clergyman, I came to the firm conclusion that:

- The Catholic Church is the same institution that was founded by Jesus Christ through His apostles to continue His mission.
- What the Catholic Church definitively teaches we can trust to be true as a matter of divine revelation, and embracing that truth keeps us on the road to salvation.
- Divine grace for healing our rift with God comes through the sacraments of the Catholic Church.
- For all these reasons and more, I had to enter the Catholic Church, whatever the cost.

I became Catholic nearly fourteen years ago, and I have never looked back. I continue to find in the Catholic tradition an abundance of spiritual riches that is inexhaustible. For more details, I often direct readers to my personal Web site.[1]

DM: You hold an earned doctorate in theology, which is rare for a contemporary creative writer. Looking back through the history of Christian thought, whose views do you most value and why?

PT: I fell in love with St. Augustine upon reading the very first page of his classic spiritual autobiography, *Confessions*. It was as if my personal journey to that point (especially the thirsty, restless spiritual wandering) had been just a pale, distant reflection of his journey, and in gazing at his, I encountered a brilliant, compelling illumination of mine. Later, as a result of my immersion in the *Summa Theologiae* of St. Thomas Aquinas, I found that the "Dumb Ox" (as his fellow students nicknamed him) unpretentiously but relentlessly rearranged my entire intellectual landscape. He provided me a new philosophical context for the world and a new set of tools to examine it.

The creative, formative presence of the works of these two theological giants has always generated a certain tension within the Christian tradition because of certain differences in their approach to knowledge. I live happily within that tension. You might say that I am an Augustinian by nature and a Thomist by training; I constantly experience God and the world through a kind of passionate Augustinian intuition, but then I go on to examine and understand more deeply what I have experienced through a careful Thomist analysis.

Gehenna, of course, presents a largely Thomist vision of hell (and the universe), by way of Dante. The protagonist could be viewed, I suppose, as a still-pagan Augustinian of sorts, and his companion is rather Augustinian as well.

As for other Christian thinkers who have been most formative in my life, I would note St. Catherine of Siena, St. Teresa of Avila, John Henry Cardinal Newman, G. K. Chesterton, Lewis, and Thomas Merton.

DM: Who are some of your literary influences? And whom do you read these days?

PT: Dante, obviously. In addition, I can never stay away very long from Flannery O'Connor; she haunts me just as she seems to haunt my city (Savannah—she was a member of my parish during her childhood and attended college with my mother, though I never knew her personally). I return to her stories repeatedly, riveted by her startling (and convincing) vision of good and evil, and her sobering depiction of the tireless assault of divine grace upon human depravity. If *she* had written *Gehenna*, I might well have had nothing left to say about the subject. As for others, J. R. R. Tolkien made me a captive of Middle Earth a long time ago, and I've never quite been able to escape. Nor do I want to. The same goes for Lewis' Narnia. From time to time I revisit Charles Dickens, Mark Twain, and Edgar Allen Poe. I've been having fun recently (as I have many times before) with Robert A. Heinlein, Chesterton (his Father Brown mysteries), Dorothy Sayers, and Dean Koontz's more exotic tales. I should note that I can only speak of sources of inspiration or entertainment here. It would be wonderful to think that careful readers might actually discern some measurable influence of great writers on my work, however meager; but that's really more than I can hope for.

DM: Some might say that theology and literature are strange bedfellows. Others see them as natural conversation partners. How do you understand the relationship between these two disciplines?

PT: We cannot separate literature from theology any more than we can separate word from thought. Every work of literature breathes out a particular theological vision of reality. Even an atheistic vision speaks about God by denying Him, and a secular vision speaks about God by ignoring Him. At the same time, every enduring theology ultimately finds a voice in literature. The Christian gospel especially is at its heart a living story, not an abstract system. In the image of the God it proclaims, its thought must be expressed as a word that becomes flesh and dwells among us (cf. John 1:14).

Think of Geoffrey Chaucer, Edmund Spenser, William Shakespeare, John Milton, John Donne, George Herbert, Nathaniel Hawthorne, Dickens, just to mention a few literary giants of our native tongue. Can we imagine that any of these would have ever dared suggest that theology and literature are strange bedfellows? I can still recall studying works by these and other writers in my freshman lit. class at Yale. In every class discussion, I would end up noting scriptural figures, allusions, and parallels I found in the texts. (As a child, I had learned my Sunday school lessons well.) But the secular students who made up most of the class were clueless about much of what was going on in the texts because they had little religious background from which they could draw.

DM: Writing in his recent anthology on Christian literature, theologian Alister E. McGrath poses some questions to his ideal reader; I would like to ask you two of them: "Is the essentially 'Christian' element in literature related to its content, its form, or the interpretation offered?" And "must a piece of writing be *exclusively* Christian to count as 'Christian literature?'"[2]

PT: I suppose an argument could be made for any of those. But let's return to the image of thought and word. When I say that "every work of literature breathes out a particular theological vision of reality," I'm not saying that it will have a particular literary form, nor even, necessarily, a particular content (in the sense of particular declarations that must be made). Rather, it will breathe a certain atmosphere, operate on certain assumptions, view the world from a certain angle. It seems to me, then, that "Christian" literature, to one degree or another, explicitly or implicitly, will somehow reflect the vision at the heart of the gospel. It will operate on the assumption that despite our brokenness, despite the apparent futility of much that takes place in our world, life is ultimately meaningful, because we are not the result of chance, we are not alone, we are in fact loved; and because we are loved, we too can love. Christian literature will view the world in a way that reveals its sacramental reality. It will breathe an atmosphere with the scent of divine grace. In addition, I think a Christian work can operate at several levels simultaneously, with one level that is (explicitly or implicitly) Christian and another level that expresses the viewpoint of a different theological tradition—to the extent that the two religious visions converge. Think, for example, of Lewis' *Till We Have Faces* and *Perelandra*, or even Dante's *Divine Comedy*. Though I would call them all Christian works, they also present sympathetically certain aspects of the classical Western pagan tradition.

DM: Thinking more specifically about the eschatological content of your own Christian literature, let me ask you about evil's personification. In your experience, what are the main reasons for belief in the devil today? Which of these do you find most persuasive and why? Which do you think are less than convincing and why?

PT: First, I should note that I understand the Devil in traditional Christian terms, not as some god of evil or some pure evil force who is an equal or near-equal opponent of the good God (the classic Dualist view). He is an extremely powerful angel who turned against God and now hates the human race made in God's image, doing all in his power to drag us down to damnation with himself and his fallen-angel allies.

My guess is that the majority of people who believe in the Devil today do so because his existence is a tenet of their religious faith, whose teaching they accept as true and authoritative. Christians accept the testimony of Christian Scripture, Christian Tradition, or both about this matter as they do about many other matters. And references to demonic powers of one sort or another are of course almost universally found in the sacred texts and oral traditions of religions around the world: not just Christianity and its derivatives, but also Judaism, Islam, Hinduism, animism and others.

A number of other contemporary believers in the Devil who aren't particularly religious may simply assume his existence because they have imbibed this particular notion from the surrounding culture without questioning it.

Still others, however, are convinced of the Devil's existence because of personal experience that compels them to believe. Through involvement in certain occult practices, mind-altering drug abuse, or other activities that made them spiritually vulnerable—or through their acquaintance with others with such an involvement—they have encountered dark forces that they conclude are the demonic powers described in Jewish and Christian Scripture or in the sacred texts of other religious traditions.

In my case, both religious faith and personal experience have been compelling in this regard. While I was still an atheist teenager, my involvement in occult practices led to certain extremely disturbing experiences that convinced me my materialist views were inadequate to explain all the aspects of reality I was encountering. I won't go into detail, but suffice it to say that I witnessed a number of preternatural phenomena that seemed impossible to explain scientifically. (Given the circumstances, I was easily able to rule out hoax, hallucination, and other common explanations.) More specifically, I tangled with what I am convinced were non-human, non-corporeal intelligences of malicious intent. In a sense, then, you might say that as a young adult, I came to believe in the Devil before I came to believe in God. Immediately after my first experience of this sort, I recalled that the Scripture, which I had imbibed deeply as a child, described the kind of evil I had encountered. So I went back to the sacred texts to see whether they might tell me more about my predicament and a way out of it.

After my reconversion to faith, I came to understand more fully and clearly how Christian teaching about the Devil's origins, activities, and destiny fit within the larger context of what divine revelation tells us about God, ourselves, and the world. In later years I also had several further encounters with demonic powers in the lives of some acquaintances; among other experiences, I was present at an exorcism. These experiences only confirmed what I already firmly believed: The Devil does in fact exist, and with his demonic allies he is powerfully active in our world. But the power of God's goodness and grace is infinitely greater, and the Devil is doomed in the end to utter defeat.

DM: Recent studies, and here I am thinking of Jeffrey Burton Russell's *Paradise Mislaid: How We Lost Heaven and How We Can Regain It,* suggest that today's understanding of heaven and hell is off-center— either modern folk yearn for some vague, New Age bliss or else they fear an arena of endless fire and brimstone, Russell says.[3] Are you sympathetic to such a claim?

PT: Actually, I think that in most ages, including ours, popular notions about heaven and hell have probably tended to be off-center (assuming, as I do, the Catholic Church's traditional authoritative teaching to be the "center"). For example, even in the early Christian centuries, some theologians criticized common notions of heaven as merely a sensual paradise. Where folks most often miss the point about heaven and hell, I believe, is in their failure to understand that heaven's joy and hell's torment aren't just some kind of ultimate reward and punishment applied to us by God, coming to us willy-nilly from outside ourselves. Rather, heaven is the final, definitive encounter with God for those who have become like Him, who see Him immediately face-to-face, and who are welcomed into the eternal love and life of the Blessed Trinity—that glorious divine community of three Persons: Father, Son, and Holy Spirit. The joy they know in heaven thus flows from *who they are and who they have become*—creatures made in the image of God, made for complete and eternal fellowship with their Creator, whose entire lives on earth have been spent in preparation for such a destiny through their own choices, with the help of divine grace.

Hell, on the other hand, is the final, definitive separation from God, who is the very Source of all life, love, peace, joy, and every good thing. The torment suffered by those who end up there also flows inescapably from who they are and who they have become: shattered, disordered, empty, terrified, enraged, miserable creatures who have abandoned—

without hope of recovery—the very goal of their existence. They too have spent their lives on earth in preparation for their fate through their own choices, and in refusal of the grace that was offered to them.

This understanding of heaven and hell can help clarify for us the weighty decisions we face even now, and their eternal consequences. It is critical to my novel, and I hope it is somehow communicated through the story. Though I use such biblical imagery as fire, ice, and worms to picture the horrors of damnation (as Dante and others did before me), it should be clear that beyond all such agony lies the truest and deepest torment of all. As one of the damned in the story puts it: "But the worst of all is to be afraid of yourself. The monster isn't under the bed like it was when you were a kid, or even in the bed beside you. The monster is in you, and you're in the monster. That's the final horror, isn't it?"

DM: I'd like you to address the three books you have written on the theology underneath the *Left Behind* novels. How do you explain the current enthusiasm for LaHaye's and Jenkins' imagined apocalypse? Are their eschatological expectations overheated? And are you worried, as some cultural critics appear to be, that a potent form of so-called right-wing political Christianity seems all too content to see world events through the rapture's prism, so to speak?

PT: Beginning in colonial times, apocalyptic fervor has been perennial and cyclical in American culture. Though interest in the end times is a constant for many American Evangelical denominations and other groups such as Jehovah's Witnesses, we see from time to time a heightening of such fervor. That happened, for example, in the 1970s, when Hal Lindsey's book *The Late Great Planet Earth* (nonfiction, but presenting an end-time scenario similar to that of LaHaye and Jenkins) became the best-selling American book of the decade.

Often end times fever heats up when fear of the future and despair about the present state of the world become widespread in a society. The worse things seem to be, and the more clearly out of our control, the more comforting it is to focus on the hope of a decisive and permanent divine intervention in the world's affairs. Catastrophes may be coming to sweep the globe, but they will merely sweep it clean in preparation for a new earth. The rapture scenario that lies at the heart of the *Left Behind* books is especially appealing in this regard. This historically recent teaching posits an "extra" coming of Christ, before the worst of the apocalyptic woes (and thus before His final coming in glory to judge the world), when He secretly and invisibly snatches all true believers out of the world to spare them the agony to come. For Christians who look at the world today and conclude it is falling apart—and I believe there are many of them—the prospect of such a cosmic escape can offer considerable relief.

The rapture idea—which is alien to the thought of most Christians throughout history, whether Catholic, Protestant, or otherwise—was soundly criticized by many when it first gained attention in America, for the same reasons it provokes critics today. Not only is it difficult to justify on a scriptural basis; it easily leads to an attitude of indifference toward the world and its problems. If Jesus is coming soon to snatch us out of this mess, why should we invest ourselves in trying to change society for the better?

At the same time, as you have noted, if rapture believers are nevertheless inclined to be politically active, then their apocalyptic scenario typically compels them to expect, as inevitable and imminent, a global war centered in the Middle East. Foreign policy based on such an expectation could be disastrous.

I might also note that problems can result as well when national policies are shaped by eschatological assumptions of the postmillennial sort. This religious vision of the future, which historically has been held more by people on the left end of the political spectrum (socialists in particular), erroneously asserts that human beings, acting in an essentially messianic role, will bring about the prophesied "millennial kingdom" on earth. (Marxism, many have argued, is actually a form of secular postmillennial messianism.) The common result of this vision is that those who view themselves in such a messianic role end up accumulating to themselves too much power and viewing their critics as dangerous, malicious dissidents who must be silenced for the "good" of the society.

DM: Could you comment on the research that helped you reimagine Dante's moral topography for *Gehenna*?

PT: Dante's *Inferno* was my first encounter with the ancient genre of literature known as "tours of hell." Martha Himmelfarb's *Tours of Hell: An Apocalyptic Form in Jewish and Christian Literature* was quite helpful in leading me to other works of this genre, such as *The Apocalypse of Peter* (2nd century), *The Acts of Thomas*, and *The Apocalypse of Paul* (both 3rd century).

I found Dante's magnificent work, shaped of course by the moral theology of St. Thomas Aquinas, to be most compelling at a number of levels. So I decided to adopt his moral topography of hell, so to speak.

To set the story in modern times, however, I did have to make a fundamental adjustment in the imagery. In Dante's time, the wilderness was widely viewed as a dark and dangerous place, the haunt of demons and witches, wild beasts and mysterious powers of nature, faerie folk and brigands. The city, on the other hand, was a place of refuge from all such things. In our time and culture, however, the values have been reversed: The city is often viewed as the locus of crime, moral degeneracy, decay, noise, pollution, artificiality, barrenness, ugliness, chaos. This leaves the wilderness as our refuge—the place of beauty and peace where we go on holiday to be refreshed and revitalized. Not surprisingly, then, in the *Inferno* the infernal imagery is nearly all that of the wilderness. To achieve a more dark and diabolical setting for a contemporary audience, in my novel I attempted to translate such images into their urban counterparts. For example, I replaced the "natural" forest of the suicides with an artificial "forest" of telephone poles whose connecting wires were all severed (suggesting the suicides' self-imposed isolation).

I also spent a great deal of time researching the age-old theological debates among Christians about the nature of hell and damnation. I studied as well the writings of universalists, annihilationists, and others who challenged or outright rejected the very notion of eternal punishment, along with the response of Christian apologists for the traditional teachings of the Church in this matter. *The Great Divorce* (of heaven and hell) by C. S. Lewis was immensely helpful in this regard. The most important of his many useful observations, I think, was his insistence that "the gates of hell are locked on the inside."

DM: *Gehenna's* introduction indicates that you wrote the novel because you thought North America's "moral compass" was "skewed." Given the years since the novel's publication and reception, noting especially the emergence of the "value voters" in recent elections, have times changed?

PT: As long as more than a million American children are killed in the womb each year, I think we can safely assume that the nation's moral compass remains skewed. It seems to me that the clearest indicator of a society's moral health is how it treats its most weak and vulnerable members.

DM: Some of my undergraduate students, not to mention several folk in various Adult Christian Education classes I have worked with, wonder if you did not set out to overdramatize hell in order to stress its importance for us. How do you react to this reflection?

PT: I guess I'm simply following in an age-old literary tradition that employed the same kind of "over-dramatization," to good effect. No doubt some, perhaps even most, readers will find it overdone. In any case, it's certainly sobering to consider, as I noted in the book's introduction, that "my pictures of Gehenna are no doubt pale and tame next to the terrifying reality."

DM: Miss C is Thomas' Virgil—very generally, what made you draw her character the way you did?

PT: I needed someone who could serve as a classic figure of the "noble pagan" for an American setting. That could have been a Native American, of course, but since the protagonist's racism is one of the themes the book explores, I decided that an eighteenth-century African slave would be a good choice. Though the protagonist wasn't particularly sexist, I decided it was also important that my "Virgil" be a woman whose personal story reflected the tragic consequences of the sins of misogyny.

DM: Miss C strikes me as a theologian of grace. Like Augustine, she knows that God's severity could send us all to hell; however, it is a measure of God's goodness that God extends mercy to some of us. Is this a fair observation?

PT: Yes, in large part she is Augustinian, I think, and she understands deeply the meaning of grace as he did. Of course, the bittersweet irony here is that despite her convictions about divine mercy, she still remains rather pessimistic about the fate of those in limbo. In this regard as well she is thoroughly Augustinian.

DM: "The Neutrals" are morally indifferent people. They refuse to make choices. Why does Thomas appear to protest their treatment? Is it because here, as elsewhere, he voices so much of what we read and hear about in today's theology? Or did you have something else in mind?

PT: He reflects a contemporary mindset (largely secular) that assumes the only real sins, if we may speak of sin at all, are those that actively injure other people. Could watching too much television *really* be evil in any sense? How could it possibly play some role in leading a person into eternal misery? At this point, Thomas has yet to understand that hell is the internal ripened fruit of a lifetime of choices, not simply a divine punishment externally applied. Of course, this scene represents just the beginning of his education about the nature and consequences of sin.

DM: The early scene concerning Jesus as the Harrower, rescuing people who lived before Christ, raises the question of religious pluralism. What are you experimenting with at this point? Are you asking your readers to ponder questions like: Should non-Christians who struggle to live a life of truth be condemned? Is there more to the Christic activity of God than Jesus of Nazareth? If so, how would you answer such inquiries?

PT: I would simply point inquirers to the statements of the Second Vatican Council with regard to this matter, which lay out in clear and simple terms what I affirm as a Catholic. In particular, let me quote two important documents—first, the Decree on the Mission Activity of the Church (*Ad Gentes*, no. 7):

> This missionary activity [of the Church] derives its reason from the will of God, "who wishes all men to be saved and to come to the knowledge of the truth. For there is one God, and one mediator between God and men, Himself a man, Jesus Christ, who gave Himself as a ransom for all" (1 Tim. 2:45), "neither is there salvation in any other" (Acts 4:12). Therefore, all must be converted to Him, made known by the Church's preaching, and all must be incorporated into Him by baptism and into the Church which is His body. For Christ Himself "by stressing in express language the necessity of faith and baptism (cf. Mark 16:16; John 3:5), at the same time confirmed the necessity of the Church, into which men enter by baptism, as by a door. Therefore those men cannot be saved, who though aware that God, through Jesus Christ founded the Church as something necessary, still do not wish to enter into it, or to persevere in it." (17) Therefore though God in ways known to Himself can lead those inculpably ignorant of the Gospel to find that faith without which it is impossible to please Him (Heb. 11:6), yet a necessity lies upon the Church (1 Cor. 9:16), and at the same time a sacred duty, to preach the Gospel. And hence missionary activity today as always retains its power and necessity (7).

Second, from *Nostra Aetate* (Declaration on the Relation of the Church to Non-Christian Religions, no. 2):

> Likewise, other religions found everywhere try to counter the restlessness of the human heart, each in its own manner, by proposing "ways," comprising teachings, rules of life, and sacred rites. The Catholic Church rejects nothing that is true and holy in these religions. She regards with sincere reverence those ways of conduct and of life, those precepts and teachings which, though differing in many aspects from

the ones she holds and sets forth, nonetheless often reflect a ray of that Truth which enlightens all men. Indeed, she proclaims, and ever must proclaim Christ "the way, the truth, and the life" (John 14:6), in whom men may find the fullness of religious life, in whom God has reconciled all things to Himself.

DM: What are your thoughts on Pope Benedict XVI's apparent reversal of traditional Catholic teaching on limbo?

PT: The document that appeared in late April 2007 is from a Vatican theological commission that is appointed, not to issue authoritative dogmatic statements on such matters (it doesn't have that kind of authority), but rather to serve as theological consultants for the Pope and the Curia. So first we have to keep in mind that no authoritative statement on the doctrine of limbo has been issued—not by Pope Benedict nor by anyone else in the Vatican. (As usual, the news media are overplaying the story. It sells more papers.)

Second, we must keep in mind, as Pope Benedict has pointed out in the past, that even though the doctrine of limbo has been widely accepted among Catholics for generations, the Church has never formally defined it as a dogma, a teaching that her members are obliged to accept. In fact, popes and councils have been careful to avoid doing so in order to allow the Church time for further reflection. In complex theological matters such as this, the Church often thinks and acts over a period of centuries. This means that the teaching is still open to being officially confirmed, revised or rejected as formal, authoritative Church dogma. If the Church (through a solemn pronouncement of a Pope or general council) were to reject the teaching definitively, that would be a rejection of a position commonly held by Catholics, but not a reversal of dogmatic, definitive teaching. This is a critical distinction for Catholics. The Church doesn't reverse herself on such issues; she chews over them for a long, long time, sifting traditional, popular, and more recent notions before she pronounces judgment (if at all). And if God doesn't give her the light to speak definitively, she will continue to remain silent on the matter.

Third, even the statement of the theological commission was careful not to reject the doctrine of limbo outright; it simply questioned the traditional notion in light of theological developments in the Church's understanding of grace and the breadth of Christ's salvific role. Such an approach is proper to the commission's role as a consultative rather than magisterial body. The commission's statement thus affirms, with some elaboration, what was already taught by the Second Vatican Council more than forty years ago: despite the damning consequences of original sin, and the normal role of baptism in washing away original sin, we nevetheless have grounds for hoping that at least some of the unbaptized, including those who died as infants, will still be able to attain heaven.

Finally, I should note that *My Visit to Hell* has already taken into account the more recent theological developments in this regard. That's why, rather than depicting limbo as a place where unbaptized young children (and what were traditionally called the "noble pagans") are all destined to remain eternally, the story has limbo's "residents" slowly disappearing, with those adults remaining behind hopeful (or at least speculating about the possibility) that the ones who have vanished have somehow made it to heaven. As I noted above, this is in keeping with the possibilities envisioned by the Second Vatican Council, with which I was quite familiar when I first wrote the book. It also reflects my own fervent hopes as the father of a child who died in the womb.

DM: My students find "The Seminary of Dis" both hilarious and thought-provoking. And this is because they read primary sources by the theologians you place there. Also, they know Dante was not above consigning his contemporaries to the underworld. You do not appear to pull any punches either. Now, while there is no question that intellectual pride, *hubris*, is covered by what traditional Christians have said about sin, what prompted you to reserve a place in hell for Gnostics, Arians, Rudolf Bultmann, Paul Tillich (if it is fair to infer his presence from the "Tomb of the Ultimate Concern" reference), various existentialist, Death of God, feminist, and liberation theologians? And what made you dispatch non-Trinitarian groups to this circle?

PT: First, let me note a clarification I offer in the now-revised introduction:

> In no way should references here to real historical figures be interpreted as expressing my private judgment that these particular people are in fact now in hell. Only God knows the final destiny of each soul. As a novelist, I'm simply using these well-known figures to represent in a compelling way certain sinful human tendencies that, if unchecked, could lead any one of us to damnation.

Having said that, I should note that in the Seminary of Dis, sins of the intellect find their ultimate conclusion. Of course, I recognize that in our culture, the very notion of an intellectual sin seems foreign:

The only thing that matters, goes the common refrain, is that a person be sincere in what he or she believes. But this notion is misguided in several regards.

(a) "the heart is deceitful above all things, and desperately corrupt; who can understand it?" (Jer 17:9). Can we truly be so confident of our sincerity? Our reason is not divorced from our will. Even in what may seem to be the purest of intellectual processes, our will is involved, directing our attention in certain directions, choosing to consider certain types of evidence and to dismiss others, making some connections but ignoring others—all based not simply on reason but also on personal agendas shaped by pride, sloth, greed, and other vices. Those who have ever worked for any length of time as journalists, if they are honest with themselves, know this to be true. Complete objectivity in journalism is a romantic myth, and the same is true in philosophical inquiry or scientific method. In ways both large and small, we all tend at times to avoid or reject the truths that make us uncomfortable, and the more we do that, the greater the damaging cumulative effect on what we come to believe. The character Dr. Perdido best illustrates this truth.

As you wisely note, *hubris* is most often the problem here. Take for example Bultmann. He is aware of the testimony of reliable witnesses over many generations that genuine miracles can take place. He must certainly understand it is reasonable to assume that if God truly exists, then miracles are surely possible; what could be more obvious? Yet he proudly disdains the ancient and constant teaching of the Church about the Virgin Birth, the miracles of Christ, the Resurrection, and so on, claiming that he knows better than all the rest, even the eyewitnesses of Christ's generation. He thinks he has somehow penetrated to the heart of the *true* meaning of the gospel in a way that others have never been able to do. What arrogance! Is Bultmann now in hell? Only God and Bultmann know. But I sketch him here as a warning to us all, because I believe that the kind of *hubris* he demonstrated could finally lead to eternal woe.

The same could be said of certain feminist theologians. (I recognize that "feminist" can be defined in various ways.) Jesus spoke of God as His Father in exclusively masculine terms. A consistent theologian who claims that it is inappropriate to use masculine language for God must admit that according to this view, Jesus was wrong about one of the most important aspects of His teaching—how we understand and address the God He claimed to know intimately, the God He came to reveal. In doing so, the theologian is insisting that he or she knows better than Jesus Christ himself how we should speak of God. Again—utter *hubris*, which easily leads to a loss of faith in Christ and the substitution of a self-made religion for the traditional faith of the Christian community. After all, who in their right mind would want to put their confidence in a teacher who got it wrong with regard to the most essential element of His teaching?

The same could be said of the claim that we can't be held responsible for our wrong beliefs about God because "we didn't know any better." The Catholic tradition wisely distinguishes between *vincible* and *invincible* ignorance. The latter is a state of ignorance we could not by our own efforts overcome. The former is a state of ignorance we could indeed have overcome if we had invested the time and effort to do so with honesty and courage.

In this novel, those who while on earth sought the truth as honestly as they could and were *invincibly* ignorant of the gospel arrive in limbo, with a hope of heaven (as Lakshmi sees it). Those who end up in Dis don't have the excuse of invincible ignorance, nor were they as sincere about their beliefs, nor as morally pure in their reasoning, as they thought themselves to be.

Remember: The assumption here isn't that every Christian Scientist or Unitarian or Mormon is now in hell, but rather that certain beliefs characteristic of these groups could lead people in this direction, especially if they lacked sincerity or were vincibly ignorant of the truth. I'm not condemning individuals; I'm identifying beliefs that I'm convinced are dangerously in error.

(b) Which brings us to another point about the problem with assuming that "sincerity" will save us: Even someone who is sincere can be sincerely mistaken, and given that ideas have consequences, the mistake can lead to disaster. If I drink arsenic, sincerely thinking it is milk, I will be poisoned despite my sincerity. If I follow a map that leads to Miami, sincerely thinking it will lead me to Niagara Falls, I will end up, not in Niagara, but in Miami, despite my sincerity—and it's *hot* in Miami. Thus sincerity is most certainly *not* the only thing that matters. The *truth* matters. We're talking here not about merely imaginative intellectual constructs, but about ideas that actually correspond more or less to reality—ideas that shape who we are and where we are headed. If you cling to the idea, for example, that central to God's will for the human race is the creation of socialist societies through armed revolution—a false idea, I am convinced—then you will end up losing your way in your understanding of who God truly is and how to serve Him. The same is true if you believe that God created people of color inferior, or that white people are literally "blue-eyed devils," or that God will "rapture" true believers out of the world so they can escape catastrophe, or that a self-proclaimed prophet or palm reader has accurate and divinely inspired knowledge about your future. As Miss C puts it: "Those who worship a bigoted god and live accordingly will spend eternity, not with the true God, but with the bigots. We become what we worship."

All this could lead to cynicism and despair about the possibility of ever knowing the truth if it weren't for divine grace. As a Catholic, I'm convinced that the Church has been made a channel of that grace, offering us the sacraments, along with sacred Scripture, sacred Tradition and the sacred Magisterium, which lead us to the truth and help us live according to the truth. But that's another matter, and a rather complicated one, involving such issues as material vs. formal heresy—all of which is really beyond the view of this novel.

By the way, I purposely did not put Paul Tillich in Dis, though some aspects of his personal life might well have given other circles in hell a claim on him. By speaking of "the Tomb of the Ultimate Concern," I wanted to hint playfully in passing at the limitations of existential theologies, which I'm convinced tend all too often toward narcissism, isolation, Pelagianism, despair, and other problems.

DM: A profoundly important question is raised at one point in your story: "How could a God of love allow His own creatures to suffer everlasting torture"? And Miss C answers that this is part of the cosmic scale of justice, the way fairness is seen in God's eyes. Could you respond to my students who, paraphrasing the late process philosopher Charles Hartshorne, think that if the power of God lies in the worship God inspires, then Miss C's God displays questionable moral worthiness?

PT: I probably should have placed a few process theologians in Dis as well. As far as I can tell, the process god is not in any sense a deity that the ancient Jews, Jesus, the apostles, or Christians up until recent times would have recognized. It certainly inspires no worship from me.

In opposition to the Hartshorne remark, I would insist—with Jews and Christians of all the ages—that the power of God lies in His very nature: He is Almighty, Creator and Sustainer of all things, which He has created *ex nihilo*. Whether or not we are wise enough to worship Him makes no difference at all to His absolute omnipotence. Nevertheless, it is to our duty to worship Him: to recognize and confess the truth that He is not only perfectly powerful, but also perfectly good, perfectly holy, perfectly wise, perfectly loving. Such worship is right and just, because it gives God the honor and recognition He is due. (The classic definition of justice, of course, is "giving to each his due.") Such worship is also of everlasting benefit to us, because through it we participate in the most important truth of all, and that truth sets us free.

The specific point debated in this conversation between Miss C and Thomas is the matter of whether the torments of hell are everlasting or eventually come to an end. (The latter is of course the position called annihilationism.) Miss C does not attempt to give a thoroughgoing defense of the (traditional) position toward which she leans: that the torments do not come to an end. She concludes, rather, that the issue cannot really be resolved without knowing what it means for human beings to leave time and enter into eternity. If "everlasting" or "endless" are strictly temporal terms, then the duration of torment may be simply a moot point, she notes, once time as we know it has come to an end for us.

The larger issue here, of course, is whether a loving God (who is also omnipotent) could allow a creature to suffer in hell at all. But if hell is actually a place of our own making, through our scorning of God's friendship and our refusal to live in accordance with the way we are made, then God's moral character isn't on trial here; *ours* is. The issue centers on the mystery of human free will.

Would it have been better for God to create robots that were programmed to obey Him perfectly, rather than creating sons and daughters in His own image with a free will, who could freely choose to love Him—or not? The Christian affirmation is that, as terrible as the risk of damnation might be, the great good of a free-willed creature with the ability to love must be worth the risk, since this is in fact what God has done. He is all-wise, so He *knows* what is the greatest good; He is all-powerful, so He is *able to do* what is the greatest good; and He is all-loving, so He is *willing* to do what is the greatest good. If He fails in any of these regards (as the process theologians claim He does), then He is something less than God.

In addition, God didn't just create us with the potential for choosing eternal life or death. When we chose death, He made a way for us to turn back toward Him, toward Life, and be healed—in fact, He made a way for us to share in the very life of the Godhead for eternity, a gift far beyond any possessed by our first parents at their creation. To para-phrase St. Augustine: God gave His very Self to save us; what more could He have given? What more could He have done?

DM: Thomas and Miss C eventually separate. However, this is not without Thomas being told that he must tell people in "the upperworld" about the dangers of acting without fear of ultimate recrimination. Why is this? He is told that it is only through the fear of hell that we will be drawn to God. But, is fear (or even hope) an adequate reason for believ-ing in God? What can or should we say about disinterested piety—the sort that, ironically, Satan asks after in Job 1 (the "Does Job fear God for nothing?" question).

PT: Read that passage carefully. Miss C says: "On your story will hang the fate of thousands of souls; for *many*, only the fear of hell's clutches will drive them into the love of God's embrace" (italics added). She didn't say that only through the fear of hell will we be drawn to God. She says that for *many*, that's what provokes them to start running, so to speak, in God's direction, as they flee the thing they fear. (My imagery here was carefully chosen.) For many *others*, however, fear is not the catalyst.

St. Augustine said that fear is like a sewing needle, and love is like the thread it pulls along behind it. The fear of evil and its consequences makes a place in us for loving God, and when that place is filled with love, the "needle" (fear) is no longer necessary, and the "thread" (love) remains in place permanently ("love abides").

To speak with more nuance: We must keep in mind that the kind of fear we're talking about—the fear that leads to salvation—manifests itself in certain transformational stages. Several ancient and medieval Christian writers pondered the apparent contradiction between the scriptural commands to fear God and the scriptural statement that "fear has to do with punishment, and he who fears is not perfected in love" (1 John 4:18). The solution to this dilemma, they concluded, lies in recog-nizing that the initial fear of punishment, though useful and often nec-essary, must give way in the end to something else so that love may be "perfected." They identified the three stages in what can be called, using the biblical expression, "the fear of God."

First is the fear of a *slave*. He serves his master because he fears punishment if he does not. This is a wise choice, because the threat of punishment is real: Rebelling against his Master, who is the Source of all goodness and life, does in fact lead to self-destruction, and that is most certainly a fate to be feared. But this stage is only the beginning of the process that is salvation; the "slave" has not yet been perfected in love.

Second is the fear of a *hired servant*. He serves his Master because he fears losing his wages, the reward of his service. This too is a wise choice, because the possibility of losing his reward is real. It is a better condition to be in than the service of a slave who fears punishment. But the "hired servant" is not yet perfected in love; he is still primarily interested in what he can get from his Master.

Third, and finally, is the fear of a *friend*. (As Jesus told His apostles at the conclusion of His time on earth with them: "No longer do I call you servants . . . but I have called you friends"—John 15:15). The "friend" serves his Master because he loves his Master for who He is; he wants to be with Him, to join his will to the Master's will. For the friend, the Master Himself is His own reward. So the friend fears, not punishment or loss of wages, but anything that comes between him and his Master, anything that would diminish their friendship. And in this way, the friend has become perfected in love.

Many people start off in the second stage without needing to work through the first. Most Christians are perhaps working their way through the second stage in most regards. The people Miss C was referring to, however, are those who for one reason or another can't seem to get to those second and third stages without starting at the first one—the fear of punishment. For them, "the fear of the Lord is the beginning of wisdom" (Prov 9:10). They encounter the evil consequences of spurning the Giver of life, and when they run away in fear of those consequences, they eventually run right into the arms of God.

DM: India surfaces as a subtext in your novel. Consider Lakshmi. Is there any significance in the fact that her name evokes a famed figure in Hindu mythology?

PT: Yes, indeed! She is of course Miss C's companion, a second "noble pagan" like Virgil, representing Asia as Miss C represents Africa, and Hinduism/Buddhism as Miss C represents animism. In Hindu mythology, Lakshmi is the goddess of divine knowledge, and the Lakshmi in this story acts as a kind of prophetess, speaking for God to those in limbo. The Hindu Lakshmi is also goddess of wisdom, light, courage and good fortune. What better name for a noble pagan from India?

Every name in the story was of course carefully chosen for the rich meanings in its etymology or symbolism. "Thomas," the doubter, is surnamed "Travis," which means "at (or from) the crossroads," the place of decision. Coach Schweiss' name means "sweat" in German, Dr. Perdido's name means "lost" or "damned" in Spanish, and so on.

DM: Also, your ending situates Thomas in India—what is intended by this finale? Some students have suggested to me that India represents Christianity in the Global South, so they wonder if you are suggesting that Christianity's future lies with our non-Western brothers and sisters. Other students point out that one of the early Christian legends places Thomas, the doubting disciple, in India after Christ's death. Are you drawing parallels, then, between Scripture's Thomas and your own skeptical Thomas? Or is there some other reason why Travis ends up in India after coming out the other side of hell?

PT: Your students are wonderfully perceptive—I would say yes to all of the above. In addition, I chose India because we could say that it lies on the opposite side of the world from Georgia. As was the case in Dante's *Divine Comedy*, when the traveler through hell exits the infernal regions, he comes out on the other side of the earth. That's a visual reminder that his world has been turned upside down by his experience—his beliefs and values in many ways inverted. In short, he has been converted.

Also note that once Thomas emerges in the upper world, his skin is brown. No longer the white racist, he has achieved a certain solidarity with people of color, even to the point of recognizing and embracing his African heritage through Capopia.

Please note that this change in skin color does *not* intend to suggest that Thomas has been reincarnated, as a few of my readers have speculated. In fact, the theory of reincarnation (which admittedly has roots in India) is antithetical to the theological premises of the novel. Rather, Thomas clearly has the same body he's always had, complete with scars from the Burger Demon's barbecue fork. But now his skin has been darkened by his experience; roasted in the flames of hell, he is now "well done." (Cf. the story of the ancient Christian martyr St. Lawrence, who joked with his tormenters, telling them they could turn him over on his red-hot griddle—the instrument of his martyrdom—because the cleansing fire had made him "well done" on that side.)

DM: Theologians like Gabriel Fackre enjoin tellers of the Christian story to resist the temptation to think they possess cognitive precision when it comes to the question of what happens after we die.[4] Do you still think the time is right for us to talk about eschatology openly? Or do you think we should suspend our eagerness for knowing about such ultimate things?

PT: I agree that we don't "possess cognitive precision" about the next life. (That's one reason why, when I decided to write a book about hell, I chose to make it a novel rather than nonfiction.) But we have nevertheless received, through divine revelation, a certain fundamental and extremely valuable knowledge about the next life that merits our reflection on its implications and our witness to its reality. If it's true that we have been made by a good and loving God with the intended destiny of living in joyful communion with Him forever, then the knowledge of that truth has thoroughgoing implications for the way we live right now. Our culture tends to focus almost entirely on the present or the short-term future. Such spiritual myopia is dangerous; it leads people astray as they invest themselves in things that will fail them and pass away, or things that will distract them from their true purpose. For this reason, though we shouldn't be speaking beyond what we know about the next life, we certainly must be telling whatever we *do* know. To remain silent would be a sin against charity!

DM: Finally, could you comment on your future plans as a creative writer? What can we expect next?

PT: I would love to write a sequel to *Gehenna/My Visit to Hell*, in which Thomas makes his way through purgatory and to heaven as Dante did in the other parts of his *Divine Comedy* (*Purgatorio* and *Paradiso*). But that may have to wait until I retire and have much more time than I do now. As for nonfiction: because I believe that eschatological issues are so important for Christians to ponder, in my writings I continue to return to the traditional "four last things" of Christian theology: death, judgment, hell, and heaven.

Appendix II

Further Reading

"Some stories leave a train of light behind them, meteor-like, so that much later than they strike our eyes we may see their meaning like an aftereffect," writes Eudora Welty.[1] Such has been the case for the stories I scrutinize in my book. On first reading I was smitten with them as art forms of human yearning, moved by each narrator's felicitous telling of views. Then, however subtly, for better or for worse, I began to overhear the big questions about God, life, reality, and meaning. Theology came *after* reading. Other Christians I have met and, in some cases, taught, say something similar. They frequently surrender to good or great literature, feel their sympathies enlarged by its beauty and passion, and many find that fiction abounds in what makes for serious theological reflection. I wrote my book for such people, and I hope it stimulates Christians to recognize and appreciate how our doctrines are expressed as themes in the works of modern fiction I commend.

I also hope it inspires my fellow believers to listen for similar stories elsewhere. There are many novels like the ones I feature here, stories that prowl at the edges of theology and literature, but I had to begin as well as end somewhere. For the Christian who relishes further reading, and I hope there are many of you, I close by offering a selected bibliography, which I structure around the schematic used throughout my book. I trust it will serve as a source of interest and challenge for some time to come.

GOD

Laurence Cossé, *A Corner of the Veil*
E. L. Doctorow, *City of God*
Franco Ferrucci, *The Life of God: As Told By Himself*
Bernard Malamud, *God's Grace*
Toni Morrison, *Paradise*
Iris Murdoch, *The Time of the Angels*
Arundhati Roy, *The God of Small Things*
Mark Saltzman, *Lying Awake*
Frank Turner Hollon, *The God File*
John Updike, *Roger's Version*
Alice Walker, *The Color Purple*

HUMANITY

J. M. Coetzee, *Disgrace*
Shusaku Endo, *Scandal*
Graham Greene, *Brighton Rock*
Graham Greene, *The Heart of the Matter*
Kathy Hepinstall, *The House of Gentle Men*
Mary Rakow, *The Memory Room*
Philip Roth, *The Human Stain*
Carol Shields, *Unless*
John Updike, *In the Beauty of the Lilies*
Evelyn Waugh, *Brideshead Revisited*
Jeanette Winterson, *Oranges Are Not The Only Fruit*

JESUS

Peter De Vries, *The Blood of the Lamb*
William Faulkner, *A Fable*
Robert Graves, *King Jesus*
Oscar Hijuelos, *Mr Ives' Christmas*
John Irving, *A Prayer for Owen Meany*
D. H. Lawrence, *The Man Who Died*
Norman Mailer, *The Gospel According to the Son*
Roger Mais, *Brother Man*

Ian McEwan, *Atonement*
Anne Rice, *Christ the Lord: Out of Egypt*
Michele Roberts, *The Wild Girl*
José Saramago, *The Gospel According to Jesus Christ*
Lee Smith, *Saving Grace*
Gerd Theissen, *The Shadow of the Galilean*
Gore Vidal, *Live from Golgotha*

CHURCH

Chinua Achebe, *Things Fall Apart*
Michael Arditi, *Easter*
James Baldwin, *Go Tell It On the Mountain*
Mongo Beti, *The Poor Christ of Bomba*
Willa Cather, *Death Comes for the Archbishop*
Martin Clark, *Plain Heathen Mischief*
Margaret Craven, *I Heard the Owl Call My Name*
Clyde Edgerton, *Where Trouble Sleeps*
Shusaku Endo, *Silence*
Ernest Gaines, *In My Father's House*
Denise Giardina, *Saints and Villains*
Gail Godwin, *Evensong*
Graham Greene, *Monsignor Quixote*
Graham Greene, *The Honorary Consul*
Graham Greene, *The Power and the Glory*
Jeannette Haien, *The All of It*
Ron Hansen, *Mariette in Ecstasy*
P. D. James, *Death in Holy Orders*
Nikos Kazantzakis, *The Greek Passion*
Barbara Kingsolver, *The Poisonwood Bible*
David Lodge, *Souls and Bodies*
Brian Moore, *Black Robe*
Alan Paton, *Cry, the Beloved Country*
Marilynne Robinson, *Gilead*
Jane Rogers, *The Voyage Home*
Elizabeth Strout, *Abide with Me*
Anne Tyler, *Saint Maybe*
A. N. Wilson, *The Vicar of Sorrows*

ESCHATOLOGY

William Faulkner, *As I Lay Dying*
Ernest Gaines, *A Lesson Before Dying*
Tim LaHaye and Jerry Jenkins, *Left Behind*, multiple volumes
David Lodge, *Paradise News*
Walter M. Miller Jr., *A Canticle for Leibowitz*
Toni Morrison, *Beloved*
Walker Percy, *Love in the Ruins*
Walker Percy, *The Second Coming*
Muriel Spark, *Memento Mori*
David Searcy, *Last Things*
Alice Sebold, *The Lovely Bones*
Graham Swift, *Last Orders*

Christian doctrine and modern fiction are never far apart from one another, as my book demonstrates, and in studying theology's alliance with literature, we have discovered how stories help us think through our faith. Certain novels open up a riverbed of meaning within us, or so it seems, and into them pours multiple, divergent, and vibrant values, beliefs, and ideas. Some Christians may find it hard to favor such things with their faith. It is hard. And I appreciate their predicament. But I also think it is worth the effort to surrender oneself, to listen *for* the story and not just *to* it, and then, after reading, to find that little hermitage within and reflect theologically on fiction's approximation of human—even divine—truth. Reading literature *as well as* theology gives Christians more choice in how to think about matters of the spirit; therein lies no small virtue.

NOTES

INTRODUCTION

1   Here and elsewhere I refer to "us." Clearly my book's implied reader is any Christian, clergy or laity, who desires to think about the faith imaginatively. I have shared my work with Adult Christian Education groups around the country, so I write with such folk in mind. I also teach a "theology and literature" class at my university; many of the students I have taught across the years have read the novels featured in my book and both admire as well as challenge the interpretations I offer—they, too, influence my sense of an audience.

2   See Darrell L. Bock, *Breaking the Da Vinci Code: Answers to the Questions Everybody's Asking* (Nashville, Tenn.: Thomas Nelson, 2004) and Bart D. Ehrman, *Truth and Fiction in The Da Vinci Code: A Historian Reveals What We Really Know About Jesus, Mary Magdalene, and Constantine* (Oxford: Oxford University Press, 2004). On the Left Behind series: Bruce David Forbes and Jeanne Halgren Kilde, eds., *Rapture, Revelation, and the End Times: Exploring the Left Behind Series* (New York: Palgrave Macmillan, 2004); Amy Johnson Frykholm, *Rapture Culture: Left Behind in American Culture* (Oxford: Oxford University Press, 2004); Glenn W. Shuck, *Marks of the Beast: The Left Behind Novels and the Struggle for Evangelical Identity* (New York: New York University Press, 2004); and, finally, see Michael Standaert, *Skipping Towards Armageddon: The Politics and Propaganda of the Left Behind Novels and the LaHaye Empire* (New York: Soft Skull Press, 2006).

3 On objections to Kazantzakis, for example, see Darren J. N. Middleton, ed., *Scandalizing Jesus?: Kazantzakis's* The Last Temptation of Christ *Fifty Years On* (New York: Continuum, 2005).

4 I have discussed their uneasy faith(s) elsewhere. See Darren J. N. Middleton, *Broken Hallelujah: Nikos Kazantzakis and Christian Theology* (Lanham, Md.: Lexington Books, 2007), 1–10. Also see Darren J. N. Middleton, "Graham Greene's Teilhardian Vision," in Darren J. N. Middleton, ed., *God, Literature and Process Thought* (Burlington, Vt.; Aldershot, Hampshire: Ashgate Publishing, 2002), 157–71. For an insightful as well as eloquent defense of forgiveness toward literary art that offends, see J. M. Coetzee's "Taking Offense" in William H. Gass and Lorin Cuoco, eds., *The Writer and Religion* (Carbondale and Edwardsville, Ill.: Southern Illinois University Press, 2000), 136–46.

5 George Eliot, *Middlemarch*, complete and unabridged and with an introduction by A. S. Byatt (New York: Modern Library, 1994), 799.

6 Readers should not interpret me as saying that this book's featured novelists self-identify as Christians. Some do and some do not; others set the issue of spiritual formation to one side, choosing to let the fiction speak for itself. My point is that I read our novelists the way I read people in general—Christianly, as it were, or as people whose life and work carries the potential to open out to something transcendent.

7 See Genesis 32:22-32. I have been greatly instructed on this topic by Valentine Cunningham's work, especially his "It Is No Sin To Limp," *Literature and Theology*, 6.4 (1992): 303–9. Also see Middleton, *Broken Hallelujah*, 125–43.

8 For an excellent and very thorough analysis of this practice of reading, see the essays and excerpts in Leland Ryken, ed., *The Christian Imagination: The Practice of Faith in Literature and Writing*, rev. and exp. ed. (Colorado Springs, Colo.: Shaw Books, 2002), to which I am frequently indebted for this section. I have also found the following sources most helpful: Michael Edwards, *Towards a Christian Poetics* (Grand Rapids, Mich.: W. B. Eerdmans, 1984), 1–13; Luke Ferretter, *Towards a Christian Literary Theory* (New York: Palgrave, 2004), 140–90; Nigel Forde, *The Lantern and the Looking-Glass: Literature and Christian Belief* (London: SPCK, 1997), 1–14; Susan V. Gallagher and Roger

Lundin, *Literature through the Eyes of Faith* (San Francisco: Harper & Row, 1989), 29–60; Gene Edward Veith, Jr., *Reading Between the Lines: A Christian Guide to Literature* (Wheaton, Ill.: Crossway Books, 1990), 17–25, and Terry Wright, "Religion and Literature from the Modern to the Postmodern: Scott, Steiner and Detweiler," *Literature and Theology*, 19.1 (2005): 3–21.

9   Other critics make this point also. It may not be out of place to note Dan B. Allender's recent work, for example, which complements my own. Allender urges Christians to trace the themes that God has written into our own narratives by taking the time to listen to our stories. See Allender, *To Be Told: Know Your Story, Shape Your Future* (Colorado Springs, Colo.: WaterBrook Press, 2005). Arnold Weinstein also claims that we can better grasp our own life stories by reading novels that mirror our world. See his *Recovering Your Story: Proust, Joyce, Woolf, Faulkner, Morrison* (New York: Random House, 2006). Finally, see Edward Mendelson, *The Things That Matter: What Seven Classic Novels Have to Say About the Stages of Life* (New York: Pantheon, 2006).

10   A. S. Byatt, *On Histories and Stories: Selected Essays* (Cambridge, Mass.: Harvard University Press, 2000), 166.

11   Cited in Susan Ketchin, ed., *The Christ-Haunted Landscape: Faith and Doubt in Southern Fiction* (Jackson: University of Mississippi Press, 1994), 57.

12   Eudora Welty, *On Writing*, with an introduction by Richard Bausch (New York: Modern Library, 2002), 28.

13   Roberto Calasso, *Literature and the Gods*, translated by Tim Parks (New York: Alfred A. Knopf, 2001), 192.

14   For additional commentary on how and why creative writers gesture toward Mystery, see Paul S. Fiddes, *Freedom and Limit: A Dialogue between Literature and Christian Doctrine* (Macon, Ga.: Mercer University Press, 1999), 3–46. Also see Matt Guynn, "Theopoetics: That the dead may become gardeners again," *CrossCurrents*, 56.1 (2006): 98–109.

15   Calasso, *Literature and the Gods*, 116.

16   Calasso, *Literature and the Gods*, 183.

17   Calasso, *Literature and the Gods*, 181. One might even boil it down to this observation: the end of reading is the end of life.

18   Rowan Williams, *On Christian Theology* (Malden: Mass.: Blackwell, 2000), 3–15.

19   Williams, *On Christian Theology*, 14. Emphasis in original.

20   I have been greatly instructed on this model of theology and its approach to reading literature by the following scholars and texts: David S. Cunningham, *Reading Is Believing: The Christian Faith through Literature and Film* (Grand Rapids, Mich.: Brazos Press, 2002); John R. May, *Nourishing Faith through Fiction: Reflections of the Apostles' Creed in Literature and Film* (Franklin, Wisc.: Sheed and Ward, 2001); William H. Willimon, *Reading with Deeper Eyes: The Love of Literature and the Life of Faith* (Nashville, Tenn.: Upper Room Books, 1998); and T. R. Wright, *Theology and Literature* (Oxford: Basil Blackwell, 1988).

21   For a fuller treatement of this motif, see Robert Detweiler, *Breaking the Fall: Religious Readings of Contemporary Fiction* (Louisville, Ky.: Westminster John Knox, 1989). I am also indebted to Margo Jefferson's "We Are All Tourists," *New York Times Book Review*, July 8, 2001, 27.

22   C. S. Lewis, *An Experiment in Criticism* (Cambridge: Cambridge University Press, 1961), 19.

23   Lewis, *An Experiment in Criticism*, 86.

24   Switch my metaphor for this fourth point—novels as foreign countries—and my point still stands: fiction changes things for us. Consider Louis Menand. "Novels, notoriously, are not about making peace or cultivating domesticity. Novels are about the demons that wreck happiness inside the bubble by whispering that there is something better for us outside it." See Menand, "The Earthquake," *The New Yorker*, February 6, 2006: 91. In addition, Milan Kundera argues that our preconceived notion(s) of the world—something we work with every day and certainly bring to our reading—is like a curtain that the novelist, assuming she or he performs well, rips through and reveals what it hides. See Kundera, *The Curtain: An Essay in Seven Parts* (New York: HarperCollins, 2007).

25   Mark Edmundson, *Why Read?* (New York: Bloomsbury, 2004), 129.

26   I do not mean to suggest that Edmundson and I are opposed to one another's interpretative strategies. A careful comparison of our work reveals that we are not so different—Edmundson self-identifies as a democratic humanist who recognizes that "the literature we have come to value, most especially the novel, is by and large antitranscendental. It does not offer a vision of the world under a deity's guidance." He also notes that "my sort of teaching assumes that a most pressing spiritual and intellectual task of the moment is to cre-

ate a dialogue between religious and secular visions of the world"
(Edmundson, *Why Read?*, 129, 136–43). I agree with him. There is
little question about today's novels; most are antitranscendental. But
some continue to gesture toward Mystery. And those are the novels that interest me. For an elaborate discussion of why we need to
blend humanist and theological considerations in our appreciation of
literature, see Jens Zimmermann, "*Quo Vadis?*: Literary Theory after
Postmodernism," *Christianity and Literature* 53.4 (2004): 495–519. Also
see Dennis Taylor, "The Need for a Religious Literary Criticism,"
Religion and the Arts 1.1 (1996): 124–50.

27 See Augustine, *On Christian Doctrine*, translated by D. W. Robertson,
Jr. (Upper Saddle River, N.J.: Library of Liberal Arts, 1958).

28 See Valentine Cunningham, *Reading after Theory* (Malden, Mass.:
Blackwell, 2002); Alan Jacobs, *A Theology of Reading: The Hermeneutics
of Love* (Boulder, Colo.: Westview Press, 2001); and Nancy M.
Malone, *Walking a Literary Labyrinth: A Spirituality of Reading* (New York:
Riverhead, 2003). Also see Kevin J. Vanhoozer, *Is There a Meaning
in This Text?: The Bible, The Reader, and the Morality of Literary Knowledge*
(Grand Rapids, Mich.: Zondervan Publishing House, 1998), 13–36,
367–468. Finally, see Michael Vander Weele, "What Is Reading For?"
Christianity and Literature 52.1 (2002): 57–83. As he puts it: "Reading is
first of all an exchange between people, an exchange whose dynamic
reminds us that we were created as limited human beings who are
enriched by fellowship with others" (81).

29 Malone, *Walking a Literary Labyrinth*, 164.

30 For an example of literature's life-changing effects, consider *Freedom
Writers*. See Stephen Henderson, "Film brings new life to Anne
Frank's diary," *Baptists Today* 25.2 (2007): 27. Also see http://www.
freedomwriters.com. While I have made every effort to provide accurate Internet addresses at the time of publication, neither I nor the
publisher assumes any responsibility for errors or changes that occur
after publication.

31 Noted in Alan Jacobs, "How to Read," *Books & Culture: A Christian
Review* (March/April 2007): 12–13.

32 Wayne C. Booth, *The Company We Keep: An Ethics of Fiction* (Berkeley:
University of California Press, 1988). Also see his "Story as Spiritual
Quest," *Christianity and Literature* 45.2 (1996): 163–90.

33 This is the thesis of Carl Ficken's helpful study, *God's Story and Modern
Literature: Reading Fiction in Community* (Philadelphia: Fortress, 1985).

See part one especially.

34   Malone, *Walking a Literary Labyrinth*, 176. Emphasis in original. Also see Romans 8:24-25.

35   See Richard Lansdown, *The Autonomy of Literature* (New York: St. Martin's Press, 2001). On the need to move beyond autonomy—because literary art so often stimulates us to do so—and read fiction theologically, see Andrew Shanks, *"What Is Truth?": Towards a Theological Poetics* (New York: Routledge, 2001), 3–38.

CHAPTER 1

1   To N.

2   A. F. Cassis, ed., *Graham Greene: Man of Paradox*, with a foreword by Peter Wolfe (Chicago: Loyola University Press, 1994), 125.

3   Cassis, ed., *Graham Greene: Man of Paradox*, 216. See Isaiah 40:1ff. Here God is a terror and a shepherd.

4   See Leopoldo Duran, *Graham Greene: An Intimate Portrait by His Closest Friend and Confidant*, translated by Euan Cameron (San Francisco: HarperSanFrancisco, 1994), 43–52, 94–116. Here Duran discusses Greene's literary and theological influences. Greene discusses Browning's influence in *A Sort of Life* (Harmondsworth, Middlesex: Penguin Books, 1971), 84–85.

5   See Henry J. Donaghy, ed., *Conversations with Graham Greene* (Jackson: University of Mississippi Press, 1992), 41. Most critics agree that Greene's life is best seen in three parts. For his early years, see Greene, *A Sort of Life*, and Norman Sherry, *The Life of Graham Greene Volume I: 1904–1939* (New York: Viking, 1989). Greene's *Ways of Escape: An Autobiography* (New York: Simon and Schuster, 1980) covers the second part of his life. Also see Norman Sherry, *The Life of Graham Greene Volume II: 1939–1955* (New York: Viking, 1994). The third and final part is covered by Norman Sherry, *The Life of Graham Greene Volume III: 1955–1991* (New York: Viking, 2004). For a useful, well-written summary of Greene's life and work, see Andrew W. Hass, "God and the Novelists 5. Graham Greene," *Expository Times* 110.3 (1998): 68–72.

6   See William Cash, *The Third Woman: The Secret Passion that Inspired Graham Greene's The End of the Affair* (New York: Carroll and Graf, 2000), 70, 219–20; Cassis, ed., *Graham Greene: Man of Paradox*, xvi, 74, 107, 127, 154, 168, 258; Donaghy, ed., *Conversations with Graham Greene*, 17, 152; and, finally, Duran, *Graham Greene: An Intimate Portrait*, 257, 285, 289.

7   Robert Browning, "Bishop Blougram's Apology," in *The Complete Poetical Works of Browning*, edited by Horace E. Scudder (Cambridge, Mass.: Houghton Mifflin, 1895), 353. Also see Scudder's "Biographical Sketch" of Browning's life and work, which appears at the onset of this volume. For an excellent account of how Browning's poem influences Greene's fiction, see Alan Warren Friedman, "'On the Dangerous Edge': Beginning with Death," in *Graham Greene: A Revaluation*, edited by Jeffrey Myers (New York: St. Martin's Press, 1990), 131–55.

8   Greene, *A Sort of Life*, 84–88. Also see Cassis, ed., *Graham Greene: Man of Paradox*, 277; Donaghy, ed., *Conversations with Graham Greene*, 140. For a discussion of uncertainty in Greene's fiction, see David H. Hesla, "Theological Ambiguity in the 'Catholic Novels,'" in *Graham Greene: Some Critical Considerations*, edited by Robert O. Evans (Louisville, Ky.: University of Kentucky Press, 1963), 96–111. Finally, a commitment to paradox links Greene with Søren Kierkegaard, the nineteenth-century Danish Lutheran theologian. For further information, see Anne T. Salvatore, *Greene and Kierkegaard: The Discourse of Belief* (Tuscaloosa: University of Alabama Press, 1988), 35–43.

9   Donaghy, ed., *Conversations with Graham Greene*, 152. Greene often sends out conflicting signals. Thus, I think we must be careful not to trust his storytelling completely. American novelist Reynolds Price says it well: "There are some early novels of Graham Greene's in the thirties after he was converted to Catholicism that as much as I admire them, I feel as if a hand is reaching into my pocket for my wallet. He's trying to seduce me with the story and also have me wind up down at St. Christopher's Catholic Church." See Reynolds Price, "Interview," in Susan Ketchin, ed., *The Christ-Haunted Landscape: Faith and Doubt in Southern Fiction* (Jackson: University Press, of Mississippi, 1994), 77.

10   Donaghy, ed., *Conversations with Graham Greene*, 17, 35. It is worth recalling that *Ways of Escape* is the title for Greene's second autobiography. Such a title suggests his own eagerness for emotional and spiritual liberation. Also see Cash, *The Third Woman*, 10, 70, 219; Cassis, ed., *Graham Greene: Man of Paradox*, 107–8, 168; and Francis L. Kunkel, "The Theme of Sin and Grace in Graham Greene" in Evans, ed., *Graham Greene: Some Critical Considerations*, 49–60. Finally, see K. C. Joseph Kurismmootil, S.J., *Heaven and Hell on Earth: An Appreciation of Five Novels of Graham Greene* (Chicago: Loyola University Press, 1982), 199–214. Kurismmootil provides an excellent outline of Greene's

theological convictions, especially the twin notions of sin and salvation, gathered together in a chapter he calls "A Novelist's Creed."

11 See Cash, *The Third Woman*, 139; Donaghy, ed., *Conversations with
Graham Greene*, 18, 38, 57, and Duran, *Graham Greene: An Intimate
Portrait*, 257. For a book-length treatment of Greene's "novels of pursuit," see Georg M. A. Gaston, *The Pursuit of Salvation: A Critical Guide to
the Novels of Graham Greene* (Troy, N.Y.: Whitson Publishing, 1984).

12 Cash, *The Third Woman*, 138. On this issue, readers will notice the sim-
ilarity between Greene and Thomas Hardy. As far as I am aware, the
connection between Greene and Thomas Hardy by way of an ironic
God first appears in Laurence Lerner, "Graham Greene," in *Graham
Greene: The Power and the Glory: Text, Background, and Criticism*, edited
by R. W. B. Lewis and Peter J. Cohn (New York: Viking, 1970),
395–414. Unlike Lerner, I intend to discuss Greene's ironic God in
some detail.

13 Duran, *Graham Greene: An Intimate Portrait*, 97, 100. Also see Cassis,
ed., *Graham Greene: Man of Paradox*, 252, 339, 347, 420, 465. Finally, see
Donaghy, ed., *Conversations with Graham Greene*, 169, 171.

14 Browning, "Bishop Blougram's Apology," 351.

15 Marie-Françoise Allain, *The Other Man: Conversations with Graham
Greene*, translated from the French by Guido Waldman (New York:
Simon and Schuster, 1981), 162–63. Also see Thomas A. Wassmer,
S.J., "Faith and Reason in Graham Greene," *Studies* 48 (1959):
163–67. Finally, see Cassis, ed., *Graham Greene: Man of Paradox*, xxix,
391, 420–1, 437.

16 Many patristic theologians drew the picture sketched in this section.
Among other places, their views on God are recorded in J. Stevenson,
ed., *A New Eusebius: Documents Illustrative of the History of the Church to A.D.
337*, based upon the collection by the late B. J. Kidd (London: SPCK,
1957), 63, 68, 100, 121, 123, 131, 138, 171, 216, 277, 340–78. Also
see Henry Chadwick, *The Early Church* (Harmondsworth, Middlesex:
Penguin Books, 1967), 77, 86–87, 89–90, 105, 114, 130, 141, 146, 148,
198–212, 235.

17 In this section, as with similar sections in subsequent chapters, it is
only possible to selectively sketch a particular doctrine's lengthy and
wide-ranging history. While I note certain landmark dates, personalities, and issues, I concentrate on those theologians whom Greene both
read and, in some cases, admired. This chapter's "for further reading"
section recommends several books featuring more background and

detailed information. My sources for this specific summary include: Karen Armstrong, *A History of God: The 4000-Year Quest of Judaism, Christianity and Islam* (New York: Alfred A. Knopf, 1994), 107–31; Hans Küng, *On Being a Christian*, translated by Edward Quinn, complete and unabridged version (New York: Doubleday, 1984), 57–88, 295–318; Jack Miles, *God: A Biography* (New York: Alfred A. Knopf, 1997); David A. Pailin, *God and the Processes of Reality: Foundations of a Credible Theism* (New York: Routledge, 1989), 1–56; Keith Ward, *The Living God* (London: SPCK, 1984), 1–35; and Maurice Wiles, *Reason to Believe* (Harrisburg, Pa.: Trinity Press International, 1999), 1–18. Greene read and admired Küng's work. See Cassis, ed., *Graham Greene: Man of Paradox*, 335–40, 425. In addition, see Allain, *The Other Man*, 80.

18   See R. W. Southern, *Western Society and the Church in the Middle Ages* (Harmondsworth, Middlesex: Penguin Books, 1970), 190, 202–4, 277–79. Also see Alister E. McGrath, *Historical Theology: An Introduction to the History of Christian Thought* (Malden, Mass.: Blackwell, 1998), 94–96, 101–5, 113–15, 118–21. The remainder of this section focuses on Anselm and Aquinas. For biographical sketches, see Bernard McGinn, *The Doctors of the Church: Thirty-Three Men and Women Who Shaped Christianity* (New York: Crossroad Publishing, 1999), 103–6, 124–30.

19   Anselm of Canterbury, *The Prayers and Meditations of St Anselm with the Proslogion*, translated and with an introduction by Sister Benedicta Ward, S.L.G., with a foreword by R. W. Southern (Harmondsworth, Middlesex: Penguin Books, 1973), 91.

20   Anselm of Canterbury, *The Major Works*, edited and with an introduction by Brian Davies and G. R. Evans (Oxford: Oxford University Press, 1998), 12, 26, 66–67, 72, 78–81.

21   Anselm, *The Major Works*, 88.

22   Anselm, *The Major Works*, 84–89, 111–22. Also see R. W. Southern, *Saint Anselm: A Portrait in Landscape* (Cambridge: Cambridge University Press, 1990), 15, 113–37.

23   For further information on the ontological argument and its critics, see John Hick, *Philosophy of Religion* (Englewood Cliffs, N.J.: Prentice-Hall, 1963), 15–30; David A. Pailin, *Groundwork of Philosophy of Religion* (London: Epworth Press, 1986), 159–80, and, finally, B. R. Tilghman, *An Introduction to the Philosophy of Religion* (Cambridge, Mass.: Blackwell, 1994), 46–96.

24 For additional biographical details, see Anthony Kenny, *Aquinas* (Oxford: Oxford University Press, 1980), 1–33.

25 See David Smith, "Thomas Aquinas," in *The Christian Theological Tradition*, edited by Catherine A. Cory and David T. Landry (Upper Saddle River, N.J.: Prentice Hall, 1999), 213–27. Also see Jeffery Hopper, *Understanding Modern Theology II: Reinterpreting Christian Faith for Changing Worlds* (Philadelphia: Fortress, 1987), 97–125.

26 For Aristotle's influence on Aquinas, see F. C. Copleston, *Aquinas* (Harmondsworth, Middlesex: Penguin Books, 1955), 63–69, 156–80, 213–19.

27 St. Thomas Aquinas, *Summa Theologiae*, complete English edition in five volumes, translated by the Fathers of the English Dominican Province (Notre Dame, Ind.: Christian Classics, 1981; 1948), 1.12.12, 1.12.13, 2-2.2.3, 2-2.2.7, 2.2.28, 2-2.2.10 (theological sources—faith and reason); 1.2.1, 1.2.2, 1.2.3, 1.3.4 (God's existence and nature). For those who find Aquinas' *Summa* daunting to follow, and I confess that I am one of them, I recommend the eminently readable translation and commentary by Frederick Christian Bauerschmidt, *Holy Teaching: Introducing the* Summa Theologiae *of St. Thomas Aquinas* (Grand Rapids, Mich.: Brazos Press, 2005). Finally, I should add that Aquinas' attempt to establish God's existence proceeds out from the provocative claim that Anselm's earlier proof rests on a mistake. It is impossible, Aquinas insists, for Anselm to know the divine *nature* before the divine *existence*. Such a claim may be likened to placing the cart before the horse. It's muddle-headed. And according to Aquinas, *contra* Anselm, God's existence is far from self-evident; it must, in fact, be ascertained by observing nature, particularly the dynamics of everyday experience, and seeing if anything *there* points to God. Only after this Aristotelian method of reflection is complete, Aquinas holds, can we then say we comprehend God's *existence*, making it feasible for us to return to what Anselm has to say about the divine *nature*.

28 For an excellent overview of Aquinas' arguments, see Anthony Kenny, *The Five Ways* (New York: Schocken Books, 1969).

29 Aquinas, *Summa Theologiae*, 1.2.3.

30 For additional biographical details, see D. LeMahieu, *The Mind of William Paley: A Philosopher and His Age* (Lincoln: University of Nebraska Press, 1976), 1–28, 55–90.

31 William Paley, *Natural Theology, or, Evidences of the Existence and Attributes of the Deity Collected from the Appearances of Nature*, illustrated by the

plates and by a selection from the notes of John Paxton; with additional notes, original and selected, for this revised American edition, and a vocabulary of scientific terms, by John Ware (Boston: Gould and Lincoln, 1863), 5. Emphasis in original.

32   Paley, *Natural Theology*, 13–30, 45–51, 207–11, 229–91. In responding to Paley and Aquinas, subsequent philosophers and theologians note the limitations involved in any attempt to argue to God from an observation of the world's teleology. For every instance of teleology in the world, they say, there are numerous examples of distelelogy, or moments of seemingly gratuitous evil and suffering, which serve to problematize the confident claim that our world is the product of a *benevolent* deity. See Anthony Flew and Alasdair MacIntyre, eds., *New Essays in Philosophical Theology* (London: SCM Press, 1955), 47–75, 96–130, 144–69; Brian Hebblethwaite, *Evil, Suffering and Religion* (London: Sheldon Press, 1976), 68–81, and, finally, John Hick, *An Interpretation of Religion: Human Responses to the Transcendent* (New Haven, Conn.: Yale University Press, 1989), 73–125.

33   Greene discusses Newman's influence in interviews with critics Alex Hamilton, Maria Couto, John Cornwall, Père Jouve, Marcel Moré, and V. S. Pritchett. See Cassis, ed., *Graham Greene: Man of Paradox*, 230, 425, 459. Also see Donaghy, ed., *Conversations with Graham Greene*, 19–20, 117. In Cornwall's interview, Greene praises von Hügel.

34   John Henry Cardinal Newman, *Apologia Pro Vita Sua* (London: Longmans, Green and Company, 1921), 1, 147, 149. For an exhaustive Newman biography, see Ian Kerr, *John Henry Newman: A Biography* (Oxford: Clarendon Press, 1988). For an instructive though brief overview, see Geoffrey Rowell, "Newman," in *The Blackwell Encyclopedia of Modern Christian Thought*, edited by Alister E. McGrath (Cambridge, Mass.: Blackwell, 1993), 405–8.

35   On the Enlightenment background to English religious thought in Newman's time, see Gerald R. Cragg, *The Church and the Age of Reason 1648–1789* (Harmondsworth, Middlesex: Penguin Books, 1960), 117–73, 234–55; Don Cupitt, *The Sea of Faith: Christianity in Change* (London: British Broadcasting Corporation, 1984); and A. N. Wilson, *God's Funeral* (New York: W. W. Norton, 1999). In addition, see Patrick Allitt, *Catholic Converts: British and American Intellectuals Turn to Rome* (Ithaca: Cornell University Press, 1997), 1–12, 54, 76, 94, 97–98, 104–5, 122, 168, 174, 188, 196, and, finally, David A. Pailin, *The Way to Faith: An Examination of Newman's* Grammar of Assent *as*

a Response to the Search for Certainty in Faith (London: Epworth Press, 1969), 1–96.

36 John Henry Cardinal Newman, *An Essay in Aid of A Grammar of Assent*, edited and with a preface and introduction by Charles Frederick Harrold (New York: Longmans, Green and Company, 1947), 11–74, 261–91. Also see Pailin, *The Way to Faith*, 144–60. Faith as internal assent stands in contrast to the claim, implicit in Anselm, that dialectical reasoning provides the grounds for faith. See Norman Pittenger, *Picturing God* (London: SCM Press, 1982), 141: "As St Ambrose put it, *non in dialectica complacuit deo salvum facere populum suam*: 'it was not in 'dialectic' that God has been pleased to save his people'. This was one of Cardinal Newman's favourite quotations; and rightly so."

37 Since faith involves internal assent, our thoughts about God, even whole theological doctrines, inexorably develop across time. In *An Essay on the Development of Christian Doctrine*, first published in 1845 and then revised in 1878, Newman wrestles with the issue of variation and constancy in the formulation of Christian doctrine. Christianity is "suited not simply to one locality or period, but to all times and places," Newman claims, and so "it cannot but vary in its relations and dealings towards the world around it, that is, it will develop." Changes in our theological understanding are inevitable, Newman asserts, because our environments and we change. And while specific tests—Newman suggests there are seven of them—for "ascertaining the correctness of developments [in doctrine] may be drawn out," the "large and complicated" nature of Christianity entails that such tests "may aid our inquiries and support our conclusions in particular points" only; such tests serve as "instruments rather than warrants of right decisions." The evolution of our ideas about God is to be expected, then, even encouraged, which implies that skepticism— Newman calls this "loving inquisitiveness"—has a place within the discipline of Christian formation. As we will see, Greene warmed to Newman's notion of the evolution of ideas, because *The End of the Affair* features several characters who are driven by a bizarre set of "coincidences" (or "miracles") to move out from under their dogmatic atheism in order to consider the possibility that God exists. Assuredly, *An Essay on the Development of Christian Doctrine* is Newman's hymn to the importance of growth in our knowledge of God. However much we think we know about the divine, Newman appears to say, God is always more than what we can say about God. See John Henry

Cardinal Newman, *An Essay on the Development of Christian Doctrine* (Westminster, Md.: Christian Classics, 1968), 58, 78, 169–206, 337. For Newman's notion of God and mystery, see *A Grammar of Assent*, 97–102, 267. Greene read and admired Newman's *Essay*. See Cassis, ed., *Graham Greene: Man of Paradox*, 467.

38   Baron Friedrich von Hügel, *The Mystical Element of Religion as Studied in Saint Catherine of Genoa and Her Friends*, vol. 1 (London: J. M. Dent and Sons; New York: E. P. Dutton, 1923), v, 50–82. Von Hügel believes Jesus, Catherine of Genoa, and St. John of the Cross exemplify religion's mystical element.

39   L. V. Lester-Garland, *The Religious Philosophy of Baron F. von Hügel* (New York: E. P. Dutton and Company, Inc., 1933), 17. For additional information on von Hügel's biography, see Michael De La Bedoyere, *The Life of Baron von Hügel* (New York: Charles Scribner's Sons, 1951).

40   Baron Friedrich von Hügel, *The Mystical Element of Religion as Studied in Saint Catherine of Genoa and Her Friends*, vol. 2 (London: J. M. Dent and Sons; New York: E. P. Dutton, 1923), 395.

41   Graham Greene, *The End of the Affair*, collected edition, with an introduction by the author (London: William Heinemann and The Bodley Head, 1974), viii–ix. See von Hügel, *The Mystical Element of Religion*, vol. 2, 375–76. I should add that although Greene implies that a passage unconnected with *The Mystical Element of Religion* provides him with the quotation that he cites for his readers, careful research shows that he does, in fact, quote the second volume of von Hügel's theological masterpiece. I am not aware of any Greene scholar, past or present, who has noted this intriguing fact. Even the most recent critic—William Cash—seems to have overlooked it. After citing Greene's 1974 introduction to *The End of the Affair*, Cash enjoins critics to deal "satisfactorily with the sources of his [Greene's] moral and religious thinking." See *The Third Woman*, 194, 219. My attempt to tie Greene to von Hügel's *The Mystical Element of Religion* is a modest start to this endeavor.

42   See von Hügel, *The Mystical Element of Religion*, vol. 2, 336–40, 372–87. Also see Greene, *The End of the Affair*, collected edition, ix. Finally, see Lester-Garland, *The Religious Philosophy of Baron F. von Hügel*, 63–76.

43   Graham Greene, *The End of the Affair* (Harmondsworth, Middlesex: Penguin Books, 1962), 35–36. Also see 56, 59–60, 101. Note Sarah's belief that Bendrix is motivated by love, not hate, which only serves to problematize Bendrix's narration. On the subject of Greene's penchant

222 Notes to pp. 32-33

for unreliable narration, see Carlos Villar-Flor, "Unbelieving Narrators: A Comparative Study of Graham Greene's *The End of the Affair* and C. S. Lewis's *Till We Have Faces*," in Wm. Thomas Hill, ed., *Perceptions of Religious Faith in the Work of Graham Greene* (New York: Peter Lang, 2001), 315–47. Furthermore, William Cash describes Greene as "the unreliable narrator of his own life—a deliberately self-delusional voyager-on-the-edge." And Cash's recent book, an engrossing account of Greene's tempestuous relationship with Lady Catherine Walston (the "C" to whom Greene's novel is dedicated), "is an inquiry into the theme of unreliable narrative." See Cash, *The Third Woman*, 22. Incidentally, I should say that I am inclined to side with Cash, who sees *The End of the Affair* as an example, perhaps the best there is, of the debt literature owes to adultery. Having acknowledged this, it strikes me as much too simplistic to identify Greene with Bendrix and Lady Walston with Sarah, even if *something* is going on there. See Cash, 16, 38. Finally, Greene's novel was first published in 1951 by William Heinemann Ltd, and then re-released as part of the collected edition of his novels in 1974. Readers will note that I have cited Greene's "Introduction" to the collected edition elsewhere in this chapter. In citing from the novel proper, as it were, I use the standard Penguin edition, readily available in bookstores and libraries. Since the collected edition of *The End of the Affair* is not so readily available, and since students and teachers very often use the latter and not the former, I quote from the Penguin edition.

44   Greene, *The End of the Affair*, 7.

45   Greene, *The End of the Affair*, 50. Also see 20–23, 30–31, 36–41.

46   Greene, *The End of the Affair*, 69. Laplace made his remark—"Sir, I have no need of *that* hypothesis"—to Napoleon, after the latter asked him why God was absent from his theory of the universe (*Celestial Mechanics*). Such words helped to sustain a modern worldview, an enlightened perspective, where it is thought God no longer plugs the gaps in our knowledge, for we have come to understand our world, not by invoking providence, but by engaging in scientific inquiry. See Edward W. H. Vick, *Quest: An Exploration of Some Problems in Science and Religion* (London: Epworth Press, 1975), 79. In choosing to eliminate God from their world, Bendrix and Sarah epitomize this modern sensibility, which Greene seems eager to question with the strange incident of the V1 blast.

47   Greene, *The End of the Affair*, 42, 52–59. For appropriate biblical references, see Exodus 20:5; 34:14. Finally, see Francis Thompson, "The

Hound of Heaven," in *Chapters into Verse: Poetry in English Inspired by the Bible, Volume Two: Gospels to Revelation*, assembled and edited by Robert Atwan and Laurance Wieder (New York: Oxford University Press, 1993), 186–91.

48   Greene, *The End of the Affair*, 69.

49   Greene, *The End of the Affair*, 71, 72.

50   Greene, *The End of the Affair*, 73.

51   Greene, *The End of the Affair*, 69.

52   Greene, *The End of the Affair*, 74. Also, see Roland A. Pierloot, "The Experiential God Representations and the God Concept in the Writings of Graham Greene," in Hill, ed., *Perceptions of Religious Faith in the Work of Graham Greene*, 349–89. In my view, it is impossible to over-state Sarah's interiority at this point in Greene's story. After all, the perception that God saves Bendrix and now expects Sarah to keep her bargain belongs to Sarah only; Bendrix does not render his experience the way Sarah does—he thinks he passed out for a few seconds. In the novel as in life we are not privy to God's view of the world, only to what takes place within ourselves, and Greene makes this point about theological and epistemic ambiguity very clear. Finally, I wish I had the space to problematize this apparent tension between reason and experience; in my view, a rationally defensible God need not be at odds with religious experience, though in this chapter I aim to be faithful to Greene's own stress on their apparent incompatibility.

53   Greene, *The End of the Affair*, 105.

54   Greene, *The End of the Affair*, 109.

55   Greene, *The End of the Affair*, 115.

56   Greene, *The End of the Affair*, 83.

57   While many believers assume that Anselm, Aquinas, and Paley show rational grounds for God's existence and activity, Greene disagrees. In *A Sort of Life*, the first of two autobiographies, he revisits his 1926 conversion to Catholicism and questions the value of theological rea-soning vis-à-vis his own spiritual struggles:

> If I were ever to be convinced in even the remote possibility of a supreme, omnipotent and omniscient power I realized that noth-ing afterwards could seem impossible. It was on the ground of a dogmatic atheism that I fought and fought hard. It was like a fight for personal survival.
>
> My friend Antonia White many years later told me how, when she was attending the funeral of her father, an old priest,

who had known her as a child, tried to persuade her to return to the Church. At last—to please him more than for any other reason—she said, 'Well then, Father, remind me of the arguments for the existence of God.' After a long hesitation he admitted to her, 'I knew them once, but I have forgotten them.' I have suffered the same loss of memory. I can only remember that in January 1926 I became convinced of the probable existence of something we call God, though now I dislike the word with all its anthropomorphic associations and prefer Chardin's Omega Point, *and my belief never came by way of those unconvincing philosophical arguments* which I derided in a short story called *A Visit to Morin*.

See Greene, *A Sort of Life*, 120–21; emphasis added. Such "unconvincing philosophical arguments" find their way into Greene's *The End of the Affair*, which appears nine years before "A Visit to Morin." They surface, for example, in Smythe's claim that none of these arguments, taken by themselves or cumulatively, constitutes anything approaching reasonable proof that God exists. And they materialize in Bendrix's contention that the universe and its so-called design is the result of blind, mindless chance. For information on "A Visit to Morin," see R. A. Wobbe, *Graham Greene: A Bibliography and Guide to Research* (New York: Garland, 1979), 120. On Greene and Teilhard de Chardin, see Darren J. N. Middleton, "Redeeming God: Traces of Catholic Process Theism in Graham Greene's *The Honorary Consul*," in Hill, ed., *Perceptions of Religious Faith in the Works of Graham Greene*, 523–47.

58 Greene, *The End of the Affair*, 122. Also see Richard Kelly, *Graham Greene* (New York: Frederick Ungar Publishing, 1984), 63–64. Finally, see Kurismmootil, *Heaven and Hell on Earth*, 154.

59 Greene, *The End of the Affair*, 115.

60 Greene, *The End of the Affair*, 188.

61 Greene, *The End of the Affair*, 177–79.

62 I think this is a false dichotomy. In my view, it seems possible to develop a theology of divine providence that is not obliged to view God intervening in the world on specific occasions only. See Darren J. N. Middleton, "David Pailin's Theology of Divine Action," *Process Studies* 22.4 (1993): 215–26.

63 Additional information on Greene's territory of uncertain meanings may be found in Thomas A. Wendorf, S.M., "Allegory in Postmodernity: Graham Greene's *The Captain and the Enemy*," *Christianity and Literature* 50.4 (2001): 657–77. Also see Greene, *The End of the Affair*, 92, 97, 144,

178–79, 184–89. In my view, Neil Jordan's 1999 cinematic adaptation of Greene's novel persuasively renders this shift in point of view, filming the V1 blast twice, as it were, so that the viewer comes to see the dilemma at the heart of the story. The DVD version of Jordan's film features some fairly instructive audio commentary on this same issue, even if it strikes me that the commentators take unnecessary pains to accentuate the moral—not the theological—issues at stake in the film. See *The End of the Affair* (Culver City, Calif.: Columbia Tri-Star Home Video, 2000). An earlier version of *The End of the Affair*, directed by Edward Dmytryk, was released in 1955. This 1955 version has been re-released on DVD. See *The End of the Affair* (Culver City, Calif.: Columbia Tri-Star Home Video, 2000). For more information on both films, see Quentin Falk, *Travels in Greeneland: The Complete Guide to the Cinema of Graham Greene*, rev. and updated 3rd ed., with a foreword by Neil Jordan (London: Reynolds & Hearn, 2000), 78–81, 137–41. For Greene's approach to the 1955 film, see David Parkinson, ed., *The Graham Greene Film Reader: Reviews, Essays, Interviews and Film Stories* (New York: Applause Books, 1994), 555, 706.

64   Greene, *The End of the Affair*, 95. Is this a sort of stigmata?

65   See Blaise Pascal, *Pensées*, edited by Brunschvicg, No. 233 (London: J. M. Dent & Sons; New York: E. P. Dutton, 1932), 66. Connecting Sarah to Pascal is instructive, I believe, because she seems more concerned with the God of living theistic faith, not the God of the philosophers, and also because Greene has Henry reference Pascal and Newman in the same sentence. See Greene, *The End of the Affair*, 111.

66   Greene, *The End of the Affair*, 102, 104, 120–21.

67   Greene, *The End of the Affair*, 91, 94, 100, 102. Note that Sarah walks in the rain when she realizes that God is working in her life, moving in the pain, sending a burst of divine love to fall on the desert of her disbelief (113). It is also worth noting that Sarah's reference to spiritual dryness connects her to the mystical writings of St. John of the Cross, whose *The Dark Night of the Soul* outlines three types of dryness, along with exercises to overcome each, and that Bendrix himself speaks of experiencing his own kind of *noche oscura*, dark night of the soul (47). See St. John of the Cross, *The Dark Night of the Soul*, edited by Halcyon Backhouse (London: Hodder and Stoughton, 1988). For a useful summary of St. John of the Cross, see McGinn, *The Doctors of the Church*, 148–52.

68   Greene, *The End of the Affair*, 89.

69 Greene, *The End of the Affair*, 109.

70 Greene, *The End of the Affair*, 122, 185, 188–90. This is Sarah's third miracle, so to speak, and is a clear sign that Greene intends us to see her in saintly terms.

71 Cash, *The Third Woman*, 190–91. Also see Saint Thérèse of Lisieux, *The Story of A Soul*, translated and with an introduction by John Beevers (New York: Doubleday, 1989). For a short summary of Thérèse's life and work, see McGinn, *The Doctors of the Church*, 169–73. Interestingly, Georg M. A. Gaston notes that "there are elements in the story of Sarah Miles which make it resemble a conventional hagiography." See Gaston, *The Pursuit of Salvation*, 44.

72 Greene, *The End of the Affair*, 123. As I see it, Sarah's words echo Luke 15. No one can ever will or act himself outside the story that God inscribes.

73 Kenneth Tynan, "An Inner View of Graham Greene," in Cassis, ed., *Graham Greene: Man of Paradox*, 107.

74 Greene, *The End of the Affair*, 125. Also see 126–31.

75 Greene, *The End of the Affair*, 128. Emphasis in original. Even though I discuss Greene's novel in the context of the doctrine of God, it is important to recognize that one of the ways God manifests Godself before Sarah and Bendrix is in the figure of Jesus, the crucified God, and especially in the images associated with this figure, like the crucifix, which means there are features of Greene's novel that provoke *christological* as well as *theological* reflection (109, 111–12, 119–20).

76 Greene, *The End of the Affair*, 131.

77 William Cash follows "the tough Jesuit intellectual" Father Martindale in likening Bendrix to the Apostle Paul, particularly at this point in Greene's narrative, since Bendrix appears to be kicking against the good, especially the good represented by Sarah. See Cash, *The Third Woman*, 223. I am inclined to connect Bendrix to the character of Jacob in Genesis 32–33. In my reading, Jacob is a disabled theologian, one who wrestles with God, and who is left lame for his efforts. With his own limp, Bendrix resembles Jacob, because his life seems like one long row with God, or himself, and he is left wounded and disabled from his struggles. Having offered this reading, I should acknowledge that we can trace Bendrix's limp to a childhood accident. See Greene, *The End of the Affair*, 57.

78 Doris Betts, quoted in W. Dale Brown, *Of Fiction and Faith: Twelve American Writers Talk About Their Vision and Work* (Grand Rapids, Mich.: W. B. Eerdmans, 1997), 10. If Betts (Job), Cash (Paul) and I (Jacob) are fair-minded in our assessment of Greene's narrative, then *The End of the Affair* possesses a biblical background. Finally, I should add that my notion of "seeing-as" has been greatly influenced by three books: John Berger, *Ways of Seeing* (London: British Broadcasting Corporation, 1972); John Hick, *An Interpretation of Religion*, 129–230; and, finally, Ludwig Wittgenstein, *Culture and Value*, edited by G. H. von Wright and translated by Peter Winch (Oxford: Blackwell, 1980), 82–86.

79 Greene, *The End of the Affair*, 136, 137.

80 Greene, *The End of the Affair*, 137.

81 Greene, *The End of the Affair*, 142, 146–48, 152–55. Also see Cates Baldridge, *Graham Greene's Fictions: The Virtues of Extremity* (Columbia: University of Missouri Press, 2000), 49–89. Also see Alan Warren Friedman, "'The Dangerous Edge': Beginning with Death," 150.

82 Greene, *The End of the Affair*, 146–47.

83 Greene, *The End of the Affair*, 72–3, 178, 184. I think Greene invites us to ask the question that Bendrix himself is forced to make toward the end of the novel: are these weird and wonderful events miracles or coincidences? And yet, regardless of what we say about the *source* of these events, I think Greene's signal contribution lies in his subtle suggestion that any such evaluation, theological or not, reveals more about the evaluator—their way of seeing-as, their overlay—than the *thing* being evaluated.

84 Greene, *The End of the Affair*, 162–65. For Mrs. Bertram's provocative simile (the sacrament of baptism is like a vaccination), see 164. Finally, see Psalms 23:6 and Romans 8:28. I find it utterly absorbing that Sarah compares faith to a disease while her mother compares it to a vaccination.

85 Greene, *The End of the Affair*, 173. Also see Psalms 139.

86 Greene, *The End of the Affair*, 192. Also see von Hügel, *The Mystical Element of Religion*, vol. 2, 375–76.

87 Julia Llewellyn Smith, *Traveling on the Edge: Journeys in the Footsteps of Graham Greene* (New York: St. Martin's Press, 2000), 99.

88 I am borrowing the "gesture toward mystery" phrase from the work of Thomas A. Wendorf. See his "Allegory in Postmodernity," 658.

89   Graham Greene, *Brighton Rock*, collected edition, with an introduc-
      tion by the author (London: William Heinemann and The Bodley
      Head, 1970), 389. Interestingly, one scholar has recently encouraged
      Christians to rethink the model of the "God of thunder" as an alterna-
      tive to the "domestic God" that permeates much modern Christianity.
      See Denis Donoghue, *Adam's Curse: Reflections on Religion and Literature*
      (Notre Dame, Ind.: University of Notre Dame Press, 2001), 14–28.

90   Miles, *God: A Biography*, 408. For similar literary assessments of the
      Hebrew Bible's God, see Richard Elliott Friedman, *The Hidden Face of
      God*, originally published as *The Disappearance of God* (San Francisco:
      HarperSanFrancisco, 1995); W. Lee Humphreys, *The Character of God
      in the Book of Genesis: A Narrative Appraisal* (Louisville, Ky.: Westminster
      John Knox, 2001); and, finally, Bernard Lang, *The Hebrew God: Portrait
      of an Ancient Deity* (New Haven, Conn.: Yale University Press, 2002).

91   David Penchansky, *What Rough Beast?: Images of God in the Hebrew Bible*
      (Louisville, Ky.: Westminster John Knox, 1999) 1–2.

92   Penchansky, *What Rough Beast?*, 93–94. Also see 15.

Chapter 2

1   I owe this insight to David A. Pailin, *The Anthropological Character of
      Theology: Conditioning Theological Understanding* (Cambridge: Cambridge
      University Press, 1990).

2   Kevin Vanhoozer makes this point throughout his "Human Being,
      Individual and Social" in Colin Gunton, ed., *The Cambridge Companion
      to Christian Doctrine* (Cambridge: Cambridge University Press, 1997),
      158–88.

3   For an excellent survey of this salient feature of the Christian doc-
      trine of humanity, see Tatha Wiley's *Original Sin: Origins, Developments,
      Contemporary Meanings* (Mahwah, N.J.: Paulist Press, 2002).

4   I am indebted to Jill Matus for my biographical sketch. See Matus,
      Toni Morrison (Manchester: Manchester University Press; St. Martin's
      Press, 1998), xii–36.

5   Besides ploughing through the novels themselves, which can prove
      difficult initially, readers interested in an engaging, if sometimes idio-
      syncratic, introduction to Morrison's literary art might consult Ron
      David, *Toni Morrison Explained: A Reader's Road Map to the Novels* (New
      York: Random House, 2000).

6   See Danille Taylor-Guthrie, ed., *Conversations with Toni Morrison*
      (Jackson: University of Mississippi Press, 1994), 58. Also see Toni

Morrison, *Playing in the Dark: Whiteness and the Literary Imagination* (Cambridge, Mass.: Harvard University Press, 1992), 1–28.

7   Taylor-Guthrie, *Conversations*, 10–29. Readers interested in a general introduction to the role religion plays in the African American community might consult Albert J. Raboteau, *African American Religion* (Oxford: Oxford University Press, 1999). Raboteau is Morrison's Princeton colleague.

8   Taylor-Guthrie, *Conversations*, 137.

9   Taylor-Guthrie, *Conversations*, 47.

10   Taylor-Guthrie, *Conversations*, 235. For criticism on community's place in Morrison's work, see Elizabeth Ann Beaulieu, ed., *The Toni Morrison Encyclopedia* (Westport, Conn.: Greenwood Press, 2003), 83–88 (entry on "community"); Patrick Bryce Bjork, *The Novels of Toni Morrison: The Search for Self and Place Within the Community* (New York: Peter Lang, 1992), 1–15, 55–82, and, finally, Therese E. Higgins, *Religiosity, Cosmology, and Folklore: The African Influence in the Novels of Toni Morrison* (New York: Routledge, 2001), 75–139.

11   Taylor-Guthrie, *Conversations*, 151.

12   Comprehensive materials on Morrison and Christianity are few and far between. I have been helped by the entry on "spirituality" in Beaulieu, ed., *The Toni Morrison Encyclopedia*, 324–29. In addition, Josiah Ulysses Young III's recent study contains some useful remarks. See *Dogged Strength Within the Veil: Africana Spirituality and the Mysterious Love of God* (Harrisburg, Pa.: Trinity Press International, 2003), 45–56. Even here, though, Young takes pains to separate Morrison and Christianity. He cites, for example, her sense that theology ties itself to racism (5). Books on Morrison, cosmology, and traditional African religions fair much better by comparison.

13   For example, Morrison frequently describes Scripture's role in her family's and community's life. See Taylor-Guthrie, *Conversations*, 80, 97, 104, 115, 126, 238, and 277. Furthermore, some of her characters—Hagar, Pilate, Shadrack, Hannah, and First Corinthians—bear names illustrating the Bible's impact "on the lives of black people, their awe of and respect for it coupled with their ability to distort it for their own purposes" (126). Finally, Morrison holds that "transcending love" lies at the New Testament's heart. And she claims that this quality renders the Christian Scriptures "so pertinent to black literature—the lamb, the victim, the vulnerable one who does die but nevertheless lives" (117).

14   Taylor-Guthrie, *Conversations*, 100, 165.

15   As with the Christian doctrine of God section in chapter one, it is
      only possible to selectively sketch our featured doctrine's lengthy and
      wide-ranging history. Thus, after discussing certain traditional theo-
      logical themes and personalities, I highlight those thinkers—especially
      the womanist writers—whose work intersects with Morrison's most
      directly. This chapter's "for further reading" section recommends
      several books featuring more background and detailed information.

16   B.C.E. signifies the religiously neutral designation for viewing his-
      tory prior to Jesus of Nazareth.

17   Genesis benefited from at least one editor. And many scholars hold
      that this person placed the two creation stories alongside one another
      because he found religious and existential insights in both—insights
      about life's total dependence on God, who orders and declares all
      things good.

18   For a brief biography of Irenaeus, see Eric Osborn, "Irenaeus of Lyon"
      in G. R. Evans, ed., *The First Christian Theologians: An Introduction to
      Theology in the Early Church* (Malden, Mass.: Blackwell, 2004), 121–26.
      Regarding Irenaeus and heresy, see Alister E. McGrath, *Historical
      Theology: An Introduction to the History of Christian Thought* (Malden, Mass.:
      Blackwell, 1998), 17–93. Also see Michael Hollerich's "Christianity
      after the Apostles" in Catherine A. Cory and David T. Landry, eds.,
      The Christian Theological Tradition, 2nd ed. (Upper Saddle River, N.J.:
      Prentice Hall, 2003; 2000), 108–22.

19   Cited in Alister E. McGrath, ed., *The Christian Theology Reader*, 3rd ed.
      (Malden, Mass.: Blackwell, 2007; 2001, 1996), 179–80, 404.

20   McGrath, ed., *The Christian Theology Reader*, 414–19. Augustine upholds
      predestinationism. And this belief—in the primacy and adequacy of
      God's saving action—colors what he says about free will. Augustine
      certainly thinks we have free will, for he declares that Adam acted
      freely in tasting the fruit of the tree of knowledge of good and evil. But
      he also thinks that freedom's power and range lessens after the Fall.

21   For an accessible introduction to Augustine, see Stephen A. Cooper,
      Augustine for Armchair Theologians (Louisville, Ky.: Westminster John
      Knox, 2002). I also recommend Sandra Lee Dixon, *Augustine: The
      Scattered and Gathered Self* (St. Louis, Mo.: Chalice Press, 1999). Finally,
      see David Hunter, "Augustine of Hippo" in Cory and Landry, eds.,
      The Christian Theological Tradition, 141–52.

22   See McGrath, ed., *The Christian Theology Reader*, 199–200, 416–19. One way to appreciate the difference between Irenaeus and Augustine is to view them as representing dissimilar, yet entirely legitimate, strands in the Christian doctrinal tradition of thinking about humanity. They disagree on the function freedom plays in the formation of our interactions with one another and with God. However, as can be seen, both acknowledge freedom's existence and worth in just such a process. For additional information on the notion of sin in the early Christian tradition, see Wiley, *Original Sin*, 37–75.

23   Taylor-Guthrie, *Conversations*, 168.

24   Wiley, *Original Sin*, 128. Other theologians include: Douglas J. Hall, *God and Human Suffering: An Exercise in the Theology of the Cross* (Minneapolis, Minn.: Augsburg Publishing House, 1986), 73–92; Jerry D. Korsmeyer, *Evolution and Eden: Balancing Original Sin and Contemporary Science* (Mahwah, N.J.: Paulist Press, 1998), 112–32, and, finally, Marjorie Hewitt Suchocki, *The Fall to Violence: Original Sin in Relational Theology* (New York: Continuum, 1995), 16–29.

25   For an anthology of Niebuhr's writings consult Larry Rasmussen, ed., *Reinhold Niebuhr: Theologian of Public Life* (Minneapolis, Minn.: Fortress, 1991). This anthology's biographical introduction contextualizes Niebuhr's social and pastoral theology quite helpfully.

26   Reinhold Niebuhr, *The Nature and Destiny of Man: A Christian Interpretation*, 1 vol. ed. (New York: Charles Scribner's Sons, 1941), 1–18.

27   Niebuhr, *The Nature and Destiny of Man*, 16.

28   Niebuhr, *The Nature and Destiny of Man*, 182.

29   Niebuhr, *The Nature and Destiny of Man*, 185.

30   Niebuhr, *The Nature and Destiny of Man*, 186–240.

31   Niebuhr, *The Nature and Destiny of Man*, 208.

32   Niebuhr, *The Nature and Destiny of Man*, 213.

33   Taylor-Guthrie, *Conversations*, 67–68.

34   Unlike elsewhere in this and other chapters, space prohibits me from providing specific biographies of individual theologians in my discussion of feminist theology. Here I paint with broad brushstrokes, since I think feminist theology is a style of thinking that owes much to many scholars, not just one or two. Something similar might be said of womanist theology, which I discuss a little later in this section.

35   I owe this insight to Sarah Coakley, "Creaturehood before God: Male and Female," in Robin Gill, ed., *Readings in Modern Theology: Britain and*

America (Nashville, Tenn.: Abingdon Press, 1995), 329–41. Similar thoughts appear in the many essays associated with Catherine Mowry LaCugna, ed., *Freeing Theology: The Essentials of Theology in Feminist Perspective* (San Francisco, Calif.: HarperSanFrancisco, 1993); see especially Mary Aquin O'Neill's essay, "The Mystery of Being Human Together: Anthropology," 139–60. Also see Denise L. Carmody, *Christian Feminist Theology* (Cambridge, Mass.: Blackwell, 1995), 139–72.

36 Daphne Hampson makes this point in her work. See *Theology and Feminism* (Oxford: Blackwell, 1990), 121–24.

37 Valerie Saiving, "The Human Situation: A Feminine View," 37. Reprinted in Carol P. Christ and Judith Plaskow, eds., *Womanspirit Rising: A Feminist Reader in Religion* (San Francisco: Harper and Row, 1979), 25–42.

38 For an overview of the rise and development of womanist theology, see Dwight N. Hopkins, *Introducing Black Theology of Liberation* (Maryknoll, N.Y.: Orbis Books, 1999), 125–56. And for a compelling womanist critique of feminist theology, see Jacquelyn Grant, *White Women's Christ and Black Women's Jesus: Feminist Christology and Womanist Response* (Atlanta, Ga.: Scholars Press, 1989), 195–201. Also see Kelly Brown Douglas, *The Black Christ* (Maryknoll, N.Y.: Orbis Books, 1994), 92–96.

39 These various quotes summarize Walker's four-part definition, which is quite detailed. See Alice Walker, *In Search of Our Mothers' Gardens: Womanist Prose* (New York: Harcourt Brace Jovanovich, 1983), xi–xii.

40 For an outline of such theologians and their views, see James H. Evans Jr., "Black Theology in America," in James C. Livingston and Francis Schüssler Fiorenza with Sarah Coakley and James H. Evans Jr., *Modern Christian Thought: Volume II: The Twentieth Century*, 2nd ed. (Upper Saddle River, N.J.: Prentice Hall, 2000; 1997), 443–68. It is worth noting Morrison's own emphasis upon black female experience. See Taylor-Guthrie, *Conversations*, 129.

41 See Grant, *White Women's Christ and Black Women's Jesus*, 202–18. "The daily struggles of poor black women must serve as the gauge for the verification of the claims of womanist theology," Grant maintains (209–10). For similar views on this issue, see Teresa L. Fry Brown, *God Don't Like Ugly: African-American Women Handing on Spiritual Values* (Nashville, Tenn.: Abingdon Press, 2000), 34, Cheryl J. Sanders,

ed., *Living the Intersection: Womanism and Afrocentrism in Theology* (Minneapolis, Minn.: Fortress, 1995), 68–73, and, finally, Emilie M. Townes, *In a Blaze of Glory: Womanist Spirituality as Social Witness* (Nashville, Tenn.: Abingdon Press, 1995), 9–10. As James H. Evans Jr. points out, though, it is important not to view womanist theology as a reaction to sexism, racism, and classism only: "It is a movement of the Spirit. It celebrates the distinctive historical and contemporary gifts of black women in the churches and the world." See Evans Jr., "Black Theology in America," 460.

42   For various womanist approaches to relationality, see Fry Brown, *God Don't Like Ugly*, 39, 50–52, 80, 114–32, 158–81; Townes, *In a Blaze of Glory*, 48–49, and, finally, Emilie M. Townes, ed., *Embracing the Spirit: Womanist Perspectives on Hope, Salvation, and Transformation* (Maryknoll, N.Y.: Orbis Books, 1997), 72–94, 97–121.

43   Katie G. Cannon, *Katie's Canon: Womanism and the Soul of the Black Community* (New York: Continuum, 1995), 58. Also see Katie G. Cannon, *Black Womanist Ethics* (Atlanta, Ga.: Scholars Press, 1988), 144–45.

44   Cannon, *Katie's Canon*, 91.

45   Cannon, *Katie's Canon*, 63. Also see 92.

46   Cannon, *Black Womanist Ethics*, 99–157.

47   Cannon, *Katie's Canon*, 92.

48   Cannon, *Black Womanist Ethics*, 144.

49   Cannon, *Black Womanist Ethics*, 144.

50   Toni Morrison, *Sula* (New York: Plume, 1973), 5. In citing from the novel proper, I use the standard Plume edition, readily available in bookstores and libraries.

51   Morrison, *Sula*, 5.

52   Morrison, *Sula*, 4. Also see Cannon, *Katie's Canon*, 58–60.

53   Morrison, *Sula*, 18.

54   Morrison, *Sula*, 18.

55   Morrison, *Sula*, 18.

56   Morrison, *Sula*, 29. The only time Hannah appears to lose her moral grip on the world is when she visits relatives in New Orleans; here she stumbles, because going outside the Bottom places her in a world she seems unable to control (17–29). Nel accompanies Hannah on this trip, interestingly enough, and then returns to the Bottom invigorated, with a new sense of self (29). She figuratively unbinds the apron strings that tie her to Hannah, at least from this point on, and sets about knowing people outside her home, including Sula.

57 Morrison, *Sula*, 30, 32–37. Eva sounds like Eve, of course, and one wonders if Morrison intends us to read some provocative theology into such naming. Hannah is another biblical name. See Genesis 3:20 and 1 Samuel 1.

58 Morrison, *Sula*, 31, 34, 47, 72, 93.

59 Morrison, *Sula*, 42.

60 Morrison, *Sula*, 41.

61 Morrison, *Sula*, 7–16. Notice that Shadrack resembles John the Baptizer (15).

62 Morrison, *Sula*, 41–44. Eva's and Hannah's feistiness shows up sexually. But sexuality does not exhaust womanism. And in one sense, womanists might question the way Eva and Hannah express their sexuality. Both seem unable to love relationally, for example, and insofar as relationality represents womanism's story and song, Eva and Hannah's selfishness seems problematic. Without referencing womanism, Morrison makes a similar point in an interview with Betty Jean Parker. See Taylor-Guthrie, *Conversations*, 61–64.

63 Living with little or no recourse to community values represents part of the problem. See Higgins, *Religiosity, Cosmology, and Folklore*, 89–94.

64 See Diane Gillespie and Missy Dehn Kubitschek, "Who Cares? Women-Centered Psychology in *Sula*," in David L. Middleton, ed., *Toni Morrison's Fiction: Contemporary Criticism* (New York: Garland Publishing, 1997), 82–87. Also see Deborah E. McDowell, "The Self and the Other: Reading Toni Morrison's *Sula* and the Black Female Text," in Nellie Y. McKay, ed., *Critical Essays on Toni Morrison* (Boston: G. K. Hall, 1988), 77–90.

65 Morrison, *Sula*, 18, 29, 83.

66 Morrison, *Sula*, 57.

67 Morrison, *Sula*, 52.

68 Morrison, *Sula*, 54–55. I am persuaded that this kind of sacrifice is best viewed religiously. See Walter Burkert, *Creation of the Sacred: Tracks of Biology in Early Religions* (Cambridge, Mass.: Harvard University Press, 1996), 34–55.

69 Morrison, *Sula*, 61, 80.

70 Morrison, *Sula*, 80.

71 Morrison, *Sula*, 83.

72 Morrison, *Sula*, 85. Some critics think Sula's community casts her out. See Patricia McKee, "Spacing and Placing Experience in Toni Morrison's *Sula*," in Nancy J. Peterson, ed., *Toni Morrison: Critical and*

Thoretical Approaches (Baltimore, Md.: The Johns Hopkins University Press, 1997), 44–46.

73 Morrison, *Sula*, 92.

74 Morrison, *Sula*, 92–93.

75 See John Milton, *Paradise Lost and Paradise Regained*, edited and with notes by Christopher Ricks and with a new Introduction by Dr. Susanne Woods (New York: Signet, 2001), I:33–49. Also see Isaiah 14:12.

76 Vanhoozer, "Human Being, Individual and Social," 177. Also see Carmody, *Christian Feminist Theology*, 148–53.

77 Morrison, *Sula*, 94, 102–18.

78 Morrison, *Sula*, 121–22.

79 Cannon, *Katie's Canon*, 67.

80 Cannon, *Katie's Canon*, 91.

81 Cannon, *Katie's Canon*, 63.

82 Taylor-Guthrie, *Conversations*, 13–14. Here Morrison makes the point that Nel is the Bottom community, because she embodies so many of its values.

83 Cannon, *Katie's Canon*, 92. Also see Cannon, *Black Womanist Ethics*, 99–157, especially 144.

84 Taylor-Guthrie, *Conversations*, 13.

85 Taylor-Guthrie, *Conversations*, 14.

86 Carmody, *Christian Feminist Theology*, 145. Technically, Sula is not the subject of Carmody's reflection; however, I find her felicitous phrase instructive when thinking about Sula, when she returns to the Bottom after ten years away.

87 Morrison, *Sula*, 95.

88 Morrison, *Sula*, 113. Also see 122.

89 Morrison, *Sula*, 113–14.

90 Morrison, *Sula*, 115.

91 Morrison, *Sula*, 117–18. Also see McKee, "Spacing and Placing," 54–58. It is perhaps ambitious to say that Sula displays Christ-like qualities at this point. However, I think it is worth noting the argument, even if I judge it best to confine it to an endnote, since much of what follows is entirely speculative. It is fairly commonplace to note, for example, that the word "Christ," separate from the name Jesus, means "anointed one." It can also mean "smeared one" or "one who is marked," usually for some special or chosen purpose. See W. R. F. Browning, ed., *A Dictionary of the Bible* (Oxford: Oxford

University Press, 1997), 63. Morrison's fiction is replete with biblical allusions, as I have noted, but *Sula* nowhere explicitly indicates that Sula is Christ-like. The closest Morrison comes to thinking in such terms is in an interview she gave in 1983; here she thinks of Sula as pre-Christ-like. See Taylor-Guthrie, *Conversations*, 165. But readers of *Sula* would do well to notice Morrison's epigram: "Nobody knew my rose of the world but me . . . I had too much glory. They don't want glory like *that* in nobody's heart." This inscription is from "The Rose Tattoo," a play by Tennessee Williams. But what does it signify? I think it refers to Sula's "evil birthmark," which takes the shape of a "stemmed rose that hung over" her eye. See Morrison, *Sula*, 115, 135. Morrison is an ironic writer, one whose striking literary imagination often inverts things and turns them upside down. In her hands, as we have seen, evil can sometimes appear good, and good can sometimes appear evil. In any event, this observation about the rose birthmark allows us to describe Sula as smeared or marked by something. If we yoke this description to the definition of "Christ" as one who is marked *and* to Sula's ability to stimulate goodness in others, then we have some reason to think of Sula as Christ-like. Morrison's narrator gives us warrant for such an interpretation. See Morrison, *Sula*, 117–18. Finally, compare with Brown Douglas, *The Black Christ*: "I affirm that Christ is found where Black people, men as well as women, are struggling to bring the entire Black community to wholeness" (109). And again: "So, is Christ a Black woman? Yes, when Black women are acting to establish life and wholeness for the Black community" (110).

92   Morrison, *Sula*, 120.
93   Morrison, *Sula*, 119, 139.
94   Morrison, *Sula*, 52.
95   Morrison, *Sula*, 52.
96   Gillespie and Kubitschek, 86.
97   Morrison, *Sula*, 52–53, 128, 174. Also see Gillespie and Kubitschek, 87–88.
98   See Genesis 4:1-26; 25-33. Also see Carolyn M. Jones, "*Sula* and *Beloved*: Images of Cain in the Novels of Toni Morrison," in Harold Bloom, ed., *Modern Critical Interpretations: Toni Morrison's* Sula (Philadelphia: Chelsea, 1999), 133–48.
99   I have been helped in this insight by McKee, "Spacing and Placing," 40–44.

100 I owe the phrase "spirituality of persistence" to Hopkins, *Introducing Black Theology of Liberation*, 128.

101 Cannon, *Katie's Canon*, 58.

102 Cannon, *Black Womanist Ethics*, 75–98. Also see Cannon, *Katie's Canon*, 77–100. For other womanists on the black woman's literary tradition, see Brown Douglas, *The Black Christ*, 90, 117; Fry Brown, *God Don't Like Ugly*, 64–76, 169–78; Grant, *White Women's Christ and Black Women's Jesus*, 204–9; Youtha C. Hardman-Cromwell, "Living the Intersection of Womanism and Afrocentrism: Black Women Writers," in Sanders, ed., *Living the Intersection*, 106–16, and, finally, Townes, *In a Blaze of Glory*, 47–119.

103 Cannon, *Katie's Canon*, 59–60. Womanist theologians draw on literature quite freely. And they heed how black women—in community groups, church committees, kitchen table conversations, book clubs, etc.—interpret such literature. See Hopkins, *Introducing Black Theology of Liberation*, 134. Also see Fry Brown, *God Don't Like Ugly*, 158–81.

104 These words reflect Morrison's writerly self-understanding. See Hardman-Cromwell, "Living the Intersection," 108.

105 Cannon, *Katie's Canon*, 61. Morrison expresses her commitment to the notion that narrative both creates and sustains community in her Nobel Lecture. See Toni Morrison, *The Nobel Lecture in Literature 1993* (New York: Alfred A. Knopf, 1994), 7. Morrison also uses this lecture to comment on what she calls "theistic language," which she groups together with sexist and racist discourse as part of "the policing languages of mastery" (16–17). Now, theology can be a totalizing language, at least in the hands of some, promising Final Meaning, but it need not be, especially if theologians read more narrative and, as a result, come to appreciate how story is one of the best tools we have in our work of gesturing toward Mystery. "Language can never 'pin down' slavery, genocide, war. [I would add God to this list.] Nor should it yearn for the arrogance to be able to do so. Its force, its felicity, is in its reach toward the ineffable" (21).

106 I owe the "storytelling bipeds" phrase to Kathleen Norris. See *Amazing Grace: A Vocabulary of Grace* (New York: Riverhead Books, 1998), 3.

107 Eugene H. Peterson, *Take and Read: Spiritual Reading–An Annotated List* (Grand Rapids, Mich.: W. B. Eerdmans, 1996), ix–x. Compare Peterson's remarks with the basic thesis in Toni Morrison's *The Dancing Mind* (New York: Alfred A. Knopf, 1997).

108 Cannon, *Katie's Canon*, 63.

CHAPTER 3

1   Completed in 1951, Kazantzakis' novel was published in Greek in
     1955. For the Greek text, see Nikos Kazantzakis, *O teleftaíos peirasmós*
     (Athens: Difros, 1955). Even though the Greek title does not include
     the "of Christ" favored by the U.S. publisher, I am writing for non-
     Greek readers primarily. For the U.S. publication of the English trans-
     lation, see Nikos Kazantzakis, *The Last Temptation of Christ*, translated
     by Peter A. Bien (New York: Simon and Schuster, 1960). In keeping
     with the strategy adopted in previous chapters, I use the most acces-
     sible version of the main novel under scrutiny. To this end, I cite Bien's
     translation. For the controversies surrounding Kazantzakis' work,
     see *God's Struggler: Religion in the Writings of Nikos Kazantzakis*, edited
     by Darren J. N. Middleton and Peter A. Bien (Macon, Ga.: Mercer
     University Press, 1996), 23–35. For criticism of the film version of
     Kazantzakis' novel, see John Ankerberg and John Weldon, *The Facts
     on "The Last Temptation of Christ": The True Story Behind the Controversial
     Film* (Eugene, Ore.: Harvest House Publishers, 1988). In addition, see
     Michael Medved, *Hollywood vs. America: Popular Culture and the War on
     Traditional Values* (New York: HarperCollins and Zondervan, 1992),
     37–49. For the DVD version of the film, which features instructive
     audio commentary by Martin Scorsese, Willem Dafoe, Paul Schrader,
     and Jay Cocks, see *The Last Temptation of Christ* (Universal City, Calif.:
     Criterion Home Collection, 2000). For an intriguing reception his-
     tory of the film, see Robin Riley, *Film, Faith, and Cultural Conflict: The
     Case of Martin Scorsese's* The Last Temptation of Christ (Westport,
     Conn.: Praeger Publishers, 2003). Also see the essays in Darren J. N.
     Middleton, ed., *Scandalizing Jesus?: Kazantzakis's* The Last Temptation of
     Christ *Fifty Years On* (New York: Continuum, 2005).

2   When discussing Jesus' significance for the Christian faith, theolo-
     gians frequently divide their time between Christology and soteriol-
     ogy (an examination of salvation). Those concerned with Christology
     reflect on Jesus' *person and significance* while those involved with
     soteriology deliberate on Jesus' *saving work*. Although this distinc-
     tion is instructive, most accounts of Jesus include elements of each.
     Theologians recurrently find it difficult, if not altogether impossible,
     to assess Jesus' person without incorporating an analysis of his work,
     and vice versa. For the purposes of this book, I discuss Christology
     and soteriology together, since experience teaches me that this aca-

demic distinction ultimately dissolves in the mind and heart of most believers. For more details on why theologians distinguish between Christology and soteriology, see Alister E. McGrath, *Christian Theology: An Introduction*, 4th ed. (Malden, Mass.: Blackwell, 2007; 2001, 1996, 1993), 272–359.

3   For more detailed information on Kazantzakis' biography, see the following texts: Peter A. Bien, *Kazantzakis: Politics of the Spirit*, vol. 1 (Princeton, N.J.: Princeton University Press, 1989); Peter A. Bien, *Kazantzakis: Politics of the Spirit*, vol. 2 (Princeton, N.J.: Princeton University Press, 2007); Helen Kazantzakis, *Nikos Kazantzakis: A Biography Based on His Letters*, translated by Amy Mims (New York: Simon and Schuster, 1968); James F. Lea, *Kazantzakis: The Politics of Salvation*, (Tuscaloosa: University of Alabama Press, 1979), 1–34; Morton P. Levitt, *The Cretan Glance: The World and Art of Nikos Kazantzakis* (Columbus: Ohio State University Press, 1980), 3–19; and, lastly, Pandelis Prevelakis, *Nikos Kazantzakis and His Odyssey: A Study of the Poet and the Poem*, translated by Philip Sherrard (New York: Simon and Schuster, 1961). Kazantzakis wrote an autobiography, *Report to Greco*, but it is a misleading source, because it blends experience and hyperbole. See Nikos Kazantzakis, *Report to Greco*, translated by Peter A. Bien (New York: Simon and Schuster, 1965), 9.

4   The following sources describe the Bergsonian-Nietzschean background to Kazantzakis' thought: Bien, *Kazantzakis: Politics of the Spirit*, vol. 1, 23–53; Daniel A. Dombrowski, *Kazantzakis and God* (Albany: State University of New York Press, 1997), 9–26, 145–53; B. T. McDonough, *Nietzsche and Kazantzakis* (Washington, D.C.: University Press of America, 1978). Also see Kazantzakis, *Report to Greco*, 317–39. For details regarding Kazantzakis' lecture on Bergson, see Bien, *Kazantzakis: Politics of the Spirit*, vol. 1, 295.

5   Kazantzakis was born and raised in the Greek Orthodox Church. For an introduction to Greek Orthodoxy, see Demetrios J. Constantelos, *Understanding the Greek Orthodox Church: Its Faith, History, and Practice* (New York: Seabury Press, 1982). For the unfamiliar, there are over 250 million Orthodox Christians around the world, and Orthodox Christians are divided into one of two groups, the Eastern and the Oriental. Based in Istanbul in modern-day Turkey, the Ecumenical Patriarch of Constantinople leads both groups. Larger than the Oriental group, the Eastern group includes Russian, Romanian, Bulgarian, Serbian, and the

Greek Churches. Mount Athos is crucial to any understanding of Eastern Orthodoxy. While it is a deeply mysterious place, one very informative and readable account of its monastic life is: Graham Speake, *Mount Athos: Renewal in Paradise* (New Haven, Conn.: Yale University Press, 2003). For details on Kazantzakis' visits to Athos, see Darren J. N. Middleton, *Broken Hallelujah: Nikos Kazantzakis and Christian Theology* (Lanham, Md.: Lexington Books, 2007), 11–29. His sense of Christ was extraordinarily strong during his visits. See Kazantzakis, *Report to Greco*, 188–234.

6   Bien, *Kazantzakis: Politics of the Spirit*, vol. 1, xxiii.

7   Further details on this friendship may be found in Middleton, *Broken Hallelujah*, 45–56.

8   Henri Bergson, *Creative Evolution*, translated by Arthur Mitchell (New York: Henry Holt, 1911), 128. Emphasis in original.

9   Bergson, *Creative Evolution*, 270–71.

10   Bergson, *Creative Evolution*, 50–55, 85–87, 98–105, 128, 247–52, 260. It is helpful here, I think, to note Bergson's view that matter is not a separate entity but a coagulation of the *élan vital* (252).

11   In traditional Eastern Orthodox and Roman Catholic doctrine, transubstantiation refers to the dynamic process whereby bread and wine become, through divine action, the body and blood of Jesus Christ at the sacrament of the Eucharist. See Nikos Kazantzakis, *The Saviors of God: Spiritual Exercises*, translated and with an introduction by Kimon Friar (New York: Simon and Schuster, 1960), 100, 105–6, *passim*. Also see Kazantzakis, *The Last Temptation of Christ*, 3, 152, 197.

12   Kazantzakis names the *élan vital* "God" because "only this name, for primordial reasons, can stir our hearts profoundly." See Kazantzakis, *The Saviors of God*, 101. In addition, I identify "traditional Christianity" and "traditional Christian doctrine" with the Platonic-Aristotelian-Augustinian tradition, which I outline in chapter one, and where the picture of God's unchangeability prevails against all other ways of modeling the divine. For additional information on the place of God's unchangeability in Christian doctrine, see Roger E. Olson, *The Mosaic of Christian Belief: Twenty Centuries of Unity and Diversity* (Downers Grove, Ill.: InterVarsity Press, 2002), 111–54.

13   See *Report to Greco*, 109–26. Here Kazantzakis recounts his "adolescent difficulties" with the religious implications of evolutionary theory and heliocentric astronomy. I have written elsewhere

of the way Kazantzakis absorbs evolutionary theory, especially Bergsonian vitalism, and how he therefore anticipates *process theology*, whose influence on Christian doctrine has been felt mainly in North America. See Darren J. N. Middleton, *Novel Theology: Nikos Kazantzakis's Encounter with Whiteheadian Process Theism* (Macon, Ga.: Mercer University Press, 2000). Also see Middleton, *Broken Hallelujah*, 83–99.

14   Kazantzakis, *The Saviors of God*, 56. Also see 49–50, 55.

15   Kazantzakis, *Saviors of God*, 59.

16   Kazantzakis, *Saviors of God*, 63–68, 83, 87, 105, 110, 112. Also see Kazantzakis, *Report to Greco*, 291–92.

17   For instance, see Matthew 25:6; Acts 23:9; Hebrews 5:7; and Revelation 14:18; 21:4.

18   Kazantzakis, *The Last Temptation of Christ*, 25–27, 44, 126, 186. Also see Kazantzakis, *The Saviors of God*, 84. Here Kazantzakis depicts God as a merciless vulture who, advancing from carcass to carcass for something to feed on, flies forward on a journey unfinished. I should add that ravens appear in the Bible. See 1 Kings 17:1-7 and Luke 12:24. Now, I offer biblical references here and elsewhere because, as many Kazantzakis scholars know, several critics charge that Kazantzakis' portrait of Jesus, not to mention his general religiosity, is unbiblical. I disagree; in my view, there is a biblical background to Kazantzakis' work. As an aside, interested readers will note that Kazantzakis joins Graham Greene in depicting God's agency ambiguously. Finally, note that references to Kazantzakis' Jesus refrain from capitalizing the pronoun, to accentuate Jesus' humanity, Kazantzakis adopted this style in his novel, and I wish to honor his choice.

19   Kazantzakis, *The Saviors of God*, 80–81.

20   Kazantzakis, *Saviors of God*, 100. Also see 106.

21   In the next section, as with similar sections in earlier chapters, it is only possible to selectively sketch our featured doctrine's lengthy and wide-ranging history. While I note certain landmark dates, personalities, and issues, I concentrate on two thinkers—Cabasilas and Renan—whom Kazantzakis both read and admired. Both thinkers symbolize Christians working from different ecclesiastical traditions—Orthodox and Catholic—and across the centuries. Despite their differences, they believe that Jesus is not only an important human figure but that he is a living, if mysterious, presence who

shares in our daily lives. This chapter's "for further reading" section recommends several books featuring more detailed information on the doctrine concerning Jesus.

22 My sources for this summary include: John Bowden, *Jesus: The Unanswered Questions* (London: SCM Press, 1988), 32–50, 72–90, 133–64; Henry Chadwick, *The Early Church* (Harmondsworth, Middlesex: Penguin Books, 1967), 125–51, 192–205; Catherine A. Cory and David T. Landry, eds., *The Christian Theological Tradition*, 2nd ed. (Upper Saddle River, N.J.: Prentice Hall, 2003; 2000), 75–166; John Dominic Crossan, *Jesus: A Revolutionary Biography* (San Francisco: HarperSanFrancisco, 1995); David F. Ford and Mike Higton, eds., *Jesus* (Oxford: Oxford University Press, 2002); Martin Forward, *Jesus: A Short Biography* (Oxford: Oneworld, 1998); Paula Fredricksen, *From Jesus to Christ: The Origins of the New Testament Images of Christ*, 2nd ed. (New Haven, Conn.: Yale University Press, 2000; 1988); Robert Funk and the Jesus Seminar, *The Gospel of Jesus according to the Jesus Seminar* (Santa Rosa, Calif.: Polebridge Press, 1999); Justo L. González, *Church History: An Essential Guide* (Nashville, Tenn.: Abingdon, 1996), 23–40, 59–66, 83–88; Christian E. Hauer and William A. Young, eds., *An Introduction to the Bible: A Journey into Three Worlds*, 5th ed. (Upper Saddle River, N.J.: Prentice Hall, 2001; 1986), 214–363; Roy W. Hoover, ed., *Profiles of Jesus* (Santa Rosa, Calif.: Polebridge Press, 2002); McGrath, ed., *The Christian Theology Reader*, 257–400; Alister E. McGrath, *Historical Theology: An Introduction to the History of Christian Thought* (Malden, Mass.: Blackwell, 1998), 30–33, 45–61; Marvin Meyer and Charles Hughes, eds., *Jesus Then and Now: Images of Jesus in History and Christology* (Harrisburg, Pa.: Trinity Press International, 2001); Olson, *The Mosaic of Christian Belief*, 223–42; Jaroslav Pelikan, *The Illustrated Jesus through the Centuries* (New Haven, Conn.: Yale University Press, 1997), and, finally, A. N. Wilson, *Jesus* (London: Sinclair-Stevenson, 1992).

23 See Stevenson, ed., *A New Eusebius*, based upon the collection by the late B. J. Kidd, 45–48, 96–97. In addition, see Chadwick, *The Early Church*, 23, 37. I suspect politics intersects with Christianity at this point, if not before, and recent studies makes this point forcefully. See Gregory J. Riley, *One Jesus, Many Christs: How Jesus Inspired Not One True Christianity, but Many* (San Francisco, Calif.: HarperSanFrancisco, 1997), 71, 99, 113–37.

24   For brief and basic information on *theosis* and deification, see Ken Parry, David J. Melling, Dimitri Brady, Sidney H. Griffith and John F. Healey, eds., *The Blackwell Dictionary of Eastern Christianity* (Malden Mass.: Blackwell, 1999), 5, 98, 109, 159, 205, 241, 310, 333, 404, 452, 459. A more detailed but still accessible explanation of both ideas may be found in Donald Fairbairn, *Eastern Orthodoxy through Western Eyes* (Louisville, Ky.: Westminster John Knox, 2002), 68–77, 79, 81, 84–95, 99, 102, 107–9, 117–18, 122–26, 153–54, 176. Fairbairn suggests that deification lies at the heart of the Orthodox vision. He is correct. As we will see, the Eastern Orthodox church has favored *theosis* for several centuries. Cabasilas, the Byzantine mystic, promoted *theosis* in his writings. And Kazantzakis was fond of him. See Bien, *Kazantzakis: Politics of the Spirit*, vol. 1, 246n43. Also see Middleton, *Broken Hallelujah*, 31–44. I should note that the Western Christian tradition is not unfamiliar with *theosis*. See A. M. Allchin, *Participation in God: A Forgotten Strand in the Anglican Tradition* (Wilton, Conn.: Morehouse-Barlow, 1988).

25   Stevenson, ed., *A New Eusebius*, 340–90. Many Christians refer to Arianism as the heresy that beats all heresies. See Rowan Williams, *Arius: Heresy and Tradition*, rev. ed. (Grand Rapids, Mich.: W. B. Eerdmans, 2002; 1987).

26   McGrath, ed., *The Christian Theology Reader*, 10. Also see Ford and Higton, eds., *Jesus*, 76–91.

27   McGrath, ed., *The Christian Theology Reader*, 9–12, 281–83. Also see Tyron L. Inbody, *The Many Faces of Christology* (Nashville, Tenn.: Abingdon Press, 2002), 43–67.

28   McGrath, ed., *The Christian Theology Reader*, 269.

29   McGrath, ed., *The Christian Theology Reader*, 270.

30   Also see Ford and Higton, eds., *Jesus*, 91–101.

31   Kazantzakis, *The Last Temptation of Christ*, 281.

32   Of course, it is much more than a difference in "starting point"—it includes modern views on the past, the nature of history, the scientific method, etc. Space prohibits me from discussing such matters.

33   For biographical details, see Andrew Louth, "Postpatristic Byzantine Theologians," in G. R. Evans, ed., *The Medieval Theologians: An Introduction to Theology in the Medieval Period* (Malden, Mass.: Blackwell, 2001), 37–54; Jan Michael Joncas, "Eastern Christianity," in Cory and Landry, eds., *The Christian Theological Tradition*, 153–66, and McGrath, *Historical Theology*, 123–26.

34   Nicholas Cabasilas, *The Life in Christ*, translated from the Greek by
      Carmino J. deCatanzaro, with an introduction by Boris Bobrinsky
      (Crestwood, N.J.: St. Vladimir's Seminary Press, 1974). This is
      the most accessible version of Cabasilas' work. For introductory
      accounts of Byzantine spirituality, focusing on hesychasm, see John
      Anthony McGuckin, *Standing in God's Holy Fire: The Byzantine Tradition*
      (Maryknoll, N.Y.: Orbis Books, 2001); John Meyendorff, *Byzantine
      Theology: Historical Trends and Doctrinal Themes* (New York: Fordham
      University Press, 1974), 4, 96, 104, 107–9, 118, 147–48, 163, 171–75,
      191–94, 201–8, and, finally, Rowan Williams, "Eastern Orthodox
      Theology," in David F. Ford, ed., *The Modern Theologians: An Introduction
      to Christian Theology in the Twentieth Century*, 2nd ed. (Malden, Mass.:
      Blackwell, 1997; 1996), 499–513.

35   Athanasius, *On the Incarnation*, cited in Cabasilas, *The Life in Christ*,
      63. Much Byzantine theology and spirituality proceeds out from this
      Athanasian emphasis on deification (*theosis*). See Ford and Higton,
      eds., *Jesus*, 105–13, 123–32, 397, 441–43, 503–4, 508–9.

36   Nikos Kazantzakis, *Journey to the Morea: Travels in Greece*, translated
      by F. A. Reed (New York: Simon and Schuster, 1965) 31–32. For
      Kazantzakis' quotations, compare: "This world labors unceasingly
      with the birthpangs of the new man" (*Morea*, 32) with ". . . It is this
      world which is in travail with that inner man which is 'created after
      the likeness of God' [Ephesians 4:24]" (*The Life in Christ*, 44). And
      again compare: "Not only did he bring new light, but he created a
      new eye" (*Morea*, 32) with "By means of Himself He forms an eye
      for them and, in addition, gives them light and enables them to see
      Himself" (*The Life in Christ*, 47). In an e-mail message on July 20,
      2003, Peter Bien informs me that "in one of the [Kazantzakis' unpub-
      lished] notebooks in my possession, Kazantzakis devotes a full page,
      just about, to reading notes from Kavasilas [Cabasilas], written in his
      very cramped Greek handwriting. Yes, Kazantzakis was very enam-
      ored of Cabasilas."

37   Cabasilas, *The Life in Christ*, 44. Also see Kazantzakis, *Report to Greco*,
      24.

38   For the biblical references often cited in favor of *theosis*, God's descent
      to us, our ascent to God, and creation being reunified in God, see
      Matthew 17:1-8; John 1:12; 10:35; Romans 8:14, 22-23; Colossians
      1:15-23, and 2 Peter 1:4.

39   Cabasilas, *The Life in Christ*, 66. Also see Kazantzakis, *The Saviors of God*, 43–44. In addition, see Helen Kazantzakis, *Nikos Kazantzakis: A Biography Based on His Letters*, 55. For further discussion of this ascent and descent language, see Bien, *Kazantzakis: Politics of the Spirit*, vol. 1, 268n43; Boris Bobrinsky, "Introduction: Nicholas Cabasilas: Theology and Spirituality," in Cabasilas, *The Life in Christ*, 17–42; Demetrios J. Constantelos, "Nikos Kazantzakis: Orthodox or Heterodox? A Greek Orthodox Appreciation," in Middleton and Bien, eds., *God's Struggler*, 47, 51–52; Daniel A. Dombrowski, "Kazantzakis and Mysticism," in Middleton and Bien, eds., *God's Struggler*, 89–91; Lambros Kamperidis, "The Orthodox Sources of *The Saviors of God*," in Middleton and Bien, eds., *God's Struggler*, 63, and, finally, Lewis Owens, *Creative Destruction: Nikos Kazantzakis and the Literature of Responsibility* (Macon, Ga.: Mercer University Press, 2002), 29–66. I should add that Cabasilas and Kazantzakis read and admired Palamas and Symeon the New Theologian. Finally, some brief but instructive commentary on Athos, Gregory Palamas, heyschasm, and Symeon the New Theologian may be found in Parry, *The Blackwell Dictionary of Eastern Christianity*, 69–71, 225, 230–32, 465.

40   Both Cabasilas and Kazantzakis endorse Gregory of Nazianzus' observation, cited earlier, that "what has not been assumed has not been healed."

41   Cabasilas, *The Life in Christ*, 122, 178, 181, 187. Also see Kazantzakis, *The Last Temptation of Christ*, 1–4. In addition, see Helen Kazantzakis, *Nikos Kazantzakis: A Biography Based on His Letters*, 477–78, 495–96, 502, 505, 509, 515, 523–24, 548.

42   Cabasilas, *The Life in Christ*, 122–23. Also see Kazantzakis, *The Last Temptation of Christ*, 281.

43   Cabasilas, *The Life in Christ*, 164. Also see Kazantzakis, *The Last Temptation of Christ*, 4. On this point of consanguinity, there is much to be said, even if here I paint with broad brushstrokes. Interested readers who scrutinize the following references will not fail to note how Kazantzakis' language resembles Cabasilas' discourse; indeed, similar tropes abound. For example, both describe Jesus: as marked by a dual substance, or hypostatic union, to use credal (Chalcedonian) terminology; as our co-struggler; and, finally, as the hero who secures our victory. See Cabasilas, *The Life in Christ*, 48, 58, 60, 62, 72, 89, 123, 133–35, 141, 176, 187, 189, 190–91, 226. Compare these refer-

ences to Kazantzakis' prologue in *The Last Temptation of Christ*, 1–4. For Kazantzakis' Chalcedonian language, see Constantelos, "Orthodox or Heterodox," 46. Finally, for the idea that we are partners with God in a heavenly calling, see Hebrews 3:1.

44   Cabasilas, *The Life in Christ*, 47–49, 110, 159–95, 228–29. Also see Kazantzakis, *The Last Temptation of Christ*, 1–4. In addition, see Helen Kazantzakis, *Nikos Kazantzakis: A Biography Based on His Letters*, 55. For a full range of Cabasilas' thoughts on *theosis*, see *The Life in Christ*, 51–54, 58, 63, 65–66, 72, 122, 181, 217, 224.

45   Renan was not alone in approaching Jesus historically rather than doctrinally. In fact, he was one of several eighteenth- and nineteenth-century writers to appeal to the historical Jesus in a struggle against perceived ecclesiastical tyranny. Known collectively as the so-called Life of Jesus research movement, these thinkers focused on Jesus' teaching, particularly his ethical remarks. And they emphasized his high moral character, which reaches out—mystically—from across the centuries, seeking to transform us. This movement included Ferdinand C. Baur, Hermann S. Reimarus, David F. Strauss, Johannes Weiss, William Wrede, and Martin Kähler. For useful surveys on the *Leben-Jesu Forschung*, see Alasdair I. C. Heron, *A Century of Protestant Theology* (Cambridge: Lutterworth Press, 1980), 18–21, 42–67. Also see James C. Livingston, *Modern Christian Thought: Volume I: The Enlightenment and the Nineteenth Century*, 2nd ed. (Upper Saddle River, N.J.: Prentice Hall, 1997; 1988), 30–39, 127–29, 215–21.

46   For biographical details, see Richard M. Chadbourne, *Ernest Renan* (New York: Twayne Publishers, 1968). For the wider context of nineteenth-century European thought on religion, see James C. Livingston, *Modern Christian Thought*, 142–61. Even though *Vie de Jésus* appeared in ten editions by the end of 1863, most scholars, or at least the ones I consulted for this book, cite the second edition. See Ernest Renan, *Vie de Jésus*, 2nd ed. (Paris: Michel Lévy, 1863). In keeping with my practice of citing accessible versions of major works under study, I use the Modern Library's 1955 edition of Renan's book, which is widely available. See Ernest Renan, *The Life of Jesus*, with an introduction by John Haynes Holmes (New York: Modern Library, 1955; 1927).

47   Kazantzakis used the library in Cannes, France, for his research. See Helen Kazantzakis, *Nikos Kazantzakis: A Biography Based on His Letters*, 505–6. In this section I rely quite heavily on Peter A. Bien's essay, "Renan's *Vie de Jésus* as a Primary Source for *The Last Temptation*," in

Middleton, ed., *Scandalizing Jesus?*, 3–18. In addition to Renan's *Life of Jesus*, Kazantzakis read Renan's *Les Apôtres* (1866). However, I do not propose to discuss this second book. I want, instead, to focus on Renan's biography of Jesus. Interested readers should consult Bien's essay, for he makes much of Kazantzakis and *Les Apôtres*. Moreover, Bien describes the contents of Kazantzakis' unpublished notebooks in Peter A. Bien, *Tempted by Happiness: Kazantzakis' Post-Christian Christ* (Wallingford, Pa.: Pendle Hill Publications, 1984).

48 See Renan, *The Life of Jesus*, 33–65, 387. Also see Kazantzakis, *The Last Temptation of Christ*, 348–49, 378, 389–92, 415, 427. Current scholarly consensus affirms the priority of Mark's Gospel.

49 Renan, *The Life of Jesus*, 31. Compare Renan's claim with Kazantzakis, *The Last Temptation of Christ*, 349–50, 391. Also see Paula Fredriksen, *From Jesus to Christ*, 94–130. Fredriksen summarizes the scholarly consensus on Jesus' birth in Nazareth.

50 For Daniel's vision, see Daniel 7:13-14. Compare with Renan, *The Life of Jesus*, 77, 94–95, 150, 259–61, 266, 269, Also see Kazantzakis, *The Last Temptation of Christ*, 98–107. For other Son of Man references in the Bible, see Ezekiel 2:1, Mark 2:10, 28; 8:31, 38; 10:45; 13:26; 14:62; Matthew 12:8; Luke 5:24; 6:5; 22:69; Acts 7:56, and Revelation 14:14.

51 For both Suffering Servant and Son of Man references, see Isaiah 42:1-4; 52:13–53:12; Daniel 7; Matthew 12:18-21; Mark 1:11; 8:31, 38; 10:43-45; 14:61a; 15:5, and Acts 3:13; 8:32-33. For Renan's sense that Jesus' self-understanding evolves across time, see *The Life of Jesus*, 119–20, 123–27, 135, 149, 151–52, 235–37, 330, 367. For Kazantzakis on Daniel and Isaiah, see *The Last Temptation of Christ*, 316–17, 335, 382, 386, 420–21, 425–26. Generally, Kazantzakis' unpublished notebooks outline his Jesus' messianic formation, and Bien's work makes this aspect of Kazantzakis' evolutionary Christology very clear. See Bien, *Tempted by Happiness*. I address Bien's work in the next section.

52 Renan, *The Life of Jesus*, 135–47, 173–83, 329–30, 337–43, 370–75. Also see Kazantzakis, *The Last Temptation of Christ*, 282–93, 326, 328–30, 335, 337–38, 377–78, 391–92, 415, 420–21, 425–27, 439, 448–457, 455, 490–95.

53 Renan, *The Life of Jesus*, 126, 148–59, 219, 225–27, 302. Also see Kazantzakis, *The Last Temptation*, 217, 316–17, 366–67, 372–73.

54 Renan, *The Life of Jesus*, 248–58. Compare with Kazantzakis, *The Last Temptation of Christ*, 307–8.

55 Renan, *The Life of Jesus*, 367. Also see Kazantzakis, *The Last Temptation of Christ*, 443–96. For biblical accounts of Jesus' death, see Matthew 27:32-56; Mark 15:16-40; Luke 23:26-43, and John 19:17-24.

56 Renan, *The Life of Jesus*, 65, 193, 205, 336, 368, 374–75, 381–93. Compare with Kazantzakis, *The Last Temptation of Christ*, 1–4. Also see Kazantzakis, *Report to Greco*, 289. Finally, see Matthew 28:20.

57 Renan, *The Life of Jesus*, 65.

58 Kazantzakis, *The Last Temptation of Christ*, 496. Also see Renan, *The Life of Jesus*, 239–47, 392–93. Interestingly, Renan cites the biblical passages noted by those who support the doctrine of *theosis*. See *The Life in Jesus*, 240n5. In my view, Kazantzakis expresses his commitment to *theosis* throughout his work. At least one Greek Orthodox prelate agrees. See Archbishop Stylianos of Australia, "Prologue," in Middleton and Bien, eds., *God's Struggler*: ". . . I would be happy if even a very tiny portion of today's so-called 'faithful' throughout the world possessed the sensitivity, vigilance, and thirst for θέωσις ('deification') shown by this idiosyncratic ascetic of vast horizons" (xi). Carnegie Samuel Calian makes a similar point in *Theology without Boundaries: Encounters of Eastern Orthodoxy and Western Tradition* (Louisville, Ky.: Westminster John Knox, 1992), 80–91. Finally, in Pauline and Deutero-Pauline language, we are children (sons and daughters) of God by adoption. For spirit of adoption language, see Romans 8:15-17, 23; 9:4; Galations 4:1-15; Ephesians 1:5-6; and Hebrews 3:1.

59 See Renan, *The Life of Jesus*, 100. Similar remarks may be found throughout the same text. See *The Life of Jesus*, 78, 273, 278–79, 382–84.

60 Helen Kazantzakis, *Nikos Kazantzakis: A Biography Based on His Letters*, 505.

61 Helen Kazantzakis lent these notes to Peter Bien. See Bien, *Tempted by Happiness*, 5. I think of these four categories as "vocational stages" for Jesus, as he works out his sense of messiahship—evolving spiritually, as it were. As such, these four stages remain the best illustration we have that Kazantzakis' novel is an evolutionary Christology in a narrative form.

62 Kazantzakis, *The Last Temptation of Christ*, 25. Note how God's Spirit troubles Jesus' uncle as well. Rabbi Simeon doubts whether Jesus is "the One" and so God's Spirit descends on him in a similarly savage manner (58).

63   I should add that "saw the heavens torn apart/split/cloven" is a correct rendering of Mark's Koine Greek.

64   Compare to the "voice" of Kazantzakis' "spiritual grandfather" in *Report to Greco*:

> They paint the Holy Spirit descending upon the Apostles' heads in the form of a dove. For shame! Haven't they ever felt the Holy Spirit burning them? Where did they find that innocent, edible bird? How can they present that to us as spirit? No, the Holy Spirit is not a dove, it is fire, a man-eating fire which clamps its talons into the very crown of saints, martyrs, and great strugglers, reducing them to ashes. Abject souls are the ones who take the Holy Spirit for a dove which they imagine they can kill and eat. (508)

65   Kazantzakis, *The Last Temptation of Christ*, 33.

66   Kazantzakis, *The Last Temptation of Christ*, 64. Also see 30, 59–60, 64, 71–72, 78, 91, 95. For Kazantzakis' Jesus, comfort, not adversity, is Lucifer's bait, and spiritual struggle illustrates one's providential ascent to God. Significantly, this feature of Kazantzakis' characterization mirrors developments in Kazantzakis' own religious life. See Kazantzakis' conversation with the Eastern Orthodox monk in *Report to Greco*, 296–97. Also see Middleton, *Broken Hallelujah*, 129–32.

67   See Adèle Bloch, "Kazantzakis and the Image of Christ," *Literature and Psychology* 15.1 (1965): 6–7. Kazantzakis' approach to women is deeply troubling, I think, yet it represents an aspect of his thought that is best examined separately. See Jen Harrison, "An Unholy Trinity: Woman in Pre-Easter Patriarchy," in Middleton, ed., *Scandalizing Jesus?*, 125–33.

68   Richard W. Chilson, "The Christ of Nikos Kazantzakis," *Thought* 47 (1972): 82.

69   Kazantzakis, *The Last Temptation of Christ*, 69.

70   Kazantzakis, *Report to Greco*, 483. Bergson also inspires Kazantzakis' larva-insect trope. See Bergson, *Creative Evolution*, 72, 139, 181–82. Very generally, Kazantzakis thinks the butterfly mimics God's law within creation—spirit's dematerialization. See *Report to Greco*, 465.

71   Tom Doulis, "Kazantzakis and the Meaning of Suffering," *Northwest Review* 6/1 (1963): 46–48. Compare to Kazantzakis, *The Last Temptation of Christ*: "'Look how he [Jesus] walks. He puts out his arms and flaps them like wings. God has swelled his head and he's trying to fly'" (307). In addition: "Jesus sat down among his disciples and divided

the bread but did not speak. Within him, his soul still anxiously flapped its wings as though it had just escaped an immense danger or completed a great and unexpected exploit" (325).

72   Kazantzakis, *The Last Temptation of Christ*, 126–27. Also see Doulis, "Kazantzakis and the Meaning of Suffering," 47.

73   Also see Doulis, "Kazantzakis and the Meaning of Suffering," 47:

> The butterflies are of course winged, but so is the golden eagle, the traditional Byzantine (and therefore Russian and modern Greek) symbol of God and Monarch; thorn-claws refer to the sensation Jesus feels when He sees an object of temptation, or when He weakens in His discipline (He is still in the cocoon stage of His life), and they also foreshadow the thorns He will wear in His Passion, when He will have broken the cocoon.

74   Dombrowski, *Kazantzakis and God*, 27–40. Also see Andreas K. Poulakidas, "Kazantzakis and Bergson: Metaphysic Aestheticians," *Journal of Modern Literature* 2.2 (1971–72): 275–83.

75   Dombrowski, *Kazantzakis and God*, 32. Kazantzakis' own thoughts on this trinity of metaphors are recorded in Kazantzakis, *Report to Greco*, 454 (flying fish), 465 (caterpillar-butterfly), 480 (silkworm), and 483 (all three together). As an aside, note how Kazantzakis' Magdalene applies the flying-fish image of self-transcendence and processive becoming to Jesus. See Kazantzakis, *The Last Temptation of Christ*, 374. Finally, see Kazantzakis, *The Saviors of God*, 100, 105–6, 119–121.

76   See Dombrowski, *Kazantzakis and God*, 38.

77   Dombrowski, *The Last Temptation of Christ*, 3.

78   Poulakidas, "Kazantzakis and Bergson," 278.

79   Although "Son of Man" is a complex term in the Hebrew Bible, Kazantzakis accepts Renan's emphasis on Daniel's vision. See Kazantzakis, *The Last Temptation of Christ*, 98–101. Also see Bien, *Tempted by Happiness*, 9.

80   See Kazantzakis, *The Last Temptation of Christ*, 150–51, 180–86. This reverence for life links Kazantzakis to Renan by way of what one might call "religious aestheticism." See Bien, *Tempted by Happiness*, 20. Reverence for life also connects Kazantzakis to his good friend Albert Schweitzer, whose philosophy falls under this title. See Albert Schweitzer, *Reverence for Life*, translated by Reginald H. Fuller (New York: Harper and Row, 1969). For a lucid commentary on

Schweitzer's philosophy, see Walter L. Ensslin, *Reverence for Life: Albert Schweitzer's Spiritual Message to Mankind* (Fresno, Calif.: Pioneer Publishing, 1983).

81 Kazantzakis, *The Last Temptation of Christ*, 169. For additional temptations to happiness, see 131, 146, 169, 190.

82 Kazantzakis, *The Last Temptation of Christ*, 188.

83 Kazantzakis, *The Saviors of God*, 68.

84 Jesus' insouciance devastates Mary and yet, in a rare instance of a woman assisting the *élan vital*'s progress in Kazantzakis' literary art, Salome, wife of the mean-spirited and thrifty Zebedee, criticizes Jesus' mother for her theological shortsightedness. See Kazantzakis, *The Last Temptation of Christ*, 189–90.

85 Kazantzakis, *The Last Temptation of Christ*, 191; emphasis added.

86 Kazantzakis, *The Last Temptation of Christ*, 205.

87 Kazantzakis, *The Last Temptation of Christ*, 203–4. Be sure to note Kazantzakis' symbol of the partridge in the gilded cage (85), which seems to be another device for the matter-spirit dialectic.

88 Kazantzakis, *The Last Temptation of Christ*, 241–43.

89 Kazantzakis, *The Last Temptation of Christ*, 248.

90 Kazantzakis, *The Last Temptation of Christ*, 255. Also see 248–55.

91 Kazantzakis, *The Last Temptation of Christ*, 298–99.

92 Kazantzakis, *The Last Temptation of Christ*, 300.

93 Kazantzakis, *The Last Temptation of Christ*, 392. For the spiritually facile disciples, see 377–78.

94 Chilson, "The Christ of Nikos Kazantzakis," 84.

95 As Chilson writes, "The spiritual, represented by Jesus, is the higher level wherein salvation rests, but it must work and struggle through the material order and this involves crucifixion of the spirit. The whole relationship of Jesus to Judas is on this level of allegory" ("The Christ of Nikos Kazantzakis," 84–85).

96 Kazantzakis, *The Last Temptation of Christ*, 356.

97 Kazantzakis, *The Last Temptation of Christ*, 354. Also see 380. Kazantzakis uses fire and flames throughout his work. They signify dynamism, animation, and zest in both the earth's and God's evolution. See Kazantzakis, *Report to Greco*, 176, 279. Also see Kazantzakis, *The Saviors of God*, 128.

98 Kazantzakis, *The Last Temptation of Christ*, 387.

99 Bien, *Tempted by Happiness*, 10.

100 Bien, *Tempted by Happiness*, 12.

101 Kazantzakis, *The Last Temptation of Christ*, 386–88, 411, 420–21, 425–433.
102 Kazantzakis, *The Last Temptation of Christ*, 444–48. Also see Genesis 22:1-24.
103 Kazantzakis, *The Last Temptation of Christ*, 461. Also see 450, 459–60.
104 Kazantzakis, *The Last Temptation of Christ*, 467–81.
105 Kazantzakis, *The Last Temptation of Christ*, 491.
106 Kazantzakis, *The Last Temptation of Christ*, 496. Critic Morton Levitt links this dream at the novel's conclusion with the dream at the novel's start:

> [H]e [Jesus] struggles to wake from his last temptation—as earlier he had fought out of his dream of the Redbeard and the dwarfs— and aided by Judas, he wakes and dies on the cross, affirming the life he has chosen to lead and denying the one he might have enjoyed. He truly lives and dies with his visions. In the silence at the edge of the precipice, confronting himself across the abyss of human desires and forgetfulness, he has at last sprouted wings, his life a dramatization of all men's struggles, a living metaphor that grows from the rhetorical imagery of *The Saviors of God*. (*The Cretan Glance*, 79)

107 Bowden, *Jesus: The Unanswered Questions*, 83.
108 Cunningham, *Reading Is Believing*, 62.
109 McGrath, ed., *The Christian Theology Reader*, 6.

CHAPTER 4

1 See Matthew 14–18.
2 See the introductory comments on ecclesiology in Alister McGrath, *Theology: The Basics* (Malden, Mass.: Blackwell, 2004), 105–22. Also see Maurice F. Wiles, *Reason to Believe* (Harrisburg, Pa.: Trinity Press International, 1999), 85–96. For a recent, general survey of different approaches to the doctrine of the church, see Veli-Matti Kärkkäinen, *An Introduction to Ecclesiology: Ecumenical, Historical and Global Perspectives* (Downers Grove, Ill.: InterVarsity Press, 2002).
3 See Luke 3:17; Revelation 21:1-4.
4 See Genesis 1:25; John 3:16; Colossians 1:15-23.
5 The classic study in this aspect of Christian doctrine is H. Richard Niebuhr's *Christ and Culture* (New York: Harper and Row, 1951). More specifically, two contemporary monographs on the church's relationship to the world have helped shape my articulation of the

two models in this paragraph. See Ruth Page, *God With Us: Synergy in the Church* (London: SCM Press, 2000), 4, 31, 37–40, 42, 84, 154–56. Also see Ralph C. Wood, *Contending the Faith: The Church's Engagement with Culture* (Waco, Tex.: Baylor University Press, 2003). Wood's book has proved to be especially helpful to me, because he draws on specialties in theology and literature to invoke poets and writers for ecclesiological wisdom; I try to model his approach in this chapter.

6   For a general survey, see Christopher Rowland, *The Cambridge Companion to Liberation Theology* (Cambridge: Cambridge University Press, 1999). Also see Curt Cadorette et. al., *Liberation Theology: An Introductory Reader* (Maryknoll, N.Y.: Orbis Books, 1992).

7   It is not without significance that writers in the Christian theological tradition have used literary devices to describe this task of continuing Jesus Christ's work. The Apostle Paul pictures the church as God's temple and as Christ's body, for example, and the Deutero-Pauline author of Ephesians uses love imagery to think of the church as Christ's bride. John's Gospel likens the church to a vine, moreover, and Revelation's apocalyptic seer describes the church as a city, the new Jerusalem. In later theology, Cyprian of Carthage suggests that since the Latin word "ecclesia" is feminine, we would do well to think of the church as our mother. This third century Roman rhetorician also describes the church using nature imagery, such as the sun, trees, and streams. The sixteenth-century Anglican divine, Richard Hooker, utilizes Matthew's parable of the tares to suggest that the church is like a field in which wheat and weeds grow alongside one another. And, finally, Leonardo Boff, the contemporary Brazilian liberation theologian, speaks of "grassroots" or "base communities." See Matthew 13:24; John 15:1-6; 1 Corinthians 3:10-17; 12:12-27; Ephesians 5:25-33; Revelation 21. Also see McGrath, ed., *The Christian Theology Reader*, 492–93, 511–12, 534–39. All these tropes, theological as well as biblical, attempt to capture something that remains difficult to explain, mystical even, and hidden from immediate view.

8   See Earl Lovelace, *The Wine of Astonishment*, with an Introduction by Marjorie Thorpe (Oxford: Heinemann, 1982). This novel was published in the United States of America in 1984 (New York: Vintage). Both versions have the same pagination. They are also freely available.

9   Texts that advance this claim include: Philip Jenkins, *The Next Christendom: The Rise of Global Christianity* (Oxford: Oxford University Press, 2002); Alister E. McGrath, *The Future of Christianity* (Malden,

Mass.: Blackwell, 2002), 22–39; Lamin Sanneh, *Whose Religion Is Christianity?: The Gospel beyond the West* (Grand Rapids, Mich.: W. B. Eerdmans, 2003), and, finally, Andrew F. Walls, *The Cross-Cultural Process in Christian History* (Maryknoll, N.Y.: Orbis Books; Edinburgh: T&T Clark, 2002), 3–81.

10   Earl Lovelace, *A Brief Conversion and Other Stories* (Oxford: Heinemann, 1988).

11   Funso Aiyejina, "Introduction: Finding the Darkness in Which to Grow: The Journey Towards Bacchanal Aesthetics," in Earl Lovelace, *Growing in the Dark: Selected Essays*, edited by Funso Aiyejina (Trinidad and Tobago: Lexington Trinidad, 2003), v–xx.

12   The text of the 1917 law, together with the 1951 repeal, is available online. For full information see http://library2.nalis.gov.tt/Default.aspx?PageContentID=271&tabid=174.

13   Lovelace, *Growing in the Dark*, 163.

14   Lovelace, *Growing in the Dark*, 163.

15   In the 1950s, Lovelace worked for a brief spell as a proofreader for the *Trinidad Guardian*.

16   See Matthew 28:18-19.

17   I am painting with broad brushstrokes at this point. For more detailed information, see Henry Louis Gates Jr., *Wonders of the African World* (New York: Alfred A, Knopf, 1999), 193–229. Also see Roland Oliver, *The African Experience: Major Themes in African History from Earliest Times to the Present* (New York: HarperCollins, 1991), 116–29.

18   Support for this outline may be found in Dale Bisnauth, *History of Religions in the Caribbean* (Trenton, N.J.: Africa World Press, 1996), 80–100. Also see Margarite Fernández Olmos and Lizabeth Paravisini-Gebert, *Creole Religions of the Caribbean: An Introduction from Vodou and Santería to Obeah and Espiritismo* (New York: New York University Press, 2003), 1–23.

19   Lovelace, *Growing in the Dark*, 167.

20   Lovelace, *Growing in the Dark*, 167.

21   Lovelace, *Growing in the Dark*, 167.

22   Lovelace, *Growing in the Dark*, 167.

23   Lovelace, *Growing in the Dark*, 172.

24   Lovelace, *Growing in the Dark*, 172.

25   See 2 Kings 12:5, 7-8, 12; 22:5-6; Ezra 9:9; Isaiah 61:4.

26   See 2 Corinthians 5:18-20.

27   See Kelly Hewson, "An Interview with Earl Lovelace," *Postcolonial*

Text 1.1 (2004). This is an interview available online at http://postcolonial.org/index.php/pct/article/viewArticle/344/122.

28 Hewson, "An Interview."

29 Hewson, "An Interview."

30 Lovelace, *Growing in the Dark*, 173–75.

31 It is not without significance that the New Testament writers link reconciliation to atonement. We may isolate the meaning of atonement by breaking the word into three parts: at-one-ment. This concept suggests that atonement brings people together, connects an otherwise disconnected set of individuals, or links people previously separated. In Christian theology, as I note in earlier chapters, God uses Jesus of Nazareth to atone for humanity's sinfulness. Separated from God on account of our sin, we are made at one with God through what God accomplishes on the cross in Jesus of Nazareth. Reconciled believers who live in light of such atonement must, therefore, assume the ministry of reconciliation through the church. See 2 Corinthians 5:14.

32 See 1 Thessalonians. Also see Bradley P. Nystrom and David P. Nystrom, *The History of Christianity: An Introduction* (Boston: McGraw-Hill, 2004), 22–47.

33 Nystrom and Nystrom, *The History of Christianity*, 48–112.

34 Nystrom and Nystrom, *The History of Christianity*, 125–30, 133–47, 192–95.

35 Nystrom and Nystrom, *The History of Christianity*, 197–200, 225–83. Also see Shirley E. Jordan's "Martin Luther" and David S. Cunningham's "Other Protestant Reformers" in Catherine A. Cory and David T. Landry, eds., *The Christian Theological Tradition*, 2nd ed. (Upper Saddle River, N.J.: Prentice Hall, 2003; 2000), 259–95.

36 Nystrom and Nystrom, *The History of Christianity*, 225–47. Also see Margaret R. Miles, *The Word Made Flesh: A History of Christian Thought* (Malden, Mass.: Blackwell, 2005), 243–60. For a general survey of the era, see Carter Lindberg, ed., *The Reformation Theologians: An Introduction to Theology in the Early Modern Period* (Malden, Mass.: Blackwell, 2002).

37 See Lindberg, ed., *The Reformation Theologians*, 85, 87, 90–91, 120, 138, 150–51, 213. Also see Alistair E. McGrath, *Christianity: An Introduction*, 2nd ed. (Malden, Mass.: Blackwell, 2006; 1997), 271–72.

38 Lovelace, *The Wine of Astonishment*, 3, 5, 13–14, 16, 30–34, 48–49, 58–63, 73, 76–77, 122–34, 145–46. I intend to make these references more explicit in the next section.

39   The documentary details behind this outline may be found in A. G. Dickens and Dorothy Carr, eds., *The Reformation in England to the Accession of Elizabeth I* (London: Edward Arnold, 1967). For a narrative overview, see J. J. Scarisbrick, *The Reformation and the English People* (Oxford: Basil Blackwell, 1984).

40   For a close and careful study, I recommend B. R. White, *The English Baptists of the Seventeenth Century* (London: The Baptist Historical Society, 1983), and Raymond Brown, *The English Baptists of the Eighteenth Century* (London: The Baptist Historical Society, 1986). As a young man training for the Baptist ministry in Manchester, England, in the mid-1980s, I was told these texts were required study; I still like them.

41   Statistics courtesy of the Baptist World Alliance. http://www. bwanet.org/.

42   Once again, I paint with broad brushstrokes. For details, see H. Leon McBeth, *The Baptist Heritage: Four Centuries of Baptist Witness* (Nashville, Tenn.: Broadman Press, 1987).

43   McBeth, *The Baptist Heritage*, 22, 47, 67–68, 74, 80–81, 90, 97, 308.

44   McBeth, *The Baptist Heritage*, 69–91. My list abbreviates McBeth's observations, which are commonplace in Baptist studies. Let me add that I know there is tremendous variety among Baptists, today as in the past, so I do not intend to oversimplify matters at this point.

45   See Mark 16:16; John 3:16; Ephesians 1:4, 12.

46   For additional information on this aspect of being Baptist, see E. Jeffrey Mask, *At Liberty Under God: Toward a Baptist Ecclesiology* (Lanham, Md.: University Press of America, 1997). Also see Kärkkäinen, *An Introduction to Ecclesiology*, 142–50.

47   McBeth, *The Baptist Heritage*, 79.

48   McBeth, *The Baptist Heritage*, 83.

49   For detailed, primary sources for Baptist beliefs and behaviors, see Curtis Freeman, James Wm. McClendon Jr., and C. Rosalie Velloso da Silva, eds., *Baptist Roots: A Reader in the Theology of a Christian People* (Valley Forge, Pa.: Judson Press, 1999).

50   Brian Stanley, *The History of the Baptist Missionary Society, 1792–1992* (Edinburgh: T&T Clark, 1992), 14.

51   Stanley, *The History of the Baptist Missionary Society*, 15–29, 36–67.

52   Stanley, *The History of the Baptist Missionary Society*, 68–105.

53   Stanley, *The History of the Baptist Missionary Society*, 68.

54   Stanley, *The History of the Baptist Missionary Society*, 94. Also see Lorna McDaniel, "Memory Spirituals of the Ex-Slave American Solidiers

in Trinidad's 'Company Villages,'" *Black Music Research Journal* 14.2 (1994): 119–43. For details on black Baptists in America, see McBeth, *The Baptist Heritage*, 776–90.

55 Stanley, *The History of the Baptist Missionary Society*, 95.

56 Stanley, *The History of the Baptist Missionary Society*, 102–5.

57 Stanley, *The History of the Baptist Missionary Society*, 251–54, 264–68. For more information on the Southern Baptist Convention's missions work, see William R. Estep, *Whole Gospel Whole World: The Foreign Mission Board of the Southern Baptist Convention 1845–1995* (Nashville, Tenn.: Broadman and Holman Publishers, 1994).

58 James T. Houk, *Spirits, Blood, and Drums: The Orisha Religion in Trinidad* (Philadelphia: Temple University Press, 1995), 71–85. Houk discusses four theories of origins for the movement (71–75). He appears most persuaded by the notion that the Spiritual Baptists in Trinidad were influenced by immigrants from St. Vincent during the twentieth-century's first few years (75).

59 Kenneth Anthony Lum, *Praising His Name in the Dance: Spirit Possession in the Spiritual Baptist Faith and Orisha Work in Trinidad, West Indies* (Amsterdam: Harwood Academic Publishers, 2000). Lum mentions Lovelace in passing (7).

60 Besides Houk and Lum, I draw my observations from material provided by Melville J. Herskovits and Frances S. Herskovits, *Trinidad Village* (New York: Alfred A. Knopf, 1947), 181–223. While this latter text is dated, it is regarded as a classic in the field.

61 For a diagram, see Herskovits and Herskovits, *Trinidad Village*, 191, 197. Also, see Houk, *Spirits, Blood, and Drums*, 84–85. Finally, see Lum, *Praising His Name in the Dance*, 41–47.

62 Herskovits and Herskovits, *Trinidad Village*, 210.

63 Herskovits and Herskovits, *Trinidad Village*, 194–97. In addition, see Lum, *Praising His Name in the Dance*, 51–81.

64 See Acts 2:2-4.

65 See Herskovits and Herskovits, *Trinidad Village*, 181, 193, 217. Also, see Houk, *Spirits, Blood, and Drums*, 77. Finally, see Lum, *Praising His Name in the Dance*, 49–89.

66 More detailed information on spirit possession in traditional African religions, especially those associated with West Africa, may be found in Benjamin C. Ray, *African Religions: Symbol, Ritual, and Community*, 2nd ed. (Upper Saddle River, N.Y.: Prentice Hall, 2000; 1999), 41–44, 73–76, 83, 89–91.

67   Herskovits and Herskovits, *Trinidad Village*, 199–207. Also, see Houk, *Spirits, Blood, and Drums*, 78–80. Finally, see Lum, *Praising His Name in the Dance*, 62–79.

68   Cited in Herskovits and Herskovits, *Trinidad Village*, 183–84. The writers describe attending a prohibited service elsewhere in their text (218–23).

69   Herskovits and Herskovits, *Trinidad Village*, 187.

70   Herskovits and Herskovits, *Trinidad Village*, 189.

71   Lovelace, *Growing in the Dark*, 54.

72   As with my discussion of feminist and womanist theologians in chapter 2, space prohibits me from providing specific biographies of individual theologians in this section. Here I paint with broad brushstrokes, since I think Caribbean theology is a style of thinking that owes much to many scholars, not just one or two. For representative texts, see Kortright Davis, ed., *Moving into Freedom* (Bridgetown, Barbados: Cedar Press, 1977); Kortright Davis, *Emancipation Still Comin': Explorations in Caribbean Emancipatory Theology* (Maryknoll, N.Y.: Orbis Books, 1990); Noel L. Erskine, *Decolonizing Theology: A Caribbean Perspective* (Maryknoll, N.Y.: Orbis Books, 1991); Idris Hamid, *In Search of New Perspectives* (Bridgetown, Barbados: Caribbean Ecumenical Consultation for Development, 1971); Idris Hamid, ed., *Troubling of the Waters* (San Fernando, Trinidad: Rahaman Printery, 1973); Romney E. Moseley, "Decolonizing Theology in the Caribbean: Prospects for Hermeneutical Reflection," in William R. Barr, ed., *Constructive Christian Theology in the Worldwide Church* (Grand Rapids, Mich.: W. B. Eerdmans, 1997), and William Watty, *From Shore to Shore: Soundings in Caribbean Theology* (Kingston, Jamaica: Cedar Press, 1981). While I rely quite heavily on Moseley's analysis in this section, I bring other voices into discussion when and where it seems appropriate.

73   Erskine, *Decolonizing Theology*, 85.

74   Caribbean theology shares significant points of consanguinity with the black womanist theology discussed in chapter 2, and with black theology in general. For additional information, see J. Deotis Roberts, *Black Theology in Dialogue* (Philadelphia: The Westminster Press, 1987), 11–42. Also see Josiah U. Young III, *Black and African Theologies: Siblings or Distant Cousins?* (Maryknoll, N.Y.: Orbis Books, 1986). In addition, see Young's later text, *A Pan-African Theology: Providence and the Legacies of the Ancestors* (Trenton, N.J.: Africa World Press, 1992), 3–20, 79–167.

75 For details, see Moseley, "Decolonizing Theology in the Caribbean," 78–81. Also see Davis, *Emancipation Still Comin'*, 1–28. Compare with similar themes in Lovelace, *Growing in the Dark*, 22–29, 38–45, 56–60, 107–17, 147–57, 197–204.

76 See Davis, *Emancipation Still Comin'*, 140–41; Erskine, *Decolonizing Theology*, 81–85, and, finally, Robert E. Hood, *Must God Remain Greek?: Afro Cultures and God-Talk* (Minneapolis, Minn.: Fortress, 1990), 43–76. Compare with similar themes in Lovelace, *Growing in the Dark*, 1–13, 30–37, 51–55, 93–97, 102–6, 217–28.

77 Davis, *Emancipation Still Comin'*, 103. Emphasis in original.

78 Davis, *Emancipation Still Comin'*, 30–40, 102–4; Erskine, *Decolonizing Theology*, 69–86; and Moseley, "Decolonizing Theology in the Caribbean," 75–77. Compare with the essays on reparation theory in Lovelace, *Growing in the Dark*, 163–216. Also compare with Louis James' reflections on the search for personhood in Lovelace's work. See James, *Caribbean Literatures in English* (London: Longman, 1999), 192–98.

79 Moseley, "Decolonizing Theology in the Caribbean," 78.

80 Moseley, "Decolonizing Theology in the Caribbean," 80, 81.

81 Lovelace, *Growing in the Dark*, 230.

82 Since 1995, for example, islanders have celebrated the government-mandated Spiritual Baptist (Shouter) Liberation Day annually. This event occurs on March 30. See Frances Henry, *Reclaiming African Religions in Trinidad: The Socio-Political Legitimation of the Orisha and Spiritual Baptist Faiths* (Kingston, Jamaica: University of West Indies Press, 2003), 30–44.

83 Lovelace, *The Wine of Astonishment*, 18–31.

84 Readers will notice that Mother Eva speaks in patois, her mother tongue, and critics praise this use of the vernacular for its authenticity. I should add that she tells her tale through the use of *analepsis* (flashbacks) and *prolepsis* (flashforward), which explains why my analysis sometimes covers the same ground or events more than once.

85 Lovelace, *The Wine of Astonishment*, 3–5, 8, 9–10, 15, 30.

86 Lovelace, *The Wine of Astonishment*, 13. As we will see, Leader Bee (Dorcas), together with Mother Eva, will help resurrect the church at the novel's end (146). Also see Acts 9:36-43.

87 Lovelace, *The Wine of Astonishment*, 11, 13–16.

88 Lovelace, *The Wine of Astonishment*, 17.

89 Lovelace, *The Wine of Astonishment*, 21.

90 Lovelace, *The Wine of Astonishment*, 22.

91 Lovelace, *The Wine of Astonishment*, 22–24. A "chantwell" is an enthused vocalist, someone who leads others in singing the praises of a stickfighter.

92 Lovelace, *The Wine of Astonishment*, 25.

93 Patrick Colm Hogan, *Colonialism and Cultural Identity: Crises of Tradition in the Anglophone Literatures of India, Africa, and the Caribbean* (Albany: State University of New York Press, 2000), 138.

94 Hogan, *Colonialism and Cultural Identity*, 146–52. Hogan identifies these mimeticists as Ivan Morton; Mitchell, Mother Eva's cousin; and Colonel Prince, the policeman who eventually raids and arrests the Bonasse congregation for breaking the law.

95 Lovelace, *The Wine of Astonishment*, 27.

96 Lovelace, *The Wine of Astonishment*, 30–31.

97 Lovelace, *The Wine of Astonishment*, 32.

98 Lovelace, *The Wine of Astonishment*, 32.

99 Lovelace, *The Wine of Astonishment*, 32.

100 Lovelace, *The Wine of Astonishment*, 32.

101 Moseley, "Decolonizing Theology in the Caribbean," 77–79. Also see 2 Corinthians 1:15.

102 Lovelace, *The Wine of Astonishment*, 1, 3, 13–14, 34, 122–29.

103 Lovelace, *The Wine of Astonishment*, 33.

104 Lovelace, *The Wine of Astonishment*, 32.

105 Lovelace, *The Wine of Astonishment*, 33.

106 Lovelace, *The Wine of Astonishment*, 33.

107 Stanley, *The History of the Baptist Missionary Society*, 68.

108 Lovelace, *The Wine of Astonishment*, 62.

109 Lovelace, *The Wine of Astonishment*, 34.

110 Lovelace, *The Wine of Astonishment*, 33–37.

111 Lovelace, *The Wine of Astonishment*, 39–46. The three-way tussle between Morton, Eulalie, and Bolo seems allegorical—two men jousting for the attentions of one woman, two ideological powers contending for the mind and heart of the community. Morton defeats Bolo, fathers a child with Eulalie, but then leaves her for someone who symbolizes the island's privileged, emerging mulatto leadership (46). Morton's departure not only angers Bolo, though; it crushes Eulalie emotionally. And it seems telling that her loss causes her to prostitute herself before American soldiers. Colonialism engulfs everyone and everything. Of course, this is Bolo's point!

112 Lovelace, *The Wine of Astonishment*, 48.

113 Lovelace, *The Wine of Astonishment*, 49.

114 Lovelace, *The Wine of Astonishment*, 50, 55, 57–58.

115 For additional information, see George M. Mulrain, "Is There a Calypso Exegesis?" in R. S. Sugirtharajah, ed., *Voices from the Margin: Interpreting the Bible in the Third World* (Maryknoll, N.Y.: Orbis Books, 1995), 37–47. Also see George Mulrain, "Hermeneutics within a Caribbean Context," in R. S. Sugirtharajah, ed., *Vernacular Hermeneutics* (Sheffield: Sheffield Academic Press, 1999), 116–32. Calypso exegesis forms part of the so-called postcolonial approach to biblical interpretation. For a general survey, see R. S. Sugirtharajah, *Postcolonial Reconfigurations: An Alternative Way of Reading the Bible and Doing Theology* (St. Louis, Mo.: Chalice Press, 2003).

116 Mulrain, "Hermeneutics within a Caribbean Context," 123. Compare with Erskine's understanding of the merits of the Calypso worldview. See *Decolonizing Theology*, 84.

117 For Leader Bee's sermon, see Lovelace, *The Wine of Astonishment*, 58–63. Also see Hogan, *Colonialism and Cultural Identity*, 156–57.

118 Lovelace, *The Wine of Astonishment*, 73. For the wider context behind these remarks, see 65–74.

119 Lovelace, *The Wine of Astonishment*, 78.

120 Lovelace, *The Wine of Astonishment*, 80, 83, 87–105. Characters like Bolo find themselves caught betwixt and between. They remember the old world with nostalgia and yet shudder at the new world's onslaught. This liminality produces anomie, or general social rootlessness.

121 Lovelace, *The Wine of Astonishment*, 116–20.

122 Lovelace, *The Wine of Astonishment*, 122–29. Muriel actually dies during the altercation. In addition, it is worth noting that Lovelace presents Leader Bee as the novel's other Christ figure (1–3). In his *Colonialism and Cultural Identity*, Hogan points out that Bolo violates an actual law on Trinidad's statute books in 1924. The law said that a man is strictly forbidden from taking and keeping an underage unmarried woman against her will. If convicted of this unlawful behavior, the criminal was sent to jail for two years. "Note that this puts Bolo's crime in exactly the same category as the prostitution of underage women by U. S. servicemen, just as Bolo indicates. And no one calls the police to attack the America GIs" (165). Finally, Hogan has an extremely interesting and entirely persuasive reading of Bolo: he sees Bolo as one part Jesus, one part Ogun [the Yoruban warrior god]. "Bolo may

draw his name from the Shango [Trinidadian neo-African religion] name for Jesus: Abalophon or Obalophone—the unstressed initial vowel dropped in a typical phonetic development" (169). Further: "Ogun is one of the central deities for Shangoists. When possessed by Ogun, men act, precisely, like Bolo . . . His weapon, like Bolo's, is a wooden sword—one of the ritual objects shared by Shango and Spiritual Baptism. And his object, in possessing a worshipper, is most often retributive. He watches for transgressions, then possesses a devotee to challenge the transgressor, again Bolo's function" (169–170).

123 Lovelace, *The Wine of Astonishment*, 133. Theologically speaking, we might say that Bolo's untimely death represents a kenotic outpouring of self, which inspires the church to recover its dignity.

124 Young III, *A Pan-African Theology*, 165. Compare with Hood's understanding of how God's Spirit works in black religions. See Hood, *Must God Remain Greek?*, 204–10. I find it fascinating to think that Lovelace's Spiritual Baptists typify Hood's understanding.

125 Lovelace, *The Wine of Astonishment*, 146.

126 Norman Reed Cary, "Salvation, Self, and Solidarity in the Work of Earl Lovelace," *World Literature Written in English* 28.1 (1988): 107–8.

127 Trinidadian theologian George Mulrain has done much to emphasize how music, especially calypso, reggae, and general hymnody, helps Caribbean women and men think theologically. That there is a general Caribbean preparedness to see God's Spirit in music, then, only supports my theological reading at this point. For more information, see Mulrain, "The Music of African Caribbean Theology," *Black Theology in Britain* 1 (1998): 35–45.

128 Davis, *Emancipation Still Comin'*, 49. Compare with Erskine's idea that the Caribbean church functions best as the bearer of new identity. See Erskine, *Decolonizing Theology*, 81–86.

129 Hogan, *Colonialism and Cultural Identity*, 140.

130 There is no question that this observation about Europe holds true for, say, Great Britain, where Christianity is not so much in decline as it is in free fall. See Callum Brown, *The Death of Christian Britain* (New York: Routledge, 2002). On the subject of Christianity in Africa, I recommend Kwame Bediako, *Christianity in Africa: The Renewal of a Non-Western Religion* (Edinburgh: Edinburgh University Press; Maryknoll, N.Y.: Orbis Books, 1995).

131 I have found the following studies most instructive: Philip Jenkins, *The New Faces of Christianity: Believing the Bible in the Global South* (Oxford:

Oxford University Press, 2006); Jenkins, *The Next Christendom*; Hugh McLeod, ed., *World Christianities 1914–2000* (Cambridge: Cambridge University Press, 2006) and, finally, Lamin Sanneh, *Whose Religion Is Christianity?* Facts and figures on the Global South trend may be found in *The Next Christendom*.

132 Sanneh, *Whose Religion Is Christianity?* 95–130. I have evaluated one example of such mother tongue theology, from Africa actually, in a recent article. See Darren J. N. Middleton, "Jesus of Nazareth in Ghana's Deep Forest: The Africanization of Christianity in Madam Afua Kuma's Poetry," *Religion and the Arts* 9.1–2 (2005): 116–34. For a book length study of similar trends, see Diane B. Stinton, *Jesus of Africa: Voices of Contemporary African Christology* (Maryknoll, N.Y.: Orbis Books, 2004).

133 Philip Jenkins, "Downward, Outward, Later: A Superb New History of Christianity," *Books and Culture*, September/October 2006, 10.

134 Lovelace, *Growing in the Dark*, 230.

135 I have in mind the following, selected novels: Chinua Achebe, *Things Fall Apart*; Mongo Beti, *The Poor Christ of Bomba*; Margaret Craven, *I Heard the Owl Call My Name*; Shusaku Endo, *Deep River*; Graham Greene, *The Honorary Consul*; Ivan Klima, *The Ultimate Intimacy*, and, finally, Barbara Kingsolver, *The Poisonwood Bible*.

CHAPTER 5

1 See Ernest Becker, *The Denial of Death* (Boston: Free Press, 1997).

2 For general information, see Harold Coward, ed., *Life after Death in World Religions* (Maryknoll, N.Y.: Orbis Books, 1997) and Alan F. Segal's *Life after Death: A History of the Afterlife in Western Religion* (New York: Doubleday, 2004).

3 In what follows I summarize part of David Ferguson's essay, "Eschatology," in Colin E. Gunton, ed., *The Cambridge Companion to Christian Doctrine* (Cambridge: Cambridge University Press, 1997), 226–44. I am also indebted to McGrath, *Christian Theology: An Introduction*, 464–85.

4 See 1 Corinthians 15:51-55, 1 Thessalonians 4:13-18, and Revelation 1:17-18.

5 See Matthew 5:12, 25:31-46; Mark 9:47-48; and Revelation 21:21.

6 See Matthew Philips and Lisa Miller's "Visions of Hell," *Newsweek* (November 6, 2006): 52–53.

7 Scholars have been especially drawn to the Left Behind series: Bruce David Forbes and Jeanne Halgren Kilde, eds., *Rapture, Revelation, and the End Times: Exploring the Left Behind Series* (New York: Palgrave Macmillan, 2004); Amy Johnson Frykholm, *Rapture Culture: Left Behind in American Culture* (Oxford: Oxford University Press, 2004); Glenn W. Shuck, *Marks of the Beast: The Left Behind Novels and the Struggle for Evangelical Identity* (New York: New York University Press, 2004), and, finally, see Michael Standaert, *Skipping Towards Armageddon: The Politics and Propaganda of the Left Behind Novels and the LaHaye Empire* (New York: Soft Skull Press, 2006).

8 Published by Creation House in 1992, this novel's original title was *Gehenna*. See Paul Thigpen, *Gehenna* (Lake Mary, Fla.: Creation House, 1992). Creation House is now Charisma House, though, and its editors recently asked Thigpen to revise *Gehenna* for publication in May 2007. The revised version bears a new title: *My Visit to Hell*. Since this revised version replaces *Gehenna*, and is more readily available than the 1992 text, readers should note that I take *My Visit to Hell* into explicit consideration for my analysis. See Paul Thigpen, *My Visit to Hell* (Lake Mary, Fla.: Realms, 2007).

9 Thigpen and I conducted this e-mail interview just before the May 2007 release of *My Visit to Hell*. I prepared and sent my questions in the summer of 2006, Thigpen provided his answers in early 2007, and then we wrapped things up later in the spring. When Thigpen speaks about *Gehenna* during his interview, readers should recall the information in the previous endnote. Needless to say, I am very grateful to Dr. Thigpen for his time, grace, and considerate as well as nuanced responses to my questions.

10 Patrick Madrid, ed., *Surprised by Truth: Eleven Converts Give the Biblical and Historical Reasons for Becoming Catholic* (Irving, Tex.: Basilica Press, 1994).

11 See Paul Thigpen, *Last Words: Final Thoughts of Catholic Saints and Sinners* (Cincinnati: Servant Books, 2006) and *Blood of the Martyrs, Seed of the Church: Stories of Catholics Who Died for Their Faith* (Ann Arbor: Servant Publications, 2001), 9–31, 195–206. For Thigpen's trilogy of texts on end times fiction, see *The Rapture Trap: A Study Guide* (West Chester, Pa.: Ascension Press, 2003), *Responding to the Rapture: A Catholic Critique of Rapture Fever* (West Chester, Pa.: Ascension Press, 2002), and, finally, *The Rapture Trap: A Catholic Response to "End Times" Fever* (West Chester, Pa.: Ascension Press, 2001).

12 See especially Thigpen, *The Rapture Trap: A Catholic Response*, 25–37, 173–84.

13 Thigpen's *What the Bible Says About the End of the World* is due out in early 2008.

14 As with similar discussions in previous chapters, it is only possible to selectively sketch our featured doctrine's lengthy and wide-ranging history in what follows. Our primary focus will be the notion of hell. After introducing certain traditional theological themes and figures, I chart those thinkers whose work intersects with Thigpen's most directly. This chapter's final section recommends several books featuring more background and more detailed information.

15 Thigpen's novel addresses hell, not heaven, so I must focus on hell from this point forward. Readers interested in exploring the history of heaven, at least among Christians across the centuries, should consult Alister E. McGrath's *A Brief History of Heaven* (Malden, Mass.: Blackwell, 2003).

16 Here I try to capture something of the popular understanding of what Scripture has to say about hell; I am not trying to be exegetically precise with the particular words I use. In what follows, my sources include Jonathan L. Kvanvig, *The Problem of Hell* (Oxford: Oxford University Press, 1993), 3, 5, 6, 14, 16–21, 25–66, 74–76, 107–11, 135–37; Hans Schwarz, *Eschatology* (Grand Rapids, Mich.: W. B. Eerdmans, 2000), 36–40, 59, 67, 102, 274, 278, 296, 338, 340, 354, 401–2, and, finally, Alice K. Turner, *The History of Hell* (New York: Harcourt Brace, 1993), 40–45, 52–70.

17 See Job 3:11-19; Psalms 6:5, 88:3-12, and Proverbs 9:18.

18 See 2 Maccabees 7:7-11.

19 Concerning punishment, see Matthew 13:42, 50; Luke 16:28; Jude 7, and Revelation 19:20.

20 See McGrath, ed., *The Christian Theology Reader*, 647. For the biblical background to *Gehenna*, see 2 Kings 23:10; Jeremiah 7:31-33, and Matthew 25:41.

21 See Psalms 88; Ecclesiastes 9:10; Isaiah 38:10; Matthew 16:18; Mark 9:47-48; Luke 16:23, and Revelation 1:18.

22 See 1 Peter 3:18-20, 4:6 and Revelation 20:13.

23 See McGrath, ed., *The Christian Theology Reader*, 11. Later creeds omit the descent into hell clause. Turner suspects this is due to "uneasiness with the Harrowing story at higher intellectual levels." See *The History of Hell*, 69. Both Augustine and Aquinas, theologians who

shape Thigpen's novel, expressed some concerns about the topic. For additional details, see http://www.christianitytoday.com/history/features/ask/2002/nov15.html.

24   As we will see, Augustine and Aquinas subscribe to Christ's descent into hell. For the biblical background, see Isaiah 53:4; Zechariah 9:11; Acts 2:24; Ephesians 4:9, and Colossians 2:15. Jesus harrows the limbo of the patriarchs, not hell itself, according to the *Gospel of Nicodemus*, which serves as the main text for this aspect of the Christian story. Here Christ liberates the Hebrew Bible's holy figures. See Turner, *The History of Hell*, 67.

25   My summary relies on material in Henry Angsar Kelly, *Satan: A Biography* (Cambridge: Cambridge University Press, 2006) and T. J. Wray and Gregory Mobley, *The Birth of Satan* (New York: St. Martin's Press, 2005).

26   In some texts, like Job 1 and Zechariah 3, "Satan" is not a proper name; he is an agent of God only. 1 Chronicles 21:1 is the only passage in the Hebrew Bible where the word appears as a proper name.

27   See Job 1:6-12. I owe "prosecuting attorney" to Christian E. Hauer and William A. Young, *An Introduction to the Bible: A Journey into Three Worlds*, 6th ed. (Upper Saddle River, N.J.: Prentice Hall, 2005; 2001, 1998, 1994, 1990, 1986), 172.

28   For biblical references to the devil, Satan, and other names that he has been associated with across the centuries (e.g., Beelzebul and Lucifer), see Isaiah 14:12; Matthew 12:26; Mark 3:23-27; Luke 9:42; 10:18; 22:3, and Revelation 12:9; 20:10-15.

29   The church condemned Origen's universalism at the Second Council of Constantinople, which occurred in 553 C.E. For all its unorthodoxies, though, his theology influenced Eastern Christianity greatly. See Stevenson, ed., *A New Eusebius*, based upon the collection by the late B. J. Kidd, 219. Also see Henry Chadwick, *The Early Church* (Harmondsworth, Middlesex: Penguin Books, 1967), 100–115. In addition, see Paul Thigpen, "Hell," in George H. Shriver and Bill J. Leonard, eds., *Encyclopedia of Religious Controversies in the United States* (Westport, Conn.: Greenwood Press, 1997), 209. For more detailed information on Origen, including the issue of whether or not the church gave his theology a fair hearing, see Rowan Williams, "Origen," in G. R. Evans, ed., *The First Christian Theologians: An Introduction to Theology in the Early Church* (Malden, Mass.: Blackwell, 2004), 132–42.

30 See Ferguson, "Eschatology," 240–41. Also see McGrath, *Christian Theology: An Introduction*, 464–85. On annihilationism, see Kvanvig, *The Problem of Hell*, 22, 68–71, 75, 121–42, 149–54, 168–70, For recent attempts to promote universalism, see Philip Gulley and James Mulholland, *If Grace is True: Why God Will Save Every Person* (San Francisco: HarperSanFrancisco, 2004). On annihilationism in Thigpen's novel, see *My Visit to Hell*, 262–65. For the corresponding pages in the first edition, see *Gehenna*, 239–42. A close reader will notice some small but significant changes, which illustrate Thigpen's change in theological understanding—in particular, note the deletion of the original point number three in the Author's Note to *Gehenna* (6).

31 Since brief biographies for Augustine and Aquinas appear earlier in this book, I will focus on the eschatological component in their theologies.

32 On how Augustine warmed to neo-Platonism and later to the writings of the Apostle Paul, see *The Confessions*, translated by Maria Boulding, O.S.B., with a preface by Patricia Hampl (New York: Vintage Books, 1998), VII and VIII.

33 Primary sources for this summary include St. Augustine, *The City of God*, translated by Marcus Dods and with an introduction by Thomas Merton (New York: The Modern Library, 1993), XII–XIV, and *Confessions*, XIII. Secondary sources include David Hunter, "Augustine of Hippo," in Catherine A. Cory and David T. Landry, eds., *The Christian Theological Tradition*, 2nd ed. (Upper Saddle River, N.J.: Prentice Hall, 2003; 2000), 141–52; McGrath, *Christian Theology: An Introduction*, 362–68; Bradley P. Nystrom and David P. Nystrom, *The History of Christianity: An Introduction* (Boston: McGraw-Hill, 2004), 100–106, and John Rist, "Augustine of Hippo," in G. R. Evans, ed., *The Medieval Theologians: An Introduction to Theology in the Medieval Period* (Malden, Mass.: Blackwell, 2001), 3–23.

34 Thomas Merton, "Introduction," to Augustine, *The City of God*, xiv.

35 See Augustine, *The City of God*, XX.

36 John Milton, *Paradise Lost and Paradise Regained*, edited and with Notes by Christopher Ricks and with a new introduction by Dr. Susanne Woods (New York: Signet, 2001), I,263. The devil's fall from heaven is addressed in Isaiah 14:12. Here he is Lucifer, the Light-Bearer or the Day Star. Jesus seems to have this name and notion in mind in Luke 10:18. Identifying Satan or the devil with Lucifer becomes widely accepted after the fifth century.

37 Augustine, *The City of God*, XXI–XXII.

38   St. Thomas Aquinas, *Summa Theologiae*, complete English edition in
      five volumes, translated by the Fathers of the English Dominican
      Province (Notre Dame, Ind.: Christian Classics, 1981; 1948), 1.45.5,
      1-2.3.8, 1-2.5.1, 3.1.2. For those who find Aquinas' *Summa* daunting
      to follow, and I confess that I am one of them, I recommend the emi-
      nently readable translation and commentary by Frederick Christian
      Bauerschmidt, *Holy Teaching: Introducing the* Summa Theologiae *of St.
      Thomas Aquinas* (Grand Rapids, Mich.: Brazos Press, 2005). Other
      sources include: Nicholas M. Healy, *Thomas Aquinas: Theologian of the
      Christian Life* (Burlington, Vt.; Aldershot, Hampshire: Ashgate, 2003);
      Fergus Kerr, "Thomas Aquinas," in Evans, *The Medieval Theologians*,
      201–20, and David Smith, "Thomas Aquinas," in Cory and Landry,
      eds., *The Christian Theological Tradition*, 215–29.
39   Aquinas, *Summa Theologiae*, 1-2.109.2.
40   Robert Barron, *Thomas Aquinas: Spiritual Master* (New York: Crossroad,
      1998), 122–23.
41   Aquinas, *Summa Theologiae*, 1.73.1, 1-2.109.2, 3.1.2.
42   Aquinas, *Summa Theologiae*, 1-2.91.4, 1-2.109.2, 1-2.109.6, 2-2.23.1.
43   Aquinas, *Summa Theologiae*, 1.49.3.
44   Aquinas, *Summa Theologiae*, 1.2.3 *ad* 1.
45   Aquinas, *Summa Theologiae*, 1-2.4.6, 2-2.17.2, 3.59.5.
46   See Augustine, *The City of God*, XX, 25. Compare to Aquinas, *Summa
      Theologiae*, 3.
47   See Luke 16:19-31.
48   For the account of Dante's life in this section I rely particularly upon
      Peter S. Hawkins, *Dante: A Brief History* (Malden, Mass.: Blackwell,
      2006), 1–28.
49   Hawkins, *Dante*, 102–5.
50   This apt terminology is used by literary critic Theodore Ziolkowski.
      See his *Fictional Transfigurations of Jesus* (Princeton, N.J.: Princeton
      University Press, 1972), 6–7.
51   Although numerous translations of Dante's poem exist, I prefer the
      Everyman's Library edition. See Dante Alighieri, *The Divine Comedy*,
      translated by Allen Mandelbaum, with an introduction by Eugenio
      Montale and notes by Peter Armour (New York: Alfred A. Knopf,
      1995). Besides Hawkin's commentary, I also recommend Rachel
      Jacoff, ed., *The Cambridge Companion to Dante*, 2nd ed. (Cambridge:
      Cambridge University Press, 2007; 1993) for an accessible introduc-
      tion to Dante's life and literary art.

52 Dante, *Inferno*, I, 3–16, 70–79, 112–20. Dante appears to have found temporary solace in philosophy, like Augustine, before realizing that unaided reason is unable to help us acquire the true knowledge of God. See Hawkins, *Dante: A Brief History*, 106.

53 Dante, *Inferno*, III, 9, 36–37, 64–69, 77, 83, 94–98. Dante faints on the ferry, so the reader receives no description of this part of his journey.

54 A recent document from the Catholic Church now questions the concept of limbo. For more details, see http://www.originsonline.com. On Thigpen's own response to this document, see the second part of my interview with him.

55 Dante, *Inferno*, IX, 127–29.

56 Dante, *Inferno*, XXXIV, 28, 61–67, 112–17, 139.

57 Thigpen, *My Visit to Hell*, ix. This quotation comes from the novel's introduction, which appears critical to understanding the book correctly, Thigpen avers.

58 Thigpen, *My Visit to Hell*, x–xi.

59 Thigpen, *My Visit to Hell*, x.

60 Thigpen, *My Visit to Hell*, x.

61 Thomas Travis is 33, two years younger than Dante, but still roughly half the biblically allotted age. See Psalms 90:10. In *Gehenna*, Thomas is 42. See Thigpen, *Gehenna*, 11.

62 For hints regarding childhood abuse, see Thigpen, *My Visit to Hell*, 8, 18, 29. Much of the novel explores some fairly intense father-son issues: 118–19, 122, 153, 208, 230, 236–37, 248, 250, 267, 273, 293–94. On racism and sexism, see 3, 11–14, 37.

63 Thigpen, *My Visit to Hell*, 242. Miss C compares Thomas to the doubting disciple at one point. On Thomas' surname, it is possible that Thigpen's own father, Travis, to whom he dedicates at least one of his earlier books, explains the name choice. Thomas is also part of Paul Thigpen's name; he sometimes publishes as T. Paul Thigpen.

64 Thigpen, *My Visit to Hell*, 1–3. "With one foot in the field of theology and the other in a field of collard greens," Thomas self-identifies as "a cultural half-breed" (2).

65 Thigpen, *My Visit to Hell*, 2.

66 Thigpen, *My Visit to Hell*, 4. God answers Thomas' prayer, as Miss C implies, and her belief inspires him to pray in exactly the same fashion at the novel's end (25, 302).

67 Thigpen, *My Visit to Hell*, 7,

68 Thigpen, *My Visit to Hell*, 37–39, 46–48. Notice that Thigpen draws on 1 Peter 3:18-20 and the Apostles' Creed to explain this event.

69 Thigpen, *My Visit to Hell*, 1–3, 8–10, 25–26, 34–35, 40, 54.

70 Thigpen, *My Visit to Hell*, 10. Other references have Thomas as well as others converse, so to speak, with Dante's original text, which only serves to underscore *My Visit to Hell*'s postfigurative qualities. See 28–30, 35, 40, 50, 60–61, 67, 92, 99–100, 127, 148, 156, 176, 178, 183, 188, 196, 198, 212, 218, 231, 236, 288–89.

71 One remark by Thomas makes this quite clear: "Here I am, with my life in your [Miss C's] hands at every turn, traveling with you through a forsaken heap of ruins I have no choice now but to conclude is really hell, even though up till now I didn't even *believe* in hell" (Thigpen, *My Visit to Hell*, 40).

72 Thigpen, *My Visit to Hell*, 11–14, 18, 24–25, 28, 30, 40–41, 44–45, 48, 54–55.

73 To make it easier for my reader to journey with Thomas and Miss C, and thus visualize their movements, I am reproducing the "map of hell" that appears at the outset of Thigpen's novel (see p. 151). I wish to thank his editors, Christianne Squires and Elizabeth Cardone, for assistance in securing permission to use this illustration.

74 Thigpen, *My Visit to Hell*, 19.

75 Thigpen, *My Visit to Hell*, 19.

76 Thigpen, *My Visit to Hell*, 20. Emphasis in original.

77 Thigpen, *My Visit to Hell*, 16–21. Cousin Virgil died watching late-night TV (2). Also, in *Gehenna*, cousin Virgil is named cousin Bubba. See Thigpen, *Gehenna*, 10, 26.

78 Thigpen, *My Visit to Hell*, 23–26.

79 Thigpen, *My Visit to Hell*, 34.

80 Thigpen, *My Visit to Hell*, 34–35. For Augustine on memory, see *Confessions*, X. It may not be out of place to note that the late French deconstructionist philosopher Jacques Derrida provoked fresh intellectual interest in Augustine and his theology. See the essays in John D. Caputo and Michael J. Scanlon, eds., *Augustine and Postmodernism: Confessions and Circumfession* (Bloomington and Indianapolis: Indiana University Press, 2005).

81 Thigpen, *My Visit to Hell*, 35. Emphasis in original.

82 Thigpen, *My Visit to Hell*, xi–xii, 38, 122, 291, 301–3.

83 Thigpen, *My Visit to Hell*, 44–48.

84 Thigpen, *My Visit to Hell*, 51. This structure resembles the biblical Tower of Babel. See Genesis 11. We are told that hell's harrowing cracked limbo's temple down the middle, and this detail evokes the Jerusalem temple's curtain-ripping when Christ dies on Good Friday (52). Also see Mark 15:38. In addition, note that Thigpen has Thomas look at the structure and weep (53). Is this a play on John 11:35?

85 Thigpen, *My Visit to Hell*, 54.

86 Thigpen, *My Visit to Hell*, 54.

87 Thigpen, *My Visit to Hell*, 56. In the end, Miss C reveals that heaven's messengers come and take the children to a better place. When Thomas asks why they do not simply go to heaven immediately, soon after they die, Miss C explains that they have a task to perform in hell (57). Intriguingly, *Gehenna* explains that despite this purpose, "even heaven's patience has its limits, and He is eager to hold them." See Thigpen, *Gehenna*, 60. This line is omitted from *My Visit to Hell*.

88 Thigpen, *My Visit to Hell*, 62.

89 Thigpen, *My Visit to Hell*, 65, 67–73.

90 Thigpen, *My Visit to Hell*, 73.

91 Thigpen, *My Visit to Hell*, 74. Compare with Aquinas, *Summa Theologiae*, 1-2.84.2.

92 Thigpen, *My Visit to Hell*, 71, 88. Again, compare with Aquinas, *Summa Theologiae*, 1-2.84.4. Here Aquinas cites Pope Gregory the Great when listing the capital or so-called deadly sins: pride, envy, anger, sloth, greed, gluttony, lust.

93 Thigpen, *My Visit to Hell*, 85–86. If I understand Thigpen correctly, and here I am thinking of his interview with me as well as his many writings, he is a novelist of divine mercy rather than of sin. I wonder, then, if Romans 5:20 might serve as his work's motto.

94 Thigpen, *My Visit to Hell*, 86.

95 Thigpen, *My Visit to Hell*, 86.

96 Thigpen, *My Visit to Hell*, 90–93, 95.

97 Thigpen's reference to the Tomb of Ultimate Concern alludes to Paul Tillich, one of the last century's most significant theologians. As an existentialist, Tillich abandoned belief in a personal God, defined faith as ultimate concern, and understood God as the ground of our being. For an accessible anthology of Tillich's writings, see Mark Kline Taylor, ed., *Paul Tillich: Theologian of the Boundaries* (Minneapolis, Minn.: Fortress, 1991). Space prohibits me from discussing Tillich's

work, or the way it was popularized by John A. T. Robinson's *Honest to God*, which appeared in 1963, but I think it is safe to say that Thigpen problematizes the existentialist and death-of-God theologians.

98 Thigpen, *My Visit to Hell*, 97–101, 110.

99 See Frederick Christian Bauerschmidt, "Shouting in the Land of the Hard of Hearing: On Being a Hillbilly Thomist," in *Aquinas in Dialogue: Thomas for the Twenty-First Century*, edited by Jim Fodor and Frederick Christian Bauerschmidt (Malden, Mass.: Blackwell, 2004), 171–72. This is an intriguing article, one that places O'Connor and Aquinas into conversation, so to speak, and when one considers how Thigpen's voyager-narrator hails from the country, and occasionally passes Thomistic commentary on what he sees, I suspect "hillbilly Thomist" is not that out-of-place in any assessment of Thomas Travis' character. I would not want to stretch the point too far, to be sure, but there is some interpretive fun to be had with this term. For more information on O'Connor's theological views, see Flannery O'Connor, *Mystery and Manners*, edited by Sally and Robert Fitzgerald (New York: Farrar, Straus & Giroux, 1969). Also see Sally and Robert Fitzgerald, eds., *Flannery O'Connor: Collected Works* (New York: Library of America, 1988).

100 Thigpen, *My Visit to Hell*, 111–12. In Dante, the heretics are encased in burning tombs. Here, in Thigpen's novel, they are forced to eat their own words—"books *flambé*" (103).

101 Rudolf Bultmann, "New Testament and Mythology," in H. W. Bartsch, ed., *Kerygma and Myth* (London: SPCK, 1953), 1–16. For selected texts and commentary, see Roger A. Johnson, ed., *Rudolf Bultmann: Interpreting Faith for the Modern Era* (Minneapolis, Minn.: Fortess Press, 1991).

102 Thigpen, *My Visit to Hell*, 102. Emphasis in original. Some readers might find Thigpen irreverent to include humor in his story. (Thigpen tells me that at least one reviewer of *Gehenna* harbored this concern.) In face of such an objection, however, I think it is only fair to offer the following two thoughts. First, anyone who has ever read Dante's work knows that it is replete with humor. Any attempt to acknowledge *My Visit to Hell*'s postfigurative qualities must, therefore, recognize Thigpen's appropriate use of jokes and puns to get his point across. Second, I would encourage any and all perturbed readers to engage in a close reading of Thigpen's other work to set his fondness for comedy in wider context. Perhaps the place where his work's two main

themes—salvation/eternal life and joy/humor—come together is in the introduction to his book of readings from the martyr St. Thomas More, *Be Merry in God*, which Thigpen published in 1999. Luckily, this introduction is available at Thigpen's Web site: http://www. paulthigpen.com/saints-history/thomasmore.html. A more extensive look at the subject can be found in a lecture Thigpen once gave at the Franciscan University. This is also posted online. See http://www. paulthigpen.com/humor/causetolaugh.html.

103 See Thigpen, *My Visit to Hell*, 107: "You knew, Dr. Perdido. I knew. We all knew. We were all self-serving, but we fooled ourselves into thinking we were serving the truth."

104 Thigpen, *My Visit to Hell*, 114.

105 Thigpen, *My Visit to Hell*, 120–26. I should clarify the necklace's history at this point. A man in limbo gives Apangela's crucifix to Miss C. She then offers it to the Al Capone-like demon guarding circle seven's middle ring, as part of her bid to move on down through hell, but she never really hands it over, for it scares the demon tremendously. Later, Miss C reunites with Apangela and returns the crucifix (243, 289).

106 Thigpen, *My Visit to Hell*, 125.

107 Thigpen, *My Visit to Hell*, 126. Also see 291, 301–2.

108 Thigpen, *My Visit to Hell*, 127–32. Also see Dante, *Inferno*, XIII.

109 Thigpen, *My Visit to Hell*, 131.

110 Thigpen, *My Visit to Hell*, 136.

111 Thigpen, *My Visit to Hell*, 146–47. The slavers are affected by the radiation in this circle; ironically, it turns their skin black (193).

112 Thigpen, *My Visit to Hell*, 149–56, 159–63. For Dante on the inner ring and Geryon, see *Inferno*, XIV–XVI. In Dante, Geryon is half-man, half-scorpion; Thigpen's portrayal retains the scorpion-like traits but renders Geryon as an exotic woman.

113 Thigpen, *My Visit to Hell*, 165–71. Miss C even mentions how "the theologians speak of original sin, of a brokenness that pervades all creation ever since the first human said no to God," and with this remark she quite clearly alludes to Augustine (169). It is a measure of Thigpen's skill as a novelist that he resists an easy didacticism at this point and, instead, fair-mindedly represents both points of view—a sensitivity personified by Thomas, who favors Miss C *and* Stone with his friendship (170–71). For my part, I think Thomas gives us every indication to think Stone represents an unsteady cry for redemption as well as understanding: "Stone was like a wounded butterfly, flit-

ting back and forth between hope and a hard heart. Did so wobbly a will as his have any chance of getting out?" (195).

114 Thigpen, *My Visit to Hell*, 180. And Thomas notes: ". . . ever since I'd met Miss C, it seemed easier to speak my mind, whatever the consequences" (191).

115 Thigpen, *My Visit to Hell*, 181. This said, Thomas invites Stone to pray a sinner's prayer with God right there, on the cusp of pit two, but Stone fudges the issue and moves on.

116 Thigpen, *My Visit to Hell*, 191. Little wonder, then, that justice remains hell's only guarantee, an oft-cited notion in Thigpen's novel.

117 Thigpen, *My Visit to Hell*, 194. Thigpen makes much of this perspective in my interview's second part, which appears shortly.

118 Thigpen, *My Visit to Hell*, 196–98, 209–12, 217–25. Note that the trousers Stone stole from Thomas turn gold (224).

119 Thigpen, *My Visit to Hell*, 228.

120 Thigpen, *My Visit to Hell*, 200–208, 215–25, 237–40.

121 Thigpen, *My Visit to Hell*, 239.

122 Thigpen, *My Visit to Hell*, 245–57. In Dante's version of pit nine, the poet encounters the prophet Muhammad, the architect of Islam. See Dante, *Inferno*, XXVIII. In *My Visit to Hell*, Thomas describes a new character's appearance and gait, and Miss C comments on his life, but "the Prophet" says nothing and does not interact with Thigpen's protagonists (247). For Augustine on the love of God and neighbor, see *Confessions*, X.

123 Thigpen, *My Visit to Hell*, 260.

124 Thigpen, *My Visit to Hell*, 261.

125 Compare Thigpen, *Gehenna*, 239, with Thigpen, *My Visit to Hell*, 262.

126 Compare Thigpen, *Gehenna*, 241 with Thigpen, *My Visit to Hell*, 264; emphasis mine. Space prohibits me from capturing Capopia's and Thomas' nuanced discussion about time and eternity, which adds to the debate over annihilationism, and does so in a way that evokes what we read in Augustine's *Confessions*, XI.

127 Thigpen, *My Visit to Hell*, 279.

128 Thigpen, *My Visit to Hell*, 288–89. For Dante's account, see *Inferno*, XXXIV.

129 Thigpen, *My Visit to Hell*, 301.

130 Thigpen, *My Visit to Hell*, 303. Emphasis in original. Kissing this crucifix makes us wonder if Apangela finished her journey after all.

131 See Jürgen Moltmann, *Theology of Hope: On the Ground and Implications of a Christian Eschatology*, translated by J. W. Leitch (London: SCM Press, 1967). Also see Richard Bauckham, "Jürgen Moltmann," in David F. Ford with Rachel Muers, eds., *The Modern Theologians: An Introduction to Christian Theology Since 1918*, 3rd ed. (Malden, Mass.: Blackwell, 2005; 1996, 1989), 147–62.

132 See Jürgen Moltmann, *Religion, Revolution, and the Future* (New York: Charles Scribner's Sons, 1969), 60.

133 Personal interview, 2007. These remarks belong with the material included in Appendix I. I reproduce them here and not elsewhere because they serve as an instructive point of agreement between Thigpen and Moltmann.

134 Thigpen, *Last Words*, 94.

135 Thigpen, *Last Words*, 186.

APPENDIX I

1 http://paulthigpen.com/paulthigpen/howibecamecatholic.html.

2 See Alister E. McGrath, ed., *Christian Literature: An Anthology* (Malden, Mass.: Blackwell, 2001), xiv.

3 Jeffrey Burton Russell, *Paradise Mislaid: How We Lost Heaven and How We Can Regain It* (Oxford: Oxford University Press, 2006).

4 See Gabriel Fackre, *The Christian Story: A Narrative Interpretation of Basic Christian Doctrine*, rev. ed. (Grand Rapids, Mich.: W. B. Eerdmans, 1984; 1978), 223–25.

APPENDIX II

1 Eudora Welty, *On Writing*, and with an introduction by Richard Bausch (New York: The Modern Library, 2002), 7.

SELECTED BIBLIOGRAPHY

CHRISTIAN DOCTRINE: HISTORIES, OVERVIEWS, READERS

Bagchi, David, and David C. Steinmetz, eds. *The Cambridge Companion to Reformation Theology*. Cambridge: Cambridge University Press, 2004.

Baum, Gregory, ed. *The Twentieth Century: A Theological Overview*. Maryknoll, N.Y.: Orbis Books, 1999.

Bellitto, Christopher M. *The General Councils: A History of the Twenty-One Church Councils from Nicaea to Vatican II*. Mahwah, N.J.: Paulist Press, 2001.

Bollier, John A. *The Literature of Theology: A Guide for Students and Pastors*. Philadelphia: Westminster Press, 1979.

Brown, Peter. *The Rise of Western Christendom: Triumph and Diversity 200–1000*. Malden, Mass.: Blackwell, 2002.

Bruyneel, Sally, and Alan G. Padgett. *Introducing Christianity*. Maryknoll, NY: Orbis Books, 2003.

Carey, Patrick W., and Joseph T. Lienhard, eds. *Biographical Dictionary of Christian Theologians*. Westport, Conn.: Greenwood Press, 2000.

Charry, Ellen T., ed. *Inquiring After God: Classic and Contemporary Readings*. Malden, Mass.: Blackwell, 2000.

Cobb, John B. *Becoming a Thinking Christian*. Nashville, TN: Abingdon Press, 1993.

Dunn, Marilyn. *The Emergence of Monasticism: From the Desert Fathers to the Early Middle Ages*. Malden, Mass.: Blackwell, 2003.

Elton, Geoffrey. *Reformation Europe: 1517–1559*. Malden, Mass.: Blackwell, 1999.

Evans, G. R., ed. *The First Christian Theologians: An Introduction to Theology in the Early Church*. Malden, Mass.: Blackwell, 2004.

———. *The Medieval Theologians: An Introduction to Theology in the Medieval Period*. Malden, Mass.: Blackwell, 2001.

Ford, David F. *Theology: A Very Short Introduction*. Oxford: Oxford University Press, 2000.

Ford, David F., ed. *The Modern Theologians: An Introduction to Christian Theology in the Twentieth Century*. 3rd ed. Malden, Mass.: Blackwell, 2005; 2001, 1997.

Gill, Robin, ed. *Readings in Modern Theology: Britain and America*. Nashville, Tenn.: Abingdon Press, 1995.

González, Justo L. and Zaida Maldonado Perez. *An Introduction to Christian Theology*. Nashville, Tenn.: Abingdon Press, 2002.

Graham, Elaine, Heather Walton, and Frankie Ward, *Theological Reflection: Sources*. London: SCM Press, 2007.

———. *Theological Reflection: Methods*. London: SCM Press, 2005.

Gunton, Colin E. *The Cambridge Companion to Christian Doctrine*. Cambridge: Cambridge University Press, 1997.

———. *The Christian Faith: An Introduction to Christian Doctrine*. Malden, Mass.: Blackwell, 2002.

Gunton, Colin E., Stephen R. Holmes, and Murray A. Rae, eds. *The Practice of Theology: A Reader*. London: SCM Press, 2001.

Harries, Richard, and Henry Mayr-Harting, eds. *Christianity: Two Thousand Years*. Oxford: Oxford University Press, 2001.

Hastings, Adrian, Alistair Mason, and Hugh Pyper, eds. *Christian Thought: A Brief History*. Oxford: Oxford University Press, 2003.

Inbody, Tyron. *The Faith of the Christian Church: An Introduction to Theology*. Grand Rapids, Mich.: W. B. Eerdmans, 2005.

Jones, Gareth, ed. *The Blackwell Companion to Modern Theology*. Malden, Mass.: Blackwell, 2003.

Jones, W. Paul. *Theological Worlds: Understanding the Alternative Rhythms of Christian Belief*. Nashville, Tenn.: Abingdon Press, 1989.

Kelsey, David H. *Proving Doctrine: The Uses of Scripture in Modern Theology*. Harrisburg, Pa.: Trinity Press, 1999.

Lambert, Malcolm. *Medieval Heresy: Popular Movements from the Gregorian Reform to the Reformation*. Malden, Mass.: Blackwell, 2002.

Lindberg, Carter., ed. *The Pietist Theologians: An Introduction to Theology in the Seventeenth and Eighteenth Centuries.* Malden, Mass.: Blackwell, 2004.

———. *The Reformation Theologians: An Introduction to Theology in the Early Modern Period.* Malden, Mass.: Blackwell, 2001.

Luck, Donald G. *Why Study Theology?* St. Louis, Mo.: Chalice Press, 1999.

Luebke, David. *The Counter Reformation: The Essential Readings.* Malden, Mass.: Blackwell, 1999.

McGrath, Alister E. *Historical Theology: An Introduction to the History of Christian Thought.* Malden, Mass.: Blackwell, 1998.

———. *Reformation Thought: An Introduction.* Malden, Mass.: Blackwell, 1999.

McGrath, Alister E., ed. *The Blackwell Encyclopedia of Modern Christian Thought.* Malden, Mass.: Blackwell, 1995.

McGrath, Alister E. and Darren C. Marks. *The Blackwell Companion to Protestantism.* Malden, Mass.: Blackwell, 2003.

McKim, Donald K. *The Westminster Dictionary of Theological Terms.* Louisville, Ky.: Westminster John Knox, 1996.

McManners, John, ed. *The Oxford History of Christianity.* Oxford: Oxford University Press, 2002.

Miles, Margaret. *The Word Made Flesh: A History of Christian Thought.* Malden, Mass.: Blackwell, 2004.

Olson, Roger E. *The Mosaic of Christian Belief: Twenty Centuries of Unity and Diversity.* Downers Grove, Ill.: InterVarsity Press, 2002.

Parrinder, Geoffrey. *A Concise Encyclopedia of Christianity.* Oxford: Oneworld, 1998.

Pattison, George. *A Short Course in Christian Doctrine.* London: SCM Press, 2005.

Pelikan, Jaroslav. *Credo: Historical and Theological Guide to Creeds and Confessions of Faith in the Christian Tradition.* New Haven, Conn.: Yale University Press, 2003.

Penner, Myron, ed. *Christianity and the Postmodern Turn: Six Views.* Grand Rapids, Mich.: Brazos Press, 2005.

Petersen, Rodney L. with Nancy M. Rourke, ed. *Theological Literacy for the Twenty-First Century.* Grand Rapids, Mich.: W. B. Eerdmans, 2002.

Placher, William C., ed. *Essentials of Christian Theology.* Louisville, Ky.: Westminster John Knox, 2003.

Reid, Patrick V., ed. *Readings in Western Religious Thought.* New York: Paulist Press, 1987.

Richardson, Alan, and John S. Bowden, eds. *The Westminster Dictionary of Christian Theology*. Philadelphia: Westminster Press, 1983.

Riggs, John W. *Postmodern Christianity: Doing Theology in the Contemporary World*. Harrisburg, Pa.: Trinity Press International, 2003.

Russell, Letty M., and J. Shannon Clarkson, eds. *Dictionary of Feminist Theologies*. Louisville, Ky.: Westminster John Knox, 1996.

Seitz, Christopher, ed. *Nicene Christianity: The Future for a New Ecumenism*. Grand Rapids, Mich.: Brazos Press, 2002.

Solle, Dorothee. *Thinking About God: An Introduction to Theology*. London: SCM Press, 1990.

Ward, Graham. *The Blackwell Companion to Postmodern Theology*. Malden, Mass.: Blackwell, 2001.

Ward, Keith. *Christianity: A Short Introduction*. Oxford: Oneworld, 2000.

Webster, John, Kathryn Tanner, and Iain Torrance, eds. *The Oxford Handbook of Systematic Theology*. Oxford: Oxford University Press, 2007.

Wiles, Maurice F. *Reason to Believe*. Harrisburg, Pa.: Trinity Press International, 1999.

Wilken, Robert Louis. *The Spirit of Early Christian Thought: Seeking the Face of God*. New Haven, Conn.: Yale University Press, 2003.

Williams, Rowan. *On Christian Theology*. Malden, Mass.: Blackwell, 2000.

Willis, David. *Clues to the Nicene Creed: A Brief Outline of the Faith*. Grand Rapids, Mich.: W. B. Eerdmans, 2005.

Wilson, Jonathan R. *A Primer for Christian Doctrine*. Grand Rapids, Mich.: W. B. Eerdmans, 2005.

Woodhead, Linda. *An Introduction to Christianity*. Cambridge: Cambridge University Press, 2004.

GOD

Bauerschmidt, Frederick. *Holy Teaching: Introducing the* Summa Theologiae *of St. Thomas Aquinas*. Grand Rapids, Mich.: Brazos Press, 2005.

Bowker, John. *God: A Brief History*. London: DK Publishing, 2002.

Brizee, Robert. *Where in the World Is God?: God's Presence in Every Moment of Our Lives*. Nashville, Tenn.: The Upper Room, 1987.

Cahn, Steven M. and David Shatz, ed. *Questions About God: Today's Philosophers Ponder the Divine*. Oxford: Oxford University Press, 2002.

Callen, Barry L. *Discerning the Divine: God in Christian Theology*. Louisville, Ky.: Westminster John Knox, 2004.

Capetz, Paul E. *God: A Brief History*. Minneapolis, Minn.: Fortress, 2003.

Hemming, Laurence Paul, and Susan Frank Parsons, eds. *Restoring Faith in Reason with a New Translation of the Encyclical Letter, Faith and Reason of Pope John Paul II, Together with a Commentary and Discussion*. London: SCM Press, 2002.

Houtepen, Anton. *God: An Open Question*. New York: Continuum, 2002.

Howard-Snyder, Daniel, and Paul K. Moser, eds. *Divine Hiddenness: New Essays*. Cambridge: Cambridge University Press, 2002.

O'Malley, William J. *God, the Oldest Question: A Fresh Look at Belief and Unbelief—and Why the Choice Matters*. Chicago, Ill.: Loyola Press, 2000.

Pattison, George. *A Short Course in the Philosophy of Religion*. London: SCM Press, 2001.

Pederson, Ann. *God, Creation, and All That Jazz: A Process of Composition and Improvisation*. St. Louis: Chalice Press, 2001.

Renick, Timothy M. *Aquinas for Armchair Theologians*. Louisville, Ky.: Westminster John Knox, 2002.

Sanna, Ellyn. *Touching God: Experiencing Metaphors for the Divine*. Mahwah, N.J.: Paulist Press, 2002.

Ward, Keith. *God: A Guide for the Perplexed*. Oxford: Oneworld, 2002.

HUMANITY

Bazyn, Ken. *The Seven Perennial Sins and Their Offspring*. New York: Continuum, 2002.

Card, Claudia. *The Atrocity Paradigm: A Theory of Evil*. Oxford: Oxford University Press, 2002.

Chadwick, Henry. *Augustine: A Very Short Introduction*. Oxford: Oxford University Press, 2001.

Clark, Mary T., ed. *Augustine of Hippo: Selected Writings*. New York: Paulist Press, 1984.

Cooper, Stephen Andrew. *Augustine for Armchair Theologians*. Louisville, Ky.: Westminster John Knox, 2002.

Dixon, Sandra Lee. *Augustine: The Scattered and Gathered Self*. St. Louis, Mo.: Chalice Press, 1999.

Ellingsen, Mark. *Blessed Are the Cynical: How Original Sin Can Make America A Better Place*. Grand Rapids, Mich.: Brazos Press, 2003.

Larrimore, Mark, ed. *The Problem of Evil: A Reader*. Malden, Mass.: Blackwell, 2000.

Mathewes, Charles T. *Evil and the Augustinian Tradition*. Cambridge: Cambridge University Press, 2001.

McFadyen, Alistair L. *Bound to Sin: Abuse, Holocaust, and the Christian Doctrine of Sin*. Cambridge: Cambridge University Press, 2000.

McMinn, Mark R. *Why Sin Matters: The Surprising Relationship Between Our Sin and God's Grace*. Wheaton, Ill.: Tyndale House Publishers, 2004.

Middleton, J. Richard. *The Liberating Image: The Imago Dei in Genesis 1*. Grand Rapids, Mich.: Brazos Press, 2005.

Morone, James A. *Hellfire Nation: The Politics of Sin in American History*. New Haven, Conn.: Yale University Press, 2003.

Neiman, Susan. *Evil in Modern Thought: An Alternative History of Philosophy*. Princeton, N.J.: Princeton University Press, 2002.

Paffenroth, Kim, and Robert P. Kennedy, eds. *A Reader's Companion to Augustine's* Confessions. Louisville, Ky.: Westminster John Knox, 2003.

Portmann, John, ed. *In Defense of Sin*. New York: Palgrave, 2001.

Stump, Eleonore, and Norman Kretzmann, eds. *The Cambridge Companion to Augustine*. Cambridge: Cambridge University Press, 2001.

Townes, Emilie M., ed. *A Troubling in My Soul: Womanist Perspectives on Evil and Suffering*. Maryknoll, N.Y.: Orbis Books, 1993.

Wiley, Tatha. *Original Sin: Origins, Developments, Contemporary Meanings*. Mahwah, N.J.: Paulist, 2002.

JESUS

Altizer, Thomas J. J. *The Contemporary Jesus*. Albany: State University of New York Press, 1997.

Bartlett, Anthony W. *Cross Purposes: The Violent Grammar of Christian Atonement*. Harrisburg, Pa.: Trinity Press International, 2001.

Battles, Ford Lewis. *Interpreting John Calvin*. Grand Rapids, Mich.: Baker Books, 1996.

Berquist, Jon L. *Incarnation*. St. Louis, Mo.: Chalice Press, 2000.

Bockmuehl, Markus, ed. *The Cambridge Companion to Jesus*. Cambridge: Cambridge University Press, 2001.

Boersma, Hans. *Violence, Hospitality, and the Cross: Reappropriating the Atonement Tradition*. Grand Rapids, Mich.: Baker Books, 2004.

Borg, Marcus J. *Jesus in Contemporary Scholarship*. Valley Forge, Pa.: Trinity Press International, 1994.

Catanzaro, C. J. de, ed. and trans. *Symeon The New Theologian: The Discourses*. New York: Paulist Press, 1980.

Coakley, Sarah. *Re-thinking Gregory of Nyssa*. Malden, Mass.: Blackwell, 2003.

Cowdell, Scott. *Is Jesus Unique?: A Study of Recent Christology*. New York: Paulist Press, 1996.

Crossan, John Dominic. *The Jesus Controversy: Perspectives in Conflict*. Harrisburg, Pa.: Trinity Press International, 1999.

Dupuis, Jacques. *Who Do You Say I Am?: Introduction to Christology*. Maryknoll, N.Y.: Orbis, 1994.

Finlan, Stephen J. and Vladimir Kharlamov, eds. *Theosis: Deification in Christian Theology*. Eugene, Oreg.: Pickwick Publications, 2006.

Ford, David F., and Mike Higton, eds. *Jesus*. Oxford: Oxford University Press, 2002.

Forward, Martin. *Jesus: A Short Biography*. Oxford: Oneworld, 1998.

Green, Joel B. *Salvation*. St. Louis: Chalice Press, 2003.

Grün, Anselm. *Images of Jesus*. New York: Continuum, 2002.

Hayes, John Haralson. *Son of God to Super Star: Twentieth-Century Interpretations of Jesus*. Nashville,: Abingdon Press, 1976.

Heyer, C. J. den. *Jesus and the Doctrine of the Atonement: Biblical Notes on a Controversial Topic*. Harrisburg, Pa.: Trinity Press International, 1998.

Howard, Marshall I. *The Origins of New Testament Christology*. Downers Grove, Ill.: InterVarsity Press, 1990.

Inbody, Tyron L. *The Many Faces of Christology*. Nashville, Tenn.: Abingdon Press, 2002.

Johnson, Luke Timothy. *The Real Jesus: The Misguided Quest for the Historical Jesus and the Truth of the Traditional Gospels*. San Francisco: HarperSanFrancisco, 1996.

Kärkkäinen, Veli-Matti. *Christology: A Global Introduction*. Grand Rapids, Mich.: Baker Academic, 2003.

La Due, William J. *Jesus Among the Theologians: Contemporary Interpretations of Christ*. Harrisburg, Pa.: Trinity Press International, 2001.

Meyer, Marvin, and Charles Hughes, eds. *Jesus Then and Now: Images of Jesus in History and Christology*. Harrisburg, Pa.: Trinity Press International, 2001.

Pelikan, Jaroslav. *Jesus through the Centuries: His Place in the History of Culture*. New Haven, Conn.: Yale University Press, 1999.

Reno, Russell R. *Redemptive Change: Atonement and the Christian Cure of the Soul*. Harrisburg, Pa.: Trinity Press International, 2002.

Rybarczyk, Edmund J. *Beyond Salvation: Eastern Orthodoxy and Classical Pentecostalism on Becoming Like Christ*. Bletchley, UK: Paternoster Theological Monographs, 2004.

Stackhouse, John G. Jr., ed. *What Does It Mean to Be Saved?: Broadening Evangelical Horizons of Salvation*. Grand Rapids, Mich.: Baker Academic, 2002.

Townes, Emilie M., ed. *Embracing the Spirit: Womanist Perspectives on Hope, Salvation, and Transformation*. Maryknoll, N.Y.: Orbis Books, 1997.

Weaver, J. Denny. *The Nonviolent Atonement*. Grand Rapids, Mich.: W. B. Eerdmans, 2001.

Weaver, Walter P. *The Historical Jesus in the Twentieth Century: 1900–1950*. Harrisburg, Pa.: Trinity Press International, 1999.

Wildman, Wesley J. *Fidelity with Plausibility: Modest Christologies in the Twentieth Century*. Albany: State University of New York Press, 1998.

Wiles, Maurice F. *Archetypal Heresy: Arianism through the Centuries*. Oxford: Clarendon Press, 1996.

CHURCH

Bettenson, Henry and Chris Maunder, ed. *Documents of the Christian Church*. Oxford: Oxford University Press, 1999.

Binns, John. *An Introduction to the Christian Orthodox Churches*. Cambridge: Cambridge University Press, 2002.

Davies, J. G., ed. *The New Westminster Dictionary of Liturgy and Worship*. Philadelphia: Westminster Press, 1986.

Dowley, Tim, ed. *Introduction to the History of Christianity*. Minneapolis, Minn.: Fortress, 2002.

Harries, Richard, and Henry Mayr-Harting, eds. *Christianity: Two Thousand Years*. Oxford: Oxford University Press, 2001.

Hinson, E. Glenn. *The Early Church: Origins to the Dawn of the Middle Ages*. Nashville, Tenn.: Abingdon Press, 1996.

Kärkkäinen, Veli-Matti. *An Introduction to Ecclesiology: Ecumenical, Historical and Global Perspectives*. Downers Grove, Ill.: InterVarsity Press, 2002.

McGinn, Bernard. *The Doctors of the Church: Thirty-Three Men and Women Who Have Shaped Christianity.* New York: Crossroad Publishing, 1999.

McKim, Donald K., ed. *Encyclopedia of the Reformed Faith.* Louisville, Ky.: Westminster John Knox, 1992.

McManners, John, ed. *The Oxford History of Christianity.* Oxford: Oxford University Press, 2002.

Miller, Glenn T. *The Modern Church: From the Dawn of the Reformation to the Eve of the Third Millennium.* Nashville, Tenn.: Abingdon Press, 1997.

Parrinder, Geoffrey. *A Concise Encyclopedia of Christianity.* Oxford: Oneworld, 1998.

Prusak, Bernard P. *The Church Unfinished: Ecclesiology through the Centuries.* Mahwah, N.J.: Paulist Press, 2004.

Volz, Carl A. *The Medieval Church: From the Dawn of the Middle Ages to the Eve of the Reformation.* Nashville, Tenn.: Abingdon Press, 1997.

ESCHATOLOGY

Alcorn, Randy. *Heaven.* Wheaton, Ill.: Tyndale House Publishers, 2004.

Braaten, Carl E., and Robert W. Jenson, eds. *The Last Things: Biblical and Theological Perspectives on Eschatology.* Grand Rapids, Mich.: W. B. Eerdmans, 2002.

Buckley, James J. and L. Gregory Jones, eds. *Theology and Eschatology at the Turn of the Millennium.* Malden, Mass.: Blackwell, 2002.

Davies, Douglas. *A Brief History of Death.* Malden, Mass.: Blackwell, 2005.

McDannell, Colleen, and Bernhard Lang, eds. *Heaven: A History.* New Haven, Conn.: Yale University Press, 2001.

McGrath, Alister E. *A Brief History of Heaven.* Malden, Mass.: Blackwell, 2003.

Sanford, Peter. *Heaven: A Guide to the Undiscovered Country.* New York: Palgrave, 2004.

Sauter, Gerhard. *What Dare We Hope?: Reconsidering Eschatology.* Harrisburg, Pa.: Trinity Press International, 1999.

Walls, Jerry L, ed. *The Oxford Handbook of Eschatology.* Oxford: Oxford University Press, 2007.

Walls, Jerry L. *Heaven: The Logic of Eternal Joy.* Oxford: Oxford University Press, 2002.

Wright, J. Edward. *The Early History of Heaven.* Oxford: Oxford University Press, 2000.

CHRISTIAN DOCTRINE AND THE LITERARY ARTS

Begbie, Jeremy, ed. *Sounding the Depths: Theology through the Arts.* London: SCM Press, 2002.

Borgman, Erik, Bart Philipsen and Lea Verstricht, eds. *Literary Canons and Religious Identity.* Aldershot, Hampshire; Burlington, Vt.: Ashgate Publishing, 2004.

Buechner, Frederick. *Speak What We Feel (Not What We Ought to Say): Reflections on Literature and Faith.* San Francisco: HarperSanFrancisco, 2001.

Cary, Norman Reed. *Christian Criticism in the Twentieth Century: Theological Approaches to Literature.* Port Washington, N.Y.: Kennikat Press, 1975.

Cunningham, David S. *Reading Is Believing: The Christian Faith through Literature and Film.* Grand Rapids, Mich.: Brazos Press, 2002.

Cunningham, Valentine. *Reading after Theory.* Malden, Mass.: Blackwell, 2002.

Edwards, Michael. *Towards a Christian Poetics.* Grand Rapids, Mich.: W. B. Eerdmans, 1984.

Ferretter, Luke. *Towards a Christian Literary Theory.* New York: Palgrave Macmillan, 2003.

Ficken, Carl. *God's Story and Modern Literature: Reading Fiction in Community.* Philadelphia: Fortress, 1985.

Fiddes, Paul S. *The Promised End: Eschatology in Theology and Literature.* Malden, Mass.: Blackwell, 2000.

Hass, Andrew, David Jasper, and Elisabeth Jay, eds. *The Oxford Handbook of English Literature and Theology.* Oxford: Oxford University Press, 2007.

Hawley, John C., ed. *Through a Glass Darkly: Essays in the Religious Imagination.* New York: Fordham University Press, 1996.

Jacobs, Alan. *A Theology of Reading: The Hermeneutics of Love.* Boulder: Westview Press, 2001.

Jasper, David. *The Sacred Desert: Religion, Literature, Art, and Culture.* Malden, Mass.: Blackwell, 2004.

Jasper, David, and Stephen Prickett, eds. *The Bible and Literature: A Reader.* Malden, Mass.: Blackwell, 1999.

Jeffrey, David Lyle. *Houses of the Interpreter: Reading Scripture, Reading Culture.* Waco, Tex.: Baylor University Press, 2003.

Lansdown, Richard. *The Autonomy of Literature.* New York: St. Martin's Press, 2001.

Mallard, William. *The Reflection of Theology in Literature: A Case Study in Theology and Culture.* San Antonio: Trinity University Press, 1977.

McGrath, Alister E., ed. *Christian Literature: An Anthology.* Malden, Mass.: Blackwell, 2001.

McFague, Sallie. *Literature and the Christian Life.* New Haven, Conn.: Yale University Press, 1966.

Merrill, Thomas F. *Christian Criticism: A Study of Literary God-Talk.* Amsterdam: Rodopi, 1976.

Neary, John. *Like and Unlike God: Religious Imaginations in Modern and Contemporary Fiction.* Atlanta: Scholars Press, 1999.

Ryken, Leland, ed. *The Christian Imagination: Essays on Literature and the Arts.* Grand Rapids, Mich.: Baker Book House, 1981.

Schroth, Raymond A. *Dante to Dead Man Walking: One Reader's Journey through the Christian Classics.* Chicago: Loyola Press, 2001.

Shanks, Andrew. *'What Is Truth?:' Towards a Theological Poetics.* New York: Routledge, 2001.

Sherry, Patrick. *Images of Redemption: Understanding Soteriology through Art and Literature.* New York: Continuum, 2003.

Smith, James K. A. and Henry Isaac Venema, eds. *The Hermeneutics of Charity: Interpretation, Selfhood, and Postmodern Faith.* Grand Rapids, Mich.: Brazos Press, 2004.

Thiessen, Gesa Elsbeth, ed. *Theological Aesthetics: A Reader.* Grand Rapids, Mich.: W. B. Eerdmans, 2005.

Vanhoozer, Kevin J. *Is There a Meaning in This Text?: The Bible, the Reader, and the Morality of Literary Knowledge.* Grand Rapids, Mich.: Zondervan, 1998.

INDEX OF NAMES AND TERMS